ORDNANCE SURVEY
LEISURE GUIDE

IRELAND

Produced jointly by the Publishing Division of the
Automobile Association and the Ordnance Survey
of Ireland and the Ordnance Survey of Northern Ireland

Cover: Near Ardgroom, Beara Peninsula, Cork.
Photo by Bryan Lynch
Back cover: The Vale of Avoca, Wicklow
Title page: Ardmore Round Tower, Waterford
Opposite: Parknasilla, Kerry
Introductory page: Lough Erne, Fermanagh

Editors: Antonia Hebbert and Betty Sheldrick
Additional editorial: Gail Harada

Art Editor: Bob Johnson
Design concept by Dave Austin

Editorial contributors: Victor Kelly (The Story of
Ireland), C Douglas Deane (Natural History and
Landscape), Peter Somerville-Large (Literary
Ireland), Ted Bonner (Fountains of the Water of Life),
Theodora Fitzgibbon (A Taste of Ireland), Lyn
Gallagher (Gazetteer: Northern Ireland), Adrian
MacLoughlin (Gazetteer: Republic of Ireland),
Rebecca Snelling (Directory), Wilfrid Capper (Walks:
North), David Herman, Joss Lynam, JB Malone
(Walks: Republic)

Picture researcher: Wyn Voysey

**Printed and bound in Great Britain by Purnell Book
Production Ltd, Paulton, Bristol**

Maps extracted from:
the Ordnance Survey of Northern Ireland's 1:50,000
First Series, 1:25,000 Outdoor Pursuits Map and
1:250,000 Holiday Map, with the permission of the
Ordnance Survey of Northern Ireland. Crown
Copyright reserved.
the Ordnance Survey of Ireland's 1:63,360 Series and
1:250,000 Holiday Maps, with the permission of the
Government of Ireland.
the Automobile Association's 1:1,000,000 Map of
Great Britain and Ireland.
Additions to the maps by the Ordnance Survey of
Northern Ireland and the Cartographic Department of
the Automobile Association.

Produced by the Publishing Division of the
Automobile Association, Fanum House, Basingstoke,
Hampshire RG21 2EA.
Distributed by the Publishing Division of the
Automobile Association, Fanum House, Basingstoke,
Hampshire RG21 2EA

Published by the Automobile Association, the
Ordnance Survey of Ireland and the Ordnance Survey
of Northern Ireland.

ISBN 0 86145 375 1 (hardback)
AA reference 59488
ISBN 0 86145 357 3 (softback)
AA reference 57642

IRELAND

Contents

Using this Book

The entries in the Gazetteer have been carefully selected to reflect the interest and variety of Ireland. For reasons of space, it has not been possible to include every community, but the selection of places has been made on the basis of their importance to the cultural and social life of Ireland as a whole.

Each entry in the A to Z Gazetteer has the atlas page number on which the place can be found, and its Irish National Grid reference included under the heading. An explanation of how to use the Irish National Grid is given on pages 120–121. This system of reference is also given for each place name in the index.

Beneath many of the entries in the Gazetteer are listed AA-recommended hotels, guesthouses, town and country homes (T&C), farmhouses, restaurants, garages and camping sites in the immediate vicinity of the place described. Hotels, restaurants and camping sites are also given an AA classification.

HOTELS

1-star	Good hotels and inns, generally of small scale and with good furnishing and facilities.
2-star	Hotels with a higher standard of accommodation. There should be 20% private bathrooms or showers.
3-star	Well-appointed hotels. Two-thirds of the bedrooms should have private bathrooms or showers.
4-star	Exceptionally well-appointed hotels offering high standards of comfort and service. All bedrooms should have private bathrooms or showers.
5-star	Luxury hotels offering the highest international standards; in provincial 5-star hotels, some of the services may be provided on a more informal and restricted basis.
Country House	Used to denote AA Country House hotels, often secluded, but not always rurally situated, where a relaxed, informal atmosphere and personal welcome prevail. However, some of the facilities may differ from those found in urban hotels of the same classification.
Red Star Hotels	These hotels are considered by the AA to be of outstanding merit within their classification. The award is reviewed annually.

GUESTHOUSES

These are different from, but not necessarily inferior to, AA-appointed hotels, and they offer an alternative for those who prefer inexpensive and not too elaborate accommodation. They all provide clean, comfortable accommodation in homely surroundings. Each establishment must usually offer at least six bedrooms and there should be a general bathroom and a general toilet for every six bedrooms without private facilities.

Parking facilities should be reasonably close.

Other requirements include:
Well maintained exterior; clean and hygenic kitchens; good standard of furnishing; friendly and courteous service; access at reasonable times; the use of a telephone and full breakfast.

TOWN AND COUNTRY HOMES (T & Cs)

This type of accommodation is offered in the Republic of Ireland only. T & Cs are similar to guesthouses but generally smaller and run more as family concerns. Each establishment must provide at least four bedrooms and a general bathroom and toilet for every six bedrooms without private facilities.

RESTAURANTS

1-fork	Modest but good restaurant
2-fork	Restaurant offering a higher standard of comfort than above
3-fork	Well-appointed restaurant
4-fork	Exceptionally well-appointed restaurant
5-fork	Luxury restaurant

CAMPSITES

1-pennant	Site with six or more pitches for the touring caravanner or camper and full range of basic facilities
2-pennant	Site with extended range of facilities including hot water
3-pennant	Site with improved facilities and limited range of services
4-pennant	Well-equipped site with wider range of services
5-pennant	Very well-equipped and well laid-out site with full range of services

TELEPHONE NUMBERS

Area codes shown against telephone numbers in the Republic of Ireland are applicable within the Republic. To dial from the UK consult your local Dialling Code book. Similarly, codes in Northern Ireland and Great Britain to be verified for calls from the Republic of Ireland.

IRELAND

Introduction

Ireland is a land of green pastures, peaceful roads and welcoming people. Whether you look for the beauty of its countryside, the spectacular scenery of its coastline, or prefer to go in search of the past, this guide will provide the key. Exploring the history, traditions, literature and wildlife of Ireland, it also lists and describes the towns, villages and hamlets. Walks and motor tours seek out the hidden corners and the finest scenery. Written by people who live and work in Ireland, backed by the AA's research expertise and the Ordnance Survey's mapping, this guide is as useful to local residents and the faithful who return to Ireland year after year, as it is to first-time visitors.

The Story of Ireland

VICTOR KELLY

Ireland lay on the edge of the Old World, the ultimate destination for successive migratory waves of early and medieval peoples driven westward from Europe to seek refuge, subsistence and fortune in this green, wet, forbidding and remote landscape. Inevitably, geography and environment have shaped the culture of the Irish. From 4000 BC till the colonisation of the New World in the 17th century, the barrier of the great Atlantic Ocean discouraged fresh conquests beyond the Western Sea and hemmed the Irish within their island home. With outlet denied and limited space to manoeuvre, new and permanent settlements were built on the old, and created rich strata of varied and contrasting cultures.

For some, this cold and remote land proved too inhospitable. New colonies were not supported with sufficient impetus and were absorbed within the indigenous culture. Yet during the early and medieval period Irish society was continuously enriched and renewed by the contributions and genius of new settlers; the merging of the old with the new created an invigorating cross-fertilisation of cultures. It is only a partial truth to say that the newcomers became 'more Irish than the Irish', and in a more modern age Ulster settlers have strenuously preserved their separate identity.

Cut off from the mainland of Europe and separated from North America by 3000 miles of sea, the land of Ireland has imbued its inhabitants with a sense of loneliness and isolation and turned their feelings and emotions inward. A special relationship has built up between the people and the land. The emigrants of the 18th and 19th centuries left Ireland reluctantly and retained a nostalgic longing for their homeland. It is the land that has moulded the character of the Irish, and in turn people have shaped the environment.

The earliest colonists were the Mesolithic people. Fearful of the dark forests and central bogs, they clung to the coasts, the flint bearing cliffs, the river valleys and the lake shores. Food gatherers and fisherfolk, they were the prisoners of the environment and made no impression upon it.

The megalith builders

From about 3500 BC and for more than a thousand years, European society experienced a radical transformation. Restless groups of people were on the move, and one migratory route was the perilous journey from the Mediterranean through Iberia and Western France to Ireland. Along this route travelled countless companies of Neolithic peoples, who were much more creative and adventurous in thought and deed, technology and organisation than their Mesolithic predecessors. In Ireland, to meet their economic needs, they created agricultural and technological revolutions, clearing parts of the forests for arable farming and stock raising, manufacturing stone axes and producing high quality pottery. Above all, they were a deeply religious people, who, mostly on inaccessible sites on hill tops, buried their dead in enduring and spectacular megalithic ('great stone') tombs,

The Rock of Cashel – principal stronghold of the Kings of Munster from the 4th to the 12th century

with votive offerings to their gods and goddesses. No other group has left in the Irish countryside such vivid, mysterious and compelling traces of their social, spiritual and material culture as the Neolithic people. In religious zeal alone, perhaps the Irish owe more to them than they realise.

There are two main types of tomb, the gallery grave and the passage grave, each with variations. The gallery graves have narrow burial chambers, sometimes segmented and with forecourts for rituals. The passage graves are more imposing, with long narrow passages, usually with corbelled roofs, as entrances to the burial chambers. In some instances passage graves are grouped in cemeteries; the most notable concentration is in the Boyne Valley, and the most famous passage grave in this complex is New Grange.

Celts and Christians

During the half millenium before Christ, waves of people with Indo-European roots and loose linguistic and cultural links swept across Europe to Ireland. In a broad sense they were known as Celts. Much of Ireland's Celtic past is hidden in the mists of mythology and sentiment, due in part to highly imaginative but largely unreliable medieval sources, but it is generally agreed that the last of these Celtic invaders were the Gaels, a superior iron-working warrior aristocracy.

The Celts held military prowess in high esteem. Minstrels sang in praise of heroic deeds, poets honoured the warrior in verse, and plunder was regarded as due reward for victory in war. Emphasis on military valour encouraged political disunity. There were hundreds of petty kings ruling local kingdoms, or tuatha, more powerful over-kings of three or four tuatha, and the 'Ard-Ri' or High King. Yet being Ard-Ri meant no more than the claim to be the greatest of the kings of Ireland, the King of Kings who would constantly be challenged by his nearest rivals. Divine wrath was never far away: the land shaped the destiny of even the greatest of these kings, for famine, the dryness of cows and the scarcity of corn could be interpreted as signs of divine disfavour and false kingship. Thus the Druids (and later the abbots) could ordain religious sanctions, while the Brehons; the judges of the political, social and economic provisions of the law tracts, could apply legal curbs to royal power. In this way religion and law created a form of social and cultural control and unity.

The typical Celtic dwelling was a small farmstead, encircled by a ditch and a bank of earth which served as a hedge for livestock, but could be used for defence in emergency. There were some 30,000 to 40,000 of these earth ring forts, or 'raths', with adjacent fields. Much more substantial, and more common in the stonier west, were the stone forts (or 'cashels') like Staigue (in County Kerry); and quite distinct again were the great hill forts encircling summits with enormous ramparts, banks and fosses, the residences of aspiring Supreme Kings, as at Eamain Macha, Tara and Cashel.

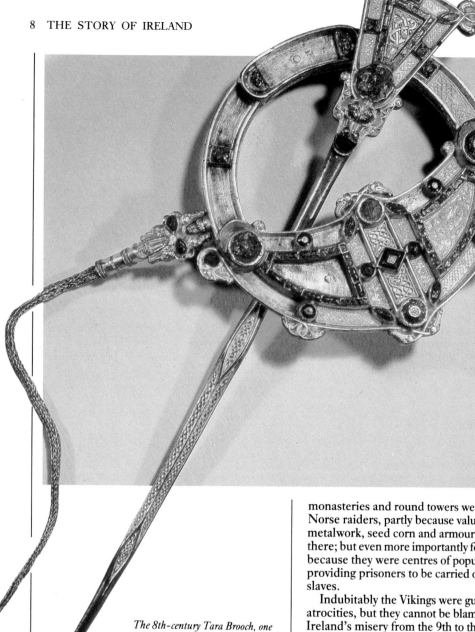

*The 8th-century Tara Brooch, one
of the finest examples of Celtic art. It
is now in the National Museum of
Ireland, Dublin*

It was in the field of art that the Celts excelled.
Poised on the brink of the known world and
spared from Roman legions and barbarian
invaders, they developed in relative peace the art
form of spirals and curves known as 'La Tène'.
From the fifth to the ninth centuries AD, after St
Patrick had brought the Christian Gospel to
Ireland, the sheltered monastic retreats and
schools developed a most remarkable and
original fusion of abstract Celtic and Christian
representations in sculpture, in illuminated and
decorated manuscripts and in metalwork. The
Tara brooch, the Ardagh Chalice, the Bealin
Cross and the Book of Kells are a few of the many
wonderful examples of this almost perfect art.

The Vikings
The reputation of the Vikings has suffered at the
hands of the Irish churchmen. Their hostile pens
give contemporary but distorted views of the
Norse invaders of ninth- and tenth-century
Ireland, describing them as mere marauders,
pillagers of church property, murderers,
incendiaries, destroyers and plunderers.
    The reality was very different. Certainly the

monasteries and round towers were targets for
Norse raiders, partly because valuables like
metalwork, seed corn and armour were stored
there; but even more importantly for the Vikings,
because they were centres of population,
providing prisoners to be carried off and sold as
slaves.
    Indubitably the Vikings were guilty of
atrocities, but they cannot be blamed for all
Ireland's misery from the 9th to the 11th
centuries. Secular sources show large scale
butchery and villainy by the Irish themselves, and
some of these reports concern monastic houses
where saintly qualities had evaporated as house
fought against house or took sides in lay quarrels
and battles.
    The ninth and tenth centuries can justifiably
be called the Viking Age. For the first 50 years,
from AD 830 to 880, the Viking raids devastated
large areas and subjected the country to
tremendous pressure; AD 880 to 980 were years
of comparative peace. Treasures from the raids
were taken to Scandinavia where they are still
being discovered in Viking graves today. There
was a resurgence of Viking military activity from
AD 920 to 980, but by this time the symbols of the
Norsemen's peaceful pursuits, the warehouses
and trading centres, were open to Irish attack and
the Vikings were as much defenders as attackers.
By the 11th century, the Viking menace had
vanished.
    At no time did the Vikings come in sufficient
numbers to colonise Ireland; nor did they even
contemplate such a conquest. Their aim was to
establish trading bases and settlements in a few
great coastal towns and their hinterlands. In this
they were very successful. Their lasting
monuments are ports like Dublin and Limerick;
their less conspicuous legacy to the Irish was the

transmission of trading, maritime and marketing skills, the use of coins and the enjoyment of civilised town life.

The Anglo-Normans
Temporarily united against the Vikings by the legendary warrior-king Brian Boru, by the 12th century Ireland was once more being torn by rivalries between kings. Political disunity invited intervention. In 1166 Dermot McMurrough, King of Leinster, driven into exile by the Kings of Connacht and Breiffni, appealed for help to Henry II of England. His call was answered by the Anglo-Norman knights of the Welsh border, the greatest being Richard Strongbow, Earl of Pembroke, whose reward was the hand of Eva McMurrough and Dermot's kingdom. Other Norman barons were quick to build upon Strongbow's successes, like John de Courcy, who from 1177 to 1185 carried out a highly successful private military adventure into East Ulster, consolidating his hold upon the area by building the great stone castles of Carrickfergus and Dundrum, and atoning for his sins by creating the beautiful Cistercian Abbey at Inch, near Downpatrick. From the start of this Anglo-Norman enterprise, Henry II had looked anxiously across the Irish Sea at the growing power of his overmighty barons and in 1171 the crown assumed the Lordship of Ireland.

Some medieval and modern scribes have blamed Dermot for all of Ireland's woes, accusing him of introducing English oppression and destroying Erin's soul. Others argue that the failure to complete the conquest was Ireland's tragedy.

By 1250 the invaders had won most of the east, the centre and the south, about two-thirds of the land, but that was the extent of their triumphs. After that an Irish resurgence recovered most of the lost territory. Land and people stood in the way of a complete Norman victory. The inhospitable terrain of West Ulster and Connacht proved difficult to subdue and the Irish were stubbornly opposed to Anglo-Norman ways. Abandoned for long periods by the English crown and being thin on the ground, many Norman knights gave up the struggle, married into Irish families, followed Irish customs and became 'more Irish than themselves'.

Yet the Anglo-Normans left a legacy: towns and villages the Irish were loath to inhabit; systematic manorial agriculture the pastoral Irish refused to adapt; centralised government alien to Irish thought and habits, a jury system, an economy based on rents and money, magnificent castles, cathedrals and abbeys.

The Tudors and the Plantation of Ulster
By early Tudor times the Irish military revival had swept back English rule to 'the Pale', a narrow stretch around Dublin. 'Beyond that the Great Captains, without licence of the King,' made war and peace for themselves and obeyed 'only such as may subdue them by the sword,' wrote Daniel O'Connell in a later history. This situation was intolerable to the Tudors. Mary Tudor began a policy of 'planting' loyal settlers in Ireland, and with the Reformation making a Catholic Ireland strategically significant to England's continental enemies and to her own security, Elizabeth I resolved upon a bloody conquest. Remote Ulster felt the full force of her

armed might and in 1607 the surrender of the great Hugh O'Neill, Earl of Tyrone, opened the way for James I's Plantation of Ulster. It changed the face and culture of Ulster and the course of Irish history.

Ulster had remained the most Gaelic of the Provinces. Isolated geographically by a drumlin belt from Dundalk to Sligo Bay, by the Mourne and Carlingford mountains and the loughs and bogs of the Erne area, and scarcely touched by the precarious English footholds at Carrickfergus and Newry, the Gaelic culture in Ulster was undisturbed until 1609. The planners of the Plantation project intended the almost complete replacement of rebellious Catholic Irish landholders with loyal Presbyterian Scots and Anglican English settlers – the 'planters'. Early in James I's reign planters poured into Counties Antrim and Down, but settlement west of the Bann proved more difficult. The adventurous, tough, land-hungry Scottish pioneers attempted to take over large, hostile, native portions; the less determined English were content to settle the more secure Lagan Valley and move up to the lower lands of Armagh, Tyrone and Fermanagh. The London Livery Companies developed County Londonderry. Though the Irish, many of whom stayed on the land as tenants, rose in rebellion in 1641 and swept away most of the original settlements, fresh waves of settlers came in the later 17th century to ensure a considerable Protestant presence in Ulster.

The planters created a landscape geared to advanced agriculture, the needs of trade and the problems of defence, and introduced a culture based on the Protestant religion and economic success. Forests were felled, farms were hewn out of the wilderness and new towns and villages, patterned on British models, were thrust into the remotest extremeties. The walls of Londonderry, a mile round and 18ft thick, were later a refuge for Protestant families fleeing from the rebels in 1641 and the Jacobite army in 1689. The success of the plantation depended on the strength of village networks clustered around castles and bawns (fortified enclosures) for defence, and around the market crosses for trade and wealth. The abiding and distinctive changes were stubbornly resisted by the native Irish, resentful of the loss of land and unwilling to conform to an alien culture.

The Anglo-Irish Ascendancy
In 1649, Cromwell followed up his victory over Charles I of England by invading Ireland. Drogheda and Wexford were sacked with brutal massacres, and thousands of Catholics were forcibly deported. Protestant settlers assumed control of most of Ireland, a process confirmed when Catholic James II was defeated by William III at the Battle of the Boyne in 1690. This was the prologue to the Ascendancy, the control of Ireland by the Anglo-Irish, Protestants of English descent.

Economically secure because they owned five-sixths of the land, on which they built large estates and great mansions, the Anglo-Irish enforced their supremacy on the Catholics by a crippling Penal Code, and on the Presbyterians by economic and religious sanctions. Georgian Dublin, with its great buildings and civilised life, became a splendid and beautiful capital city.

The elegant façade of Dublin's Old Parliament Building (c. 1729)—regarded as one of the century's finest specimens

Despite their power and status the small clique of ruling Protestant gentry was caught between two worlds: their Irishness that spurred them on towards greater independence, and their connection with England, of which they were so much a part. Their political aspirations were boosted in 1783 when the English government yielded to the threats of the Volunteers – 'the armed might of the Protestant Nation', and conceded parliamentary independence in the form of Grattan's Parliament. Their confidence was rudely shaken in 1798 by the insurrection of the United Irishmen, inspired largely by northern republican Presbyterians; and their dependence on the English connection was confirmed by the crushing of the rebellion by English armies. An ungrateful Westminster Government decided upon an Act of Union, which abolished Grattan's Protestant Parliament.

The Great Famine

The Anglo-Irish gentry had lost their Parliament, but not their land or local power and status. Tenants in pre-famine years subdivided their already tiny farms into even smaller holdings of minute fields and thatched whitewashed cottages of mud and stone; but the demands of a rapidly increasing population continued to outstrip supply. Peasants, desperate for land, encroached upon the infertile bogs and pushed up the harsh and rough mountainside with 'lazy beds' – beds of prolific potatoes – providing subsistence for their large families. Inevitably catastrophe struck. In 1845, blight partly destroyed the potato crop; total disaster followed the next year and between 1846 and 1850 famine and fever claimed one million lives. Another million fled the land.

The Famine hit hardest in the impoverished west and remote south. It had relatively little direct impact on the more prosperous Eastern Ulster, Leinster and the Midlands; but it was an event of momentous historical significance for the whole of Ireland.

Some of the bankrupt landlords, ruined by the Famine, seized the chance offered by the Encumbered Estates Acts, to sell their Irish Estates, and the Land War of 1879–1882 carried their downfall a stage further. By 1914 successive British governments had transferred the ownership of three-quarters of the soil of Ireland from landlords to tentants. From that time empty mansions and demesnes were stark reminders of a vanished Anglo-Irish ruling class.

The famine taught the peasantry the cruel

lesson of the awful consequences of subdivision of land and total reliance on the potato. The 'cottier' class of smallholders was wiped out and those who remained on the land were resolved to turn to pasture and to keep intact or even enlarge the family farms, which were passed on either to widows or to eldest sons.

Rural Ireland entered a new age of late marriages, large scale emigration of the disinherited and clerically imposed chastity.

The British Government had responded to the crisis in a manner consistent with the current economic ideas of laissez-faire and free trade, but the Great Famine is deeply embedded in the folk memories of the Irish at home and overseas.

The rise of Belfast
Meanwhile, industrialisation was changing the face and future of the north-east. From a small town of some 19,000 inhabitants in 1800, Belfast experienced an astonishing growth in population to 386,000 in 1914, unique in an Irish context and remarkable in a British one. During the second half of the 19th and early 20th centuries this proud and prosperous city and its neighbourhood outpaced by far the rest of Ireland in industrial and economic progress. Its glory was found in its great shipbuilding, engineering, ropemaking and textile concerns and its fame was due, in no small measure, to the inherent energy and intelligence of its workforce and the enterprise of its Presbyterian entrepreneurs. But its wellbeing was threatened by the Home Rule crises of 1886, 1893 and 1911. Belfast's manufacturing and commercial communities were convinced that Ulster's prosperity depended upon her links with Britain and the protection of the Westminster Parliament. They believed that government from Dublin would mean financial and industrial disadvantage to the north-east. Economic arguments were a powerful instrument in shaping their opposition to Home Rule.

Protestant zeal for wealth and power was tempered by a quest for godly favour and the puritan qualities of sobriety and hard work. Religious fervour and fear fuelled anti-Home Rule feeling, and in 1920–1921 influenced Lloyd George's decision to propose partition, as a 'temporary' solution of the Irish question.

Gael and Gall
The modern period is also the age of Irish Nationalism, a movement divided between constitutionalists seeking political independence by peaceful means and revolutionaries marching to more martial airs. In 1916 and the early 1920s the men of force drew their inspiration from a mystical Catholicism and caught their idealism from a romantic view of Gaelic culture. Their energies were directed towards the expulsion of the Gall, or foreigner, from Ireland and from their struggles there emerged in 1921 an independent Irish Free State of 26 counties, now the Republic of Ireland.

To the Irish, history is not just an account of past events and people who lived long ago, but a reality, related to their everyday experiences.

Main picture: Life was hard for the Irish peasant after the Great Famine. A family outside a sod cabin or 'black house' Co Mayo c. 1860

Inset: Today's hi-tech aircraft engineering at Short Bros, Belfast

Natural History and Landscape

C DOUGLAS DEANE

Intimate links between the land, the wildlife and the climate have made Ireland's natural history quite unique. Flowers bloom here that are otherwise found only in North America or the Mediterranean, while animals commonplace to Britain are unknown. The reasons lie far back in the making of the landscape millions of years ago.

Geology

For its size Ireland has the most varied geology in the world and visitors will find rock structures of every age and type. The highlands of Connemara and Donegal are girded by hard rocks over 3000 million years old, and are amongst the most ancient in the world, formed as the earth's crust was still hardening. The central plain has a floor of carboniferous limestone 300 million years old, rising to mountains in Fermanagh and Sligo and forming the largest limestone pavement in Europe at the Burren, in Co Clare. In the north-east, rocks are younger, more spectacular, and the Antrim coast is world famous for the geological symmetry of the Giant's Causeway. Here are beds of soft lias clay, rich in fossil shell-fish and sea lillies, and cliffs of chalk or white limestone, laid down in a warm sea when dinosaurs dominated the world. Above are great layers of black basalt poured out by volcanoes as red hot lava 40 million years ago, and later hardened and cooked into symmetrical shapes, containing beautiful crystals of the rare mineral zeolite.

In Co Down rocks are hard shales which made a useful building stone in medieval times, and in the south-west of Ireland they are arranged in great folds, as in the massive mountain ranges of Cork and Kerry. In one quarry in Kilkenny are found whole fronds of ferns 400 million years old, delicately preserved as beautiful fossils. The granites of the Wicklow and Mourne mountains, the Newry hills and Donegal were cut and polished and used for building and decoration in cities all over the British Isles. And not a little of the land surface is due to Ice Age glaciers spreading into Ireland from Scotland and smoothing and rounding the landscape. When they began to melt some 13,500 years ago, they left behind an island with an island's peculiarities in wildlife.

Climate

The climate of Ireland is more equable than in the sister island of Britain. Summers are cooler,

The limestone pavements of the Burren support rare plants such as Bloody Cranesbill

winters milder and the ripening of crops and fruit somewhat later. The Spanish chestnut and walnut seldom ripen fully in Ireland, yet in the south and west, warmed by the Gulf Stream, exotic plants from all over the world flourish in rich growth.

A unique tapestry

Irish natural history is made up of a tapestry of many different threads, all connected with the history of the landscape. After the retreat of the glaciers, many plant and animal species migrated into Ireland from Europe over land corridors left

Near Lough Sheedagh, Connemara, Co Galway. During the ice ages local glaciers scraped the land down to its underlying igneous rocks

behind by a receding ocean, but some failed to get there before the seas covered the corridors over. So Ireland has about 1400 species of flowering plants and ferns compared to 2500 species in Britain, but it also has a number of both plants and animals not found in Britain, and which reappear again only in southern Europe: the giant butterwort, Mediterranean heath, St Dabeoc's heath, kidney-leaved saxifrage and more. The arbutus or strawberry tree grows to a greater size in Ireland than elsewhere in Europe and there are a number of plants of North American origin.

The animal world, too, has gaps and differences. Ireland has no moles, harvest mice, weasels or wild cats. Ireland has seven species of bats compared with 15 species in Britain. The story is the same with birds: Ireland is not rich in woodland species and possesses half the warblers on the British list, with no woodpeckers, nightingales or nuthatches and only three of five species of owl. And yet being sited on the western rim of Europe, with a long and varied coastline of cliffs, estuaries and many inland lakes and loughs, it has a rich selection of seabirds and other aquatic species; and having a moist and milder climate Ireland also has numerous wildfowl and waders in winter.

The same sparseness of species is true of reptiles, amphibians and freshwater fish. There are no snakes in Ireland, not, sadly, because St Patrick drove them out, but probably because Ireland became an island first, leaving Britain joined to the mainland of Europe for longer. The three amphibian species in Ireland (almost certainly introduced) include the natterjack toad, confined to a small area in north Kerry. Amongst the freshwater fish, pike, roach, minnow and perhaps perch may be the result of introduction. As with the flowers, there are animal species in Ireland (like the spotted slug of Kerry and Cork) which are not found again until the Iberian Peninsula. Other species have developed characteristics best suited to local conditions, the mountain hare, stoat, jay and dipper amongst them.

It is probable that new species await discovery, as happened in 1964 with the finding of the bank vole in Kerry (almost certainly the result of recent introduction) and there is talk of water shrews and water voles being seen in Ireland, but without confirmation.

Where to go for wildlife

There are certain key places in Ireland which are especially good for studying natural history. Organisations devoted to conservation of the countryside include the Ulster Trust for Nature Conservation, the Irish Wildbird Conservancy, the Forest and Wildlife Service (in the Republic) and the Forest Service and Department of the Environment in Northern Ireland. All have developed a number of nature reserves and areas of scientific importance. Lists of places to go are available either from these organisations or from AA centres and tourist offices. The following is a small selection of sites of special interest.

The Burren

The Burren is a massive plateau of bare grey hills hunched in a hundred square miles of north Clare, a naked waterless land of massive stone pavements. It is a botanist's paradise, a meeting place of arctic-alpine plants living side by side with species from the Mediterranean. Nowhere else in the world can the white flowers of the mountain avers be seen growing beside the dense-flowered orchids of southern Europe. Here it grows with a freedom unequalled elsewhere and has a second flowering period in August. Other plants of the Burren are the rare pyramidal bugle and various orchids such as the bee, spider and fragrant orchids. There are blue seas of spring gentian, red splashes of bloody cranesbill, yellow clumps of rock roses and, hidden in 'grykes' in the stone pavement, the delicate maidenhair fern. The Burren is a place of wonder to which people from all over the world come back time and again. Animals too are surprisingly plentiful in this world of bare stone, from wild goats silhouetted against the skyline to the viviparous lizard basking in the sun.

Fermanagh Lakeland

This is a unique countryside and apart from the beauty of its lovely lakes, it has peace and tranquillity, and the wonder of the River Erne. Born in Lough Gowna 15 miles to the south of the River Shannon, it carves a great wide valley through limestone to the north and, before reaching the sea 70 miles away in Donegal Bay, it spreads itself over a third of Co Fermanagh, giving pleasure to a whole countryside. Studded with islands, the Erne is the summer breeding place of gulls, terns and wildfowl, including the common scoter (actually rather rare as a breeding bird). So big are the fish in Lough Erne that a pike must be over 25 pounds before anybody will turn his head to look at it, and there are bream, pollan and roach, with, in Lough Melvin, the Arctic charr.

Fermanagh is also a network of underground caves, of which the most important are the

Opposite top: The rich-soiled limestone lowland of the Golden Vale, Co Tipperary. Bottom left: Nesting gannets, Saltee Island. Bottom right: Spotted slugs. Above top: The eye-catching Kingfisher. Bottom: Mountain Avens, the Burren

Marble Arch Caves, a strange and fascinating underground landscape where abstract formations decorate the roofs, walls and floors of caverns.

The Kingdom of Kerry

Kerry, sited in the south-west corner of Ireland, is a land of great purple mountains, glittering lakes and a soft landscape warmed by the Gulf Stream, which produces a benign climate. Hot summers, like cold winters, are exceptional and soft warm rain is expected to fall every week of the year. The result is a lush richness of vegetation, both in the wild countryside and in grand gardens like Glanleem, where visitors can walk an avenue between tropical tree ferns. The embothrium or 'firebush' grows into a tree nearly fifty feet high, and even garden plants have spilled out into the countryside: fuchsia, balsam and New Zealand flax. But the jewel in Kerry's crown is the abundance of wild plants, from the Mediterranean and from the New World. Here can be seen the greater butterwort or 'bog violet', the grandiflora of southern Europe, a blue flower at the top of a long thin stalk and below a rosette

of insect seeking leaves. The Kerry lily grows side by side with the shy ladies' tresses orchid from North America, Canadian blue-eyed grass, American pipe-wort (on Lough Currane) and the rare naias. Some naturalists doubt that the blue-eyed grass is truly native, believing it to have been introduced with American grain during the famine periods of the 19th century. Also here are London pride, or St Patrick's cabbage, the filmy fern and the Royal fern, which grows so tall and lush it acts as a hedge between fields.

The spotted slug is confined in Ireland to Kerry and Cork and in mainland Europe to the Iberian Peninsula. On Torc Mountain are remnants of Ireland's wild red deer, though mixed with blood from British deerparks. The same mountain has a herd of Japanese Sika deer, but there is no mixing of the two species. The natterjack toad hides at the head of Castlemaine and around Lough Caragh. Kerry is still the stronghold of the threatened chough (a red-billed crow), and up around the Ring of Kerry drift 30ft long basking sharks. The islands, too, are rich in seabirds, with 20,000 gannets breeding on the Little Skellig, and Manx shearwaters, storm petrels and auks scattered in profusion round other islands.

Strangford Lough

The name means 'violent fjord', but this almost land-locked part of the sea, some 18 miles long, is rich in sanctuaries and reserves under the control of the National Trust. There are breeding colonies of terns and gulls, and the wintering wildfowl include brent geese, while numerous waders can also be seen. There is also a rich underwater life. A fine observation hide and wildfowl collection have been established at Castle Espie.

Bird watching in Ireland

As well as having a number of species like the chough which are more common than in Britain, Ireland is internationally important for its great seabird breeding colonies, with a total of 21 breeding species on cliffs and islands round its rim. It is equally famous for its hordes of wintering wildfowl and waders. Ireland is the first 'landfall' in winter for some northern species, which either use Ireland as a stepping stone to more southerly areas or spend the winter in the rich feeding areas inland and on the coast. A large proportion of the pale-breasted Brent geese which breed in the Canadian Arctic spend winter in Ireland. Down the west coast, wintering barnacle geese come to graze on grassland and on islands like Inishkea. The great sea loughs and estuaries hold vast flocks of winter waders, golden plovers, greenshanks, knots, black and bartailed godwits, dunlins and more.

Being on the western rim of Europe, the great headlands are ideal places for watching ocean species such as great and sooty shearwaters and various species of skuas, mainly from August through to October. And when severe weather hits Britain or the rest of Europe, Ireland is a haven to eastern species of birdlife from ducks to thrushes. A full list of reserves and sanctuaries is obtainable from the Irish Tourist Board (Information Sheet No 56), and a leaflet on bird watching in Northern Ireland is obtainable from the Northern Ireland Tourist Board.

Literary Ireland

PETER SOMERVILLE-LARGE

'. . . and we'll find hearteners among men
That ride upon horses'

*T*he inspiration for this reflection of Yeats' was
Galway racetrack, a fact which emphasises how
there is hardly a rock in Ireland without its literary
association. The relationship between Irish literature
and landscape is a beguiling study. There are other
cogent reasons why the literary arts flourish here: a
strong oral tradition linked with the music and poetry
of the bards continued up to the present century, and
Irish people remain good talkers and admirers of a
well-told story. Crucial also has been Ireland's
history. But the mysterious beauty of Ireland's
landscape plays a major part. Even in Dublin, which
has fostered so much literary genius, the mountains
and countryside are not far away.

Voices in a landscape

Certain writers have made parts of Ireland
particularly their own. John Synge's tramps
trudged through every part of the Wicklow Hills,
while West Kerry and the Aran Islands offered
him material about a way of life that had not been
previously recorded in written literature. The
shabby streets of Dublin gave Joyce and Sean
O'Casey their material. Although Sligo is the
mainspring of Yeats' imagination, much of his
later poetry focused on the land of limestone,
wind-bent trees and ancient towers a hundred
miles south around East Galway and Clare.

People are aware of the haunts of these great
names, but one of the delights of looking at
literature through landscape is seeking out places
where less prominent writers found their
inspiration. Such a situation is Mary Carbery's
Farm by Lough Gur, or hymn writer (*There is a
green hill far away*) Mrs Alexander's own green
hill outside Strabane, not a target for tourists. It is
not always a matter of looking for a plaque on a
house, since outside Dublin plaques are rare.
Sometimes you have to soak up a location without
finding evidence of the author it nurtured. Oliver
Goldsmith's Westmeath, for example, no longer
has any tangible trace of his presence. Some
places have minimal, yet fascinating contacts
with literary figures, and have often slipped
notice altogether. If you care about Laurence
Sterne, you will seek out the ruined mill at
Annamoe, Co Wicklow, where the infant Sterne
fell into the stream. Admirers of Thomas Carlyle
who have read his *Reminiscences of My Irish
Journey* should seek out the 'queer old house' in
Kilkenny where the fierce Scotsman on his
desolate tour of post-famine Ireland woke one
hot July morning to the sound of starlings.

Around Dublin

In Dublin the traveller finds his literary ghosts
everywhere, from Behan's pubs to Beckett's
Foxrock to Patrick Kavanagh's stretch of canal,
even to brooding Dublin Castle where Edmund
Spenser worked while writing part of *The Faerie
Queen*. The Castle is also scene of the climax of
George Moore's *Drama in Muslin* and for the
vivid opening passage of Sean O'Casey's
autobiography, where the sick child watches the
procession of carriages bound for the vice-regal
ball. In St Patrick's Cathedral, the presence of
Jonathan Swift is far more impressive than the
tattered banners and battle monuments. The
graves of Swift and his beloved Stella are marked
by bronze plaques, while nearby are his bust and
great epitaph.

Other Dublin buildings associated with Swift
are Marsh's library and St Patrick's Hospital
which he founded 'for the reception of aged
lunaticks and other diseased persons'. There is
also Trinity College, transformed since he was
there. Outside the west facade of Trinity stand

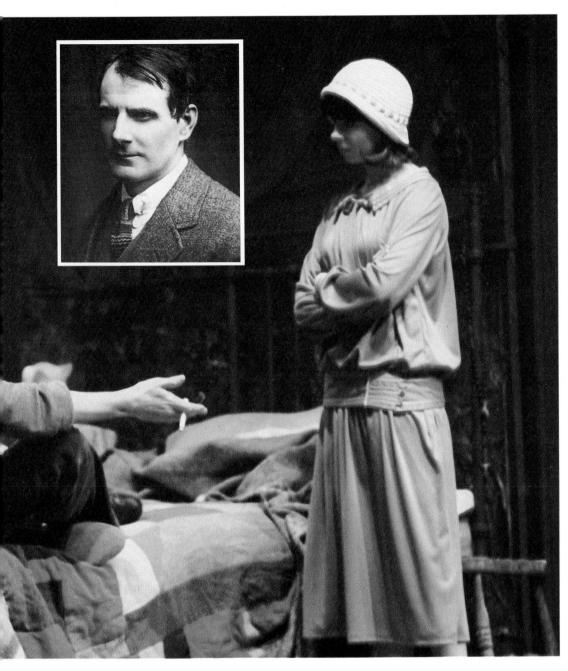

John Foley's statues of two other distinguished students, Oliver Goldsmith and Edmund Burke, philosopher and statesman. Burke was the model student who founded the Debating Society, while Goldsmith, the poor 'sizar' – awarded a meagre allowance – augmented it by writing lampoons and ballads.

A later student was Oscar Wilde, born in nearby Westland Row; when his father's medical practice prospered the family moved round the corner to smarter Merrion Square. Since Wilde's plays first appeared in London, he is not a part of Dublin's vigorous theatrical tradition, which reached its zenith with the Abbey Theatre, fostered by Yeats, Lady Gregory and friends. Across the Liffey, the modern Abbey Theatre contains a set of portraits saved from the destruction of the original, featuring those who did so much to encourage the Irish literary renaissance in the early years of this century.

On the south side of Merrion Square stands the house where Sheridan LeFanu wrote many of his ghostly fantasies. Charles Maturin and Bram Stoker also found inspiration for horror in the gas-lit city. Yeats occupied Number 82 for a time, while his friend George Russell the poet, mystic and economist (who wrote under the pseudonym Æ) edited *The Irish Homestead* at Number 84, Plunkett House. From Merrion Square it is a short distance to Ely Place, where novelist George Moore lived in simple elegance.

The fine row of buildings on the south side of Stephens Green once included University College, where poet Gerard Manley Hopkins languished as Professor of Greek and James Joyce received his higher education. Number 86, Newman House, its interior iced with elaborate plasterwork, was the home of the genial 18th-century eccentric, Buck Whaley, who walked to Jerusalem and whose name was used by Joyce in *Ulysses*, for the character based on Oliver St John Gogarty.

On the Ulysses trail

The museum in the Martello Tower and Sandycove where that stately Buck Mulligan stepped out with his shaving gear in the novel lovingly encompasses most aspects of Joyce's life. It also supplies useful maps tracing the routes of *Ulysses* characters Stephen Daedalus and Leopold Bloom during the long June day in which the novel takes place. Some places mentioned are quite intact, like the villa on Dalkey avenue where Joyce taught briefly. (Climb Dalkey Hill for another literary diversion – half way up is Torca Cottage to which young George Bernard Shaw moved with his family from dreary Synge Street.) Others have been swept away. Bloom's house in Eccles Street is gone, and all of Nighttown. Tyrone Street of the Crowded Doors succumbed long ago to morality and town planning.

The Joyce reader will also go to Bray to view Number 8 Martello Terrace on the seafront, where the Joyce family argued so bitterly on Christmas day. Bray opens on to Wicklow and the Wicklow hills, Synge's 'grey and wintry sides of many glens'.

Southward among the lush plains of Leinster, Kilkenny city harbours Kilkenny College whose pupils included Jonathan Swift, philosopher Bishop Berkeley, and playwrights William Congreve and George Farquar. Almost within sight of Kilkenny rises Slievenamon, on whose slope stands the tower of Kilcash, known by the Irish as a symbol of Ireland's lost past, a source of poetic metaphor and the subject of a renowned lament hauntingly translated by Frank O'Connor.

Two Tudor poets

Walter Raleigh lived for years in Youghal, south-east of Cork: he used to go visiting fellow poet Edmund Spenser at Kilcoman. The stump of Kilcoman Castle beside a wild lake marks the place where Spenser wrote about the surrounding hills, the 'fair forests' and rivers swimming with nymphs and silver scaly trout. At Doneraille, outside the demesne of Doneraille Court, which Spenser knew, stands the charming statue of Canon Sheehan, priest and novelist. Not far away, at Kildorrey, look hard for the ruin of novelist Elizabeth Bowen's beloved Bowen's Court.

The steep streets of Cork

In Cork City stands the red and white tower of Shandon Church, topped by a golden fish, and *The Bells of Shandon* ring to remind us of the writer of the poem, Father Prout. Writers Sean O'Faolain and Frank O'Connor were Corkmen, and O'Connor, in particular, brings to life in his short stories and autobiography the steep shabby streets of his childhood.

Westward in Carbury, low furzy hills, bogs and outcrops of rock announce the country of Flurry Knox, of *Some Experiences of an Irish RM* fame. His creators, Edith Somerville and Martin Ross (real name Violet Martin) are buried in the churchyard at Castle Townshend. Drishane, Edith's slated grey home stands at the head of the village overlooking the sea.

Islands and O'Briens

South of Roaring Water Bay, Cape Clear was the home of one of Munster's island authors,

A fine bust of James Joyce can be found on St Stephen's Green, Dublin

Conchur O Siochain, 'The Man from Cape Clear'. At Gouganebarra 'the Tailor' and 'Anstey' beguiled a passing author and created a furore: the church came down heavily on the racy stories Eric Cross wrote about these two characters. The oak trees of Glengarriff evoke Emily Lawless' *Dirge of the Munster Forest* – 'Bring out the hemlock! Bring the funeral yew!' At the foot of Hungry Hill (whose name was taken by Daphne Du Maurier for her historical romance about the Beare peninsula), the fate of the outlaw, Morty Oge O'Sullivan, anti-hero of JM Froude's poem *The Two Chiefs of Dunboy*, also inspired a fine lament by another unfashionable poet, Jeremiah Callanan. 'A curse, blessed ocean, be on thy green water . . .' he wrote, for O'Sullivan was dragged through the waves from the stern of a ship.

Off the Dingle peninsula the Blasket Islands (now uninhabited) had a fine tradition of storytelling, continued by islanders who wrote about their harsh, yet rewarding, lives – Maurice O'Sullivan, Tomas O Crohan and Peig Sayers. Synge walked among the sands of west Kerry where Armada ships had foundered and gathered speech patterns for his plays.

The town of Listowel produced the playwright George FitzMaurice, as well as two contemporary Irish voices, Bryan MacMahon and the publican-playwright John B Keane. Killarney was the goal of many distinguished literary visitors during the 19th century, including Sir Walter Scott and Tennyson, who listened to buglers entertaining tourists by the lakeside and wrote: 'Blow, bugle blow, set the wild echoes flying . . .'

Northward is O'Brien country. Novelist Kate O'Brien lived in Limerick, while Edna O'Brien used her childhood at Scarriff in *The Country Girls*. Feakle was the home of Brian Merriman, the last of the great Gaelic poets.

The sun-splashed verandah of James Joyce's house, Bray Co Wicklow

The Swans of Coole

Across the Slieve Aughty mountains the town of Gort heralds the ruin of Coole, a stark testimony to Yeats' prophecy of desolation. Here stands the Autograph Tree, scratched by vandals and men of letters, where it is just possible to make out the initials of WB Yeats and his brother Jack, Synge's lyre cypher, a decisive GBS and Æ. Beside Coole Lake, swans are still to be seen, if not the 'nine and fifty' described by Yeats. Down the road, the tower in which Yeats lived, Thoor Ballylee, has been marvellously restored – a stark contrast with the wreck of the home of Lady Gregory, who worked with him to establish the Abbey Theatre in Dublin.

The far west

Within calling distance of Coole at Ardrahan is Tullira Castle, home of Edward Martyn, friend of Lady Gregory and Yeats and another early patron of the Abbey Theatre. The path of Synge can be traced on the Aran Islands, birthplace of writer Liam O'Flaherty. In Galway city the diminutive statue of the Gaelic writer Padraic O Conair sits in Eyre Square. The churchyard of Rahoon, featured in James Joyce's *The Dead*, lies beyond a Galway suburb. On the western road from Galway city stands Ross House, the gaunt home of Violet Martin, Edith Somerville's friend and co-writer of *Some Experiences of an Irish RM*. Another lakeside mansion, Moore hall, a Georgian shell on the shores of Lough Arrow, evokes the novels and autobiographical writings of George Moore.

In Connemara, Oliver St John Gogarty purchased Renvyle House, ancestral home of the Burkes, which he loved dearly until it was destroyed in the Civil War. Richard Murphy lived at Cleggan for many years, and there found themes for his poetry about the west. A surprising cluster of literary associations is found in Roscommon. The monks of Trinity Island on Lough Key compiled the Annals of Lough Ce. Rockingham Park is the site of Rockingham House, home of Edward King, who was the subject of Milton's poem *Lycidas*. Here too is the grave of Douglas Hyde, who collected and translated Gaelic poetry with a near perfect ear. This area, beside the 'lake of many isles across whose surface pass lovers' reflected dreams' described by Kathleen Raine (friend of Gavin Maxwell) provides the background for John McGahern's early novels. Not far away at Kilronan Abbey lies the 18th-century blind bard, Turlough O'Carolan, buried in 1738 after a four-day wake and a funeral procession that included ten harpers. Among his compositions was the tune to which *The Star Spangled Banner* is sung.

Where Trollope began

At Banagher by the Shannon stands the ruin of Cuba Court, and here Charlotte Brontë's sad widower, Arthur Bell Nicholls, lived after her death, keeping the childhood diaries of the Brontë children in a cupboard. Anthony Trollope worked at Banagher as a clerk for the Post Office Surveyor, and wrote his first two novels *The Kellys and The O'Kellys* and *The Mac Dermot of Ballycloran*. He was inspired to write the latter in 1843 after a journey in the course of his duties to Drumsna, County Leitrim, where he came across a mouldering house: 'The usual story, thought I, of Connacht gentlemen; an extravagant landlord, reckless tenants, debt, embarrassment, despair, ruin.'

Trollope's observation is reminiscent of *Castle Rackrent* by Maria Edgeworth, storytelling child prodigy and friend of Walter Scott, who lived nearby at Edgeworthstown (Mostrim). Her house is now an old people's home, but St John's church and a museum in the town contain notebooks of her remarkable domineering father and her own touching memorabilia, including a knitted purse and her steel spectacles.

Ulster's clean hard names

Until recently Ulster was not particularly noted for its poets and writers, but today it is from Northern Ireland that the strongest voices are heard.

'. . . So its Ballinamallard, its Crossmaglen,
Its Aughnacloy, its Donaghadee,
Its Magherafelt needs the best of men . . .'

. . . writes John Hewitt. 'I take my stand by Ulster names, Each clean hard name like a weathered stone . . .'

County Tyrone nurtured the 19th-century novelist, William Carleton and two distinguished modern Ulster writers, Benedict Kiely and John Montague. Belfast is the setting for Brian Moore's early melancholy novels, *The Feast of Lupercal* and *The Lonely Passion of Judith Hearne*. Another Belfast writer, the poet Louis MacNeice, grew up at Carrickfergus Rectory beside the grim castle.

Top: The childhood home at Carrickfergus Co Antrim, of the Belfast poet, Louis Macneice. Above: Ruined walls at Emdale, near Banbridge Co Down, mark the birthplace of Patrick Brontë, father of the Brontë Sisters

Kavanagh country

Celbridge Abbey in Kildare was once the home of Jonathan Swift's admirer Esther van Homrigh, who followed him to Ireland and became 'Vanessa' in his poetry. It provides one of the few surviving links with Swift outside the capital. North from Dublin through Slane in County Meath (birthplace of poet Francis Ledwidge, who died in World War I) is Bective, where many of Mary Lavin's quiet and understated short stories are set. Carrickmacross and the surrounding 'hungry hills' are remembered in Patrick Kavanagh's writing, while his home town thrives on his name. His school, his house, his grave and a bar are all labelled for the pilgrim. Nowadays you would look hard for 'A dog lying on a torn jacket under a heeled-up cart, a horse nosing along the posied headland, trailing a rusty plough . . .'

Donegal memories

County Derry was Seamus Heaney's pastoral inspiration, but more recently he has been inspired by Lough Derg in Donegal and the penitential pilgrimage around the little island, whose austerities have been recorded since the Middle Ages. Patrick MacGill and Paedar O'Donnell used the experience of life in harsh Donegal for their novels. Ballyshannon, the winding banks of Erne and the surrounding countryside of Donegal and Sligo are recalled in meandering detail in the lilting poetry of William Allingham. Although he preferred to live elsewhere, he is buried at Ballyshannon, up the airy mountain in St Ann's churchyard, which has a stupendous view overlooking Sligo Bay and Ben Bulben.

In search of Yeats

Which brings us to the wedge of Sligo, with its strange flat-topped mountains teeming with ancient legend and Yeatsian associations. The literary industry, where Yeats the poet is swallowed up by Yeats the myth, becomes wearying as earnest busloads take the place of 'the passing horseman' at Drumcliff, although many people would rather wander round County Sligo seeking out Ben Bulben and Knocknarea and Rosse's crawling tide and Lissadell and Lough Gill and even the disappointing little Lake Isle of Innisfree, than walk through Dublin picking up pieces of *Ulysses.*

But in his final poems, Yeats' genius sought out memories of Sligo, and his very last poem, *The Black Tower* – possibly associated with the lighthouse on Black Rock off Deadman's Point – welding poetry, landscape and mystery in powerful incantation, is one of the greatest justifications for any obsession with the link between landscape and literature.

'There in the tomb stand the dead upright,
But winds come up from the shores:
They shake when the winds roar,
Old bones upon the mountain shake.'

One of this century's most famous epitaphs is chiselled into the headstone of Yeats's grave, Drumcliff Co Sligo

Fountains of The Water of Life

TED BONNER

*W*hen the soldiers of Henry II paid their first
visit to Ireland in the 12th century, they found
the natives consuming, with great relish, a potion
which they called Uisce beatha (*pronounced Is-Kay
Ba-Ha*) and which means 'The Water of Life'. It is
said that the soldiery in question returned to England
speaking – or, indeed, singing – of little else, although
by that time they had anglicised 'Uisce' into
'Whiskey'. It is also said that Queen Elizabeth I was
partial to a drop of uisce beatha and if this is true, she
undoubtedly acquired the taste from Sir Walter
Raleigh, who notes in his diary that at Youghal,
County Cork, on his way to what is now Guyana, he
had 'received a supreme present of a 32-gallon cask of
the Earl of Cork's home-distilled uisce beatha.'

Before all this happened, however, whiskey
had to be invented, and although no one knows
exactly when this was done, the Irish are quite
certain that missionary monks, who had spread
out through the then-known world to preach the
gospel, returned to Ireland with a form of
distilling flask, known as an 'alembic', which they
had found in the Mediterranean area being used

Old Bushmills' whiskey – Irish Gold

for the production of perfumes or aromatics.
Certainly Aristotle, who was born in 347 BC,
mentions the art of distilling, and 600 years later
one Zosimos of Alexandria describes a still.

An accidental discovery?
Some unknown Irishman (whom many consider
deserved to be, if not canonised, at least
beatified) rapidly found a better use for the
alembic than making perfume and, anyway, there
could scarcely have been a brisk market for scent
in the Ireland of the eighth and ninth centuries.
He discovered, almost certainly by accident, that
if a fermented mixture is heated in a still (as the
alembic in its revised form was to be called) the
alcohol in the liquid boils at a lower temperature
than the water and can be captured by
condensation. This fermented mixture consists,
ideally, of a mixture of pure water, yeast and
unmalted and malted barley. (Malting is the
process whereby the barley is encouraged to
sprout and then stopped and dried, in order to
encourage the formation of natural enzymes
which convert its starches into sugar.) This
mixture is 'mashed' for a period and then boiled
in the stills – a distillation process which is
undertaken three times in the case of some Irish
whiskeys.

Having discovered this, our unknown
benefactor had yet another amazing truth to
unearth and this undoubtedly came about by
accident; he found that if this liquid from
distillation were poured into wooden barrels and
then stored away for a lengthy rest, the result was
quite delicious – it was, in fact, whiskey. I say he
came across this by accident because it would
seem highly probable that he hid some of the
distillate either underground or in caves and
forgot it until years later and then stumbled on it
again by accident. Great must have been the
rejoicings thereat.

Old Bushmills
The oldest licensed distillery in Ireland – indeed,
the oldest licensed distillery in the world – is in
Bushmills – a most attractive little village in
County Antrim, right up in the north-east corner
of the island. There is evidence to show that
distilling was taking place in the Bushmills area
in 1494 but, in 1608, when the province of Ulster
was held for King James I of England by Sir
Thomas Phillips, it was decided that there was so
much distilling being done that it must be
legalised and licensed. So Sir Thomas's
considerable powers were widened to include the
issue of such licences and (Sir Thomas was no
fool) he issued the first one to himself, in respect
of what is known to this day as 'Old Bushmills'. It
is in what must surely be one of the most
beautiful parts of Ireland and one steeped in
tradition and legend. Bushmills lies on the
ancient road stretching from Dunseverick Castle
(the remains of which still stand) right down
through Ireland to Royal Tara of the Kings.
When the greatest of all distillery chroniclers – a
Londoner called Arthur Barnard – visited
Bushmills in 1886 he began his account of that
visit in this fashion:
*'We stayed over Sunday at Portrush, and on
Monday morning started for Bushmills by the
celebrated Electric Railway which, for nearly six miles,
climbs the hills and rocks overhanging the sea; after
crossing the River Bush we found ourselves . . . within*

The labels say it all. Old Bushmills' whiskey enjoys a worldwide reputation – and, of course, the secret is in the water

The public can visit old and new Midleton Distilleries, the former is now a museum

a few minutes walk of the distillery. This very old work is about two miles from the Giant's Causeway which attracts a large number of tourists during the season from all parts of the world.'

Old Bushmills is distilling to this very day and, indeed, has been greatly modernised but without in any way degrading that peculiar and particular charm that is the product of its lovely rural setting and its great history of unbroken tradition. The distillery is served by the water of Saint Columb's Rill which, they say, flows as sweetly today as it has done for all those centuries since the saint stopped to bathe his face in its coolness and purity. Visitors are very welcome at Bushmills and are shown the various processes of whiskey making, including the huge copper stills, glowing warmly in the semi-darkness, and the air is fragrant with the aroma of malt. Needless to say, no visitor is allowed to leave without being offered a sample of the product which is now world famous.

Midleton – six in one

At one time there were about 2000 mini-distilleries operating in Ireland but gradually, with the imposition of stricter and stricter Revenue controls, the number was whittled down and only the great houses survived. When Arthur Barnard visited Ireland, there were 28 major distilleries, the majority of which were in Dublin. Now, there are but two; one is Old Bushmills and the other is Midleton, in County Cork. If Bushmills, as we have seen, is the oldest distillery in the world, Midleton is amongst the most modern. It was built on the site of another very old distillery which, in turn, represented the merger of five others, the oldest of which had begun distilling in 1779. Midleton lies half-way between Cork city and Youghal (hence possibly 'Middletown', though one 'd' got dropped somewhere) and is also in a beautiful rural setting: it has been carefully and fondly landscaped so that it in no way detracts from its lovely environment. It is much larger than Old Bushmills and is actually a complex of distilleries in one, so designed that it can produce the famous Irish whiskeys that were once distilled on their own individual sites – such as John Jameson and John Power and 'Paddy' and Tullamore Dew, a whiskey marketed for many years under the atrocious pun 'Give every man his Dew' and

rather charmingly confused in France where it is known as 'Tout L'Amour'.

The Still House at Midleton is almost cathedral-like with its four massive (17,000 gallons each) stills and high echoing roof. By contrast, the area in which new whiskey is poured into barrels for warehousing, or emptied from them after maturation, is computerised and the most up-to-date and innovative in the industry anywhere. So there is a pleasant contrast between old and new, and perhaps nowhere is the old and traditional better seen than in the original distillery, which remains on site and contains the largest pot still ever used – it could hold 31,000 gallons – and also a fire engine which was horse drawn and had a steam boiler for the pump. Here again they are delighted to welcome visitors and show them not only the distilling processes but also the many huge, dark and aromatic warehouses – each containing something like the equivalent of 20 million bottles of whiskey – where the barrels are arranged in tiers awaiting the day of liberation. Ireland is united in spirit at least, for Old Bushmills and Midleton Distilleries are under the aegis of the Irish Distillers Group.

The best of spirits

Many things have happened to the Irish whiskey industry since that first Irishman invented uisce beatha, and it might well be argued that one of the worst instances ever of misplaced generosity was when the Irish revealed this secret to the outside world which, as we know, fell upon it eagerly. Down the centuries it has had many stout advocates. Dr Samuel Johnson defined it, in his dictionary, in the most complimentary terms; Peter the Great, Czar of all the Russias, said simply that of all spirits, the Irish is the best, and there is no record of anyone contradicting him but, it must be admitted, Peter was not a chap people usually contradicted – and certainly not twice. Much later Oliver St John Gogarty said 'There is no such thing as a large whiskey'.

Whiskey Corner

Although no distilling is now done in Dublin, the administrative headquarters of Irish Distillers is there in a conversion of part of John Jameson's original distillery. Beside it, another part of that distillery is used as the base for an Irish Whiskey Corner, which houses not only a museum and much memorabilia, but also a bar where visitors – always welcome – are invited to taste, or discover, their favourite Irish Whiskey.

Slainte!

No story of Irish whiskey, however brief, could be told without reference to the traditions of toasting which have grown up with it. Instead of 'Cheers', the Irish say 'Slainte' (pronounced Slan-che) which means 'Good Health' but there are many more wordy, and more worthy, examples of felicitous wishes. Most people know at least some of what is perhaps the best-loved toast of all:

'May the road rise before you
May the wind be always on your back
The sun shine warm upon your face
The rain fall softly on your fields
And, until we meet again,
May God hold you in the hollow of His hand.'

There are less solemn ones:

> *'Health and long life to you*
> *The wife/husband of your choice to you*
> *A land without rent to you*
> *A child every year to you*
> *And may you be in Heaven for half an hour*
> *Before the Devil knows you're dead.'*

Or:

> *'May the roof above us never fall in*
> *And the friends beneath it never fall out.'*

And, finally, a very old one – as old, almost, as Irish whiskey itself:

> *'May you be rich in blessings*
> *Poor in misfortune*
> *Slow to make enemies*
> *Quick to make friends*
> *But rich or poor, slow or quick,*
> *May you know nothing but happiness*
> *Until we meet again.'*

Slainte!

Ireland's Finest, a bottle of 'Old JJ'. Below: Midleton Distillery has been landscaped to harmonise with its idyllic surroundings

A Taste of Ireland

THEODORA FITZGIBBON

The food of Ireland is like the Irish people: unpretentious and homely. Simple and succulent dishes have been a tradition for centuries, and are still an important part of Irish life. What Gernon, second Justice of the Province of Munster, said in 1620 could still be quoted with truth today: 'What feeds on earth, or flies in the air, or swimmeth in the water, Lo, Ireland hath it of her own.'

The visitor has only to travel a score of miles in the country to see fine cattle grazing on fertile pastures, or to find the sturdy, horned sheep of Kerry and Wicklow nibbling at the young shoots of heather which gives their meat a special flavour; or to notice that hardly anywhere in Ireland is more than a few miles from river or sea or lakes with their teeming underwater life of flavoursome fish and crustacea. This was noticed as early as the sixth century when an annalist wrote, 'Fruitful were its river mouths . . . sweet and abundant the butter from it churns.'

In the 12th century Giraldus Cambrensis, Gerald the Welshman, whose father was an Anglo-Norman chieftain and his mother a noble Welsh lady wrote, 'This Ireland is also specially remarkable for a great number of beautiful lakes abounding in fish and surpassing in size those of any other country I have visited.'

Happily this tradition still continues and Ireland is known the world over for the excellence of its salmon, both fresh and smoked, fine salmon trout and huge scallops and mussels. Traditionally these are cooked simply to retain their fine flavour, and WM Thackeray gives an appetising account in *The Irish Sketch Book* (1842) of having fresh salmon trout grilled in hot ashes on the floor of the herd's cottage at Lake Derryclear, Connemara. '. . . they were such trouts as, when once tasted, remain for ever in the recollections of a commonly grateful mind – rich, flaky, creamy, full of flavour.'

Certain parts of Ireland have their own specialities. Galway is considered one of the best places for salmon, and in the season the large, fat fish can be seen, packed like sardines, lying under Salmon Weir Bridge in Galway city. The

Galway oyster beds are internationally famous, and the beginning of the season (September) sees a grand oyster festival. Every pub and hotel for miles around serves fresh oysters with brown soda bread, butter and pints of Guinness. The mussels in Ireland, especially at Castlemaine Harbour, West Cork and Wexford reach an astonishing size and succulence and are served in many imaginative ways. The large scallops from the warm waters of Kenmare Bay are a special

Ireland enjoys an abundance of succulent seafood and the finest scallops are gathered in Kenmare Bay (main picture)

Wholesome Irish fare includes lamb and vegetable recipes as well as potato dishes and of course the world-famous Irish Stew

treat. During the summer months mackerel is plentiful, and visitors as well as local fishermen enjoy catching them.

Waterford is known for good ham, as is Limerick where it used to be cured with honey and smoked over juniper branches and oak shavings, which gave it a characteristic taste. For many centuries the general favourite was pork, and pork butchers all over the country still sell a variety of good quality cuts. The blood is used too, to make black puddings (in Cork a large type is called drisheen) which often form part of the traditional Irish breakfast with bacon, eggs and potato cakes or scones.

The potato is linked in many people's minds with the Irish diet, but up until the late 18th century it was used mainly for feeding pigs, and is thought to have given the pork a special flavour. But by the 19th century it had established a firm place in the Irish kitchen and many recipes for using potatoes exist. Popular dishes are colcannon, traditionally eaten at Hallowe'en, which consists of cooked potato, kale or cabbage, leeks, butter and cream, spiced with a little nutmeg. Dublin coddle is another one, a nourishing layered stew of sausages, bacon, onion and sliced potatoes. The real Irish stew is simply lamb, onion and potatoes all well seasoned and with a touch of thyme.

Today, perhaps the most widespread traditional food in Ireland is brown soda bread. Made from stone-ground wheaten flour, it is baked in countless houses and farmhouses all over the country. Crusty, yet soft inside, this is the perfect accompaniment to many Irish dishes. Quick and easy to make, it takes only a little over an hour including the cooking time. The same mixture can be made into scones and these form a simple meal with home-made soup.

Irish whiskey is used in cooking too, not only in cakes but also for flaming certain foods, while Guinness is used to lace beef casserole. Ireland's

delicious liqueur of whiskey, honey and herbs (Irish Mist) is popularly used with duck and ham dishes, and to flavour sweet sauces and soufflés.

Traditional Recipes

No real substitute exists for going there to discover the true taste of Ireland. These are some of the simple, yet slightly out-of-the-ordinary dishes to be found.

BEEF BRAISED WITH GUINNESS

Serves 4

2 lb (900 g) lean stewing steak
2 tablespoons oil or dripping
2 bay leaves
1 large onion, peeled and sliced
2 level tablespoons flour
¼ pint (150 ml) Guinness and ½ pint (300 ml)
  beef stock or water (mixed)
salt and freshly-ground pepper
1 tablespoon chopped parsley

A cold buffet with 'Irish Mist' and Irish whiskey. Irish alcoholic beverages are also popular with Irish cooks, notably whiskey for cakes, Guinness for casseroles and Irish Mist liqueur for delicate sweet sauces

Trim the meat and cut into suitably sized serving pieces. Heat the oil and put in the bay leaves, let them crackle a little, then add the beef and fry quickly on both sides. When brown, remove to a casserole dish and lightly saute the onion until soft but not coloured.

Sprinkle with flour and let it cook for one minute, then add the Guinness and stock mixture to barely cover. Season, then add half the parsley and pour over meat, mixing well. Bring back to the boil, cover and braise in a moderate oven *325 degrees F, 170 degrees C, Gas mark 3* for about one and a half hours. Take out to stir, adding a little more liquid if it seems to be drying up. Continue cooking a further half-hour. Before serving, lift out the bay leaves and sprinkle with the rest of the parsley. If liked, about ½ lb (225 g) of sliced carrots can be cooked with the meat.

BROWN SODA BREAD

8 oz (225 g) stoneground wholemeal flour
8 oz (225 g) plain white flour
1 teaspoon salt
3 teaspoons baking powder
1 teaspoon bicarbonate of soda
1 egg
14 fl oz buttermilk

*NOTE: If buttermilk is unobtainable, substitute
8 fl oz natural yoghurt beaten with 4 fl oz water,
and increase bicarbonate of soda to 1¼ teaspoons.*
Mix all dry ingredients together in a large mixing
bowl. Beat the buttermilk (or yoghurt and water)
with the egg and stir into a well in the dry
mixture. Turn out on to a lightly floured surface
and knead for a few minutes until it is smooth.

Shape into two round cakes, or put into a
lightly-oiled 2 lb (900 g) loaf tin. The round cake
is more traditional, but a loaf tin gives a good
shape for slicing. Cut a deep incision across the
top, making a cross on the round cake to allow for
even rising. Bake at *375 degrees F, 190 degrees C,
Gas mark 5* for about 40 to 45 minutes. To keep
crust soft, wrap in a clean tea towel when cool. A
cup of currants or sultanas can also be added for a
tea bread.

SALMON BAKED WITH CREAM

Serves 4–6

*2–3 lb (900 g–1.4 kg) salmon, preferably
    tail-end*
3 tablespoons butter
Salt and freshly-ground white pepper
½ pint (300 ml) double cream
Juice of 1 lemon
*1 tablespoon chopped parsley, or half parsley and
    half fennel*

*NOTE: Salmon trout of over 2 lb (900 g) in weight
may be used instead of salmon.*
Clean the fish and scale it with a sharp knife, then
rub all over with the butter and put into a
flameproof dish. Season and pour the cream
around the fish. Cover with foil and bake in a
moderate oven *350 degrees F, 180 degrees C, Gas
mark 4* for 15 minutes to the pound.

Remove from the oven, baste well and add half
the lemon juice and the herbs to the sauce and
stir. Put back uncovered for a further 15 minutes.
Lift out the fish and peel off the skin, then put
back in the sauce and gently reheat. Just before
serving add the remaining lemon juice.

A variation of this is to peel and chop a
cucumber and to blanch it in boiling salted water
for three minutes, then drain it. Add this to the
cream sauce when taking from the oven the first
time. The slightly crunchy cucumber acts as a foil
to the creamy sauce.

Serve the salmon by slitting the spine, then
cutting portions along the side. Lift each portion
off the bone, then turn the fish over and repeat
the process.

POTATO CAKES

'. . . While I live I shall not forget her potato cakes.
They came in hot, and hot from the pot oven . . .
they swam in salt butter, and we ate them
shamelessly and greasily, and washed down with
hot whiskey and water'. *The Holy Island*, from
Some experiences of an Irish RM by E. Somerville
and M. Ross.

This is the scone variety; the other variety is
made the same way but rolled thinner and fried in
bacon fat. In the north they are called 'fadge'.

Makes about 9

*½ lb (225 g) self-raising flour (use plain for fried
    variety)*
2 heaped tablespoons butter or bacon fat
6 oz (175 g) freshly-made mashed potato
4 tablespoons milk
salt

Mix the butter into the flour, add a pinch of salt,
then add the cooled mashed potato and enough
milk (about 4 tablespoons) to make a soft, but not
slack, dough. Turn out on to a floured surface,
roll out to ½ in (1.5 cm) thick and cut into 3-in
(8 cm) circles. Bake on a lightly-greased sheet at
400 degrees F, 200 degrees C, Gas mark 6 for 20 to
30 minutes. Eat hot, split and spread with butter.

*Oak-smoked salmon with Irish
soda bread, another treat
to tickle the palate*

IRELAND

Gazetteer

Each entry in this Gazetteer has the atlas page number on which the place can be found and its Irish National Grid reference included under the heading. An explanation of how to use the Irish National Grid is given on pages 120–121.

Blarney Castle, Cork

Achill Island, Co Mayo

Map Ref: 122 F60

The largest island off the Irish Coast, Achill is reached by the R319 from Mulrany. A bridge connects it with the mainland. It is mountainous and heather-covered; Slievemore in the north (2204ft), Croaghaun (2192ft) and Menawn (1530ft) are the highest points.

Keel has a two-mile sandy beach, ending in the Menawn Cliffs, which have an 800ft sheer drop at one place. The Cathedral Rocks are a remarkable example of erosion. Near the village, Keel Lough has sea and brown trout. Two miles beyond Keel is Dooagh, with a lovely inlet whose beach is sheltered by the steep Moyteoge Head. An ascent of Croaghaun, at the island's western extremity, may begin from here. On the mountain's seaward side is a four-mile line of cliffs, and at its highest point is a sheer drop of almost 2000ft to the Atlantic. There are magnificent views in all directions, and the Mullet peninsula, Blacksod Bay, Croagh Patrick, and even Connemara's Twelve Bens can be identified.

Dugort, at the base of Slievemore's quartzite mass, is another resort. Small villages are dotted throughout the island.

AA recommends:
Hotel: McDowells, 1-star, tel. (098) 43148
Guesthouse: Grays, tel. (098) 43244
Garages: Henry's, Achill Sound, tel. (098) 45246
E T Sweeney, Achill Sound, tel. (098) 45243

Achill Island holds a special magic for the seeker of solitude

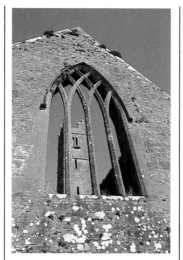

Adare, Co Limerick

Map Ref: 124 R44

Adare village is remarkable in being renowned for its own beauty rather than that of its surroundings. The old-world thatched cottages have a more English than Irish character. Ten miles from Limerick on the Killarney road Adare is on the west bank of the Maigue, a salmon and trout stream, but an ancient town of the name stood on the other bank. Near the village are ruins of two abbeys, a castle and a friary, and the magnificent Adare Manor, a neo-Gothic mansion begun in 1832 by the second Earl of Dunraven, stands in a wooded demesne.

The Dunravens, whose ancestry is said to go back to a 3rd-century king of Munster, engaged Limerick architect James Pain, a pupil of John Nash, to design the manor, later employing Pugin.

The ruined 1316 Augustinian

Remains of the 15th-century Franciscan friary include a fine Irish-Gothic transept

and 13th-century Trinitarian abbeys have been partly restored by the Dunravens as churches for the village's two religious communities. Many of Adare's dwellings were built as Dunraven estate houses. A carved Tudor rose in the Augustinian ruin is possibly the only one in the Republic. The ruinous Franciscan friary dates from 1464, and the crumbling, ivy-clad castle, built by the O'Donovans, from 1226.

AA recommends:
Hotel: Dunraven Arms, 3-star, tel. (061) 86209
Guesthouse: Woodlands, Knockanes, tel. (061) 86118
Farmhouse: Laccabawn, Drehidtarsna tel. (061) 86443

Aherlow, Co Tipperary

Map Ref: 125 R93

A lovely remote glen between the Galtee Mountains and Slievenamuck, to the left of the N24 going from Cahir to Tipperary. It has been the scene of many battles, involving the Thomond O'Brien kings and the Fitzpatricks, being once an important pass between the plains of Tipperary and Limerick. It was also a refuge of the outlawed and dispossessed, and the caves in the Galtee foothills were used as hiding-places. The O'Briens held this glen without serious challenge for 300 years.

The ruins of the Franciscan Moor Abbey are at the head of the glen near Galbally village. The

foundation, by King Donagh O'Brien was early 13th-century, but the ruined church, all that survives, probably post-dates a fire of 1472. Its narrow 70ft tower is conspicuous. The abbey was used as a fortress during the Elizabethan wars.

AA recommends:
Hotels: Aherlow House, 2-star, *tel.* (062) 56153
Glen, 3-star, *tel.* (062) 56146
Campsite: Ballinacourty House Camping & Caravan Park, Ballinacourty, 4-pennant, *tel.* (062) 56230

Annaghdown, Co Galway

Map Ref: 124 M23

On the east shore of the southern part of Lough Corrib (off N84) this is the site of a 6th-century monastery founded by St Brendan the Navigator, and of a convent founded by his sister, Brigid. St Brendan governed this monastery until he died in 577, but these ancient buildings have totally vanished. The disused parish church, however, incorporates a window which is part of a 12th-century ecclesiastical edifice, and the side pilasters of a Romanesque doorway from this also remain. A ruinous Norman castle and bishop's palace are also in the vicinity.

Annalong, Co Down

Map Ref: 123 J31

Annalong lies between the Mourne Mountains and the sea south of Newcastle. At its heart is a harbour, a natural narrow cleft of stone, which was given the protection of a double row of stone walls in the middle of the 19th century. When the fleet of 'skiffs', which fish for herring, mackerel and lobster is in, the masts and rigging make a picturesque scene in front of the stone mill, well restored to full working order. Set in a marine park, it is open to the public and busily grinds corn. Along the stone pier black guillemots fly in and out of holes used for nests. Mourne granite can be seen everywhere, and off the roads around the harbour are three granite cutting yards.

Antrim, Co Antrim

Map Ref: 123 J18

Antrim is a busy town, just to the north east of Lough Neagh, which has recently expanded into housing estates and industrial complexes.
North of the railway station in the Steeple Estate is a splendidly complete 10th-century round tower, with walls 4ft thick at the base, rising 93ft to a tapering point. A rare Ulster example of a church

This unusual shop doorway in Antrim beckons the passer-by to come inside

which is at least partially 16th-century, All Saints, stands at one end of the High Street, while at the other end is a fine 1726 courthouse with its assured and sophisticated early-Georgian architecture, facing a neo-Tudor gateway. This leads to one of the best examples of early formal landscape gardening in the country, probably dating from the end of the 17th century. The garden has been associated with the name of Le Notre and has even been described as a mini-Versailles. In its prime it must have been splendid, and it still retains walks with carefully contrived vistas, straight flat canals, clipped lime hedges, yews and a Viking mound cut with a spiral walk. Beside this lies the empty shell of Antrim Castle, originally dating from 1662 but finally burnt in 1922. Clotworthy House close by has been restored as an Arts Centre.
On the Randalstown Road (A6) is Shane's Castle, the home of Lord

The Mourne Mountains form a backdrop for Annalong Harbour

O'Neill, an estate which has a steam railway, old-fashioned fun-fair, nature reserve (RSPB) and castle ruins open to the public.

AA recommends:
Garage: Hugh Tipping Motors, 23 Crosskennan Road, *tel.* Antrim 62225

Antrim Coast Road, Co Antrim

Map Ref: 123 D31

The Antrim coast road hugs the sea from Larne to Cushendall. It was constructed in the 1830s to the designs of Ulster architect, Sir Charles Lanyon, but it was the Scottish engineer, William Bald, who cunningly conceived a way of blasting through the rock so that it fell to form a base for the road itself. Thackeray, who happened to see the road in the making considered it 'one of the most noble and gallant works of art in the country'. Although the chief aim of the construction was to ease the isolation of the people of the Glens, it also served as a form of famine relief.

The whitewashed houses of Kilronan cluster around the north-western edge of Killeany Bay

Aran Islands, Co Galway

Map Ref: 124 L80

An extension of the Burren, Co Clare, these three small Atlantic islands, about 30 miles out from Galway, are rocky and barren, with small holdings divided by unmortared stone walls. Pockets of soil have been manufactured by the islanders from sand and seaweed, to grow scanty crops for livestock. The islands, connected with Galway by air and ferry, are Inishmore (7635 acres), Inishmaan (2253 acres) and Inisheer (1400 acres). Renowned for preserving traditional ways of life, they have been celebrated in the writings of JM Synge and in the 1934 film *Man of Aran*.

Fishing, the islands' main industry, is done from currachs, frail-looking boats of laths and tarred canvas.

Gaelic is the principal language, and many of the summer visitors are language students.

The islands' capital is Kilronan on Inishmore. Also on the island is Dun Aengus, most important of the group's antiquities: a dramatic semi-circular stone fort on the edge of a sheer 300ft cliff. Its date and purpose are unknown. Dun Eoghanacht, near Kilronan, Dun Oghill, near the village of Oghil, and Doocaher, near the island's southern cliffs, are other forts worth seeing. Dun Conor on Inishmaan is another well-preserved specimen. At Killeany, Inishmore, is Teampall Bheanain, a primitive church whose interior measures a mere 10ft 9in by 7ft.

Ardara, Co Donegal

Map Ref: 122 G79

In a pretty valley where the Owentocker river enters Loughros More Bay (N56), Ardara commands a long narrow peninsula separating that bay from its twin, Loughros Beg. The area has good salmon and trout fishing, and scenic attractions include Essaranka waterfall, Maghera caves and the Slievetooney mountains. The road north from Ardara over the Owenea river transverses a wild lake-studded tract of country. **Loughros Point,** six miles west, commands splendid views. Ardara is a key centre of the Donegal homespun tweed and associated crafts, including handknits, hand embroidery and hosiery, which visitors may sometimes see in progress.

Ardee, Co Louth

Map Ref: 123 N99

Breaking the rule that an 'ard' prefix means a height, the name of this town on the N2 between Slane and Carrickmacross comes from Ath Fhirdia, Ford of Ferdia, and commemorates the legendary four-day battle between Cuchulainn, leader of the Red Branch Knights, and Ferdia. Ardee Castle, a square keep in the main street converted for use as a courthouse, was built by Roger de Pippart early in the 13th century. Both James II and William

Ardee Castle, now a courthouse, graces the main street of this market town

III slept in it on their way to the Battle of the Boyne, though not simultaneously. St Mary's Church embodies part of a Carmelite church, also built by de Pippart, and burned by Edward Bruce in 1315.

Hatch's Castle, in Market Street, is of similar date, and until about 1940 had been occupied for centuries by a family of the same name.

The Dee here is fished for salmon, trout and pike.

AA recommends:
Restaurant: The Gables, Dundalk Road, I-K & F, *tel.* (041) 53789
Garage: McCabes, Castle Street, *tel.* (041) 53291

Ardmore, Co Waterford

Map Ref: 125 X17

A pleasant seaside resort off the N25 between Youghal and Dungarvan. Ardmore is near the Ram Head end of Ardmore Bay. It is small but has extensive smooth sands. There are important remains on the site of a 7th-century monastic settlement of St Declan.

The 97ft round tower is among the country's most perfect, with each of its four storeys clearly marked on the outside by rebates and projecting string courses. The interior has a unique series of projecting grotesque heads carved in stone. This was one of Ireland's last round towers.

The patron saint is recalled in St Declan's Oratory, a very small early church, St Declan's Well and St Declan's Stone, a glacial boulder lying on the beach below the village. This is good walking country, either along the cliffs or inland, a popular route going to the Dungarvan-Youghal road (N25) at Cleary's Cross, then west via Kinsalebeg to Youghal.

AA recommends:
Hotel: Cliff House, I-star, *tel.* (024) 94106

Ardnacrusha, Co Clare

Map Ref: 124 R56

Two miles north of Limerick city the Shannon hydro-electric station here was the first built in the Republic, and is still a showpiece. Its building took from 1925 to 1929. It involved a dam behind which the waters of the Shannon and of Lough Derg, further upstream, form a huge reservoir. Two canals were also dug, to a total length of nearly nine miles, forming a head race and tail race to carry a large part of the river's volume to Ardnacrusha and later back to the Shannon above the city. To operate the turbines, a 92ft waterfall is involved. To the industrially minded, the machinery is spectacular.

Fabric Crafts

Weaving at Laragh, Co Wicklow — one of Ireland's cottage industries

The familiar *Aran jerseys*, first hand-knitted on the Aran Islands, have a long history. Of the intricate stitches, passed from mother to daughter, the cables represent the fishermen's ropes and the diamonds are nets; other patterns resemble prehistoric and early Christian designs. Some say that the patterns helped families identify bodies long at sea, in this area of many drownings. The fishermen's belt, brightly-coloured braided woollen 'crios', is also still made.

True **Irish lace** is mostly 19th century. In Carrickmacross lace, the solid areas were of muslin or cambric, but later cotton or nylon net was used. Limerick's Good Shepherd convent makes lace worked in thread on fine Brussels net, and Carrickmacross is noted for lawn appliqué on a net background. Crochet was brought to Ireland to help poverty-stricken families in Cork, by four Irish nuns who went to Paris to learn the skills in 1769. Now Irish hand crochet is much sought after by fashion designers.

Hand-spinning and weaving is still carried out as a cottage industry, mainly in Donegal. The wool of rough grazing sheep is used to make high quality tweed of medium to heavy weight, which is vegetable dyed in the mountain colours of marl and heather. Ardara, West Donegal, is the centre of what is really a cottage industry, and hand-knitting and hand-embroidery are also established crafts here.

Foxford, Co Mayo has woollen mills which are noted for **homespuns**, especially checked travel rugs.

Tapestry, rugmaking and embroidery were nurtured by the Dun Emer guild, which aimed 'to find work for Irish hands in the making of beautiful things', and was founded as part of the Celtic revival in 1902. Today some of that responsibility has been taken on by the Kilkenny Design Centre in the Republic and the Local Enterprise Development Unit in Northern Ireland. At Kilkenny, and at the Kilkenny Design Centre shop in Dublin, the best of Irish workmanship is represented and includes the work of some individual craftsmen in ceramics, glass and metalwork. There are good craft shops, featuring local craftsmen in all parts of the country. A particularly good shop in the north is at Hillsborough. For **linen** see Lagan Valley.

A fine example of the intricately hand-worked Carrickmacross lace

Arklow, Co Wicklow

Map Ref: 125 T27

One of the east coast's most important resorts – Arklow is noted as a boat-building centre, a source of pottery and as a base for coastal bird-spotting. It is also a good starting point for visiting Glendalough, Glenmalure, the Vale of Clara and the Meeting of the Waters at the Vale of Avoca, a beauty spot made famous by a Tom Moore melody.

A great Ormonde fortress stood in Arklow, but was demolished by Cromwell in 1649; its ruin is on a bluff overlooking the river mouth. A decisive battle in the 1798 Rebellion also took place here.

Strands stretch for miles north and south, with safe bathing. **Shelton Abbey,** designed by Richard Morrison, is reached along the Avoca river. This was a resting place of James II after the Battle of the Boyne, and later became a State forestry education centre.

AA recommends:
Hotel: Arklow Bay, 2-star, *tel.* (0402) 32309
Farmhouse: Killinskyduff House, *tel.* (0402) 32185

Armagh, Co Armagh

Map Ref: 123 H84

Armagh, one of the chief ecclesiastical centres of Ireland, is a small city of ancient origin and importance. Three hundred years before Christ, the fabled Red Branch Knights and Queen Macha made the capital of Ulster at Emain Macha, two miles west of the present city, and, because of the prestige of the site it is said, St Patrick chose this place for his principal church around AD 445. After some parleying with the local king, Daire, St Patrick won the best position on one of the cluster of hills. Armagh then developed into a renowned centre of learning and the important illuminated manuscript, the *Book of Armagh* (now held at Trinity College, Dublin) dates from that period. This precious book was said to have been placed in the hands of Brian Boru in 1004 when he came to Armagh and made presents of gold upon the altar. Ten years later, after the Battle of Clontarf, his body and that of his son were carried to the city. A simple stone on the Church of Ireland Cathedral recalls his burial. This cathedral dates from 1268 but after a history of damage, patching and repair it was thoroughly

'restored' in the gothic revival taste of 1834 by L.N. Cottingham. It is small and simple, with a nave at 'skew' with the chancel, which is said to denote the list of Christ's head on the cross. There are interesting and mysterious carvings and good 17th- and 18th-century church monuments.

Early Armagh is also subtly recalled in the circular street patterns which wind up the central hill, following the lines of earthen mounds now disappeared.

The appearance of Armagh today owes much to two important 18th-century figures. Francis Johnston, who became the most celebrated architect of his generation in Ireland, was born here in 1760 and contributed the dignified courthouse and a house which is now the Bank of Ireland. The courthouse stands opposite the Mall which was the gift of Archbishop Robinson (archbishop from 1765 to 95), who founded the Public Library and an Observatory as well as building the Royal School and the Archbishop's Palace. The Mall, bounded by serene Georgian architecture and lined with limes and oaks, is the scene of cricket in summer. The Armagh County Museum in the Mall houses some good local collections.

Prominent on a hill are the twin

spires of the Roman Catholic Cathedral. Seven terraces rise over two hundred steps to a building which was built over a period of sixty years, its original conception being delayed by the onset of the famine. The final completion was due to massive public subscription. The interior is splendidly decorated with lavish use of mosaics, stained glass, marble, stone, wood and paint.

Armagh Planetarium covers all aspects of astronomy and has particular interest in space travel. There are regular star shows.

Within easy reach are two pleasant and interesting National Trust properties. **Ardress** near Loughgall is a modest gentleman farmer's house with excellent 18th-century plasterwork, a good farmyard museum and pleasant gardens and walks. The **Argory**, Moy, is an 1820s house overlooking the Blackwater River, with interesting contents, including a very fine pianola organ, and gaslighting.

Ashford, Co Wicklow

Map Ref: 125 T29

Four miles north-west of Wicklow town, Ashford is a pretty village on the N11, standing among delightful scenery. A mile to its north-west is the **Devil's Glen**, a beauty spot with a deep, shrub-covered chasm along whose rocky bed rushes the River Vartry. The river on entering the glen falls nearly 100 feet into the Devil's Punchbowl, a deep rock basin. Near the waterfall high-level walks have been built, and both these and the glen's winding paths afford memorable views.

Close to the village are the celebrated **Mount Usher Gardens**, open to the public. Planned as a 'wild' garden after the ideas of William Robinson in the late 19th century, they have rare shrubs and trees, including sub-tropical varieties, along their walks.

Dunran Glen, to the north, has unusual rock formations, including the mitre-shaped Bishop's Rock. A mile east of Ashford, at **Newrathbridge**, is the lovely old-world Hunter's Hotel.

Athenry, Co Galway

Map Ref: 124 M52

The Norman de Burgos (later exceedingly numerous under the name of Burke) and Bermingham obtained vast estates west of the Shannon at the close of the 12th

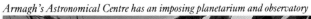

Armagh's Astronomical Centre has an imposing planetarium and observatory

The Castle and the impressive twin towers of the church of SS Peter and Paul overlook the River Shannon

century, and established Athenry as their principal town. In between Galway and Ballinasloe, it retains a market cross, part of its mediaeval wall and most of the north gate, built in 1211, as well as the rectangular keep of the 1238 castle.

Of the Dominican friary founded in 1241, the church has survived with good rows of lancet windows. The east window dates from 1324. Remains of a 15th-century Franciscan friary are fragmentary.

Athlone, Co Westmeath

Map Ref: 125 N04

Because it stands where the Dublin-Galway road crosses the country's biggest river, the Shannon, Athlone is widely, but wrongly, considered the geographical centre of Ireland. It is more notable for historical associations than what has been preserved and even its attractive Jacobean houses were demolished in this century. The Shannon here divides the eastern province of Leinster from Connaught in the west, and also separates the counties of Westmeath and Roscommon.

The polygonal remains of a 1210 castle house the museum of the Old Athlone Society. Now called Adamson Castle, it was formerly attributed to King John, but was built by John de Grey on the site of a primitive fortress. In a street called the Bawn is the birthplace of tenor John McCormack. The Duke of Wellington also lived here for a time.

The bridge in the town centre is the site of a celebrated tussle for a crossing between Jacobites and Williamites in 1691. Motor vessels can be hired nearby by arrangement, and the big Lough Ree, to the north, has many islands, good coastal scenery and noted coarse fishing. **Hare Island**, near the Westmeath shore, has a sixth-century church ruin.

Gothic St Mary's Church in the main street has associations with Oliver Goldsmith's family. **Lissoy**, his boyhood home, also called Three Jolly Pigeons from a pub name, is nine miles north-east on the N55. It may have inspired the Auburn of his poem *The Deserted Village*.

AA recommends:

Hotels: Prince of Wales, 3-star, *tel.* (0902) 726526
Royal Hoey, 2-star, *tel.* (0902) 72924
T & C: Rocwal, The Beeches, Coosan *tel.* (0902) 75640
Garages: Kenna Motors, Dublin Road, *tel.* (0902) 72726
Kenny & O'Brien, Cornafulla *tel.* (0902) 37103
Kilmartin, Dublin Road, *tel.* (0902) 75426

Athy, Co Kildare

Map Ref: 125 S69

Standing on the River Barrow and on the N78 road between Kilkenny and Naas, and on the Dublin–Waterford railway, Athy is an important market town, though the Grand Canal branch which joins the river here is no longer of commercial use. Some remains of the late 13th-century Woodstock Castle, north of the town, may be seen and the more extensive ruins of 16th-century White Castle are a National Monument. This stands at the 1796 Crom-a-Boo Bridge, whose name was a Fitzgerald warcry.

Ballitore, eight miles east, was a Quaker settlement. Orator Edmund Burke attended its school. Ruined Castle Inch lies three miles east.

Road bowls

Road bowls or 'bullets', is Ireland's most unusual sport, played now only in Counties Armagh and Cork. It entails hurling a 28oz metal ball (some say it began with cannonballs) on a set course along several miles of winding roads, in the fewest possible throws. The thrower often has a 'handler', who stands legs astride to show the best line. At one time road bowls was illegal; those who witness it now won't be in trouble with the law, but may notice the odd wager going on. It must be Ireland's most dangerous spectator sport, however, and hurtling missiles tend to scatter watching crowds.

Visitors beware that next bend on the pretty country lanes of Co Cork!

A landscape of green velvet near the picturesque village of Avoca

Avoca is dwarfed by steep wooded hills offering fine forest walks

Avoca, Co Wicklow

Map Ref: 125 T28

Widely known both through a Tom Moore song, 'The Meeting of the Waters', and for its copper, lead and zinc deposits, Avoca is between Rathdrum and Woodenbridge. The beautiful valley is at its best in late Spring, with drifts of wild white cherry blossom. Croneblane, formerly called Castle Howard, stands above the 'Meeting' formed by the union of the Avonmore and Avonberg rivers. The Lion Bridge, formerly the castle entrance, affords the best view.

AA recommends:
T & C: Ashdene, *tel:* (0402) 5327
Riverview House, *tel:* (0402) 5181

Ballina, Co Mayo

Map Ref: 122 G21

Standing between the north-east shores of Lough Conn and Killala Bay, near the estuary of the Moy – an excellent salmon and trout stream – Ballina is a noted centre for fishing and golf. General Humbert and his 1100 Frenchmen took the town after their landing in the bay during the 1798 rebellion.

Ruins of a 1427 Augustinian friary stand near the modern cathedral, which has a lovely stained glass window. The Dolmen of the Four Maols is half a mile south-west on the Lough Conn road, and marks the graves of four 6th-century foster brothers who murdered their tutor Ceallach, bishop of Kilmore-Moy, and were hanged by his brother in Ardnaree, across the river. (A standing stone at Rathcroghan, Co Roscommon, commemorates King Daithi, grand-father of this murdered bishop.)

AA recommends:
Hotel: Downhill, 3-star, *tel.* (096) 21033
Garages: Finmax, Dublin Road, *tel.* (096) 21288
Judges Auto Svc, Sligo Road, *tel.* (096) 21864

Ballinasloe, Co Galway

Map Ref: 125 M83

There were many clashes during the Elizabethan Wars, but more recently Ballinasloe has become known for its great October horse, cattle and sheep fair.

The 1824 Garbally Mansion, standing in a wooded estate and the former home of the Earl of Clancarty, became a college and some of the castle masonry was incorporated in a private house. The town is the western terminus of the Grand Canal.

Four miles south-west at Aughrim, the Jacobite army suffered a disastrous defeat by the Williamites on 12 July 1691.

AA recommends:
Hotel: Haydens, 3-star, *tel.* (0905) 42347
Garages: Fred Kilmartin, Athlone Road, *tel.* (0905) 42204
Louis Bannerton, Galway Road, *tel.* (0905) 42420

Ballinrobe, Co Mayo

Map Ref: 122 M16

Anglers and golfers are well catered for in the town, which stands on the Robe River near the eastern shore of Lough Mask and south of Lough Carra (separated by a trunk road and linked by an underground river) and also has a racecourse. **Lough Mask Castle**, a ruin almost on the lakeside, stands near **Lough Mask House**, four miles from the town. This was the residence of Captain Charles Cunningham Boycott (1832–97), the land agent whose tenants 'sent him to Coventry' during the Land League wars and gave us the word 'boycott'.

AA recommends:
Hotel: Lakelands, 1-star, *tel.* Ballinrobe 20

Ballintober, Co Mayo

Map Ref: 122 M17

Ballintubber (as it is sometimes known) has an abbey unique in the English-speaking world for having continuity of the Mass over 750 years. Henry VIII's 1542 suppression was not enforced; an unroofing by Cromwellians in 1653 was a more real hazard, but the abbey survived this too. Its restoration began in 1963. A 13th-century sacristy and internal stone-vaulted chancel roof are intact and the chapterhouse has a beautiful door. The abbey was founded for Augustinians in 1216 by Cathal O'Connor, king of Connaught, on the site of a fifth-century foundation.

South of the abbey is Lough Carra, on whose eastern shore stands the ruin of **Moore Hall**, birthplace of novelist George Moore, who wrote *A Drama in Muslin* and other works with an eye towards social reform. His ashes were scattered from an island in the lake.

Ballintoy, Co Antrim

Map Ref: 123 D04

From the main Ballycastle – Bushmills Road (A2) the strong white church tower of Ballintoy Parish dominates the little village which lies between Knocksaughey Hill and the sea. A tightly winding road down to a tiny harbour passes an amazing construction, a house eccentrically evolved cube by cube by a Belfast artist. A car park is built on old limestone kilns and looks down over the harbour.

To the east is **Carrick-a-Rede** (NT) with its swinging rope bridge. Carrick-a-Rede means 'the rock in the road' and the bridge owes its existence to the path of the salmon which are caught in nets arranged in the 60ft-wide chasm. The bridge itself, 80ft above sea level, is put up each spring and dismantled in the autumn in a tradition which dates back at least 300 years. Until recently, the fishermen who erected and used it needed only one hand rail, and viewed the addition of a second as a sign of great decadence. Now a two-handed crossing still requires courage and care but accidents are extremely rare.

Between Ballintoy and Carrick-a-Rede is the disused lime quarry of Larrybane (NT) where walks to Carrick-a-Rede give good views along the coast and also to Sheep Island where puffins nest.

To the west of Ballintoy is **Whitepark Bay** (NT) a magnificent strand backed by limestone cliffs and an arc of rich green grass and dunes. The beach can be reached only by foot. Neolithic man chose this beautiful place as an early home and a tumulus can be seen among the dunes. In the north-west corner of the Bay is the tiny cluster of houses called **Portbraddan**, which contains Ireland's smallest church, a thatched building about 10ft by 6ft dedicated to St Gobhan, the patron saint of builders.

Magnificent seascapes beckon the sailor from the peaceful harbour of Ballintoy

Ballybunion, Co Kerry

Map Ref: 124 Q84

Kerry's mountain grandeur stops short of this resort on the Atlantic, but there are many caves nearby. The extensive beach, divided by a promontory with an old Fitzmaurice castle, reaches almost to the main street and the 18-hole golf course is one of Ireland's finest. A little to the south, the Cashen river area has plentiful teal, mallard and widgeon, and inland Knockanore Hill has grouse and woodcock, with snipe in the marshes.

The range of cliffs north of Ballybunion strand extends with alternating level beaches to the Shannon estuary. Some of the caves here can be entered on foot at low tide, others must be approached by boat. In 1842, Tennyson visited the caves at **Doon**, a 15-minute walk from the town, in 1842. **Lick Castle** is an old Fitzgerald stronghold, and better preserved than that of the Fitzmaurices.

AA recommends:
Hotel: Marine, 2-star, *tel.* (068) 27139
Guesthouse: Eagle Lodge, *tel.* (068) 27224

The unspoilt coastline at Ballybunion offers sanctuary to a host of birdlife

Ballycastle, Co Antrim

Map Ref: 123 D14

Ballycastle sits in the middle of a wide bay with the crescent of Rathlin Island to the north and the outstanding headland of Fair Head to the east. The Glenshesk river runs down from the mountains of Knocklayde and reaches the sea between a good beach and some very fine lawn tennis courts. Close by on the Cushendun Road (A2) are the ruins of Bonamargy Friary. Among those buried here is Sorley Boy McDonnell, who eluded all Elizabeth I's attempts to capture him. In 1575 he had sent his wife and children to Rathlin for safety, but they were murdered by Captain John Norris, while Sorley Boy watched helplessly from the mainland. Essex told Elizabeth that he 'was likely to run mad for sorrow'. His family became the Earls of Antrim whose family seat is at Glenarm Castle.

At the other side of the bay is the harbour, recently extended, where fresh fish, including salmon in

season, may be bought. Just beyond is the memorial to Marconi, whose assistant George Kemp made early radio transmissions between Ballycastle and Rathlin.

Inland up a tree-lined avenue is the Diamond, which is transformed into a real market square in the Bank Holiday weekend of August when the Old Lammas Fair takes place. Horses and ponies are traded, there are traditional games of chance and fair goers are expected to buy and eat two local delicacies – 'dulse', or dried seaweed, and 'yellow man', sweet sticky slabs of ochre-coloured candy, to recall the song,
'You can take your Mary Ann
For some dulse and yellow man
At the Old Lammas Fair at
Ballycastle O.'

Guesthouses: Atlantic, The Promenade, *tel.* Ballycastle 62412
Hillsea, 28 Quay Hill, *tel.* Ballycastle 62385
Campsite: Moyle View Caravan Park, 2-pennant, *tel.* Ballycastle 62550

Top: Lammas Fair at Ballycastle.
Bottom: Scotland is only 14 miles off
the towering cliffs of Ballycastle

Ballyshannon, Co Donegal

Map Ref: 122 G86

On the steep banks where the Erne river becomes tidal, Ballyshannon has a large hydroelectric station at Cathleen's Fall and a 900-acre lake reservoir above that. In the estuary lies Inis Saimer islet, traditionally the spot where Partholan landed from Scythia about 1500 BC to make the first colonisation of Ireland.

Immediately north of the town's present market place was the 1423 O'Donnell castle, held for three days in 1597 by 80 men against Sir Conyers Clifford's army of 5000. In the Mall is the birthplace of prolific poet William Allingham, whose works include *The Touchstone*.

Four miles north on the coast is the ruin of **Kilbarron Castle**, fortress of the O'Clery family. One of them was Michael, chief of the Four Masters who chronicled the

detailed history of Ireland from remote times until their own day, the early 17th century.

AA recommends:
Hotel: Dorrians Imperial, 2-star, *tel.* (072) 51147
Garage: Abbey, Donegal Road, *tel.* (072) 51246

Baltinglass, Co Wicklow

Map Ref: 125 S88

In a scenic part of the Slaney valley on N81, better known as the West Wicklow road, the little town stands under 1258ft Baltinglass Hill, on top of which are the remains of a substantial cairn and passage grave, with Bronze Age burial chambers. The summit also provides superb views of the Wicklow Hills to the east.

In the riverside ruin of the 1148 Cistercian abbey of Vallis Salutis, where quite a lot of the church remains, are notable twin rows of Gothic arches. This is a national monument; its founder was Dermot MacMurrough, king of Leinster, whose invitation led to the Norman invasion of Ireland. The south nave contains some sculptures.

Grange Con Park, four miles north, is noted for the small unique herd of white fallow deer introduced there from Welbeck Abbey in Nottinghamshire.

Bandon, Co Cork

Map Ref: 124 W45

The Earl of Cork founded this town on the Bandon river in 1608, having ousted the McCarthys, O'Donovans, O'Mahonys, O'Learys, O'Driscolls and others from the surrounding lands. He walled it to keep out Roman Catholics and nonconformists, and fragments of the walls survive. Kilbrogan church (1610) is one of the earliest Irish Protestant churches erected as such and Bandon also preserves its town stocks. It has golf and angling.

Going west to Enniskean for the right turn onto the L190, a short journey brings one to the round tower of **Kinneigh**, notable in that the first 18ft of its 68ft height have a hexagonal cross-section. Further on, a right turn onto the L40 leads to **Bealnablath**, where Michael Collins, head of the Irish Free State, was ambushed and killed in the civil war of 1922.

Ballinascarthy, on the N71 south-west of Bandon, is the ancestral home of motor magnate Henry Ford.

AA recommends:
Campsite: Murry's Caravan & Camping Park, Kilbrogan Road, 2-pennant, *tel.* (023) 41232

Bangor, Co Down

Map Ref: 123 J58

Bangor is a resort which prospered with the development of rail and steamship. Neatly-painted Victorian and Edwardian villas rise in tiers around the bay with plenty of good Victorian parks (Ward Park is a favourite with children), seaside architecture and marine paraphernalia as well as modern amenities, including a marina.

In the sixth century, Bangor monastery, founded by St Comgall, was an international centre of learning and the home of 3000 monks. St Comgall sent missionary monks into Europe – St Gall went to Switzerland and St Columbanus after many travels founded his last monastery in Bobbio in Italy. It was to Bobbio that the 7th-century manuscript, the Bangor Antiphonary, was sent for safekeeping when the Vikings threatened. The site of the monastery, which would have been composed of wattle huts, is unknown, but there is a good imaginary reconstruction in the Heritage Centre, made in the old laundry of Bangor Castle. A Victorian Jacobethan House built for the Ward family, this is now Council Offices. Close by is Bangor Abbey Parish church, constructed in 1616 around a 15th-century tower. By the sea, opposite the harbour, is an imposing Customs tower house of 1637.

AA recommends:

Hotels: Ballyholme, 256–262 Seacliffe Road, 2-star, *tel.* (0247) 472807
Winston, 19–23 Queens Parade, 2-star, *tel.* (0247) 454575
Guesthouses: Ennislare, 9 Princetown Road, *tel.* Bangor 472858
Malinmore, 11 Princetown Road, *tel.* Bangor 473303
Garages: Ballyrobert Service Station, 402 Belfast Road, *tel.* Helens Bay 852262
Bangor Auto Recovery, 32–34 Belfast Road, *tel.* Bangor 457428
Car & Commercial Repair Services, 521 Belfast Road, *tel.* 450200
P W Gethin & Sons, 16 Belfast Road, *tel.* Bangor 465881
S Mellon & Sons, 40 Bingham Street, *tel.* Bangor 457525

Bangor's neat streets lead to the inner quay and a small square tower of 1637

Bantry, Co Cork

Map Ref: 124 W04

Celebrated for its setting between hills and bay, Bantry is at the end of a tortuous, looping south-easterly progress of the N71 from Kenmare. Whiddy Island blocks the view of Glengarriff Harbour across the bay, but in return makes Bantry a shelter for small vessels. The bay itself is 21 miles long and was twice used by French fleets for attempted invasions: in 1689 in support of James II and in 1796 under General Hoche. The small inlets north and north-west of Bantry, going towards Glengarriff, are not sandy but rich in limestone corals, used locally as fertiliser.

Tim Healy, first governor-general of the Irish Free State, was born in Bantry in 1855 and the spectacular **Tim Healy Pass,** north of Adrigole, is named after him. Rising to 1084ft the pass gives magnificent views across the bay to Sheeps Head and Mizen Heade, the latter of which is the 'Land's End' of Ireland.

Bantry House, standing with its Italian gardens on a wooded hill and open for tours, is a palace. It has two of Marie Antoinette's bookcases, mosaics excavated from Pompeii, priceless Russian icons and one of Waterford's finest-ever crystal chandeliers.

AA recommends:
Hotel: Westlodge, 3-star, *tel.* (027) 50360
T & C: Shangri-la, *tel.* (027) 50244
Garages: Hurley's, *tel.* (027) 50092
O'Leary's, *tel.* (027) 50127

The most beautiful of all Irish bays, Bantry Bay is a sub-tropical paradise of plants washed here by the Gulf Stream

Belfast

Map Ref: 123 J37

Belfast has grown around the River Lagan at the foot of a Lough and is almost entirely surrounded by hills so that green fields can be seen at the end of city centre streets. The traffic at the centre circulates around the **City Hall,** an impressive late Victorian building of Portland stone by London architect Sir Brumwell Thomas, who quite freely borrowed architectural features from London buildings, the most obvious being St Paul's Cathedral. Its opulence and self confidence reflects the peak of Belfast's prosperity when textile mills, engineering and shipbuilding brought full employment to the city. Around it are handsome commercial buildings which mirror the mercantile buoyancy of the turn of the century. The quiet oasis of the **Linenhall Library** in Donegall Square dates back to the late 18th century.

Standing in front of the City Hall, the view to one side is towards the **Law Courts,** down Chichester Street with a few remaining fine early 19th-century houses in the

Echoes of the City's prosperous past (High St 1880, below) can be found in the splendid Crown Liquor Saloon

Georgian style, and to the other is the 1814 façade of the **Royal Belfast Academic Institution,** a school of academic and sporting tradition. The plans were given without charge by Sir John Soane. 'Inst', as it is known, is not far from two buildings in Great Victoria Street which are as extravagant as Inst is restrained.

The **Grand Opera House** was designed by theatre architect Frank Matcham and opened its doors for a pantomime on 23 December 1895. The exterior is interesting and inviting, but the interior is exotic and lavishly decorated with the emphasis on the romantic orient: elephants' heads and eastern deities abound among Moorish and Renaissance detail and sumptuous plush and gilt. Across the road is the

Crown Liquor Saloon (NT), no ordinary pub but a 'many coloured cavern' as Sir John Betjeman described it, created with an unashamedly rich variety of materials – marble, mosaics, painted glass, mirrors, carved woodwork, granite and highly decorated tiles. On one side is a long elaborate bar and on the other is a row of wooden snugs or boxes surmounted with the mottoes, 'Love your country!' and 'Fortune favours the brave!' Among the welter of detail look for the nickel plates for striking matches and the system of bells, with letters on the snugs and on the bell boards across the centre of the bar. Perhaps the best time is an autumn afternoon when the bar may be full of a mixture of Belfast people and the

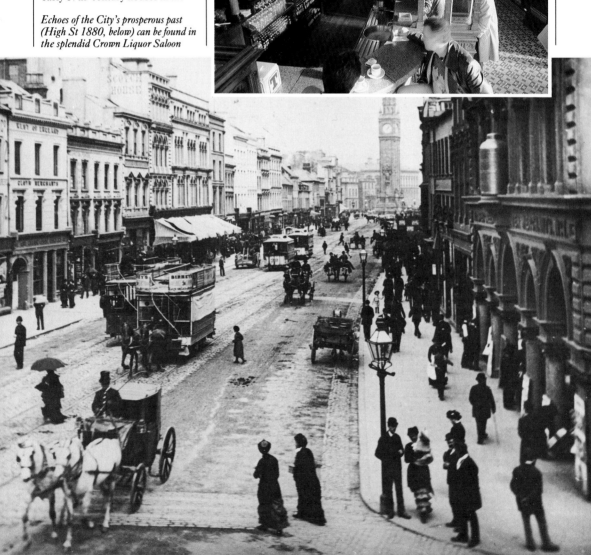

odd star from the Opera House across the way and the lamplighter comes round to light the gas lamps.

The sumptuousness of the Crown is not unlike the luxury of the great ocean liners built at Belfast at that time, when Harland and Wolff was unquestionably the greatest shipbuilding firm in the world. Today the east of the city is dominated by two gigantic cranes known to Belfast people as **Goliath and Samson,** which contribute to today's shipbuilding enterprises.

Another landmark visible from many parts of the east of the city are the white Portland stone **Parliament Buildings** at Stormont in the Holywood hills. The line of hills to the north includes **Cave Hill** with a silhouette known locally as Napoleon's Nose. The **zoo** is here and so is **MacArt's Fort** where Wolfe Tone and leading members of the United Irishmen took a 'solemn obligation' to assert the independence of Ireland in 1795. One of the United Irishmen was Henry Joy McCracken, who lived in High Street where the River Farset still flowed bringing the business of the port into the middle of the town. Between **High Street** and parallel **Ann Street** are a series of entries or alleys including interesting pubs.

Further down High Street is **St George's** church; the fine portico was taken from Ballyscullion House, one of the Irish building ventures of the great traveller, collector and eccentric Frederick Hervey, Bishop of Derry and Earl of Bristol. **St Anne's Cathedral** is nearby in Donegall Street, a simple Hiberno-Romanesque structure whose baptistry contains some fine mosaics by Gertrude Stein. In Corporation Square is the **Sinclair Seaman's** church with an unmistakable maritime atmosphere.

Other interesting city centre churches include the elegant oval-shaped **Rosemary Presbyterian** church, the elaborate Tudor Gothic **St Malachy's** in Alfred street and the imposing façade of **Donegall Square Methodists'**. At the

Above: Highlight of Belfast's Botanic Gardens is the Victorian Palm House, which predates that of Kew Gardens, London. Below: There are weekly guided tours of the City Hall, and the dome affords splendid views of Belfast

Belfast's Linenhall Library houses a fine collection of books on Ireland

bottom of High Street is the **Albert clock,** which lists a little to one side, because its foundations are on estuarine clay.

The **Queen's University** area of south Belfast has been described as a 'perfect Victorian suburb'. Around the 1845 College buildings there are institutions, schools, churches and terraces of houses full of detail to gladden the heart of the lover of Victoriana. Great set piece of the **Botanic Gardens** is the **Palm House,** one of the earliest curvilinear glass and iron constructions in the world, recently restored and stocked with exotic plants. Also in the Botanic Gardens are a **Tropical Ravine** and the **Ulster Museum.** The Museum contains the treasure reclaimed from the wreck of the sunken Spanish galleon, the *Girona*, with a comprehensive industrial archaeology. Leading Ulster artists, including Sir John Lavery, Paul Henry, William Conor and Colin Middleton, are well represented in the Art Gallery. See also **Ulster Folk Museum**.

AA recommends:
Hotels: Forum Hotel Belfast, Great Victoria Street, 4-star, *tel.* Belfast 245161 Stormont, 587 Upper Newtownards Road, 3-star, *tel.* Belfast 658621
Guesthouse: Camera, 44 Wellington Park, *tel.* Belfast 660026
Restaurants: Restaurant 44, 44 Bedford Street, 2 K & F, *tel.* Belfast 244844 Manor House Cantonese, 1-K & F, 47 Donegal Pass, *tel.* Belfast 238755 House of Moghul, 60 Great Victoria Street, 1-K & F, *tel.* Belfast 243727
Garages: A S Baird, Boucher Road, *tel.* Belfast 661811
Charles Hurst Motors, 10 Adelaide Street, *tel.* Belfast 230566
J E Coulter 58–82 Antrim Road, *tel.* Belfast 744744

Shopping, Victorian-style, along the elegant glass-topped Queen's Parade, Belfast

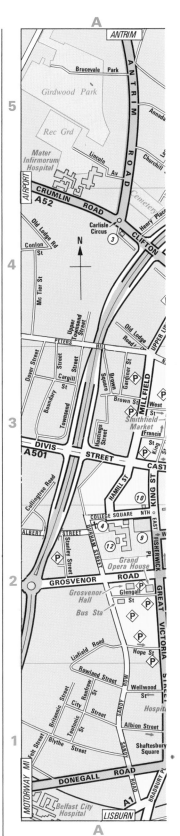

PUBLIC BUILDINGS AND PLACES OF INTEREST

Albert Memorial Clock Tower, Victoria Street 1 (C3)

Belfast Bank, Waring Street 2 (B3)

Carlisle Memorial Church, Clifton Street 3 (A4)

Christ Church (CI), College Sq North 4 (A2)

City Hall, Donegall Sq Sth 5 (B2)

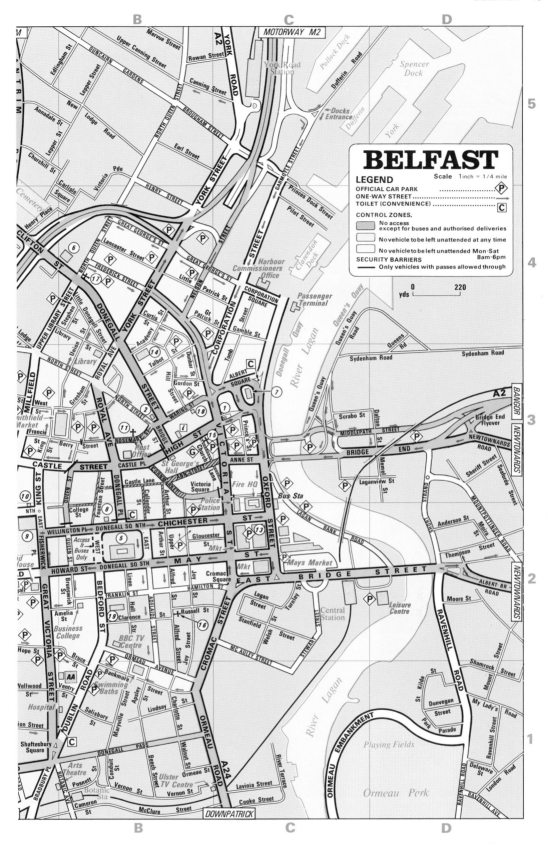

BELFAST

LEGEND

Scale 1inch = 1/4 mile

OFFICIAL CAR PARK .... Ⓟ
ONE-WAY STREET ....
TOILET (CONVENIENCE) .... Ⓒ

CONTROL ZONES.

No access
except for buses and authorised deliveries

No vehicle to be left unattended at any time

No vehicle to be left unattended Mon-Sat
8am-6pm

SECURITY BARRIERS
— Only vehicles with passes allowed through

0   220
yds

Clifton House or Old Charitable Institute, North Queen Street 6 (B4)

Custom House, 7 (C3)

Linenhall Library, Donegall Sq North 8 (B2)

Municipal College of Technology, College Sq East 9 (A2)

Old Museum, College Sq North 10 (A3)

Old Presbyterian Oval Church, Rosemary Street 11 (B3)

Royal Belfast Academic Institution, College Sq North 12 (A2)

Royal Courts of Justice, Oxford Street 13 (C2)

St Annes Cathedral (CI), Donegall Street 14 (B3)

St George's Church (CI), High Street 15 (B3)

St Malachy's Church (RC), Alfred Street 16 (B2)

St Patrick's Church (RC), Donegall Street 17 (B4)

Ulster Bank, Waring Street 18 (B3)

Ulster Hall, Bedford Street 19 (B2)

The Kilfountain Chi-Rho Pillar, Co Kerry

Standing stones and stone circles

Standing stones or gallans, the name given to stones which have been stood on end, are numerous and widely distributed. They vary in height from 3ft to 20ft tall, and they also vary in original purpose. Lines of stones, like those at Beaghmore and 'Finn Mac Cools Fingers', near Cavan, seem to have had a ritual significance. This seems most likely for stones at known religious sites such as Tara, Co Meath, and those found near or in ring forts and stone circles. The great stone of Turoe, decorated in the 'La Tène' style of the Celts, looks like a fertility symbol. A tall stone at Punchestown, Co Kildare, marked a grave, while at Lough Gur, Co Limerick, stones line a road. Other stones may record notable events; still others are boundary stones.

Christian inscriptions found on stones may have been added later and it seems likely that Ireland's elaborately carved stone crosses are descendants of earlier ritual stones. 'Ogham' writing can be seen on the Ballycrovane Ogham Stone in the Bearn peninsula, Co Cork, and on other stones in the south-west. Instead of letters, ogham has groups of up to five lines, scored or cut above, below or across a base line (usually one edge of the stone). The use of five lines suggests that it may have begun as a sign language, or it may have been developed as a code, becoming the first written form of Gaelic, dating from the first few centuries AD. Conversion into our alphabet is straightforward if the lines are clear, but the actual meaning has sometimes remained obscure. The inscription often gives the name of a person followed by that of an ancestor.

Stone circles are more regional than widespread: they are found particularly in West Cork, Limerick, Tyrone, Fermanagh and Derry. Ireland doesn't have a Stonehenge, but the concentration of circles on a site can be impressive, as at Beaghmore and Lough Gur. Like many of Ireland's circular forts they would have had a ritual use: large stones around Newgrange suggest the former presence of a circle, and at Reenagopoul, Co Kerry, a circle surrounds a chambered tomb.

Orientation towards the position of the sun seems likely, for astronomical or ritual use. Lack of evidence makes stone circles difficult to date, but it is thought they belong to the Bronze Age, about 1800 BC.

Beaghmore, Co Tyrone

Map Ref: 123 H68

Lying north-west of Cookstown, this is one of Ireland's more remarkable archaeological sites, the more so since its extent was only quite recently discovered by people cutting turf. It has three pairs of stone circles and one single circle, with stone rows and cairns. They have been dated to the early Bronze Age, but the discovery of a stone axe suggests that Neolithic people used the site.

Belleek, Co Fermanagh

Map Ref: 122 G95

Belleek is the most westerly village in Northern Ireland, sitting on the picturesque far tip of Lower Lough Erne, just on the border. The river Erne is good for trout fishing here, where sluice gates have been mounted to prevent flooding.

Belleek is best known for exquisite creamy lustre porcelain. Especially distinctive are the pretty designs in porcelain basketwork, skilfully woven from thin strands of china and generously decorated with shamrocks and roses. Belleek china is in demand throughout the world but particularly in America. The china is made in a solid three-storey factory built in 1858, and visitors may tour the pottery.

Birr, Co Offaly

Map Ref: 125 N00

Birr is another contestant for the title of Ireland's geographical centre (see Athlone), this time with the authority of surveyor Sir William Petty. It is an unusually well laid out town, with Georgian houses in Oxmantown Mall and John's Mall, and its attractions include golf, brown trout angling on the Little Brosna river, and Birr Castle.

The castle, which weathered many sieges in the 16th and 17th centuries, was originally a fortress of the O'Carrolls, but since then has been held by Normans, Cromwellians, Jacobites, Williamites and others. It dominates the town and its walled demesne encloses a lake and the meeting of the Little Brosna and Camcor rivers. In the garden are limes, chestnuts, copper beeches, redwoods, Wellingtonias, Greek and other firs, a Cedar of Goa, Himalayan juniper, Monterey cypress and box hedges which, at 35ft, may be the world's tallest.

Sir Laurence Parsons rebuilt the castle around a ruined keep in 1620, and Birr for many years was called Parsonstown. His descendant, the second Earl of Rosse, was an amateur architect and played a big

Possibly the world's tallest box hedge can be found in Birr Castle's formal gardens

part in laying out the town. The third Earl built a telescope, once the world's largest, whose remains are still here, but whose reflector is in the Science Museum in London.

Arthur Bell Nicholls, rector of Birr, married Charlotte Brontë in 1854 and the honeymoon was spent here and in **Banagher**, eight miles north on the Shannon. Anthony Trollope wrote his first novels while working in the post office in Banagher.

AA recommends:
Hotel: County Arms, 2-star, *tel.* (0509) 20791
Garage: P L Dolan & Sons, Main Street, *tel.* (0509) 20006

Blessington, Co Wicklow

Map Ref: 125 N91

This is essentially one broad and attractive village street, but it stands beside the northmost finger of the Poulaphouca reservoir, sometimes called Blessington lakes, where the water, also noted for trout, combines with woods and mountains in beautiful views. Blessington's charter dates from Charles II and there is a 1669 church.

The River Liffey formerly flowed on the town's eastern edge and Blessington was an important stop on the Dublin – Waterford mail coach route. The hotel name of 'Downshire' recalls the Marquis of Downshire; Downshire House, to the west, was burned down in 1798.

AA recommends:
Hotel: Downshire House, 3-star, *tel.* (045) 65199
Garage: Hughes, *tel.* (045) 65156

Bray, Co Wicklow

Map Ref: 125 O21

Bray is a first-class example of a railway resort, a seaside town that blossomed with the coming of excursions. Since then it has become one of the country's finest coastal holiday venues, helped by being placed between Dublin and Co Wicklow's scenic beauties. The capital is only 12 miles north by the N11, five miles more if one hugs the shore.

The town has a mile-long esplanade with 791ft Bray Head at its southern end. There are excellent views from the top of the Head; for ease of approach use the landward side, via the Greystones road. Other fine views are from the cliff walk around the base where oldhamia, the oldest fossil found in Ireland, occurs.

Bray has a nine-hole golf course and the 18-hole championship **Woodbrook** links are north of the town. The 1659ft Great Sugarloaf mountain can be seen, right of the picturesque red-roof town hall, as one looks south along the main street.

AA recommends:
Hotel: Royal, Main Street, 2-star, *tel.* (01) 862935
Restaurant: Tree of Idleness, Seafront 2-K & F, *tel.* (01) 863498

Brugh Na Boinne *see* Dowth and Newgrange.

Buncrana, Co Donegal

Map Ref: 123 C33

On the Inishowen peninsula beside a curve of Lough Swilly, Buncrana is sheltered on three sides by hills, with the 2019ft Slieve Snacht prominent to the north-east. A fine stretch of golden sand runs three miles south to Fahan, with more bathing beaches on the other side of the town.

At **Crocahaisil,** two miles north, is a Bronze Age burial cairn, with the remains of a stone circle nearby. At **Gransha,** south of the town, is a dolmen. The keep of the 1430 O'Doherty's Castle stands picturesquely at Castle Bridge, at the town's north end.

Nearby Buncrana Castle, built in 1717 by Sir John Vaughan, had Theobald Wolfe Tone as an unwilling guest after he landed from the captured French warship Hoche in 1798. Go north to Dunree Head lighthouse for unrivalled lough views.

A mile-long stretch of sandy beach curves gently round to the heather-clad Bray Head

A history of the Burren and its flora and fauna is on display at the Interpretative Centre

Rare alpine and Arctic flowers thrive in the shelter of the Burren's rocky limestone terraces

The Burren – a vast moonscape of particular interest to geologists and botanists

Lisdoonvarna, Co Clare towards Galway Bay, is one of the strangest and loneliest places in Ireland. It is a 'karst' landscape of bare limestone similar to those around Malham and Ingleborough in the Yorkshire Dales, along the north-east Adriatic shores and in the French Causses and Jura.

As in those places, caves are a feature. Four miles north-east of Lisdoonvarna along the eastern flank of 1134ft Slieve Elva, highest point in the Burren, a 100ft deep chasm leads into the Pollinagollum cave system, one of the largest in Ireland. More than seven miles of caverns have been explored here and they contain a 25ft waterfall with many underground streams.

The rock terraces shelter Ireland's rarest flora. Alpine and Arctic types grow in exceptional profusion, including brightly-hued saxifrages and gentians. Similar vegetation is found elsewhere in Ireland, in Co Kerry, Sligo and Donegal, but the extent of their distribution in the Burren is unique. They grow from the highest parts of the landscape to sea level.

Corkscrew Hill, on the Ballyvaughan–Lisdoonvarna road, gives a fine view of these stony uplands. There are many antiquities in the area: dolmens, wedge gallery graves, forts and crosses. Seven miles north-east of Kilfenora is the **Druid's Altar,** a box-like stone tomb, not the most impressive of them, but with an excellent situation for viewing the natural phenomena. At **Keelhilla** at the foot of Slieve Carran, some four miles south-west of Kinvarra and a mile inside the county's border with Co Galway, is a limestone cave below Eagle's Rock, capable of holding one reclining human. A little church ruin is nearby. The beds of eroded karstic limestone from the Road of Dishes, after a legend that a king's banquet was miraculously flown to a starving saint. The view here is splendid.

Bundoran, Co Donegal

Map Ref: 122 G85

A consistently popular seaside and golf resort on a ragged crescent inlet of Donegal Bay, Bundoran has a wide 300yd strand in the town centre, fronting a promenade. The excellent golf course has a striking situation at Aughrus Head at the town's east end. The cliffs here lead to Tullan Strand. Curiosities caused by Atlantic erosion include the Fairy Bridge, a 24ft natural arch, the Wishing Chair and the Puffing Hole.

In the cliffs west of the town are the Lion's Paw Cave fissures and grotesque rock shapes. From **Bundrowes,** where an unroofed tower called Cassidy's Folly stands at the water's edge, Michael O'Clery, chief of the Four Masters historians (see Ballyshannon), began his travels in 1627.

Finner Church, between the Fairy Bridge and the broad one and a half miles of Tullan Strand, is the ruinous marker for a new reclining pillar stone called Flaherty's Stone, named after a fairy chief of local lore.

Bunratty Castle, Co Clare

Map Ref: 124 R46

Noted both for its mediaeval candlelit banquets and for the towering arched recess of its main doorway, Bunratty Castle dates from the mid 15th century and was built by Sioda MacConmara. By 1500 it had become a stronghold of the O'Briens, kings and later Earls of Thomond. It was besieged by Cromwellian forces and later was owned by Lord Gort, who assembled the impressive collection of medieval furniture and art works, weapons and utensils which are to be seen in Bunratty today. In the folk park adjoining the castle traditional Irish farmhouses and cottages have been reconstructed and furnished in period.

The Burren, Co Clare

Map Ref: 124 M20

The Burren, an area of bare limestone hills and terraces, covering about 50 square miles and extending northwards from

Bushmills, Co Antrim

Map Ref: 123 C94

Still flourishing is Old Bushmills Distillery, reputed to be the oldest legal distillery in the world, having been granted a licence in 1608. It is said that it is the crystal clear water of St Columb's Rill combined with the local barley which gives the whiskey its special flavour. Visitors may tour the distillery from an attractive Visitor Centre made in the old malt kilns which used peat and coke as fuel for drying the malt.

Two mills can still be seen on the river Bush which gives the town its name and is full of trout and salmon. Once this water supported not only flour, paper and spade mills but generated the electricity which powered the world's first hydro-electric tramway, from Bushmills to the Giant's Causeway. It opened in 1883 and closed in 1949.

Caherdaniel, Co Kerry

Map Ref: 124 V55

Caherdaniel is a charming village on the Ring of Kerry (N70), two miles from West Cove facing the innermost point of Derrynane Bay. Its name means 'Donal's stone fort', and this still stands by the road. In the bay are several islands, including Lambs Island and Kids Island. A little to the east is the curious St Crohane's Hermitage, hewn out of the solid rock of a steep cliff, with the ruins of this saint's church.

A little west is the ruined Derrynane Abbey, standing in the well-wooded demesne of Derrynane House. For many years this was the home of patriot Daniel O'Connell, called 'the Liberator' for his championship of Catholics. Here are preserved a blunderbuss belonging to Robert Emmet, leader of the 1803 insurrection in Dublin, a pistol with which O'Connell shot one D'Esterre in an 1815 duel, a chair of the Liberator's and a bowl which contained his baptismal water.

Cahir, Co Tipperary

Map Ref: 125 S02

East of the Galtee mountains, this bright, spacious little town stands on the trout-filled Suir. The main leisure activity is obvious from a rough translation of the Gaelic name: 'fish-abounding-city-fort', but this is also the centre of a hunting district.

The *Book of Lecan* recalls the destruction of the fort, on an islet in the Suir, in the third century. King Brian Boru had a 10th-century residence here. Cahir Castle, with its massive keep and high enclosing seven-towered wall, is mainly 15th century, and includes parts of an 1142 stronghold erected by Conor O'Brien, Prince of Thomond, on the earlier fort's site.

This castle, a National Monument, with spacious hall and courtyards, was taken by the Earl of Essex after a 10-day siege in 1599, and was taken again by Cromwell in 1650.

The **Mote of Knockgraffon**, four miles north of Cahir, rising 60ft above its knoll, may have been the Munster kings' coronation place before this function was transferred to Cashel.

Cappoquin, Co Waterford

Map Ref: 125 X19

The Cistercian (Trappist) monastery of Mount Melleray was founded here in 1832. The monks cleared nearly 800 acres of moorland, establishing a farm which made them nearly self-sufficient, and still run a guesthouse at which there is no charge – although guests customarily leave an offering.

Cappoquin has good fishing for both sea and brown trout in the estuary of the Blackwater and is set in lovely wooded countryside below the southern Knockmealdown slopes. Four miles south is **Dromana House**, the Villiers Stuart mansion on the site of the Fitzgeralds' Dromana Castle (of which there are scanty remains). The neat village of **Villierstown** is south of the demesne. **Affane**, two miles south of Cappoquin, is birthplace of Valentine, 'The Stroker Greatrakes, a 17th-century healer whose mixture of massage and hypnosis greatly impressed Charles II.

Carlingford, Co Louth

Map Ref: 123 J11

Facing Co Down across Carlingford Lough, this Cooley peninsula village has a long history. King John built a castle here in 1210 (now ruinous) and Taaffe's Castle and the fortified house called the Mint are 16th-century. In the former a good spiral staircase leads to the battlements. Even the church of the 1305 priory has a battlement, in a town which once had 32 castellated buildings.

The shingle beach is unsuitable for bathing, but the little peninsula, with its Cooley Mountains, is a walkers' haven, 1935ft Carlingford Mountain being the focus.

Dominated by Slieve Foye Mountain (1935ft) the tiny town of Carlingford overlooks the lough – a popular sea fishing area

Carlingford Lough, Co Louth

Map Ref: 123 J11

Carlingford Lough is a beautiful fjord-like lough where the Cooley Mountains look across to the Mournes, both steep slopes clothed with woodland. From there are scenic drives to Omeath and Carlingford and to Warrenpoint and Rostrevor.

At the Lough's mouth is **Cranfield** where Vikings beached their ships, **Mill Bay** with some excellent wrack beds for kelp or seaweed used for fertiliser, and **Blockhouse Island** (NT) which has a colony of terns.

Legend has it that Finn MacCool threw a 40-ton hunk of granite across the Lough from the Cooleys, where he is said to be buried. **Cloughmore stone**, as it is known, was in fact carried by a glacier to rest above Rostrevor, and can be seen from the fine Forestry Division drive, close to **Kilbroney Park**, a good recreational area.

Warrenpoint is a pleasant resort with a broad promenade and tree lined avenues. Three miles west is **Narrow Water Castle** dramatically situated 16th-century towerhouse (DOE).

Carlow, Co Carlow

Map Ref: 125 S77

An enterprising but misguided doctor called Philip Middleton changed the central appearance of this county capital in 1814. He leased the castle for a mental hospital, set an explosive charge to remove inner walls for an open-plan ward system, and blew away most of a building which had withstood Cromwell's cannons. The castle dated from 1207–13; its surviving wall is like pantomime scenery.

Carlow commands a beautiful stretch of the River Barrow. A progressive town, site of Ireland's first sugar factory, it has several nicely preserved smaller premises, Dublin Street having particular charm. Sir Richard Morrison's polygonal classical courthouse of 1830 is striking, as is the 151ft octagonal tower of Cobden's neo-Gothic cathedral of the same period. Carlow's Tullow Street (and not Wexford as is sometimes said) saw the first real engagement of the 1798 rebellion. As a frontier town of the 'Pale' the town also saw many clashes from the 14th to the 17th century.

A 100-ton dolmen capstone at **Browne's Hill**, two miles east, is said to be Ireland's biggest.

AA recommends:
Hotel: Royal, Dublin Street, 2-star, tel. (0503) 31621
T & C: Dolmen House, Brownshill, tel. (0503) 42444
Garages: Deerpark Service Station, Dublin Road, tel. (0503) 31414
Statham Sheridan, Court Place, tel. (0503) 31665

Carrantouhill, Co Kerry

Map Ref: 124 V88

Ireland's highest mountain Carrantouhill (3414ft) stands in the range known as MacGillicuddy's Reeks, West of the Killarney lakes and a little south-east of Beenkeragh, which is exactly 100ft lower. The summit is roomy and on clear days the view is breathtaking, embracing other mountains, the lakes and the Atlantic inlets which are very near. The reeks are on the Inveragh peninsula, in the area surrounded by the Ring of Kerry. In the 18th century a wolf was killed here, one of Ireland's last.

The best ascent is from **Gortbue** school at the entrance to the Hag's Glen to the north, through this glen and then up the Devil's ladder. The glen approach takes one between Lough Gouragh and Lough Callee. A westerly approach from Lough Acoose makes a circuit of Caher (3200ft), Carrantouhill itself, Beenkeragh and Skregmore (2790ft), and is Ireland's best ridge walk. There are many cliffs for rock climbers. The road approach is by Beaufort Bridge.

Carrickfergus, Co Antrim

Map Ref: 123 J48

The powerful Norman John de Courcy chose the natural defence of a basalt promontory at Carrickfergus (the Rock of Fergus), to build his castle after 1180 and owing to its strategic importance the town developed. King John came in 1210, in Elizabethan times brick lined gunports were inserted in the castle walls, and the landing of William of Orange in 1690 is marked by a plaque at the harbour. Now the castle houses military museums, and a Medieval Fair is held in the summer.

St Nicholas Church, off Market Square, is also 12th-century and medieval conditions are recalled by a leper's window in the chancel. The stained glass includes a representation of St Nicholas as Santa Claus, but of particular importance is the Chichester Monument which the poet Louis

Navigating Carlow Lock on the River Barrow which flows west of the town

McNeice, whose father was rector, describes thus:

*'The Chichesters knelt in marble at the end of the transept
With ruffs about their necks, their portion sure.'*

Writer Jonathan Swift was rector of **Kilroot**, 2 miles east. Now it has a towering power station. Nearby at **Boneybefore** is a museum to US President Andrew Jackson, whose parents lived here before emigration in 1765.

Carrickmacross, Co Monaghan

Map Ref: 123 H80

Renowned for its lace, this handsome town has fine Georgian houses, a spacious main street and traditional shopfronts. St Louis convent grounds contain slight traces of a castle built by the Earl of Essex, who was granted the town by Elizabeth I. The Roman Catholic church is a good modern building, with notable Stations of the Cross. **Lough Fean House** estate, outside the town to the south-west, has some beautiful woods and a lake, and limestone caves can be

inspected at **Tiragarvan**, a mile and a half to the west.

It is seven miles north-east to **Inishkeen**, site of a sixth-century monastery founded by St Deagh but better known today as the birthplace of outspoken poet Patrick Kavanagh. The base of a round tower is the most significant

Carrickfergus Castle crowns a rocky headland overlooking the lough

surviving part of the monastery; a mile away is **Channon Rock**, once a Pale boundary mark.

American heritage

Emigration to America was already a feature of Irish life long before the great Famine, whose worst year was 1847. Andrew Jackson's parents left Boneybefore, near Carrickfergus, in 1765, and the late President John F. Kennedy's great grandfather left Ireland in 1820. But it grew to an exodus after the Famine, and continued in huge numbers for over a century, so that it became hard to find a family without relatives in the USA. Today Americans of all occupations and social strata are aware of Irish roots.

Michael Regan, great grandfather of President Ronald Reagan, was born in Ballyporeen, Co Tipperary, not far from the celebrated Mitchelstown caves. The Kennedy ancestral home is in Dunganstown, Co Wexford, some four miles south of New Ross. A Dublin Quaker named Milhous was grandmother of yet another American President, Richard Nixon, whose wife Patricia (nee Ryan) had Co Tipperary grandparents. Theodore Roosevelt's mother was descended from people of Larne, Co Antrim, and he wrote of the Irish who became American frontiersmen that 'they were a stern people, strong and simple, powerful for good and evil . . . the best fitted to conquer the wilderness'.

Wilsons still live in Dergalt, Co Tyrone, the village which Woodrow Wilson's grandfather left for America in 1807. President McKinley's ancestors came from Conagher, Co Tyrone; President Arthur's from Cullybackey, Co Antrim; President Grant's from Dergina, Co Tyrone; and President Buchanan's from Deoran, Co Tyrone. Stonewall Jackson's great grandfather left The Birches, Co Armagh, on the shores of Lough Neagh, in 1748.

Princess Grace of Monaco, formerly

Ulysses Grant, Irishman and US President 1869–77

actress Grace Kelly and Philadelphia socialite, was granddaughter of John Henry Kelly, who left Ballycroy, Co Mayo in 1867, and of Mary Costello, born in the same county. Hollywood actresses Maureen O'Hara and Maureen O'Sullivan were both born in Ireland. World heavyweight boxing champion and millionaire businessman Gene Tunney's parents came from Co Mayo, while John L Sullivan's father was from Tralee, his mother from Athlone, and James J Braddock's father was from Co Kildare. The ancestors of Neil Armstrong, first man on the moon, came from Co Fermanagh.

Motor magnate Henry Ford's father, William, emigrated from Ballinascarthy, Co Cork, in 1847. Henry later brought a hearthstone from the ancestral home to his mansion at Dearborn, Michigan, which he named Fairlane after a small street in Cork city (now called Wolfe Tone Street), where his maternal grandfather had been born. A Ford car was also named after this little street. Commodore John Barry, father of the US Navy, was born in Ballysampson, Tacumshare, Co Wexford, and William Cody, whose son of the same name was 'Buffalo Bill', in Wexford town. The lives of early settlers like these are traced at the Ulster American Folk Park, Camphill, Co Tyrone.

Interior detail of Ormond Castle, originally a 14th-century fortress, by the River Suir

Carrick-on-Shannon, Co Leitrim

Map Ref: 122 G90

Leitrim's county town stands on a crossing of the Shannon just below Lough Drumharlow and below the town the river broadens again. This makes Carrick-on-Shannon (locally 'Carrick') a natural base for the trout and coarse fish angler. The Shannon is navigable as far as Lough Allen, to the north.

This is a golf, hunting and game area. The town boasts some Georgian houses and shopfronts. At **Jamestown** a gate from the original walls still spans the road.

AA recommends:

Hotels: Bush, 2-star, *tel.* (078) 20014
County, 2-star, *tel.* (078) 20042
Guesthouses: Aisleigh House, Dublin Road, *tel.* (078) 20313
Rutledge's Old Coach Inn, *tel.* (078) 20032
T & C: Corbally Lodge, Dublin Road, *tel.* (078) 20228
Garage: Cox's, Main Street, *tel.* (078) 20217

Carrick-on-Suir, Co Tipperary

Map Ref: 125 S42

A small but attractive town – the Butlers, Earls and later Dukes of Ormonde, come to mind through the square keep of their 15th-century castle, and adjoining it is a more intriguing Elizabethan fortified mansion, a rarity in Ireland, and well preserved.

The 10th Earl, 'Black Tom', is said to have built this for a visit of Elizabeth I, before she decided not to travel. Elizabeth's grandmother (and mother of Anne Boleyn) was Margaret Butler, daughter of the seventh earl.

The Suir river is at its prettiest between here and Clonmel. There is golf, and fishing for brown trout and sometimes salmon. **Lough Coumshingaun** in the nearby Comeraghs is a noted rock-climbing centre, surrounded by a horseshoe of cliffs, 1288ft at one point, and overshadowed in the

background by the highest peak, Fauscoum (2597ft). This is one of the finest glacial cirques in the British Isles. North of it is the crag-ringed **Crotty's Lake,** with the cave hideout of William Crotty, an 18th-century highwayman and folk hero who was hanged in Waterford.

Carrigaline, Co Cork

Map Ref: 124 W76

Once renowned for its pottery, this is a village of some charm on high ground near where the Owenboy river enters Cork Harbour. A leaden effigy of Lady Newenham, who died in 1754, is one of the curiosities of its Perpendicular church. Balla Castle, a little north-west, was originally a McCarthy fort and is said to be one of the oldest castles in Ireland still lived in, but updating has obscured its early purpose and appearance. Sir Francis Drake sheltered his ships in the Owenboy estuary in 1587 when outnumbered by a pursuing Spanish Fleet, and Drake's Pool recalls the event.

Crosshaven, on Cork harbour, is a yachting and bathing resort which climbs steeply from the water's edge, with pleasant wooded walks behind it.

Carrigart, Co Donegal

Map Ref: 123 C13

Situated where the winding road passes an inlet of Mulroy Bay, Carrigart is also on the isthmus of Rosguill peninsula, and has a fine beach. Mulroy Bay has many small peninsulae, some richly clothed in pine, fir and gorse. The high ground gives splendid views of the

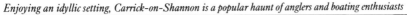

Enjoying an idyllic setting, Carrick-on-Shannon is a popular haunt of anglers and boating enthusiasts

indented shores and wooded islets.

Carrigart's sandhill prehistoric buildings, or 'kitchen middens', have yielded several finds, and there is an Ogham stone at **Meevagh**. But this is primarily resort country: the village has golf and just over a mile away are the championship **Rosapenna links,** giving 6000 yards of play. The so-called **Atlantic Drive,** a circuit of Rosguill Peninsula, encompassing the links, is possibly the best scenic drive in Donegal, especially around Tranarossan Bay.

Cashel, Co Tipperary

Map Ref: 125 S04

A round tower and church ruins make a dramatic sight on the Rock of Cashel, a limestone outcrop over 200ft tall which looms over the town's north side. Floodlit nowadays for striking night effects, the Rock, about 200 acres in extent, is one of the country's greatest historical sites.

Cashel at first seems casual about its past. Quirke's Castle, which catches the eye opposite the city hall, is 15th-century; it has been turned into first a shop and later a hotel, and the name recalls not the original owner but a late 19th-century printer who occupied it.

This ruined 13th-century cathedral crowns the 20ft-high Rock of Cashel

The Queen Anne-style deanery of 1730 also became a hotel. It is a fine building, considering that provincial building styles were usually a few years out of date.

Cashel was the seat of Munster's kings from about AD 370 to 1101, when the Rock was granted to the Church by King Murtagh O'Brien. Its visitors have included St Patrick preaching, Brian Boru being crowned, Henry II conquering, Edward Bruce holding a parliament and Gerald, Earl of Kildare, in 1495, burning. (He told Henry VII that he burned the cathedral

because he thought the archbishop was in it.)

The Rock's buildings include an 85ft 10th-century round tower, a cathedral, the Hall of Vicars Choral, St Patrick's Cross, and the lovely Cormac's Chapel, built in 1127. This is unique as a first-class example of pre-Norman Romanesque in Ireland.

AA recommends:

Hotel: Cashel Palace, 4-star (country house), *tel.* (062) 61411

Farmhouse: Knock-Saint-Lour House, *tel.* (062) 61172

Round towers

The tall slim round towers, of which about 70 survive, date mainly from the ninth century and must not be confused with the short squat Martello towers, 75 of which were built around the Irish coast in case of Napoleonic invasion. The old round towers were usually built near monastic and other ecclesiastical sites and serve as belltowers, storehouses and watchtowers, especially to warn of Viking attack.

In this last capacity they often housed the valuables which had induced the Viking to attack the monastery in the first place. In extreme cases the tower was used as a place of human refuge; quite how a community existed for the duration of a long siege, sealed in and cooped up in a stone tube, is hard to imagine. The tower which survives at Glendalough, Co Wicklow, was attacked by Norsemen in the ninth century and all its monks murdered.

The towers vary in height from 50 to 120ft, usually tapering towards a stone-capped top. (Some of the survivors have lost this stone cap.) The door is a sufficient distance from the ground to necessitate a ladder for entry, hauled in at time of siege, hidden elsewhere in the settlement at times of storage. The windows are narrow and spiral up around the tower. There are usually four windows around the top, one at each compass point, but some surviving

towers, like that beside St Canice's Cathedral in Kilkenny, have six.

Originally most towers had a number of floors linked by trapdoors and ladders but some, presumably intended as watchtowers only, had a stairway.

Towers survive, among other places, at Cashel; Glendalough, Kil-

kenny; Cloyne, Co Cork; Ardmore, Co Waterford; Monasterboice, Co Louth; Scattery Island, opposite Cappa, Co Clare in the Shannon estuary; and in Kildare town. At Roscrea, Co Tipperary and Clondalkin, in Dublin's south-west suburbs, towers have been incorporated in the streets.

An exquisite atmosphere of Celtic melancholy pervades Devenish Island

A row of sparkling whitewashed cottages overlooks the seashore in the tranquil coastal resort of Castlerock

Castlebar, Co Mayo

Map Ref: 122 M19

This pleasing, if rather plain town stands on a little river with the same name in rather flat surroundings, whose small lakes give good fishing. John Bingham, ancestor of the Earls of Lucan, founded the town in the early 17th century, and the shady, grass-covered Mall was formerly the private cricket pitch of his notorious descendant. The prima donna, Margaret Burke-Sheridan, was born here, as was Charles Haughey, the Fianna Fail politician.

The town has an airfield for pleasure flights and also hosts an international song festival (October) which has lately grown greatly in stature. At nearby **Turlough** on the N5 is a well-preserved but somewhat squat-looking round tower.

The 'Races of Castlebar' is the traditional nickname of the departure of the town's garrison, said to be exceptionally speedy, under General Lake in 1798 when Humbert's Frenchmen, who had landed in Killala, took the town. An incident of 1641 was less amusing. The town, which had received a charter from James I in 1613, was occupied by the Confederate Irish, with a promise of 'a safe conduct' given to the English garrison, who departed for Galway. En route, at Shrule, 100 of them, including clergy, were massacred although some escaped through the intervention of Ulick and Walter Burke. Lord Mayo had given the promise, and his son, who succeeded him, was tried and shot for reneging on it.

AA recommends:
Hotels: Breaffy House, 3-star, *tel.* (094) 22033
Travellers Friend, I-star, *tel.* (094) 23111
Welcome Inn, I-star, *tel.* (094) 22054
Guesthouse: Heneghans, Newtown Street, *tel.* (094) 21883

Castleisland, Co Kerry

Map Ref: 124 Q90

At the eastern end of the Vale of Tralee, the town is named after the castle built by Geoffrey de Marisco in 1226, ruins of which survive in the town. It was taken in 1345 by Sir Ralph Uffod from the Earl of Desmond, with the slaughter of the entire garrison. Red marble from Castleisland's quarries, its lovely colour coming from iron oxide, is widely used in monumental decoration. At **Ballyplymouth**, two miles east, are caves whose full extent is not yet known. Just west of Castleisland, at **Tobermainge**, the River Main flows underground.

Knight's Mountain to the north is the tallest of the Glanarudery mountains at 1097ft. Near it, but to the left of the road going north, are Glenageenty and **Desmond's Grave**. The 15th and last Earl of Desmond, Gerald, was executed here in 1583 after a betrayal. The west wind's roar in the area is still known to older people as 'Desmond's Howl'.

AA recommends:
Garage: McElligotts, Limerick Road, *tel.* (066) 41284

Castlerea, Co Roscommon

Map Ref: 122 M68

Antiquarian and oculist Sir William Wilde, father of dramatist Oscar, was born here. Lough O'Flyn and Lough Glinn are nearby lakes in the area, and an ancient high cross stands at Emlagh, two miles to the south.

Frenchpark, eight miles north, has scanty remains of 14th-century Cloonshanville Abbey (Dominican), and the shell of an 18th-century Palladian mansion in the lonely demesne which was the seat of Lord de Freyne. It has a circular brewhouse. Also here is the grave of Douglas Hyde, first President of the Republic and founder of the Gaelic League, who was born in the rectory. Within the demesne is a large souterrain.

AA recommends:
Garage: Lavins, *tel.* (0907) 20096

Castlerock, Co Londonderry

Map Ref: 123 C73

Castlerock is a quiet resort on the north east coast of Londonderry, to the west of the mouth of the River Bann. The Barmouth (NT) is good for birdwatching as many migrant species stop over here.

At the crossroads of the Coleraine–Downhill road is Hezlett House, a thatched cottage (NT) dating from 1690 – an example of 'Cruck truss' construction – a pre-fab method of building using wood frames, which were brought by planters (protestant settlers) and filled in with local materials, such as clay and rubble.

At **Downhill** (NT) is the remains of the great demesne planted by Frederick Hervey Bishop of Derry and Earl of Bristol. His house has fallen victim to the elements but there are many interesting places throughout the dramatic landscape, foremost of which is the fine rotunda Mussenden Temple built as a library and occupying a spectacular position on the edge of a cliff.

From **Gortmore** on the Bishop's road there are splendid views down to the magnificent six-mile strand at Magilligan, west to the Foyle and the Donegal hills and east to the Scottish islands.

AA recommends:
Campsite: Castlerock Caravan Park, 3-pennant, *tel.* Londonderry 848381

Castletownbere, Co Cork

Map Ref: 124 V64

Far down the north shore of Bantry Bay, this little town's natural harbour is sheltered by the long Bere Island. It is the headquarters of an area favoured by climbers, botanists and anglers, and is also known as Bere Haven. There was once rich copper mining nearby, centred on **Allihies,** to the west on the Atlantic Ballydonegan Bay, and this gave Castletownbere's harbour its original importance. A trip to Allihies nowadays is rewarded by magnificent seascapes. Further along the L61 one passes the bathing spot of **Garinish** and reaches the swirling waters of narrow **Dursey Sound,** facing Dursey Island.

Hungry Hill (2251ft) and Maulin (2044ft) are in the Slieve Miskish range north of Castletownbere. Near **Eyeries Point,** to the north-west again, is an Ogham standing stone 17ft 6in tall. **Dunboy Castle,** two miles from Castletownbere, was a stronghold of O'Sullivan Bere; its walls were shattered in 1602.

AA recommends:
Garage: Oakmount, *tel.* (027) 70264

The 19th-century parish church in Castlewellan

Castlewellan, Co Down

Map Ref: 123 J33

Castlewellan, set on a northern foothill of the Mournes, is bounded on either side by two fine spires, in contrast to the three mill chimneys in the valley of Annsborough to the east. It has broad tree lined streets and squares laid out by the Annesley family after 1750. The Annesleys also built a castle in the Scottish Baronial style in the 1850s and founded a renowned arboretum, now part of a Forest park, which includes a comprehensive collection of Chamaecyparis and Abies as well as many species from the southern hemisphere. There is a lovely lake

An imposing belfry tower is all that remains of a 14th-century friary around which Cavan grew

and walled garden. **Dromena** cashel and souterrain are at the east end of nearby Lough Island Reavey.

AA recommends:
Campsite: Castlewellan Forest Park, 3-pennant, *tel.* Castlewellan 78664

Cavan, Co Cavan

Map Ref: 123 H40

This town is the capital of the most southerly county of the province of Ulster, and one of the three which are not in Northern Ireland. It stands in an area of low hills east of Lough Oughter's baffling jigsaw of land and water. In angled Abbey Street, off Bridge Street, is the belfry tower of a Franciscan friary founded in 1300 by Giolla Iosa Rua O'Reilly. A plaque on its wall commemorates Owen Roe O'Neill, victor over Monro in the 1646 Battle of Benburgh. Cavan's 1942 Roman Catholic cathedral has a splendid interior.

Just north-west of the town are **Farnham House** and demesne, a 3000-acre spread of woodland scenery. The house dates from

1700. To its west, on an islet in Lough Oughter, is **Cloughoughter Castle,** an O'Reilly stronghold whose oldest part is 13th-century. It has been ruinous since it was taken by Cromwellian forces in April, 1653. Owen Roe O'Neill died in this castle, which had been an O'Reilly possession until the Ulster Plantation early in the 17th century.

In **Kilmore,** three miles west of Cavan, the vestry door of the cathedral is a pre-Norman Romanesque relic from a monastery on Trinity Island in Lough Oughter. Bishop William Bedell, first translator of the Old Testament into Gaelic, is buried here.

Finn MacCool's Fingers, are a group of prehistoric standing stones at Shantemon Hill, on the way to **Ballyhaise,** where the 18th-century Ballyhaise House is a work of the celebrated Richard Cassels. **Ballyjamesduff,** noted for a song, is south-east of Cavan.

AA recommends:
Hotel: Hotel Kilmore, Dublin Road, 3-star, *tel.* (049) 32288
Garages: Brady's, Dublin Road, *tel.* (049) 31833
Jacksons, Farnham Street, *tel.* (049) 31700

The most famous of Kells' five high crosses is the one dedicated to St Patrick and St Columba erected in the 9th century

had been a royal residence for centuries. The monastery was a favourite target of Vikings. The 100ft round tower, now capless, is unusual in having an odd number of windows (five) near the top, possibly to watch the five roads that enter the town.

Traces of the town walls erected by Hugh de Lacy toward the close of the 12th century remain, south of the churchyard.

St Columcille's House, a high-roofed building similar to St Kevin's Church in Glendalough, has 4ft-thick walls and measures about 24ft by 21ft externally, with a 38ft height, the roof is really a continuation of the side walls. Ceanannus Mor has five high crosses, the largest and oldest being opposite the round tower, the Cross of Patrick and Columcille. The cross in the market place was used as a gallows in 1798.

The Marquess of Headfort's wooded estate is just outside the town to the north-east.

Claremorris, Co Mayo

Map Ref: 122 M37

A prosperous agricultural town, this is an ideal base for exploring the south-eastern part of the county. The decline of railways has reduced its importance; once it was a key junction. However, since **Knock**, seven miles away to the north-east became a noted place of pilgrimage, thousands of visitors pass through

Ceanannus Mor (Kells), Co Meath

Map Ref: 123 N77

Officially Ceanannus Mor but more widely known by its anglicised name of Kells, this is the renowned source of the *Book of Kells*, an illuminated

manuscript of the Four Gospels in Latin, produced here sometime before the year 800. The town is on the N3 in a pretty, wooded district through which winds the River Blackwater.

St Columcille (Columba) set up a monastery here in AD 550 at the invitation of King Dermot; the place

The Book of Kells

'Here you may see the face of Majesty divinely drawn, . . . look more closely and you will penetrate the very shrine of art. You will make out intricacies, so delicate and subtle, so exact and compact, so full of knots and links, with colours so fresh and vivid, that you might say that all this is the work of an angel, not of a man.'

This was written in 1185, by Giraldis Cambrensis, and in all probability it describes the *Book of Kells*. It has been called the world's most complete triumph of illuminated art, and even 'the world's most beautiful book', because of its colour, detail and ornamental tracery. The *Book of Kells* is the most sumptuous of the illuminated manuscripts to have survived from the early Middle Ages, dating from the ninth century. Possibly it was started in Iona, and carried to Kells in face of threats from Viking raids. At one stage it seems that it was stolen, and its shrine wrought in gold, was never recovered. In the 17th century Bishop Henry Jones of Meath donated it to Trinity College, Dublin where it has remained and can be seen.

The *Book of Kells* was a holy work of art to be treasured in the church rather than a book for reading and

Monkish devotion created the colour and intricacy of the Book of Kells

studying. It was probably the work of several hands working in a team, to a plan which unites all four gospels in the story of the life of Christ. The wealth and variety of its decoration is famous; all the pages except two are coloured, the initial leters are beautifully worked in harmony of detail and design, full

page illustrations depict the nativity, temptation, and arrest of Christ, and the illustration of the Crucifixion and the Ascension are treated symbolically with great sensitivity. There is wit and humour too, as gaily coloured creatures, birds and animals fill the margins and empty spaces.

Clifden, a handsome market and fishing town, sits on a ridge of land at the northern end of Clifden Bay.

each year.

Apparitions of the Blessed Virgin Mary were reported in Knock in 1879, at the gable wall of its little Roman Catholic church. Church authorities were slow to commit themselves to an opinion on these phenomena, but latterly Knock has been regarded as the Lourdes of Ireland.

AA recommends:
Garage: Duggan's, Convent Road, *tel.* (094) 71610

Clifden, Co Galway

Map Ref: 122 L65

With the Twelve Pins (or Bens) rising to its east to their highest point in Benbaun (2393ft), Clifden's setting is almost alpine. Known as the capital of Connemara, it has sandy strands and coves within a mile, and Derrygimla's White Strand four miles away, while Mannin and Legaun beaches, not much further afield, are also favoured for bathing.

On the moorland inland from Mannin a monument shaped like an aircraft's vertical tail fin marks the spot where John Alcock and Arthur Whitten Brown landed at the end of the first transatlantic flight in 1919. From the air the ground here looks more solid and level than it is, a fact which later also fooled Charles Lindbergh. Surveying the west coast on behalf of the Irish Government for an airport site, he nominated this unsuitable area.

Clifden Castle was erected in

1815 by the D'Arcys. Its grounds give a fine marine view, and the Sky Road and Scardaun Hill are also prime vantage points.

AA recommends:
Hotels: Abbeyglen Castle, 3-star, *tel.* (095) 21070
Hotel Ardagh, Ardbear Bay, 3-star, *tel.* (095) 21384
Rock Glen, 3-star (country house), *tel.* (095) 21035
Garage: Brian Walsh Motors, Galway Road, *tel.* (095) 21037

Clogher Valley, Co Tyrone

Map Ref: 123 H55

The Clogher Valley is a quiet green area of south Tyrone. Augher, Clogher and Fivemiletown used to be linked by the Clogher Valley Railway, now defunct, but still regarded with affection by Ulster people. The pleasant red brick stations can be easily distinguished.

In the heart of the valley is the village of **Clogher,** an unlikely place for a cathedral and a former bishop's palace. Both are built in 18th-century classical style and recall Clogher's importance as a diocese founded by St Patrick. He is said to have consecrated St MacCairthin as first bishop of Clogher.

Fivemiletown is so called because it is five Irish miles (2240 yards) from the nearest village. South is **Fardross Forest** which has a bathing pool and is rich in wildlife like the two other forests in the area, **Knockmany** and **Favour Royal.**

Just outside the Clogher Valley, off the Ballygawley to Dungannon road at **Dergina** is the ancestral home of American President, Ulysses Simpson Grant. It is well restored with an excellent working farm, which uses traditional methods and includes flax growing in its activities.

Cheese making in the Clogher Valley

Treasures of Clonmacnoise – a beautiful Romanesque archway and (right) a bronze crucifixion plaque, c. 11th-century

Clonfert, Co Galway

Map Ref: 125 M92

Only the ruins of the cathedral remain of the monastic establishment which dated from AD 558, but its doorway is a splendid example of Irish Romanesque. Clonfert lies just west of the Shannon near the Grand Canal between roads R356 and R357. Its founder was St Brendan the Navigator. The ornately-decorated doorway which gives it lasting interest is of five orders, and its columns are alternately circular and octagonal. The entrance is crowned by a high triangular arcaded pediment. This doorway is 12th-century but the other end of the chancel, the east, is possibly 200 years older.

Clonmacnoise, Co Offaly

Map Ref: 125 N03

One of the country's most celebrated ecclesiastical sites, this is reached by turning off the N62 at Togher. It has a cathedral, eight ruined churches, three sculptured high crosses and parts of two more, two round towers and more than 200 monumental slabs. There are also castle ruins.

St Ciaran founded a monastery here in 548, which flourished under the patronage of various kings. Dermot McCarroll, soon to become High King Dermot, granted the land to the saint at a meeting point of three kingdoms, Munster, Meath and Connaught. It is also where the main esker (a glacial ridge) across Ireland touches the country's biggest river. Ireland's last high

king, Rory O'Connor, was buried here in 1198. Vikings and others plundered the place, notably Turgesius and his wife Ota who sailed up the Shannon in 844 to burn it. An attempt to restore the cathedral after a 1552 despoliation by the Athlone garrison was ill-timed at 1647, with Cromwell's forces on the way.

King Flann's Cross, also known as the Cross of the Scriptures, stands beside the west door of the cathedral. Dating from the early 10th century, it is richly decorated with scenes from the Last Judgement and the Crucifixion, animal figures around the base and two figures thought to represent St Ciaran and King Diarmid building the original wooden church. The 11th-century South Cross depicts the Crucifixion, and the North Cross, with only the shaft remaining, dates back to the 9th century and is probably the earliest cross erected there. Three sides are carved with abstract human and animal figures, much weathered. The cathedral is a simple 62ft oblong founded in 904 but with very little of the original structure surviving. The Nuns' Church was built in 1167 by Queen Dervorgilla. Its west door and beautiful chancel arch, Irish Romanesque in three orders, survive.

Clonmel, Co Tipperary

Map Ref: 125 S22

One of Munster's biggest towns, as well as one of the handsomest and best laid out, Clonmel stands on the trout-filled Suir in the extreme south of the county, its suburb of

Oldbridge being in Co Waterford. The Comeragh mountains rise in the south and Slievenamon (mountain of the women) stands in isolation seven miles to the north-east. Legend says Finn MacCool organised a race of girls up the hill, promising to marry the winner; today Clonmel is the unofficial capital of Ireland's greyhound industry.

Its central landmark, the Main Guard, was begun by the Duke of Ormonde in 1662. It is often wrongly ascribed to Wren. On its west front the town arms contain three greyhounds. The West Gate is an imaginative rebuild of 1831, but some of the town walls, including a corner bastion, survive and form a corner of the churchyard of St Mary's Church (Old), an early 13th-century foundation. Both east and west windows of the church date from about 1500. The walls, last used defensively in 1798, the church and many other structures in Clonmel are built of a pleasing yellow sandstone.

Hearn's Hotel, in Parnell St was headquarters of Carlo Bianconi, who in 1815 established a countrywide road passenger service. Laurence Sterne author of *Tristram Shandy*, was born in Clonmel in 1713; Anthony Trollope and George Borrow also lived in the town.

The town has golf, fishing, hunting, horse racing and greyhound racing. Near **Clogheen**, to the south-west, is Grubb's Cave where Samuel Grubb, owner of the local Castle Grace, is buried upright 'to overlook my land'.

AA recommends:
Hotels: Clonmel Arms, 3-star, *tel.* (052) 21233
Minella, 3-star, *tel.* (052) 22388
Hearns, 2-star, *tel.* (052) 21611
Garages: Blue Star, Cashel Road, *tel.* (052) 21177
Central, Dungarvan Road, *tel.* (052) 22399
Clonmel Service Station, Jacksons Cross, *tel.* (052) 22905

Cobh, Co Cork

Map Ref: 124 W86

Fifteen miles from Cork city, Cobh has a deepwater anchorage which once made it a stopping place for huge transatlantic liners. The *Titanic* called here on her only voyage. The facility was more recently used for marine mineral exploration. Cobh, mainly 19th-century, has a maritime museum in a converted church, with a display featuring the *Lusitania* disaster, hundreds of whose victims are buried in the town. St Colman's Cathedral, on an eminence, by Pugin and Ashlin, is built of blue Dalkey granite. The Royal Cork Yacht Club, dating from 1720, is reputedly the oldest in the British Isles.

Tim Severin's 'Brendan', designed to prove that Irish monks could have reached America in a leather-hulled craft

The Voyage of St Brendan

Founder of the monastery at Clonfert, St Brendan is best remembered for a journey which has inspired readers since it was first written as *Navigatio Sancti Brendan Abbatis*, and became one of the most popular books of medieval Europe. Perhaps it gave substance to the hopes of the 15th-century voyages of discovery. St Brendan's story tells how he and a few monks sailed from Kerry in search of isolation, and taking the 'stepping stone' route by the Faeroes and Iceland, probably reached Newfoundland.

They sailed in a 'light boat ribbed with wood and with a wooden frame . . . they covered it with ox-hides

tanned with the bark of oak and smeared all the joints of the hide on the outside with fat. They carried into the boat hides for the making of two other boats, supplies for forty days . . . Then Saint Brendan ordered the brothers in the name of the Father, Son and Holy Spirit to enter the boat.' A replica of this boat can be seen near Quinn, Co Clare.

In a classic voyage saga the monks encountered danger and drama. He described seeing 'a paradise of birds' and an incident when they landed on a bleak island to boil up a salt solution to preserve meat, when the 'island' which turned out to be a whale, started to move. He describes having burning rocks hurled at them, probably through volcanic activity, and the

experience of sailing through ice floes.

Uncannily, some of these experiences were shared in a magnificent experiment carried out by Tim Severin, a scholar, writer and sailor, in 1977. He set off with a crew in a vessel meticulously made following the methods identified in the Navigatio — they used the hides of 49 oxen. They saw a bird-covered isle, they became a magnet for whales, and they passed through icy regions, but they reached Newfoundland proving that such a small craft could cross the Atlantic.

When Brendan at last reached his destination, he was told, 'Behold, this land, which you sought for so much time. Return, then, to your native land. After many ages this land will be made known to your successors.'

Cong, Co Mayo

Map Ref: 122 M15

Beautifully placed between Loughs Mask and Corrib, Cong's Gaelic name means 'neck', a reference to this idyllic isthmus. Outdoor types are well served by fishing and boating here, and the woods are claimed to be among Europe's best for pheasant and woodcock. Ashford Castle, an imposing former Guinness family home, is now an hotel; it dates from 1715, with 1852 additions. The mountain district to the west is called Joyce's Country, and Cong is an excellent base for touring the area.

Between the village and Lough Mask the limestone has been worn into weird shapes. Horse's Discovery and the Pigeon Hole are openings through which the underground River Corrib's passage can be reached, but someone with good local knowledge should lead the party. The ruins of an 1128 Augustinian abbey are

beside **Ashford Castle**, and an inscribed stone cross in the village street is 14th-century. Just east is **Moytura's** prehistoric battlefield.

AA recommends:
Hotel: Ryans, 1-star, tel. 4

Connor Pass, Co Kerry

Map Ref: 124 Q40

This pass crosses the Dingle Peninsula from Dingle in a north-easterly direction towards Stradbally and Castlegregory, running through fine scenery between the 3127ft Brandon Mountain and the 2713ft Beenoskee. From its 1354ft summit just over four miles from Dingle are views of Brandon and Tralee Bays to the north, separated by Rough Point, with a fine view of Dingle and its bay to the south. The road descends northward past the winding base of great cliffs to a wilderness of boulders, and curves over a deep gorge. Above the pass to

the east is rock-fringed **Lough Doon**, called 'Pedlar's Lake' from a local folk tale of a drowned pedlar.

Cooley Peninsula, Co Louth

Map Ref: 123 J11

Between Dundalk Bay and Carlingford Lough, this peninsula was the scene of the Tain Bo Cuailne (cattle raid of Cooley), a celebrated heroic tale of Irish mythology. **Carlingford Mountain** (Slieve Foye), at 1935ft high, complements the Mourne Mountain scenery across Carlingford Lough in Co Down. Rocks near the harbour of the little resort of Giles's Quay are called **Queen Maeve's Stepping Stones**, another legacy of the Tain Bo legend. **Proleek Dolmen** stands near Ballymascanlon, and **Riverstown** is noted for the factory established by the Government to produce industrial alcohol from potatoes.

Cork, Co Cork

Map Ref: 124 W67

The Republic's second city, standing where the River Lee enters magnificent Lough Mahon, Cork began as a monastic settlement of St Finbar in the early seventh century, probably between 600 and 620. Later Norse invaders began by plundering this, but eventually founded a commercial city. North and South Main Streets are the backbone of this older town. Patrick Street, today's principal artery, was an open channel used by ships until the late 1780s.

A liberal use of deep red sandstone and sparkling white limestone gives the city a special charm. The flat central area is an island between twin channels of the Lee, each crossed by several bridges, with higher districts north and south of these.

Cork has a shipyard, chemical works, and a steelworks, but its Ford and Dunlop factories were victims of the recession of the early 1980s. The Ford plant at Marina, as well as making cars, was once the world's biggest tractor factory.

St Ann's Church, Shandon, in the hilly north side, with clocktower and pepper-box steeple, is called the Lion of Cork. Visitors are allowed to play tunes on its eight famous bells, which were cast in

Top: Unusual bow-windowed façade in a Cork street. Right: Patrick Street, Cork in the late 1860s. Below: The twin spires of St Finbar's Cathedral seen from the banks of the River Lee

Gloucester. Beside the church is the 1584 Skiddy's Almshouse, founded for needy widows. Watercourse Road leads through Blackpool to **Blarney**, six miles north-west, where the Blarney Stone atop a 15th-century castle of the McCarthys is said to impart, when kissed, the gift of words. Cynics claim that a 19th-century tour operator invented this story; but visitors still queue to kiss the stone, though they have to hang upside down over an abyss.

On the city's south side is the lovely French Gothic St Finbar's Cathedral, with three spires, built in 1865–80. William Burges of London was the designer. Not far away an ivy-clad wall hangs high over the houses; this is Elizabeth Fort, where in 1603 Cork's citizens gathered to defy James I. Also on this side of Cork is the university college, part of the National University, whose Tudor Gothic main buildings (1845–49) were designed by Sir Thomas N Deane, and whose campus is the most pleasant in Ireland. Past two lovely redwoods is the Honan Chapel,

based on pre-Norman designs at Roscrea and Cashel.

Nearer the city centre, the Red Abbey tower is a remnant of a 1300 Augustinian friary, and Christ Church, in South Main Street, is a Norse foundation of about 1050. Edmund Spenser is believed to have married Elizabeth Boyle here in 1594.

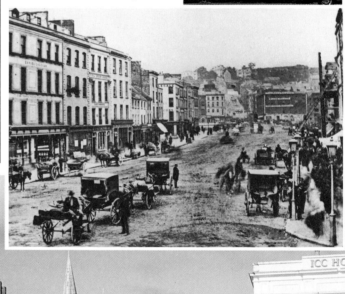

Cork's city museum is in an 1850 former home of the Beamish brewing family in Fitzgerald's Park, Mardyke. The rambling Crawford municipal art school and gallery commemorates William Horatio Crawford of the same firm. Cork's other brewery, Murphy's at Lady's Well, is on the site of a hospital whose well was said to have curative powers. The neo-Gothic Ss Peter and Paul church, off Patrick Street, is by A W Pugin, as is St Colman's Cathedral in neighbouring Cobh.

Cork has annual international choral and film festivals. Both city and hinterland are renowned for all sporting facilities.

AA recommends:
Hotels: Jury's, Western Road, 4-star, *tel.* (021) 966377
Metropole, McCurtain Street, 3-star, *tel.* (021) 508122
Silver Spring's, Lower Glanmire Road, Tivoli, 3-star, *tel.* (021) 507533
Moores, Morrison's Island, 2-star, *tel.* (021) 71291
Guesthouses: Gabriel House, Summerhill, St Lukes, *tel.* (021) 500333
Lotamore House, Tivoli, *tel.* (021) 822344
T & C: Killarney House, Western Road, *tel.* (021) 270179
Restaurant: Lovetts, Churchyard Lane, Well Road, 3-K & F, *tel.* (021) 294909
Garage: Lee, Model Farm Road, *tel.* (021) 42933
Campsite: Cork City Caravan & Camping Park, Togher Road, 2-pennant, *tel.* (021) 961866

Courtown Harbour, Co Wexford

Map Ref: 125 J15

This seaside resort was merely a sandy stretch on the wide sweep of Courtown Bay until about 1820, when construction of the harbour began, taking about 10 years. A village grew up around the harbour, but the real tourist boom began only in 1863, when the railway line from Dublin reached Gorey.

Courtown House stands in a wooded demesne north of the village, with an ancient seven-foot high cross in the grounds. Beyond it is **Ballymoney**, with another fine sandy beach, and north of this is Tara Hill, taller at 831 ft than the more famous Tara in Co Meath. Courtown, especially popular with Dublin holidaymakers, has been made more dependent on tourism through repeated silting-up of its harbour mouth, which hampers fishing.

There is golf beside the village, and the River Owenavarra offers two kinds of trout. **Ardamine**, a secluded cove, is two miles south.

AA recommends:
Hotels: Bay View, 2-star, *tel.* (055) 25307
Courtown, 2-star, *tel.* (055) 25108
Garage: Doyle's, Askingarron, *tel.* (055) 27318
Campsite: Courtown Caravan &

Camping Park, Ballinatray, 4-pennant, *tel.* (055) 25280
Parklands Caravan Park, Ardamine, 4-pennant, *tel.* (055) 25202

Craigavon, Co Armagh

Map Ref: 123 J05

Craigavon is a new city created by a linear development from Lurgan to Portadown. It has many leisure facilities including a wide variety of water sports and an artificial ski-slope. Among the many public parks is the Lord Lurgan Memorial Park with the grave of the famous greyhound, Master McGrath.

At **Coney Island** on the flat banks of Lough Neagh is a Nature Reserve and Information Centre. To the east of the city is the apple-growing area of Loughgall, which gives Armagh the title 'the orchard county of Ireland'. East are two pretty villages – **Moira** with broad main street, handsome houses and a fine 18th-century church, and **Waringstown**, which has some good 'plantation' buildings, a 17th-century church, and one of the most important big houses in Ulster, Waringstown House which was constructed of clay and rubble in the 17th century, but has an assured classical appearance.

Crawfordsburn, Co Down

Map Ref: 123 J48

Crawfordsburn is a pretty village with an old thatched inn dating from 1614. At **Crawfordsburn Country Park** (DOE) a stream runs down a steep wooded glen to the sea, passing under an impressive railway viaduct. A ten-mile coastal footpath borders the southern side of Belfast Lough, from Holywood, past Cultra and Helen's Bay, through Crawfordsburn to Bangor.

AA recommends:
Hotel: Ye Olde Inn, 15 Main Street, *tel.* Helens Bay 853255

Creeslough, Co Donegal

Map Ref: 123 C03

Creeslough stands on high ground overlooking an inlet of Sheep Haven. Duntally Bridge and waterfall, outside the village, are very picturesque. Creeslough is an ideal base for climbing Muckish Mountain (2197ft) to the west. The lovely **Glen Lough,** with its mountain background, is four miles from the village, and on a strip of land running into the sea two miles from Creeslough is **Doe Castle,** one-time fortress of the MacSweeneys, who held it against fierce opposition in the 16th century. Used as a residence until recent times, it is much altered. The adjoining graveyard, on a Franciscan monastic site, holds the ornate tomb of MacSuibhne na Doe, a chieftain of the clan.

Croagh Patrick, Co Mayo

Map Ref: 122 L98

Called 'The Reek', this mountain of pilgrimage, south of T39 between Westport and Louisburgh, owes its tradition to the fact that St Patrick spent 40 days on it in AD 441. An oratory has been built at the top of the 2510ft conical peak, and an annual mass pilgrimage is held there on the last Sunday of July. Thousands climb up, many of them barefoot.

A legend says that St Patrick used his own pilgrimage to banish snakes from Ireland. In fact it is unlikely that these reptiles ever lived there.

The view from the summit is sumptuous, especially south towards the Twelve Pins and north across island-studded Clew Bay. The climb begins at beautiful ruined **Murrisk Abbey** (14th-century Augustinian). The traditional overnight ascent is now discouraged, possibly due to the danger from broken glass (soft drink vendors at Murrisk are a tradition).

Thousands follow St Patrick to the summit of Clough Patrick each July

Crookhaven, Co Cork

Map Ref: 124 V72

Near **Mizen Head,** this resort is sheltered by Streek Head, which is like a harbour wall, with Spanish Cove a little to the east and the now fashionable Barley Cove with its fine sandy beach to the west. Mizen Head, the most south-westerly tip of Ireland, has 700ft cliffs.

Three Castle Head, to its north, has the remnants of an O'Mahony stronghold, a trio of square tower houses from whence it derives its name. Between these heads is the very scenic curving coastline at Carrigcoosheenboy Bay, with its

cliffs. Near Durrus, the innermost point of Dunmanus Bay to the north, are other ruined O'Mahony forts, Dunbeacon and Dunmanus.

For obvious reasons Crookhaven is a favourite with yachtspeople, but landlubbers can stretch their legs rewardingly in its immediate vicinity, or drive back the L56 to **Schull,** with its quaint harbour, to tackle 1339ft Mount Gabriel behind it. **Ballydehob,** east of Schull on Roaringwater Bay, has abandoned coppermines.

AA recommends:
Campsite: Barley Cove Caravan Park, 4-pennant, *tel.* (028) 35302

Reminiscent of a Cornish village, Cushenden is a cluster of black and white cottages around a village green.

Cushendun, Co Antrim

Map Ref: 123 D22

Cushendun (NT) is at the foot of Glendun, one of the nine glens of Antrim, where the river Dun flows past rich old woodland under an attractive stone bridge into a tiny harbour. A sandy beach lies to the north and the fine house prominent across the bay was the home of poet Moira O'Neill.

In the heart of the village are picturesque whitewashed, slated cottages which are often described as Cornish in appearance. Lord Cushendun built them in memory of his wife, Maud, who came from Cornwall. They were designed by the architect Clough Williams-Ellis, who created the Welsh village of Portmeirion.

There are interesting caves behind the hotels to the south.

Close to the village are the remains of two megalithic tombs, the most interesting of which lies four miles northwest at Carnamore. It is the best preserved of a group of Antrim passage graves.

AA recommends:
Campsite: Cushendun Caravan Park, 14 Glendun Road, 2-pennant, *tel.* 333

Gaeltachts

Gaelic-speaking districts — or Gaeltachts — have been given special protection since the 1920s, when the government of the Republic decided that the state should foster and encourage use of the Gaelic language. The name Gaelic originated in the seventh century as Goidelg, from Gwyddel, the Welsh name for the Irish. It was one of several languages spoken in ancient Ireland, but from the 16th century onwards English became the prevalent tongue.

Gaeltacht people have special grants and their own state-run radio. Colleges have been set up in the Gaeltachts for outsiders, mainly schoolchildren in summer, who wish to improve their command of the language, though varying dialects are a problem here. When the areas co-incide with the most scenic, though poorest, regions as in the Dingle peninsula, Connemara and the Aran Islands, they bring additional benefits from tourism.

Connemara and the Aran Islands (in Co Galway) and the Dingle Peninsula are the best-known Gaeltachts. Others are in Co Cork in a region west of Macroom embracing Ballingeary, Coolea and Ballyvourney; Co Donegal's northern area around Gortahork, Falcarragh and Derrybeg; Co Waterford at An Rinn (Ring), south of Dungarvan near Helvick Head; and

Life in the Gaeltachts in the 1870s. A mail-car waits for the horses. Clifden, Connemara

Co Meath at Gibbstown, near Donaghpatrick.

This last is a colony set up in an organised migration from the West. Similar colonies were established from time to time in urban areas, even Dublin. Some Gaelic is still spoken in Galway city without planned inducement.

Especially in the south-west, the language is accompanied by folklore and traditional music. In Connemara the visual difference is not only in

Gaelic shop signs and such, but in the preponderance of the diminutive shaggy Connemara pony, and sometimes in dress. Some Aran Islanders still make their own traditional clothes, the bainin or bauneen (a durable white homespun coat), Aran sweaters, and the crios (pronounced 'chris') a variegated woollen belt.

As the amount of spoken Gaelic varies, its areas of highest concentration are called 'Fíor' (true) Gaeltachts.

Dingle, Co Kerry

Map Ref: 124 Q40

This little town in the western half of the Dingle Peninsula sits charmingly in exquisite scenery on Dingle Bay, in a Gaelic-speaking area. To its north towers 3127ft Brandon Mountain, with Brandon Peak (2764ft), Gearhane and Ballysitteragh (both 2050ft) between. West of this chain is a coastal plain with small villages and fine marine scenery. **Dunquin** (Dun Caoin) on Blasket Sound is popular with language students, many of whom take cottage accommodation in this area. The eastern part of the peninsula is ruled by the Slieve Mish range, 2796ft Baurtregaum being the highest point, with another Gearhane (2423ft).

The central part of the peninsula rises to Beenoskee (2713ft).

Dingle, called the most westerly town in Europe, with steep streets and an old-world air, was important in Spanish trading days and walled in Elizabethan times. On the corner of Green Street and Main Street stood a house prepared to receive Marie Antoinette after a bid by its owner, Count Rice, to rescue her from prison, but she refused to travel. There are sandy beaches.

Four-mile-long **Great Blasket Island,** now uninhabited, has cliffs reaching nearly 1000ft.

AA recommends:
Hotel: Hotel Sceilig, 3-star, *tel.* (066) 51144
Guesthouses: Alpine, *tel.* (066) 51250
Milltown House, Milltown, *tel.* (066) 51372
Restaurants: Doyle's Seafood Bar, John Street, I-K & F, *tel.* (066) 51174
Half Door, John Street, I-K & F, *tel.* (066) 51600

Superb mountain and coastal scenery is a feature of the rugged Dingle Peninsula

Donaghadee, Co Down

Map Ref: 123 J57

'Six miles from Bangor to Donaghadee' is the refrain of a popular local song, but in fact because Scotland and Ireland are so close at this point – a mere 20 miles – Donaghadee has many associations with Portpatrick and the regular communications once included a mail packet service. The good harbour, sheltered by the Copeland islands (a pleasure boat will take visitors), has a handsome lighthouse. A rath, known locally as the Moat, is topped by a 1821 castellated powder house, built for the storage of explosives when the harbour was being constructed.

To the south is a recreation ground and coastal walk known as the Commons. West of nearby Millisle is **Ballycopeland Windmill** (DOE), open to the public.

Donegal, Co Donegal

Map Ref: 122 G97

A pleasant town at the head of Donegal Bay on N15, Donegal stands south of the Blue Stack Mountains, which form a horseshoe around Lough Eske. North-west is the wild Barnesmore Gap, and west is Lough Derg, or 'St Patrick's Purgatory', on whose Station Island three-day pilgrimages of the most rigorous penance take place.

Donegal was chief seat of the O'Donnell princes, and there are scant remains of a Franciscan friary founded in 1474 by Red Hugh O'Donnell and his wife Finola. An explosion wrecked it in 1601. An O'Donnell Castle (1505), incorporated into a Jacobean structure by Sir Basil Brooke in 1610, has lasted better.

AA recommends:
Hotels: Hylands Central, The Diamond, 3-star, *tel.* (073) 21027
Abbey, 2-star, *tel.* (073) 21014
T & C: White Gables House, Tirconnail Street, *tel.* (073) 21106
Ardeevin, Barnesmore, *tel.* (073) 21790
Garages: R E Johnston & Co, Quay St, *tel.* (073) 21039
J Owen Car Sales, Derry Road, *tel.* (073) 21791

Dating from c.1780 the Ballycopeland Windmill is one of the few existing in Ireland today.

Downpatrick, Co Down

Map Ref: 123 J44

It is said that when St Patrick returned to Ireland he landed at the Slaney River, north of Downpatrick, and preached his first sermon at Saul in AD 432. Now a 20th-century church stands here on high ground, in imitation of earlier architecture, and is a site of pilgrimage on St Patrick's Day. Across the valley on Slieve Patrick is the 35ft granite statue of the Saint, while close by at Struell are renowned Holy Wells. St Patrick is reputed to be buried at Downpatrick Cathedral, with the bones of St Brigid and St Columba which were carried there and interred on the orders of John de Courcy:

'In Down three saints one grave do fill Brigid, Patrick and Columcille.'

A simple slab of granite was placed here in 1900 to prevent the grave becoming worn away. A church has been on the site of the Cathedral since 520, but after pillaging, destruction and even an earthquake in 1245, it was restored with charm and simplicity at the end of the 18th century. The choir is the only medieval remnant.

Twin hills characterise Downpatrick and give it a pleasant enclosed feeling, as three roads meet in the centre where the assembly rooms stood. At the top of English Street is the former gaol and governor's residence, now the Down museum, and Southwell School, provided in 1733 for 'the reception of decayed tenants of the family and other pious uses.'

To the North west is **Quoile pondage** (DOE) which is a lovely narrow stretch of water, twisting towards Strangford Lough with good walks, picnic sites and angling stands.

Off the road to Belfast (A7) is **Inch Abbey** (DOE) established in 1180, and on the road to Newcastle is Downpatrick racecourse.

AA recommends:
Farmhouse: Havine, 51 Ballydonnell Road, *tel.* Ballykinler 242
Garage: Charles Keown Motors, 9a Ballynagross Road, *tel.* Downpatrick 3755

Dowth, Co Meath

Map Ref: 123 O07

The prehistoric burial chamber complex at Dowth, in the Boyne Valley, south of N51 east of Slane, is one of the country's largest, with some intriguingly decorated stones. Both it and Newgrange, also in this valley, were plundered by Vikings in 861. Nonetheless a Royal Irish Academy team of 1847 found human and animal bones, fibulae, bracelets, copper pins, iron tools and amber and glass beads. Grass and shrubs now grow on the great stone 'igloo' of about 2000 BC.

A 27ft-long passage of stones standing on end and roofed with

flags leads to a central chamber 9ft by 7ft by 11ft high. This forms a rough circle, but side chambers help to form a cruciform shape. Some stones are marked with concentric circles and spirals, others with lozenges and zigzags. Nearby are a stone circle and a large military rath.

Fenian poet John Boyle O'Reilly was born in Dowth.

Drogheda, Co Louth

Map Ref: 123 O07

Near the Boyne's mouth on the Dublin–Belfast road, Drogheda is bustling, industrial and historic, and also an important port. It began as a ford where St Mary's Bridge stands between the Bullring and Shop Street, and here Vikings under Turgesius settled in 911. Until 1412 the river divided two warring towns. In 1649 it was the scene of a massacre by Cromwell's troops.

St Laurence's Gate, with two four-storey drum towers, is the sole survivor of ten town gates, five on either side of the river. This is, in fact, merely the outer barbican, the best preserved of its kind in the country.

On the south side, the Millmount is a huge circular grass mound surrounded by a low wall. It dates from prehistoric times and tradition claims that it was erected over the grave of a son of Milesius in 1029 BC. The Vikings used it as a ceremonial meeting place and Hugh de Lacy built a motte-and-bailey castle here in the 12th century. Millmount House

Left: The 13th-century outer barbican of St Laurence's Gate, Drogheda.
Below: This fine 19th-century viaduct crosses the River Boyne at Drogheda

Portions of the banqueting hall and a prison are all that remain of O'Rourke's fortress Breffni Castle

Museum shows the history of the town over the past three centuries.

St Peter's Church in West Street contains the head of St Oliver Plunkett, executed in 1681. His body is in Downside Abbey. A central tower and two pointed arches remain from the 1206 Augustinian St Mary's Abbey, as does the belltower (Magdalene Tower) of the 1224 Dominican priory founded by Lucas de Netterville.

Bartholomew van Homrigh, father of Jonathan Swift's Vanessa, and Isaac Goldsmith, uncle of Oliver, are buried at St Peter's Church (Magdalene Street).

Once noted for Cairne's brewery (no longer brewing), the town has some fine Georgian architecture.

AA recommends:
Hotels: Boyne Valley, 3-star, tel. (041) 37737
Rossnaree, Dublin Road, 1-star, tel. (041) 37673
Garages: Boyne Cars, tel. (041) 38566
N Smith & Sons, North Road, tel. (041) 31106
Tara Motors, North Road, tel. (041) 38785

Dromahair, Co Leitrim

Map Ref: 122 G83

This is a neat village on the River Bonet, where the powerful O'Rourke clan had a palace. The Old Hall, built in 1626 by Sir William Villiers, adjoins the scanty ruins of this property, which was known as Breffni Castle. From here, in 1152, Dervorgilla O'Rourke, called 'the Helen of Ireland', eloped with Dermot MacMurrough, king of Leinster, while her husband was away on pilgrimage to atone for beating her with a whip.

She and her husband were reunited, but Dermot's 'black-balling' by his peers over the affair caused him to seek allies in Wales and led to the Norman invasion.

A flat-topped fern-covered eminence near the village is called O'Rourke's Table. Tom Moore wrote *The Valley Lay Smiling Before Me* about Dervorgilla; W B Yeats wrote about Inishfree island, near the Dromahair end of Lough Gill (see **Sligo**).

St Patrick

St Patrick, as portrayed in 'The Baptism at Tara' by Byam Shaw

St Patrick, Ireland's patron saint, was born in South Wales about 389 AD and may have lived 104 years, though different dates are given for his death. Pirates sold him as a boy into sheep-herding slavery on a Co Antrim mountain; six years later he escaped, trained as a missionary in Britain or France (probably Britain, as his Latin was poor), and came back to Ireland landing near present-day Downpatrick in 432 or 456. The earlier date is more likely; Dublin's annals record that he baptised Alphin MacEochaidh, city king, at a well south of the city in 448.

This well is traditionally located in the park adjoining St Patrick's Cathedral, and is the reason for the choice of this low-lying marshy site. Other wells associated with St Patrick are in Downpatrick, Clonmel, Co Tipperary, Patrickswell, Co Limerick, and elsewhere. Croagh Patrick, Co Mayo and Lough Derg, Co Donegal also have 'Patrician' traditions.

Patrick is said to have begun his mission by lighting a fire on Slane hill in Co Meath to challenge the druids of High King Leary at Tara, eventually winning the king's permission to proceed with his work. He is credited with founding the diocese of Armagh, but this may have been done by an earlier missionary named Palladius or Secundinus.

Out of respect, the early Irish never used Patrick as a first name. The Anglo-Normans brought the name Patrick, but the native Irish shunned it until the late 17th century. The feminine form, Patricia, came from Scotland in the late 18th century.

Patrick (or Paddy) is now the fourth commonest male name in Ireland, and is even the name of a brand of whiskey.

St Patrick's Day, March 17, was until recent years more an ecclesiastical feast than a joyous social occasion. Shamrocks were worn, but pubs were strictly closed and parades were usually industrial cavalcades. This has changed, mainly through Irish trips by colourful and uninhibited American bands.

Dublin, Co Dublin

Map Ref: 125 O13

The capital and largest city, Dublin sits on a splendid bay at the mouth of the Liffey, with the foothills of the Wicklow Mountains rising from its southern suburbs and an almost Dutch flatness stretching to the north. It is noted, *inter alia,* for writers, Georgian architecture, witty natives and the production of Guinness.

Since its beginning as an ecclesiastical settlement it has in turn been a key Viking raiding and trading base, a Norman stronghold, the second city of the British Empire and capital of an independent State.

Its oldest part is the **Christ Church Cathedral** area, once called the Hill of Dublin. The cathedral, begun in 1172 and clearly showing in its styles the transition from Romanesque to Gothic, replaced a wooden church erected by King Sitric in 1038. The ridge on which it stands is part of a border which divided Ireland in two about 1800 years ago, by an arrangement with Mogh, king of Munster and Conn of the Hundred Battles. (Munster and Connaught come from the names of these two.) On the same ridge, in High Street, 'Old' St Audoen's Church is claimed by some to date from AD 650.

Christ Church's restoration was financed in 1871 by Henry Roe, a

The Dublin Custom House and the Halfpenny Bridge in 1841

leading Dublin distiller. **St Patrick's Cathedral**, a little to the south, which contains the tombs of Jonathan Swift and his 'Stella' (Hester Johnson), was begun in 1191; it was restored in 1863–8 and 1901–4 by the Guinness family.

At 340ft, St Patrick's Cathedral is the longest cathedral in Ireland

Near Christ Church is Fishamble Street, where Handel gave the first public performance of his Messiah in 1742. An organ which he played at that time survives in 'Old' **St Michan's Church** across the River Liffey in Church Street; the

building is a 1686 reconstruction of a 1095 foundation by a Danish bishop. Its vaults have renowned preservative qualities; corpses lie here in a state of natural mummification for centuries, the skins brown and leathery.

Dublin has some outstanding public buildings: the massive **Four Courts**, by Gandon and Thomas Cooley, completed in 1802; the **Bank of Ireland** in College Green, with its great curving windowless Hall, by Edward Lovett Pearce (1729–39 with later additions by Gandon); the **City Hall** (Cooley, 1769–79); and the **General Post Office**, work of Francis Johnston (1815) and well worth a special stamp-buying expedition. **Leinster House**, now the seat of Parliament, was formerly the town house of the Duke of Leinster, designed by Richard Cassels and finished in 1748. Cassels used the same basic design for the Rotunda Hospital in Parnell Square (1750), the oldest maternity hospital in the world. James Gandon's classical **Custom House** was built in 1781. The port below it was partly designed by Captain Bligh, of Bounty fame; to the west at Aston Quay is the quaint pedestrians-only **Halfpenny Bridge**, once a toll bridge.

The **Royal Hospital** in Kilmainham (1680–85), designed by William Robinson, is Dublin's only monumental 17th-century building. It was restored to house a folk museum, but this was abandoned. Dublin lacks both a folk and a transport museum, though the **National Museum, National Gallery** and **National Library** are here, and the library of **Trinity College** houses the **Book of Kells**. Trinity, one of the two university colleges in the city, was founded by Elizabeth I and dates from 1592. Its oldest surviving part is a row of Queen Anne buildings called the Rubrics, begun in 1700. The imposing west front, near the Bank of Ireland, which itself was a parliament house before the 1801 Act of Union, dates from 1752–60, and may be the work of Theodore Jacobsen, architect of the London Foundling Hospital.

Almost completely destroyed in 1922, but later rebuilt, the four Courts boasts an impressive 450ft river frontage

Dublin Castle, begun in 1204, was largely rebuilt in the 18th century, and now has little suggestion of a castle. The 'record tower' is one of the few remaining original parts; the splendid State Apartments, richly appointed, are open to the public.

Dublin's elegant Georgian squares and terraces vary greatly as to preservation and surviving uniformity. The best-kept examples are in the **Fitzwilliam** and **Merrion Squares** area, but the oldest, begun in 1720, are in **Henrietta Street**. Large-scale Georgian building ended in 1818, when **Mountjoy Square**, the city's only mathematically accurate one, was completed. **St Stephen's Green** is the biggest square in Europe.

The city's best smaller gems include the **Casino** in Marino, by William Chambers, (1765–71), recognised as one of the world's most perfect Palladian buildings, and Francis Johnston's 1814 classical spired **St George's Church** in Hardwicke Place. It also has a fine range of Victorian buildings, varying greatly in style, materials and use, from churches to railway stations, schools and hospitals; some of its modern edifices, however, are unfortunate.

Of the domestic buildings associated with Dublin's native writers, who include Richard Brinsley Sheridan, George Bernard Shaw, Oscar Wilde, W B Yeats, James Joyce, Sean O'Casey and Brendan Behan, not forgetting Jonathan Swift himself, some survive, some don't. Joyce, especially in *Ulysses*, mentioned so many commercial establishments (he had a love of pubs and a seeming fixation with pork butchers) that quite a few remain. Still thriving are **Davy Byrne's pub** in Duke Street, **Mulligan's** in Poolbeg Street and **Olhausen's** German pork butchery in Talbot Street, where *Ulysses* character Leopold Bloom bought a crubeen (pig's foot) on his way to the 'Monto' red light area. It still sells them.

Dublin has a full theatrical, cultural, social and sporting life. The **Abbey Theatre** is the National Theatre; it was founded in 1904 in a former morgue and fostered by Yeats, Synge and others. Now rebuilt, it stages work by dramatists such as Synge and Shaw. Both commercial and avant garde drama can be seen at the city's other theatres. A healthy proportion of the several hundred pubs still have fine Victorian interiors. The Guinness Brewery has a display, souvenir shop and samples for visitors at St James's Gate: reservations can be made by telephone. Bewley's Cafes in South Great George Street, Westmorland Street and Grafton Street are hugely popular eating places with renowned ornate interiors. **Phoenix Park**, opened to the public by Lord Chesterfield in

Guinness

The drink — originally called porter but nowadays known universally as stout — distinguished by its creamy 'head' and unofficially regarded as Ireland's national beverage, actually originated in London, where its name was derived from the popularity it enjoyed in the 18th century with the porters from Covent Garden and Billingsgate, and is said to have been brought into Ireland by firms like Beamish and Crawford. When bad weather held up a shipment, they were forced to brew their own — a product that quickly replaced the English variety in popularity. Arthur Guinness founded his now world-famous brewery at St James's Gate on the south bank of Dublin's River Liffey in 1759. He began brewing his own porter and laid the foundations for a thriving export trade.

Stout differs from ale in that it is brewed with softer water — contrary to popular belief, Guinness stout is not made from Liffey water — and it is the roast material, made from barley grown on Irish farms, which imparts the distinctive colour and flavour.

Guinness now produces a range of stouts of different strengths depending on the markets for which they are destined, but all are produced from natural ingredients and by methods basically unchanged, despite the extensive use of modern technology, for well over 200 years.

Up to 1939, the St James's Gate Brewery was the largest in the world. It is still the largest stout-producing brewery. The 60-acre spread embraces the old sites of former rivals Manders-Powell and the Phoenix Brewery, once owned by Daniel

Distinctive badge of a unique brew, synonymous with Ireland

O'Connell Jnr, son of the Irish patriot.

Guinness — sole survivor of 55 19th-century Dublin breweries — now also has ale and lager interests in Ireland and sister breweries in many parts of the world. Its only Irish stout-brewing rivals are Murphy's and Beamish of Cork. Guinness has a fleet of ships, though its colourful Liffey barges have long since departed the scene. Its trademark is based on the O'Neill or Brian Boru Harp preserved in Trinity College, Dublin.

The firm's advertising is well known, and of all the copywriters who have helped to spread the gospel according to St James's Gate, perhaps the best known is Dorothy L Sayers, the crime writer, who penned the immortal lines:

"If he can say, as you can,
Guinness is good for you,
How grand to be a Toucan —
Just think what Toucan do."

1747, has an area of 1752 acres, a circumference of about seven miles and a racecourse just outside it. It contains the world's second oldest privately-owned zoo.

AA recommends:

Hotels: Burlington, Leeson Street, 4-star, *tel.* (01) 605222
Jury's, Ballsbridge, 4-star, *tel.* (01) 605000
Shelbourne, St Stephen's Green, 4-star, *tel.* (01) 766471
Ashling, Parkgate Street, 3-star, *tel.* (01) 772324
Blooms, Anglesea Street, 3-star, *tel.* (01) 715622
Dublin International, Dublin Airport, 3-star, *tel.* (01) 379211
Green Isle, Clondalkin, 3-star, *tel.* (01) 593476
Marine, Sutton, 3-star, *tel.* (01) 322613
Montrose, Stillorgan Road, 3-star, *tel.* (01) 693311
Royal Dublin, O'Connell Street, 3-star, *tel.* (01) 733666
Sachs, Morehampton Road, 3-star, *tel.* (01) 680995
Skylon, Drumcondra, 3-star, *tel.* (01) 379121
Tara Tower, Merrion Road, 3-star, *tel.* (01) 694666

Guesthouses: Abrae Court, 9 Zion Road, Rathgar, *tel.* (01) 979944
Ariel House, 52 Lansdowne Road, *tel.* (01) 685512
Beddington, 181 Rathgar Road, *tel.* (01) 978047
Egan House, 7/9 Iona Park, Glasnevin, *tel.* (01) 303611
Iona House, 5 Iona Park, *tel.* (01) 306217
Mount Herbert, 7 Herbert Road, *tel.* (01) 684321
St Aidans, 32 Brighton Road, Rathgar, *tel.* (01) 970559

Phoenix Park

St Jude's, 17 Pembroke Park,
tel. (01) 680483
Burtenshaw's 'Marian', 21 Upper Gardiner
Street, *tel.* (01) 744129

T & Cs: Boulevard, 8 Clontarf Road,
tel. (01) 339524
Eagle Lodge, 12 Clontarf Road,
tel. (01) 336009

Restaurants: Le Coq Hardi, 29
Pembroke Road, 4-K & F, *tel.* (01) 689070
Celtic Mews, 109a Lower Baggot Street,
3-K & F, *tel.* (01) 760796
Ernies, Mulberry Gardens, Donnybrook,
3-K & F, *tel.* (01) 693300
Killakee House, Killakee Road,
Rathfarnham, 3-K & F, *tel.* (01) 932645
Locks, 1 Windsor Terrace, Portobello,
2-K & F, *tel.* (01) 752025
Lord Edward, Christchurch Place,
3-K & F, *tel.* (01) 752557
Patrick Guilbaud, 46 St James' Place,
3-K & F, *tel.* (01) 601799
Kapriol, 45 Lower Camden Street,
2-K & F, *tel.* (01) 751235
Old Dublin, 91 Francis Street, 2-K & F,
tel. (01) 751173
Rajdoot Tandoori, Claredon Street,
Westberry Centre, 2-K & F,
tel. (01) 772441
Tandoori Rooms, 27 Lower Leeson
Street, 2-K & F, *tel.* (01) 762286
Quo Vadis, St Andrew Street, 1-K & F,
tel. (01) 773363

Garages: Bagenal Fagan & Sons, 8/12
Terenure Place, *tel.* (01) 901840
Ballsbridge Motors, 162 Shelbourne Road,
Ballsbridge, *tel.* (01) 689651
Borrowmans Breakdown Service, 17
Gortmore Road, Finglas, *tel.* (01) 694766
Cahill Motors, Howth Road, Raheny,
tel. (01) 314066
Callow Gilmore Motors, Bluebell Avenue,
tel. (01) 516877
Carroll & Kinsella, Upper Churchtown
Road, *tel.* (01) 983166
Carroll & Kinsella Motors, 164
Walkinstown Road, *tel.* (01) 508142
Cheeverstown, Nass Road, Clondalkin,
tel. (01) 514089
Clonskeagh Motors, Clonskeagh Road,
tel. (01) 694142
Dublin Automotive Services, Kilbarrack
Industrial Estate, Kilbarrack Road,
tel. (01) 390281
J Duffy Motors, Ballygall Road,
tel. (01) 342577
Emergency Breakdown Services,
55 Clonskea Road, *tel.* (01) 697985
Fairlane Motor Co, Greenhills Road,
Tallaght, *tel.* (01) 515200
T Kane Motors, 17a The Rear, Fairview
Avenue, Fairview, *tel.* (01) 338143
Gordon Kellet Services, 44 South Dock
Street, Ringsend, *tel.* (01) 689177
Huet Motors, 78–84 Townsend Street,
tel. (01) 779177
Kenilworth Motors, Harolds Cross Road,
tel. (01) 975757
Linders of Smithfield, Smithfield Square,
tel. (01) 721222
McCarville Motors, 5 Old Bawn Road,
Tallaght, *tel.* (01) 516685
E P Mooney & Co, Longmile Road,
tel. (01) 552416
Park Motors, 218 North Circular Road,
tel. (01) 792011
Sweeney & Forte, 54 Howth Road,
Clontarf, *tel.* (01) 332301
Walden Motor Co, 171–175 Parnell
Street, *tel.* (01) 747831

Plaque, Merrion Square, Dublin

PUBLIC BUILDINGS AND PLACES OF INTEREST

Abbey Theatre, Abbey St 1 (C4)

Aldborough House, Portland Row 2 (D5)

Bank of Ireland, College Green 3 (C3)

Belvedere House, Gt Denmark St 4 (B5)

Christ Church Cathedral (CI), Christ Church Place 5 (A2)

City Hall, Lord Edward St 6 (B3)

Civic Museum, William Street South 7 (B2)

Clonmel House, Harcourt Street 8 (B1)

College of Physicians, Kildare Street 9 (C2)

Customs House, Custom House Quay 10 (D4)

Dublin Castle, Cork Hill 11 (B2)

Ely House, Ely Place 12 (D1)

Four Courts, Inns Quay 13 (A3)

General Post Office, O'Connell Street 14 (B4)

Green Street Courthouse, Green Street 15 (A4)

Iveagh House, St Stephen's Green South 16 (C1)

King's Inns, Henrietta Street 17 (A4)

Leinster House, Kildare Street 18 (C2)

Mansion House, Dawson Street 19 (C2)

Marsh's Library, St Patrick's Close 20 (A2)

Methodist Centenary Church, St Stephen's Close 21 (B1)

Mornington House, Merrion Street Upper 22 (D1)

Municipal Gallery of Modern Art, Parnell Sq. North 23 (B5)

National Concert Hall Earlsfort Terrace 24 (C1)

National Gallery, Kildare Place 25 (D2)

National Library, Kildare Street 26 (D2)

National Museum and Natural History Museum, Kildare Street 27 (C2)

Newman House (University College), St Stephen's Green South 28 (C1)

Powerscourt House, William Street South 29 (B2)

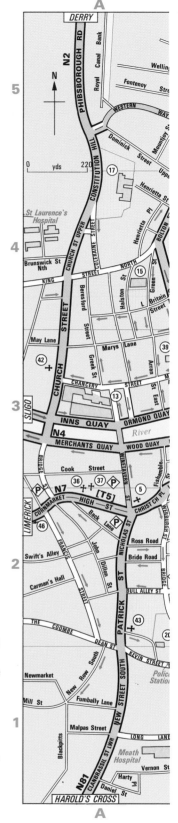

Rotunda, Parnell Street 30 (B4)

Rotunda Hospital, Parnell Sq. West 31 (B4)

Royal College of Surgeons, St Stephen's Green West 32 (B2)

Royal Irish Academy, Dawson Street 33 (C2)

St Andrews Church (RC), Westland Row 34 (D2)

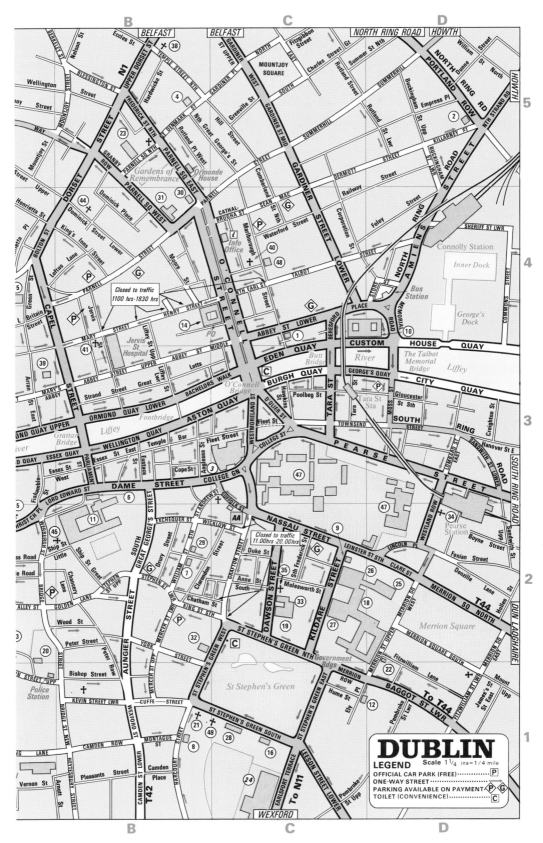

St Ann's Church (CI), Dawson Street 35 (C2)

St Audeon's Church (CI), High Street 36 (A3)

St Audeon's Church (RC), High Street 37 (A3)

St George's Church (CI), Temple Street Nth 38 (B5)

St Mary's Abbey, Mary's Abbey 39 (A3)

St Mary's Pro-Cathedral (RC), Marlborough Street 40 (C4)

St Mary's Church (CI), Mary Street 41 (B3)

St Michan's Church (CI), Church Street 42 (A3)

St Patrick's Cathedral (CI), Patrick Street 43 (A2)

St Saviours Church (RC), Dominick St Lower 44 (B4)

St Werburgh's Church (CI), Werburgh Street 45 (A2)

The Augustinian Church (RC), Cornmarket 46 (A2)

Trinity College, College Street/Westland Row 47 (D2)

Tyrone House, Marlborough Street 48 (C4)

University Church (RC), St Stephen's Green South 49 (B1)

Drumcliff, Co Sligo

Map Ref: 122 G64

Drumcliff is on the little river which drains Glencar Lough and on the Sligo–Bundoran road (N15, T18). Benbulben dominates with its long flat top (1722ft), and Glencar is noted for the waterfalls at its eastern end and for two crannog lake dwellings. St Colmcille (Columba) founded a monastery here in AD 574. A splendid 13ft High Cross stands near the church, beside which W B Yeats is buried. The poet died in France in 1939, but his body was re-interred here in 1948.

North of Drumcliff Bay, past Carney, is **Lissadell**, home of the Gore-Booth family, where Yeats was a frequent guest. A late Georgian mansion (1830–36) of Ballisodare limestone, it was designed by Francis Goodwin and has a unique music room with concealed lighting and perfect acoustics. The life-size dining room murals of the domestic staff are by the Polish Count Markievicz, who married Constance Gore-Booth, noted for her part in the 1916 rebellion.

Dundalk's fine courthouse is a granite building designed in the Doric style

Drumcliff church, famous as the burial place of the poet W B Yeats whose father served here as rector

Dundalk, Co Louth

Map Ref: 123 J00

Half-way from Dublin to Belfast (N1) and south of the Moyry Pass, (the 'Gap of the North'), Dundalk's industrial bustle and well-planned appearance gives the feeling of small city rather than town. Its 1813–18 courthouse by Edward Park and John Bowden borrowed the portico design and dimensions from the Temple of Theseus in Athens; it manages a stern, beetle-browed impressiveness. The Perpendicular church of St Patrick, usually miscalled 'the cathedral', is more elegant. It dates from 1835–50, is by Thomas Duff of Newry in Newry granite and was inspired by King's College chapel in Cambridge.

Facing the church, the Kelly memorial recalls Captain James Kelly, Gerald Hughes, James Crosby and James Murphy, who died in a sea rescue attempt in Dundalk Bay in 1858. Seatown Tower is the belltower of a 1240 Franciscan friary.

Agnes Galt, sister of poet Robert Burns, is buried in the churchyard of St Nicholas's, whose records date from 1207, and they are both recalled by an 1859 monument. Carrolls' tobacco factory, across the road, uses the Scottish poet's picture on one of their cigarette packets, with the contents named after one of his works.

Dundalk's two breweries, MacArdle's and Harp, are under the Guinness umbrella, but the latter was originally the Great Northern, named after a railway company whose engines were built in the town. Dundalk's engineering tradition has had mixed fortunes since then. Dundalk has a racecourse, and a seaside suburb in **Blackrock**, three miles south.

AA recommends:
Hotels: Ballymascanlon House, 3-star, tel. (042) 71124
Imperial, 3-star, tel. (042) 32241
Guesthouse: Failte, Dublin Road, tel. (042) 35152
Restaurant: Angela's, Rockmarshall, 1-K & F, tel. (042) 76193
Garage: Nursery, Mullararlin Road, tel. (042) 35088
Campsite: Gyles Quay Caravan Park, Riverstown PO, Gyles Quay, 4-pennant, tel. (042) 76262

Dundrum, Co Down

Map Ref: 123 J43

The Normans chose a high rocky site standing back from the inner bay of Dundrum, under the shadow of the Mournes, to build one of their most interesting castles. The 12th-century fortification, built by de Courcy or de Lacy is notable for its round keep, still in a very complete state of preservation. Other interesting features are a latrine in the outer wall and an Elizabethan gateway with pointed arch and towers.

On the seaward side of the Newcastle–Belfast road (A2) is **Murlough National Nature Reserve** (NT), Ireland's first nature reserve, which takes in dunes, a fine beach, the estuary and lovely heathland. A good place for watching birds and seals, it was the site of stone age and bronze age settlements, and finds have been made among the dunes. The reserve provides an information centre, walkways, guided walks and residential weekends.

Just opposite the main entrance to the reserve at **Slidderyford** is a dolmen, 8ft high and 4000 years old.

Dungarvan, Co Waterford

Map Ref: 125 X29

Standing on an impressive harbour between Waterford and Youghal (N25), this market town is in an area still called the 'Decies' after a Co Meath tribe who settled here in the third century. A causeway on the River Colligan connects the town with Abbeyside, and beside the river is the ruin of King John's castle of 1185, with much subsequent alteration. There are remnants of the town walls in the 'Dead Walk', and in the churchyard a strange gable-like structure, pierced by circular holes, has never been explained. In Abbeyside are remains of a McGrath castle and an Early English style tower from an Augustinian priory, incorporated in a modern church.

The area has bathing beaches and the river is best for brown trout, with occasional sea trout. Outside the town the Master McGrath memorial honours the greyhound

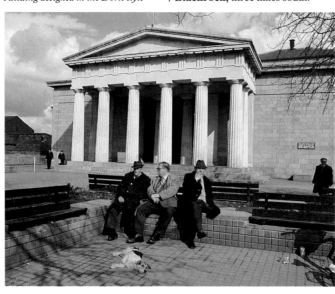

which won the Waterloo coursing cup in 1868, '69 and '71.

AA recommends:
Garage: Donnellys, 14–18 Georges Street, *tel.* 22887
Park Road Service Station, 1–7 Park Road, *tel.* 24929

Dungloe, Co Donegal

Map Ref: 122 B71

This town's area is known as the Rosses (headlands), a 60,000-acre expanse of rock-strewn terrain whose little lakes and streams draw the angler and whose geological curiosity, Talamh Briste (broken earth) is a 12ft-wide chasm more than a quarter of a mile long. This is south-west of the town, and near it, at Crohy Head, are impressive cliffs, with caves accessible only by boat. Offshore here lie Aran, Rutland and other islands. Below Crohy Head, Maghery Bay has a fine bathing strand, with good rock scenery at Termon, to the north. The ancient church of Templecrone is north of Maghery village.

Dungloe is on the N56. A side-road leads north-west to the fishing village of **Burtonport**.

AA recommends:
Hotel: Ostan Na Rosann, 2-star, *tel.* (075) 21088
Garage: Greenes, Carnmore Road, *tel.* (075) 21021
Campsite: Dungloe Caravan Park, Carnmore Road, 3-pennant, *tel.* (075) 21350

Dun Laoghaire, Co Dublin

Map Ref: 125 O22

Nine miles south-east of Dublin, Dun Laoghaire (pronounced 'Dun Leary') is a commercial centre, dormitory town, terminus of Holyhead ferries and resort.

Dun Laoghaire's two piers have a combined length of 8450ft, and the 51-acre harbour, when completed

Dun Laoghaire's magnificent harbour and two piers enclose an area of 250 acres

in 1859 after 43 years' work, was the world's biggest artificial haven. Its granite came from nearby Dalkey, where George Bernard Shaw's family had a summer home in Torca Cottage. The octagonal Victorian bandstand on the east pier, and much of the town's architecture, emphasises its late 19th-century character. Kingstown was its name then, although a fishing village, Dun Leary, was already established.

This is the national yachting headquarters, home port of three clubs, the National, Royal Irish and Royal St George. Two others, the Royal Alfred and the Dublin Bay Sailing Club, are also based here, but considered 'homeless' as they have no clubhouses. Races and regattas predominate and **Killiney** also has a popular bathing beach.

The national maritime museum is in the former Mariners' Church, and the James Joyce museum in the Martello tower at **Sandycove** contains such unexpected items as the author's guitar. At the Forty-Foot bathing spot here, the sign 'Forty-foot gentlemen only' is nowadays ignored.

AA recommends:
Hotels: Royal Marine, 3-star, *tel.* (01) 801911

Hotel Victor, Rochestown Avenue, 3-star, *tel.* (01) 853555
T & C: Ferry, 15 Clarinda Park North, *tel.* (01) 808301
Restaurants: Restaurant Na Mara, Crofton Road, 3-K & F, *tel.* (01) 806767
Trudi's, 107 Lower Georges Street, 1-K & F, *tel.* (01) 805318
Garage: J P S Motors, Ashgrove Industrial Estate, Kill Avenue, *tel.* (01) 805727

Dunmore East, Co Waterford

Map Ref: 125 S60

On the outskirts of Waterford Harbour this noted sea fishing resort stands on a bay divided by headlands into cliffs and coves. There is a 600ft pier. To the south is the promontory of Black Knob, with Merlin's Cave nearby, both accessible by path. A cairn two miles north at Harristown contains a megalithic chambered tomb. The great earthen fort or *dun* from which the resort's name derives may still be traced. Swine's Head to the south is a pleasant walk away. Dunmore East is a former mail packet station. Facing it on the Wexford side of the harbour is the prominent Hook Head.

Good fishing and sailing from Dunmore East and many sheltered coves and beaches

limestone courthouse is said to have been designed for a site in India but their plans got confused – a story often told about buildings which appear too big for their settings – see also **Enniscorthy**.

O'Connell is commemorated by a statue atop a Tuscan limestone pillar in little O'Connell Square (not a square at all – it perfectly captures the town's tortuous layout). Binden Street has Georgian houses more suited to a younger, larger town.

AA recommends:
Hotels: Auburn Lodge, Galway Road, 3-star, *tel.* (065) 21247
Old Ground, 3-star, *tel.* (065) 28127
West County Inn, 3-star, *tel.* (065) 28421

Enniscorthy, Co Wexford

Map Ref: 125 S94

Charming, hilly and historic, Enniscorthy stands at the limit of the Slaney navigation. The granite St Aidan's cathedral (1843–46) is by Pugin, its limestone spire being its best feature. The excellently preserved castle houses a comprehensive museum.

This castle is attributed to Philip Prendergast and dated 1201, but claims are also made for the earlier Raymond le Gros as its founder. One of its drum towers is an imaginative 1903 replacement of a demolished original. It was held by the Roshford and MacMorrough families before being taken over by the Crown and leased to tenants,

Ennis, Co Clare

Map Ref: 124 R37

The N18 from Limerick to Galway passes through Clare's quaintly charming county town at the centre of the county above the Fergus estuary. This is a perfect base for exploring the almost peninsular county of Clare (it's in easy reach of the Burren), and for anglers there is plenty of brown trout fishing.

Ennis is noted for its narrow 'twisters' of streets, Abbey Street, Parnell Street and O'Connell Street. Its old-world appeal has not been eroded, though its 1242

Franciscan friary had its central tower 'improved' by a concrete wash and laughable spiky finials. The carvings, representing The Passion, on a 15th-century MacMahon tomb are exceptional.

In the Fergus nearby is a rock with three painted shields and a carved lion, known as Steele's Rock after Honest Tom Steele, a farmer and friend of Daniel O'Connell, who was MP for the area in the early 19th century. Honest Tom courted Miss Crow whose home is still visible from the spot; when she rejected him he sat for countless hours on this river rock.

Ennis's big 1852 Palladian

The Musical Traditions

Top: *Traditional music can be heard at the Abbey Tavern, Howth.*
Bottom: *Irish fiddler c.1860*

Folk songs, with themes like failed revolution, beautiful girls forced to wed old men, shipwreck, drink, and seduction and desertion, are sung almost everywhere. Despite claims of great antiquity, evidence suggests that the oldest numbers date from the 16th century, when blind harpist Rory O'Cathain composed *Oh give me your hand*, still widely played.

The *sean-nos* singing style, in solo Gaelic with no accompaniment, may sound lugubrious, but has enjoyed a big revival since nearly dying out in the 1940s. The harp, Ireland's symbol, is rarely seen outside occasional concerts and at the medieval banquets in such places as Bunratty Castle. Favoured instruments are *uileann pipes* (like bagpipes), violin, accordion and tin whistle, with *bodhran* (goatskin) drums popular in west Cork and Kerry. Lovers of American bluegrass will notice its affinity with some Irish traditional airs, especially in strings.

Visitors may well find people playing traditional music in the pub, or they might get to a *ceilidh* (pronounced kay-lee) — a traditional party with boisterous dancing. Or they can visit a *fleadh* (pronounced flah), one of the numerous music festivals organised by Comhaltas Ceoltoiri Eireann, set up in 1951 to promote traditional music, song and dance. It has 200 branches and puts on the all-Ireland *fleadh* — a full blooded social event — in a different venue each August. The *Fleadh Nua* takes place in Ennis, Co Clare, in May; and the Glens of Antrim *Feis* in July. Step-dancing, with its intricate footwork, is most often seen carefully performed by girls in national costume, but a more spontaneous variety might be spotted in the Gaeltachts.

Many folksy ballads are in fact modern. A fashion in Irish imitation country-and-western is strong in the North Midlands. On the broader popular front Ireland's musical tradition is carried on by musicians as different as Dubliner Bob Geldof and Waterfordman Val Doonican. Noted musicians of the past have been Michael Balfe, composer of *The Bohemian Girl*, born in Dublin in 1808, and tenor John McCormack, born in Athlone, Co Westmeath, in 1884.

one of whom in 1581 was poet Edmund Spenser.

The Cotton Tree, beside the handsome six-arch bridge over the Slaney, is over 250 years old. English cavalry officers are said to have tethered their horses to it on their way from the Battle of Vinegar Hill in 1798. Enniscorthy was a storm centre of that year's insurrection, the rebels holding the town for several weeks. The hill rises to 390ft, is within walking distance via Templeshannon and the Curracloe road and gives a bird's eye view of the town. A windmill stump on the summit, the rebels' final headquarters, is a National Monument.

Enniscorthy has excellent Edwardian shopfronts, a triangular market 'square', and a reputation for bacon and traditional coachbuilding. St Senan's hospital, with its 300-yard Ruskinian redbrick front, is said to have been designed for an Indian site: as at Ennis, plans are said to have been transposed.

AA recommends:
Hotel: Murphy-Flood's, Town Centre, 2-star, *tel.* (054) 33413

Enniscrone, Co Sligo

Map Ref: 122 G23

A resort which had a reputation for sulphur baths, Enniscrone faces Killala across Killala Bay, with the pistol-shaped Bartragh Island between them. Its three-mile strand gives excellent surf-bathing. Nearby is Castle Firbis; one of its MacFirbises compiled the *Book of Lecan* (1416), now in the Royal Irish Academy, Dublin.

Golf and fishing on the Easkey, Moy and Killala Bay are among the attractions. A little beyond Eskey, a smaller resort to the north, is an Ice Age boulder with a deep fissure known as the 'Split Rock'. There is also a large dolmen here.

AA recommends:
Hotel: Killala Bay, *tel.* (096) 36239

Enniskerry, Co Wicklow

Map Ref: 125 O21

Enniskerry is an old-world village inland from Bray and near the Co Dublin border; its chief attraction is 34,000-acre **Powerscourt** nearby, which has one of the great gardens of Europe. This was the home of the Powerscourt family. Since their time its mansion, designed by Richard Cassels and once noted for its ballroom, has been extensively burned, but the gardens and 400ft waterfall, one of Ireland's tallest, are still open to visitors.

Giant beech trees over 200 years old line the entrance, and the estate is also noted for its conifers. The

View from the top terrace at Powerscourt to the Triton Pool

gardens were begun in 1745 – about 15 years later than the house – and finished in 1767. They include English, Japanese and Italian sections, and from the top terrace, 800ft long, the view across the Triton Pool (guarded by the winged horses Fame and Victory and with a 60ft fountain) to the Great Sugarloaf is one of Ireland's most striking vistas.

Enniskillen, Co Fermanagh

Map Ref: 123 H24

Enniskillen 'the island town' owes its fine position on the narrow neck between upper and lower Lough Erne to strategic considerations, but not until the Plantation did the town develop as an important defensive site. A handsome main street winds in snaking curves, changing its name several times from one end of the town to the other. The water of the loughs or the River Erne is often in sight and some of Fermanagh's hills have crept into the town.

On top of one of these is St MacCartan's Cathedral, essentially a building of 1841. On another is Portora Royal School, which Oscar Wilde and Samuel Beckett attended. Schoolboys 'playing' are said to have blown up a part of Portora castle in 1859 and in 1894 gales completed the ruin.

The Watergate standing back from the Lough is an impressive sight. Hugh ('the hospitable')

Maguire made a castle here first in the 15th century; in the 17th century Captain Cole built a 'fair, strong wall, 26 foot high with flankers, a parapet and a walk on the top'. Now there is a shortened keep of three storeys and a square with the air of a military barracks, where the county and regimental museums are housed. The county had two famous regiments – the Royal Inniskilling Fusiliers and the Inniskilling Dragoons.

On the Belfast road is **Castle Coole** (NT), a superb neo-classical house, the 1790s masterpiece of James Wyatt, who designed some of the furniture. After a Regency refurbishment of some of the rooms it remained substantially unaltered. It stands in parkland, some of the trees predating the house.

AA recommends:
Hotels: Killyhevlin, Dublin Road, 3-star, *tel.* Enniskillen 23481
Railway, 1-star, *tel.* Enniskillen 22084
Guesthouse: Interlaken, 54 Fort Hill Street, *tel.* Enniskillen 22274
Farmhouses: Lack-a-Boy, Tempo Road, *tel.* Enniskillen 22488
Lakeview, Drumcrow, Blaney PO, *tel.* Derrygonnelly 263
Garages: Erne Engineering Co, Queen's Street, *tel.* Enniskillen 3721
Leo McGrory & Sons, Tempo Road, *tel.* Enniskillen 24351
Modern Motors, 74 Forthill Street, *tel.* Enniskillen 22974
Patrick McNulty & Sons Motorcycles, 24–26 Belmore Street, *Tel.* Enniskillen 22423

A landmark to ancient geographers as well as modern ones, the 400ft cliffs of Fair Head

Ennistymon, Co Clare

Map Ref: 124 R18

The N67 passes through this fishing centre on the Cullenagh river, here washing a rocky bed on its way to Liscannor Bay. The town is picturesquely built in a wooded valley beside a cascade. This was the birthplace, in about 1747, of poet Brian Merryman. Around the year 1780 he wrote *The Midnight Court*, 1206 earthy lines telling of a dream in which the women of Ireland put the country's men on trial for selfishness, sexual tardiness, failing to marry until old age and then making slaves of nubile girls. The poem castigates rich clergy for staying celibate, and warns that the Irish race is on the point of extinction. Written in Gaelic, this poem is available in English.

AA recommends:
Hotel: Falls, 2-star, *tel.* (065) 71004
T & C: McMahon's, Church Street, *tel.* (065) 71078

Fair Head, Co Antrim

Map Ref: 123 D14

Fair Head, which was known to the Greek geographer, Ptolemy, forms the north eastern tip of Ireland. The bold outline of a 400ft face with a table top, makes an important landmark. The summit is wildly beautiful, exposed and barren. Three dark lakes break up the bleak headland – Lough Doo, Lough na Crannagh, with a crannog or early lake dwelling, and Lough Fadden. A herd of wild goats can sometimes be seen scrambling up the cliff face, choughs nest here and the careful walker can descend the Grey Man's Path, a dramatic plunging fissure.

If Fair Head is barren and forbidding, Murlough Bay below is green and beautiful. In a region where a tree is a rarity, this amphitheatre is well wooded with ancient scrub under the headland and belts of trees running right down to a fringe at the water's edge. At the top stands a monument to Sir Roger Casement. Waymarked paths join Fair Head and Murlough Bay.

Fermoy, Co Cork

Map Ref: 124 W89

Straddling a wide and beautiful stretch of the Blackwater, one of the country's best salmon rivers (with trout in its tributaries) Fermoy was founded by Scottish John Anderson in 1789, and continues to be of military importance. Its well-planned square betrays its relative youth among Irish towns. Tree-shaded Barnane Walk gives a view of Castlehyde House, home of the ancestors of Dr Douglas Hyde, first president of the Republic.

From here **Glanworth** can be visited, via **Labbacallee Hill,** with its huge dolmen. It stands over two burial chambers, one known as the Hag's Bed. An old Roche Castle and a 1227 Dominican abbey stand in ruins here, near the Funcheon River, with an ancient and quaintly narrow bridge on 13 arches.

AA recommends:
Garages: Fermoy Autos, Court House Road, *tel.* (025) 31455
Cavanagh's, Ashe Quay, *tel.* (025) 31211
Harry O'Sullivan, 41–43 MacCurtain Street, *tel.* (025) 31797

Fore, Co Westmeath

Map Ref: 123 N57

Traditionally called the village of seven wonders, Fore is three miles from Castlepollard, between Lough Lene and Lough Glore. The wonders, said to include unburnable wood and unboilable water, are elusive, but a hill which is said to reverse the normal gearbox procedure may be explained by

Straddling a tree-lined stretch of the River Blackwater, Fermoy was built in the 18th century by a Scottish merchant

Gallarus Oratory is the best preserved of the boat-shaped oratories in Co. Kerry

magnetic forces. As the hill, is in a field, it is hard to test the claim.

The remains of a mid-seventh-century monastery of St Feichin are here and the church has a doorway whose construction and marking resemble some in Syria. The lintel weighs over two tons. Of the damaged nearby anchorite's cell, only the eastern section is ancient.

Near Castlepollard is Pakenham Hall, also called Tullynally Castle, home of the Earls of Longford, whose family has owned it since 1655. It is the biggest castle in Ireland still lived in as a family home.

A colourful inhabitant of the Fota Wildlife Park

Fota Island, Co Cork

Map Ref: 124 W77

Nine miles east of Cork but a mile less by rail, the island has an 80-acre wildlife park, administered by the Royal Zoological Society of Ireland on land provided by University College, Cork, which has also planted an arboretum here. The first breeding in Ireland of both cheetahs and the scimitar-horned oryx has been achieved here. Other species on view include giraffes, zebras, kangaroos, wallabies, ring-tailed and other lemurs, various monkeys, gibbons, coatimundis, guanacos, Indian black buck,

ostriches, emus, penguins (breeding), pelicans, flamingoes, macaws and a wide variety of ducks and geese. The opening season is mid March to the end of October.

Gallerus Oratory, Co Kerry

Map Ref: 124 Q30

The oratory stands inland from Smerwick Harbour a few miles north-west of Dingle on an unclassified road. It is the best-preserved and possibly the most perfect early Christian church building in Ireland, and is probably 1200 years old.

About two miles south of Kilmalkedar, its outline suggests an upturned boat. Its external measurements are 22ft by 18ft by 16ft high. The 5ft 7in high entrance door narrows towards the top, as does that of the church at Fore. Inside the measurements have come down to 15ft by 10ft, with a deeply splayed loophole window at the east end. Each gable summit has a socketed stone, the bases of long-gone crosses.

The oratory's stones are

unmortared throughout, but so carefully fitted that it is even now waterproof. Nearby is the Saint's Road, an ancient trackway said to have been laid by St Brendan to the summit of Brandon Mountain.

Galtee Mountains, Co Tipperary

Map Ref: 125 R82

This is Ireland's finest inland mountain range. The highest point, **Galtymore** (3018ft), is directly north of the Mitchelstown Caves. From the Mitchelstown–Cahir road (N8), which runs along the lower slopes on the range's southern side, there are several easy routes to the summit peaks. From the northern side, bordering the Glen of Aherlow and above five tiny lakes lying in corries, steeper ascents and rock climbs may be made. West of Galtymore is **Lyracappul** (2712ft). **Greenane**, standing above Lough Muskry, one of those tiny lakes, rises to 2636ft. At the Mitchelstown–Limerick road the range merges with the Ballyhoura Hills.

Crannogs

Crannogs and other Stone Age dwellings and burial places surround Lough Gur

Crannogs are lake dwellings — artificial islands on which people built their homes from the Neolithic period until as late as the 17th century AD.

They were formed by laying down layers of logs, stones, peat and brush, or whatever other material came to hand (including animal bones), to raise a mound out of the water. The fine example at Lough-na-cranagh, Fair Head, has drystone facing rising up to 7ft above the water.

To the modern eye, crannogs may seem uncomfortable places to live, and remnants of wooden palisades suggest that they were designed for defence. But it is quite possible that they were simply a practical way of building on marshland, and that the lakes developed later.

They can be a rich source of finds,

since the prevailing damp preserves perishable substances like wood and leather. Archaeologist Sean P O Riordain reports that a crannog at Ballinderry, Co Westmeath, revealed articles from the 11th to the 17th

century in the various layers of stone, wicker floor, gravel and clay which had been used to reinforce the surface through the years. Other crannogs have survived at Drumcliff, Co Sligo and Lough Gur, Limerick.

One of Galway's best-known landmarks is the 16th-century Spanish Arch

Galway, Co Galway

Map Ref: 124 M32

Capital of Connaught, standing on Galway Bay, Galway is not only the gateway to Connemara but a city of considerable interest with much of its past preserved. Fourteen English families took over civil power from the Norman Burkes and held it until 1654; they were known as the 'Tribes of Galway'.

The area known as the Claddagh may have given its name to the Claddagh ring (two joined hands). This was until recently a fiercely independent Gaelic speaking and traditional area, but today its random array of thatched white houses has gone.

Spanish Arch is the scene of an old fishmarket; the Browne doorway in Eyre Square and Lynch window in Market Street have Spanish links. Lynch's Castle in Shop Street, now a bank, is an early 16th-century towerhouse with a staggered line of archery slits.

The weird basalt columns known as the Giant's Causeway

The oldest parts of St Nicholas of Myra Church date from 1320 and the tower from 1500. It has a rare triple nave, and is Ireland's second biggest ancient parish church. Galway Cathedral (1957–65) has touches of individuality from architect J J Robinson which could be called Celtic-Corinthian. A mosaic of J F Kennedy in a side chapel has provoked criticism.

From Galway's Salmon Weir Bridge a multitude of fish can be seen as they travel upriver in season. The city has a Gaelic theatre (An Taidhbhearc) and a colourful race week in August, but perhaps the biggest attraction is the September Oyster Festival, a highly sociable event including oyster opening championships.

AA recommends:
Hotels: Great Southern, Eyre Square, 4-star, *tel.* (091) 64041
Ardilaun House, Taylor's Hill, 3-star, *tel.* (091) 21433

Corrib Great Southern, Dublin Road, 3-star, *tel.* (091) 55281
Flannery's, Dublin Road, 3-star, *tel.* (091) 55111
Anno Santo, Threadneedle Road, Salthill, 2-star, *tel.* (091) 22110
Galway Ryan, Dublin Road, 2-star, *tel.* (091) 53181
Skeffington Arms, Eyre Square, 2-star, *tel.* (091) 63173
Warwick, Salthill, 2-star, *tel.* (091) 21244
Atlanta, Dominick Street, 1-star, *tel.* (091) 62241
Lochlurgain, 22 Monksfield, Upper Salthill, 1-star, *tel.* (091) 22884
Rockbarton Park, Salthill, 1-star, *tel.* (091) 22018
Guesthouses: Adare, Father Griffin Place, *tel.* (091) 62638
Knockrea House, 55 Lower Salthill, *tel.* (091) 21794
T & C: Roncalli House, 24 Whitestrand Avenue, Lower Salthill, *tel.* (091) 64159
Seacrest, Roscarn, Merlin Park, *tel.* (091) 57975
Restaurant: Eyre House, Eyre Square, 2-K & F, *tel.* (091) 62396
Garages: Higgins, Headford Road, *tel.* (091) 61263
J J Fleming, Tuan Road, *tel.* (091) 55451
John Kelleher, Salthill, *tel.* (091) 22463

Giant's Causeway, Co Antrim

Map Ref: 123 C94

Sixty million years ago, when extensive volcanic activity was changing the face of north west Europe, intensely hot lava flowed out of narrow vents here and spread cooling over the white chalk until it solidified into 37,000 or so columns in fantastic shapes and arrangements – the Giant's Causeway.

Most of the columns are hexagonal but others are four-, five-, seven- and eight-sided, and some have ball and socket joints. Over the centuries mystification about these formations became enmeshed with the legends of Finn MacCool, and the story that the giant built the Causeway, or

Ancient St Kevin's Church and round tower, Glendalough

stepping stones, so that he could travel dryshod to Scotland became popular. (Similar columns do in fact emerge on the other side of the sea in Staffa.) In the 18th century, with the arrival of the tourist, the guides embellished the stories. Parts of the Causeway received names – the harp, the organ, the wishing chair, Lord Antrim's parlour and the like.

Now it is possible to understand the scientific explanations without losing the romance. A bus brings visitors down to the Grand Causeway but a walk a little further round the majestic series of towering headlands and bays reveals the full glory of the Causeway, including Port na Spaniagh where Spanish Armada 'galleas' *Girona* foundered. Its treasure was recovered in 1968 and is now on show in the Ulster Museum.

Glencolumbkille, Co Donegal

Map Ref: 122 G58

This village became famous for the unique rural co-operative movement founded by a local priest to counter emigration from the area. In a secluded glen north of the 1972ft Slieve League this was a retreat of St Colmcille (Columba) and tradition says that Bonnie Prince Charlie (Charles Edward Stuart) also spent some time here. There is a folk village with cottages representing three different periods in Irish rural life. A large flagstone is pointed out as the saint's bed, and in St Columba's Oratory another stone is said to be a Columban relic. There is an engraved pillar stone, and the place is a scene of pilgrimages.

Glendalough, Co Wicklow

Map Ref: 125 S21

Two picturesque lakes rise at more than 2000ft while spread through the valley are the remains of St Kevin's early sixth-century monastic settlement, which lasted over 600 years and survived many of the usual Norse plunderings before being burned and abandoned in 1398.

St Kevin is said to have come to this beautiful spot as a hermit, to forego the joys of human love, but was pursued by Kathleen, a beautiful redhead with eyes of 'unholy blue'. The story that he flung her from a cliff into a lake may be the poetic invention of Thomas Moore, but an account by historian John O'Donovan that he cooled the ardour of both of them by rolling first himself and then Kathleen in nettles is no easier to accept. Both stories are still told.

The 103ft round tower was recapped in the original mica slate in 1876. At that time also a ruin called St Kieran's Church was unearthed from a mound of earth, having been totally forgotten. Other remains include St Kevin's Church, an early barrel-vaulted oratory with high-pitched roof, St Saviour's Church, late 11th century and also restored in 1875–6, the Caher, beside the eastern shore of the upper lake (ruin of a Bronze Age or Early Iron Age stone fort), and the Cathedral, 7th-century. The oolite (granulated limestone) east window was probably imported from England. 'St Kevin's Bed' is a 7ft by 4ft excavation in a cliff, 30ft above the water and best approached from below. Here, in this cave, St Kevin began his solitary life.

AA recommends:
Hotel: Royal, 2-star, *tel.* (0404) 5135

The Spanish Connection

The Browne Doorway, Galway

The rout of the Spanish Armada drove the fleeing ships northwards around Scotland before they could turn south, past Ireland, for home. About half of those 130 ships never reached Spain. Some simply disappeared. At least one was wrecked off Giant's Causeway, and others were wrecked off Streeda Point, Co Sligo, and near Ardara, Co Donegal. A wreck off Kerry is said to have given Ireland the Kerry Blue terrier breed.

Spanish Point on the Co Clare coast was a burial place of ship-wrecked Armada men — and a number of Spanish sailors are thought to have settled in Galway.

In fact the city had flourishing trade links with Spain and Portugal well before the Armada, which makes it hard to distinguish between the influences of shipwrecked sailors, and settlers for other reasons.

But brown eyes and olive skins are still associated with surnames of Galway provenance, and remnants of mansions in the Spanish style, from the late 15th to the 17th century, are still visible in Galway city. A notable one is the Browne doorway, preserved in Eyre Square, a fine two-storey Spanish renaissance relic, door and oriel window, part of a mansion of 1627 erected in Lower Abbeygate Street by one Martin Browne. One of the city's most prominent landmarks is still called the Spanish Arch, near the old fish quay.

A table under a window in Market Street records that in 1493 the mayor of Galway, James Lynch Fitzstephen, hanged his own son, Walter, from this window. The mayor is said to have been an extensive wine importer, and to have had the son of an important business contact in Cadiz, named Gomez, staying as a guest. Walter Lynch suspected young Gomez of trying to steal his girlfriend, Agnes, and murdered him. His father, who was also magistrate, sentenced him to death. Not only could no hangman be found, but a mob of Walter's friends threatened to break into the jail, which adjoined the house, and free him. So Lynch hanged his own son himself, and gave us the term Lynch Law (according to one tradition), though ironically in this case the mob wished to save, not take a life.

Glengarriff, Co Cork

Map Ref: 124 V95

Facing Bantry across the bay, Glengarriff is in a secluded deep valley surrounded by mountains. The name means 'rough glen' and the place is full of scattered rocks and boulders, but the roughness is countered by a profusion of greenery. Not only tall pines, elms and stately oaks, with arbutus, holly and yew in crevices and shady corners, but also many kinds of tropical shrubs and flowers grow here.

Near the middle of the big scenic harbour is Ilnacullin, more popularly known as Garinish Island, for which boat trips leave from an improbable shaded glen near the village street. A previous owner, John Annan Bryce, helped by Harold Peto, turned the desolate island into a tropical garden paradise, centred on an Italian garden comprising a lily pool with paved surround, where variegated blooms and foliage are massed. Also here are a miniature Japanese garden and an overhanging rockery. There are shady walks through trees unexpected in these latitudes, and plants with tropical, antipodean and even Antarctic origins. A simulated Grecian temple has been built and there are spectacular seaward views from the Martello tower which crowns the island. George Bernard Shaw wrote part of St Joan here; Agatha Christie visited the isle and attributed the trip to her detective Hercule Poirot, who seemingly later forgot its name.

Rewarding walks can be taken from Glengarriff to Poulgorm for the view from the heights, and to Cromwell's Bridge among its trees.

AA recommends:
Hotel: Eccles, 2-star, tel. (027) 63003

Lush green foliage and sparkling waters of Glencloy

Glenmalure, Co Wicklow

Map Ref: 125 T09

A wildly beautiful gorge, Glenmalure has mountains to the west, including Lugnaquilla (3039ft). The drive up the valley to **Baravore**, above Drumgoff, is splendid. The Military Road, so named because it was built after the 1798 rebellion to make insurgents' hideouts accessible to redcoats, runs across the valley from Aghavannagh to Laragh (eventually to Rathfarnham, Co Dublin), and gives fine vistas on its winding course. One of the old blockhouses can be seen at Drumgoff. Fiach MacHugh O'Byrne routed Lord Deputy Grey's army here in 1580. He and rebel Michael Dwyer are commemorated by a tablet in a boulder.

The Military Road runs through some spectacular mountain scenery in the beautiful valley of Glenmalure

Glens of Antrim, Co Antrim

Map Ref: 123

There are nine glens of Antrim, which follow the courses of rivers and streams rising in the Antrim Plateau. Most of these can be seen clearly by car from the Antrim Coast Road, but some parts of the mountains remain wild and inaccessible, such as the Garron Plateau. The hills are rich in old, native woodland and nature reserves have been established, while commercial forestry is also developing. Waterfalls are plentiful.

The first glen to the south is **Glenarm**, which meets the sea at the village of the same name, whose castle is the present home of the Earl of Antrim. Then comes **Glencloy**, which runs down to **Carnlough**, a village with a fine limestone harbour and buildings associated with Frances Anne Vane Tempest Stewart, third Marchioness of Londonderry. **Glenariff** is held to be the most splendid of the glens and a Forest Park has been developed there with good walks through glen, forest and exposed mountain. At the foot of Glenariff is Red Bay.

Glenballyeamon, Glenaan and **Glencorp** all meet to run into **Cushendall**, a very pretty village with a good beach and red sandstone Curfew Tower.

Glendun runs to **Cushendun**, while **Glenshesk** and **Glentaisie** meet at **Ballycastle**.

Glin, Co Limerick

Map Ref: 124 R14

On Limerick's Shannon shore (N69), the village is a dairying centre and adjoins the demesne of Glin Castle, seat of the Knight of Glin. The Georgian castle is noted for its plasterwork, furnishings and paintings and is open to parties of ten or more by arrangement. The Fitzgerald family has lived here, almost without interruption, for 700 years. The present castle was built in the 1780s, mainly by Colonel John Fitzgerald, 24th Knight of Glin. The castellations were added in the 1820s, and are merely a decoration. The ruined keep of the older castle, destroyed in 1600, stands beside the village. Glin Castle has a unique double flying staircase.

Glin Castle, a handsome 18th-century mansion belonging to the Fitzgerald family

Gorey, Co Wexford

Map Ref: 125 T15

At the western end of this pleasingly laid out town (N11) 418ft Gorey Hill was the camp of the 1798 rebels before their march on Arklow, and a granite Celtic memorial cross stands near it. The view from the summit encompasses the foothills of the Wicklow Mountains which extend this far, and there are pleasant and varied walks in the area. The N11 goes south to **Ferns**, where the Augustinian abbey built by Dermot MacMurrough in 1160 has a curious square tower with a conical roof among its remnants. West by L31–L32 is **Bunclody** (Newtownbarry), a suitable starting point for climbing the Blackstairs Mountains. Nearby is **Clonegal**, whose tree-lined street leads to the yew walk of Huntington Castle, used in the film *Barry Lyndon* and where for several years the Robertson family, practitioners and chroniclers of the Rite of Isis, have shown visitors over their shrine.

AA recommends:
Hotel: Marlfield House, 3-star (country house), *tel.* (055) 21124
Farmhouse: Woodlands, Ballynastragh, *tel.* (0402) 7125
Garage: O'Sullivans, Scarnagh, Coolgreany, *tel.* (0402) 7127

Gort, Co Galway

Map Ref: 124 M40

A pleasant little town near Lough Cutra on the N18 from Galway to Ennis, Gort was seat of Guaire, a seventh-century king of Connaught, the foundations of whose palace may still be traced. Two miles south in Lough Cutra demesne is a castle built by Viscount Gort. About two miles north of the town is **Coole Park**, home of Abbey Theatre pioneering playwright Lady Augusta Gregory. Her house has been demolished but a chestnut tree still bears the carved initials of writers she knew. W B Yeats stayed here, and a 16th-century tower house he owned, called **Thoor Ballylee**, is nearby. It is restored, and Yeats first editions may be seen there.

AA recommends:
Hotel: Glynns, Main Street, 2-star, *tel.* (091) 31047

Gougane Barra, Co Cork

Map Ref: 124 W06

Off the T64 at the Pass of Keimaneigh, this lake amid impressive, brooding scenery is the source of the River Lee, and its little island, reached by a causeway, was St Finbarr's hermitage. The saint founded a monastery here in the 7th century. Pilgrimages are made to the hermitage each September, and there is a modern oratory with stained-glass windows representing local saints. At the entrance to the causeway is an ancient cemetery. The craggy Keimaneigh Pass, with precipitous cliff-like walls hung with lush greenery, is one of Ireland's most romantic beauty spots. The Gaelic name means 'Deer's Pass', from a legend that a pursued deer once jumped across it.

AA recommends:
Hotel: Gougane Barra, 2-star, *tel.* Ballingeary 69

An annual pilgrimage takes place at St Finbarr's hermitage island in Gougane Barra

The circular stone fort has a 77ft
diameter and a wall 17ft high by 13ft
thick at the base. Two passages run
through the thickness of the wall
near the entrance, and the wall is
terraced on the inside. Elsewhere
on the hillside are three circular
embankments. The fort was built
about 1700 BC, and was later the
seat of the O'Neills, kings of Ulster.
It was restored in 1870, the rebuilt
portion being above a black line.
Splendid views of Loughs Foyle
and Swilly can be had from the
neighbourhood of the fort.

Headford, Co Galway

Map Ref: 122 M24

A neat little town east of Lough
Corrib, Headford is a favourite
angling centre, with the demesne of
Headford Castle on its outskirts.
The ruin of the Ross Errily
Franciscan friary, with its tall
battlemented tower, is a national
monument, and stands to the north-
west, off the Cong road on the Black
River. It was founded in 1351, but
the present extensive ruins are
probably about 100 years younger.
The west doorway and east window
are of special interest. The ruined
Moyne Castle, with its square tower
and spiral staircase, is nearby. The
Headford-Ballinrobe road has
lovely views of Loughs Corrib and
Mask.

AA recommends:
Hotel: Anglers Rest, I-star,
tel. (093) 35528

Greyabbey, Co Down

Map Ref: 123 J56

The little village of Greyabbey is
named after a beautiful Cistercian
monastery (DOE). It is set in
parkland, where there are specimen
trees, in a hollow overlooked by
Rosemount, the ancestral home of
the Montgomery family to whom
the abbey was granted in the 17th
century. The abbey was founded by
Affreca, wife of John de Courcy, in
1193, and the church, which
remains in a good state of
preservation, has an elaborately-
carved west door and a short
chancel lit by tall lancet windows.
There is a cloister, refectory and
chapter-house, as well as some old
and fascinating monuments.
   To the north of Greyabbey is
Mount Stewart (NT) the home of
the Marquesses of Londonderry, of

whom Lord Castlereagh is the most
famous. The house is full of family
treasures, including *Hambletonian*,
one of George Stubbs' most
celebrated works. The gardens,
designed by Edith, seventh
Marchioness of Londonderry, were
laid out in the 1920s. They each
have a theme – the Shamrock
garden, the Italian garden, the
Spanish garden and so on; the
formality of the parterres and the
elaborate topiary mixes well with the
more natural lily woods and
lakeside areas.

Grianan of Aileach, Co Donegal

Map Ref: 123 C31

Near the Derry border on an 800ft
hill, this antiquity is seven miles
south-east of Fahan, via Burrfoot.

Hillsborough, Co Down

Map Ref: 123 J25

Hillsborough is a village of
Georgian town houses, interesting
shops and bars and important large
buildings. It owes much to the

Gardens

Think of Irish gardens and think
of a landscape of natural beauty
embellished by planting, with
banks of rhododendrons and azaleas,
woodland, rocks and water. William
Robinson, author of *The Wild Garden*
in 1870, influenced the style of gardening in Ireland by advocating the com-
bination of landscape and plants as
opposed to the more artificial Victorian schemes. The climate which
makes Ireland so green favours horti-
culture and the Gulf Stream currents
in some places nurture tender and
exotic plants.
   At **Glenveagh**, Co Donegal, exotic
plants flourish among the rocks by a
dramatic lough, and a hill facing the sun

The Shamrock Garden, Mount Stewart

is extravagantly covered with rhododendrons and azaleas. **Annesgrove**, in
Co Cork, has a wonderful collection of
plants, gathered in this century by
Richard Grove-Annesley, which grow

in ordered profusion on the steep
banks of a river. At **Rowallane**,
Co Down, Hugh Armytage Moore,
another great plantsman, moulded
waves of rhododendrons and azaleas
to the drumlins and used rocky outcrops for rock gardens, and Lord
Rosse at **Birr**, Co Offaly, used the
same principal and plantsman's expertise in his demesne.
   In two of Ireland's most famous
gardens, however, natural planting
takes second place to formal schemes.
Nineteenth-century **Powerscourt**
uses statues, ornamental water, and
terraces against the backdrop of Sugar
Loaf Mountain to create one of Ireland's most celebrated vistas, while
Mount Stewart is a compartment-
alised garden, with 'rooms' featuring
different colour schemes and themes.

Bailey Lighthouse was built in 1814 on the site of an old fortress at Howth Harbour

Marquesses of Downshire who lived in Hillsborough Castle. This, standing right in the centre of the village, was the Governor's residence, but is now used for state occasions and for visiting royalty. The fine 1760 Market House looks across the Square to 18th-century gates which lead to Hillsborough Fort. Dating from early Christian times, this achieved strategic importance in 1650 and was later transformed into a picturesque toy fort which the Downshire family used for entertaining. The church, rebuilt in 1760–1774, has been described as 'the most sophisticated and uniform example of the Georgian Gothick style in Ireland'. In the churchyard is the grave of composer and conductor, Sir Hamilton Harty, whose home in Ballynahinch Street is marked by a plaque.

Holycross, Co Tipperary

Map Ref: 125 S05

A thorough restoration has been made in recent years of the 1168 Benedictine and, later Cistercián, abbey situated south-west of Thurles. But as it was much rebuilt in the first three centuries of its life, little of the original Romanesque remains, though the entrance near the south-east angle of the cloister is a fine example. Arches in the church's south aisle had to be added in the 19th century, and a tomb there was rebuilt in 1914. The Earls of Ormonde allowed the monks to remain here for more than 150 years after its supposed suppression in 1536.

Howth, Co Dublin

Map Ref: 125 O23

Forming the northern horn of the crescent of Dublin Bay, the 560ft Hill of Howth and surrounding peninsula are a beauty spot and seaside resort. The area has also become a Dublin suburb, but is still known for its fishing fleet. Fourteenth-century Howth Castle, restyled in 1910 by Sir Edwin Lutyens, has in its grounds a noted rhododendron display, best seen in May and June, and a massive dolmen known as Aideen's Grave. Howth has attractive cliff walks, and picnic excursions are made to **Ireland's Eye,** a small island a mile offshore.

AA recommends:
Hotel: Howth Lodge, 2-star, *tel.* (01) 390288
Restaurant: King Sitric, 3-K & F, *tel.* (01) 325235

Inishcealtra, Co Clare

Map Ref: 124 R68

Also called Holy Island, this islet in Lough Derg is about a mile and a half from Mountshannon. St Caimin founded a monastic settlement here in the seventh century, and there are remains of five churches, a round tower, an anchorite's cell called 'The Confessional' and a drystone structure known as 'The Cottage'. There is an earth-and-stone enclosure called the 'Saint's Graveyard', and cross-inscribed slabs dating from the eighth to the twelfth centuries, as well as three sculptured crosses. The most recent church St Mary's, has work from the late 16th century. King Brian Boru restored this settlement after Viking raids.

Inishowen Peninsula, Co Donegal

Map Ref: 123 C43

A predominately mountainous region, this peninsula stretches between Loughs Foyle and Swilly and tapers towards Malin Head, Ireland's most northerly point. Slieve Snacht (2019ft) is its most prominent summit. This area has a variety of fine scenery and several resorts. Its chief town is Buncrana. The peninsula's best scenery is along the northern and western seaboards. In **Carndonagh** is the Donagh Cross, possibly the oldest cross standing in Ireland. **Malin Head** has 200ft cliffs, rising to 800ft high at **Glengad,** further east.

Jerpoint Abbey, Co Kilkenny

Map Ref: 125 S54

Just south-west of Thomastown, this handsome ruin in the Nore Valley was founded as a Cistercian abbey in 1158, and its oldest parts, the chancel and transepts of the church, are Irish Romanesque. The chancel still has its barrel vault and stone roof, but the east window is a 14th-century insertion. The square, central tower, whose stepped battlements are distinctively Irish, was built in the 15th century. The Ormonde (Butler) family was granted the lands of this foundation after the 1540 suppression. There are some outstanding monuments with carved effigies. The curious effigy of Bishop O'Dullany (died 1202) shows him holding a crozier being chewed by a serpent.

Ireland's most northerly point, Malin Head is guarded by 200ft-high cliffs

Kilkee on the Atlantic coast of Co Clare in the centre of magnificent cliff scenery

Kanturk, Co Cork

Map Ref: 124 R30

Kanturk stands at the confluence of six small roads, where the rivers Dallua and Allow, tributaries of the Blackwater, meet. Old Court Castle, just south of the town, is a daunting five-storey pile, begun by MacDonagh MacCarthy, Lord of Dunhallow, in 1609 and never completed. It came to be known as MacDonagh's Folly. He built it after the manner of an Anglo-Norman 'city-type' castle, with a quadrangle and a massive tower at each corner. Its obvious defensive qualities aroused government suspicion, and MacCarthy was ordered to stop work on it.

AA recommends:
Guesthouse: Assolas, *tel.* (029) 50015

Kenmare, Co Kerry

Map Ref: 124 V97

At the head of Kenmare Bay on N71 and at the south-east extremity of the Ring of Kerry road, Kenmare is an excellent base for exploring the Iveragh and Beara peninsulas. At the Shrubberies, site of an old abbey, is the Druid's Circle, 15 standing stones forming a circle with a 50ft diameter, around a dolmen of three uprights and a large capstone. The town was founded in 1670 by the English government who were ousted in 1688. **Dunkerran Castle,** two miles west, is 13th century. Kenmare has a tradition of convent lacemaking, and is a focal point of many fine walks and mountain climbs.

AA recommends:
Hotels: Park, 4-star (red), *tel.* (064) 41200
Kenmare Bay, 3-star, *tel.* (064) 41300
Guesthouse: Commercial, 14 Henry Street, *tel.* (064) 41453
Farmhouses: Bay View, Greenane, *tel.* (064) 41383
Ceann Mara, *tel.* (064) 41220
Templenoe House, Greenane, *tel.* (064) 41538
Garage: Randle Brothers, Sheibourne Road, *tel.* (064) 41355

Kildare, Co Kildare

Map Ref: 125 N71

In the heart of horse-breeding territory beside the Curragh plain (N7 Dublin to Cork and Limerick), Kildare retains a slightly old-world atmosphere in some of its streets and shops. Apart from equine activities, the Curragh plain to the east has been important as a military centre for over a century and there are extensive barracks. At its eastern end is Donnelly's Hollow, scene of a celebrated boxing match in 1815, when English champion George Cooper was beaten by Irish contender Dan Donnelly. Donnelly's footprints emerging from the hollow have been preserved by countless re-treadings. East of the Curragh Camp is the 18-hole Curragh golf course, and the Cill Dara club has a nine-hole course nearer the town.

Kildare's 105ft round-tower has ill-advised modern battlements at the top. Nearby St Brigid's Cathedral incorporates parts of a 13th-century church, and contains several antiquities.

AA recommends:
Garage: T & A Boyle, Cherryville, *tel.* (045) 21898

Kilkee, Co Clare

Map Ref: 124 Q86

This Atlantic resort stands on beautiful, crescent-shaped Moore Bay. It was one of the twin termini of the quaint narrow-gauge West Clare railway, lampooned by Percy French in the song *Are you right there, Michael?* Kilrush was the alternative terminus. The line opened in 1887 but protests failed to stop its closure in 1961.

A reef called the Duggerna Rocks protects the bay from the Atlantic's full force. This can be reached on foot, and there is an Amphitheatre further west, with tiers of rocks like seats, which is often used for outdoor concerts. The Doonlicka cliffs, further on, are a smaller version of the Cliffs of Moher. From Look-Out Hill the

A history of the racehorse is on display at the National Stud Horse Museum, Kildare

Twelve Bens, Aran Islands, Shannon and Kerry Mountains are visible on clear days.

The trip to Loop Head, apex of Clare, is by way of **Carrigaholt**, a Gaelic-speaking village, and **Moneen Church**, which contains the 'Little Ark', a portable structure used by priests for religious services in time of suppression.

Hotel: Halpins, Erin Street, 1-star, *tel.* Kilkee 32

Kilkenny, Co Kilkenny

Map Ref: 125 S55

The most charming of the smaller cities, Kilkenny still has rare Elizabethan domestic architecture and quaint by-ways, known as 'slips', of great antiquity.

The castle (1192–1207) was built by William Earl Marshall, son-in-law of Strongbow. Its styles are a blend of Gothic and Classical and the conical tops of the three drum-towers are reminiscent of French chateaux. One tower, and the castle's entire south range, are missing – victims of heavy 1650 Cromwellian bombardment – and the courtyard now opens onto 15 acres of parkland.

From the windows of the castle, which houses an art gallery, one looks down on Kilkenny College, alma mater of Swift and Congreve. James II founded a university in the college in 1690, but it was disestablished five months later after the Battle of the Boyne.

The Rothe House dates from 1594 and houses a museum. The Shee almshouse, with St Mary's

Potted palms and colourful flowers brighten an attractive Kilkenny street

Steps leading to the back, dates from 1582. St Mary's 13th-century church behind it contains heraldic shields of old Kilkenny families, including Archer and Shee, ancestors of George Archer-Shee, on whose court case Terence Rattigan based his play, *The Winslow Boy*. The town's courthouse occupies the site of a one-time Grace's Castle. The stronghold was surrendered in 1566 by James Grace, who then became constable of the gaol into which it was then converted.

Battlemented St Canice's Cathedral, with its round-tower, was begun in 1251; St Mary's Cathedral in 1843; St John's Priory, now in ruins, dates from 1250; the Black Abbey from 1225 and St Francis Abbey, part of which is incorporated as an oratory in the Smithwick's brewery named after it, from 1231. Kyteler's Inn, in St

Kieran's Street, was the home of Dame Alice Kyteler, convicted of sorcery early in the 14th century after allegedly poisoning four husbands. She escaped, but her maid Petronilla was burnt at the stake in High Street, opposite the Butter Slip.

Kilkenny has 18-hole golf, angling and racing (at Gowran Park eight miles out of the city). James Hoban, architect of Washington's White House, was born nearby.

AA recommends:
Hotels: Hotel Kilkenny, College Road, 3-star, *tel.* (056) 62000
Newpark, 3-star, *tel.* (056) 22122
Springhill Court, Waterford Road, 2-star, *tel.* (056) 21122
Restaurant and Guesthouse: Lacken House (restaurant 2-K & F), Carlow Road, *tel.* (056) 65611
Garages: Kilkenny Service Station, Carlow Road, *tel.* (056) 22528
W Tallis, 1 Johns Quay, *tel.* (056) 65384

Horse Racing

The open plain of the Curragh, Co Kildare, where horses being exercised are a familiar sight, is the epicentre of Ireland's love affair with the horse. This is the course where the Irish Sweeps Derby, St Leger and Guineas are run; also here are the Aga Khan's Ballymany and Sheshoon stud farms, Brownstown Stud and the stables of leading trainer Dermot Weld. The National Stud, with its lovely Japanese Gardens, is at Tully, two miles from Kildare town, and may be visited.

The Irish Grand National is run at Fairyhouse, near Ratoath, Co Meath. The flat season begins in March and ends in November. Steeplechasing is held all year round, and point-to-points take place in spring — those at Punchestown, near Naas, Co Kildare, are considered very fashionable. The Phoenix Park course, near Dublin City, which has summer evening meetings, also has a strong social cachet, and Galway race-week is a holiday highlight.

Sunday racing was introduced in the summer of 1985.

The breeding industry is more re-nowned for jumpers than flat-racers, Arkle being the most illustrious example. Last Suspect, winner of the 1985 Aintree Grand National, was Irish-bred, as are as many as one in three winners 'over the sticks' in England. Apart from Co Kildare, the leading stud farms are to be found in Co Meath and Tipperary; Coolmore, near Fethard, being noteworthy in the

latter. The racing stables of Vincent O'Brien, probably the country's best known trainer, are also in Co Tipperary, at Ballydoyle, near Cashel. Most breeding is now controlled by syndicates such as the Robert Sangster-Vincent O'Brien combine.

The Aga Khan Trophy international competition is the showjumping highlight of the August Royal Dublin Society Horse Show.

Fun and games at the Royal Dublin Society Horse Show

The scenery around Killarney epitomises Ireland's rugged beauty

The Waterfall, Killarney

Killala, Co Mayo

Map Ref: 122 G23

On an inlet of Killala Bay, a very early church was founded, possibly by St Patrick. The 84ft round tower has been repaired, having been struck by lightning. Under the churchyard is an extensive souterrain. Two miles away are the remains of the 1460 Moyne Abbey, with almost perfect cloisters and a graceful tower. Rosserk Abbey, two miles further on near the River Moy, dates from 1400. Here too the cloisters are well preserved. Killala's 1670 cathedral has a Gothic south door from a much earlier building. A French force led by Humbert landed here on 22 August 1798, to assist the Irish rebels.

Killaloe, Co Clare

Map Ref: 124 R67

At the southern end of Lough Derg on the Shannon, Killaloe is connected with the Co Tipperary village of Ballina by a 13-arch bridge. The Bernagh mountains rise to the north-west, Moylussa (1746ft) being their highest point. The large fort of *Beal Boru*, from which King Brian Boru took his title, is nearby, as once was Brian's palace of Kincora. The cathedral of 1182 was restored in 1887; a richly carved Romanesque doorway is its

best feature. The town also has two small oratories, one of which was removed from Friar's Island in the Shannon before that was submerged for the hydro-electric scheme. Boating and brown trout angling are the main leisure pursuits.

Killarney, Co Kerry

Map Ref: 124 V99

Best-known beauty spot in Ireland, favoured by Tennyson, Wordsworth and Thackeray, Killarney lies east of Ireland's highest mountain range, MacGillicuddy's Reeks, two of whose peaks, Purple Mountain (2739ft) and Tomies Mountain (2413ft), are between the lakes and the Gap of Dunloe. The three principal lakes are Lough Leane, 5000 acres with about 30 islands, Muckross Lake, 680 acres with four islands, and Upper Lake, 430 acres with four islands. Along the Gap are the smaller Black Lake and Auger Lake, with the Black Valley to the south-west. The basins of Lough Leane and Muckross Lake were formed by the action of water on soft limestone, that of Upper Lake by ice in the glacial age. Old red sandstone rises in smooth ribs from the water's edge, and the surrounding slopes are clothed in mountain ash, birch, arbutus, oak and holly.

The town itself is north-east of the principal lakes, and its best feature is St Mary's Cathedral (1842–55), by A W Pugin. Building was delayed by the Famine. From the boat slip of the Europe Hotel, on the Killorglin road, 30 peaks can be counted. This hotel has an Olympic-sized swimming pool, and Killarney has two 18-hole championship golf courses. It is also a noted angling centre.

Beside Lough Leane, whose islands include Innisfallen, is the 14th-century Ross Castle of the O'Donoghues, an inspiration for Tennyson's *The Princess*. Sidecar

trips go to Muckross House, beside the 1440 abbey ruin, where there is a good folk museum.

AA recommends:
Hotels: Great Southern, 4-star, *tel.* (064) 31262
Aghadoe Heights, 3-star, *tel.* (064) 31766
Cahernane, Muckross Road, 3-star (country house), *tel.* (064) 31895
Castlerosse, 3-star, *tel.* (604) 31144
Glen Eagle, 3-star, *tel.* (064) 31870
International, 3-star, *tel.* (064) 31816
Lake, Muckross Road, 3-star, *tel.* (064) 31035
Torc Great Southern, 3-star, *tel.* (064) 31611
Arbutus, 2-star, *tel.* (064) 31037
Grand, 2-star, *tel.* (064) 31159
Killarney Ryan, 2-star, *tel.* (064) 31555
Guesthouses: Aisling House, Countess Road, *tel.* (064) 31112
Kathleen's Country House, Tralee Road, *tel.* (064) 32810
Loch Lein, Fossa, *tel.* (064) 31260
T & C: Green Acres, Fossa, *tel.* (064) 31454
St Rita's Villa, Mill Road, *tel.* (064) 31517
Restaurant: Gaby's, 17 High Street, I-K & F, *tel.* (064) 32519
Garages: Coffey's, Coolbane, Ballyhar, *tel.* (066) 64217
Killarney Motor Works, New Road, *tel.* (064) 31087
Murphy's, Clohane Iron Mills, Cork Road, *tel.* Headford 6
Randles, Muckross Road, *tel.* (064) 31237
Campsites: Beech Grove Camping & Caravan Park, Fossa, 3-pennant, *tel.* (064) 31727
Fossa Caravan Park, 5-pennant, *tel.* (064) 31496
White Bridge Caravan Park, Ballycasheen, 4-pennant, *tel.* (064) 31590

Killorglin, Co Kerry

Map Ref: 124 V79

On the N70, Killorglin could be called the north-east 'terminus' of the Ring of Kerry. It is also on the salmon-noted Laune river. The cattle, sheep and horse fair known as 'Puck Fair' is held on 10 August ('Gathering Day'), 11 August

('Puck Fair Day') and 12 August ('Scattering Day'). A male goat with beribboned horns presides over the proceedings from a raised platform. Normal business closing times are suspended during this fair, which has become as much a social as a commercial event, drawing thousands to the little town. Ruined Castle Conway dates from about 1240. The Laune between here and Killarney offers marvellous mountain views.

Killybegs, Co Donegal

Map Ref: 122 G77

This busy little fishing port on an inlet of Donegal Bay has a good natural harbour and a reputation for hand-woven carpets. A wall of the Roman Catholic church contains a remarkable sculptured memorial slab of Niall Mor MacSweeney, one of the clan's chiefs, which was brought here from St John's Point, to the south, and is one of only two of this kind known in Ireland. The other lies in an old cemetery in **Creeslough,** Co Donegal, and also commemorates a MacSweeney chief.

This district has both river trout and sea fishing, and Fintragh Strand, two miles away, is a splendid, sandy, bathing beach.

Killyleagh, Co Down

Map Ref: 123 J55

Sir Hans Sloane, whose collection formed the nucleus of the British Museum, was born in Frederick Street in Killyleagh in 1666, and was educated by the Rowan Hamilton family in the great library of Killyleagh Castle. His achievements are commemorated on a stone before the castle gates. The castle itself, fringed by trees and on high ground with a view of Strangford Lough, has the romantic look of a fairy tale and its evolution from 1625 to 1850 has resulted in soaring turrets, stout battlements, a sturdy bawn wall and a pretty gatehouse.

AA recommends:
Garage: T M Martin & Son, 6–8 Cross Street, *tel.* Killyleagh 828203

Kilrush, Co Clare

Map Ref: 124 R05

The main town of south-west Clare, with its careful planning, comes as a surprise after Ennis. It was laid out by the Vandeleur family, whose nearby mansion was burned down in the early 1920s. The town has a harbour on the Channon estuary and there is a pier in the suburb of Cappa. Nine-hole golf, pleasant woodland walking and a large

caravan site at Ilevarroo, beyond Cappa, are among the attractions. A car ferry runs from nearby Killimer to Tarbert in Kerry.

Scattery Island, facing Cappa, has ruins of five churches and a 122ft round-tower, reputedly Ireland's tallest and oldest. St Senan, noted misogynist, had a 6th-century monastery here. His curse condemns any woman who walks on his grave to remain childless. As late as the 1930s women went to the island to walk on it.

AA recommends:
Hotel: Inis Cathaig, 2-star, *tel.* Kilrush 36
Garage: Kilrush Motor Co, *tel.* Kilrush 48
Campsite: Aylevarroo Caravan Park, 3-pennant, *tel.* Kilrush 102

Kinsale, Co Cork

Map Ref: 124 W65

Near the mouth of the Bandon River, this yachting and sea fishing centre saw one of Irish history's most decisive battles in 1601, which Hugh O'Neill and Red Hugh O'Donnell lost to Mountjoy (Charles Blount) and Carew, thus ending a Gaelic way of life. More recently, on May 7, 1915, a German U-boat sank the Cunarder *Lusitania*

off Kinsale's Old Head, nine miles from the town; the wreck lies 12 miles south, two points west and 320ft down.

James II lodged in Kinsale in 1689, having landed here on his way to the Battle of the Boyne. The house in Lower O'Connell Street is marked.

St Multose's Church, dating from 1190 but much modified, has an original Romanesque door, the town stocks and one of the only four examples of the Lion of Nassau, a William and Mary heraldic device. The French Prison is late 15th century, and was a Desmond residence before it became a jail. The slate-fronted courthouse and town hall, a William and Mary building which had a curvilinear Queen Anne top added to the façade in 1706, boasts a museum and the room in which inquests on *Lusitania* victims were held. The huge Charles Fort (1670–77) in the lovely nearby village of **Summercove,** has a romantic 'White Lady' ghost story.

AA recommends:
Hotel: Actons, 3-star, *tel:* (021) 772135
Restaurants: Man Friday, Scilly, 2-K & F, *tel.* (021) 772260
Vintage, Main Street, 1-K & F, *tel.* (021) 772502

The slopes of Compass Hill overlook the boat-laden Bandon River at Kinsale

Knappogue Castle, Co Clare

Map Ref: 124 R47

Near Quin village, Knappogue was
built in 1467 by John MacCon
MacNamara, whose father Sioda
MacConmara, had built Bunratty.
Like Bunratty, Knappogue is the
nightly venue of medieval
banquets in summer. Visitors are
welcome all year round. The castle
was in the MacNamara family until
1815, after which a west wing was
added killing its symmetry. But the
massive central tower is the most
dominant feature. Having been
used by the Army and the Land
Commissioners, Knappogue was
bought in 1966 by Mark Edwin
Andrews of Houston, a former US
Navy assistant secretary, who set
about turning it into a social and
cultural centre.

Kylemore Abbey, Co Galway

Map Ref: 122 L75

Access to the lovely Kylemore Pass
is via the Clifden to Leenane road.
The 1736ft Duoghruagh Mountain
is north of the three Kylemore lakes,
famed for angling, with the stately
Tudor Gothic abbey standing
between the high ground and the
water. Now a girls' boarding school
run by the Benedictine nuns of
Ypres, it began life not as an abbey
but as the brainchild of Mitchell
Henry, a Liverpudlian merchant,
who cleared many acres of scrub to

*The grandeur of Kylemore Abbey is
enhanced by the beauty of its
surroundings*

build it and lay out the beautiful
grounds. He also erected the
Gothic chapel which has
Connemara-marble interior pillars.
There is a restaurant and a souvenir
shop here.

Lagan Valley, Co Down and Co Antrim

Map Ref: 123 J26

In 1812 a visitor who walked from
Lisburn to Belfast wrote 'The
country was in the highest state of
cultivation – it looked like one
continued garden, shadowed with
trees, interspersed with thickets and
neat whitewashed houses.' This is
the Lagan Valley, the site of early
plantations which brought
clearance and improvements. The
area was further developed when
the Huguenots brought linen
damask weaving, to be followed by
the bleaching industry in the 18th
century. Later the Lagan
Navigation Canal aimed to make a
navigable waterway from Belfast to
Lough Neagh.
    The towpath for this canal makes
a good walk, which passes fine parks
and a beautiful little suspension
bridge at **Lambeg**. There are
glimpses of the grand houses which
the linen magnates built for
themselves, and remnants of canal
days – a canal mile-post, a lock or a
lock-keeper's house – can be seen
along the way.
    The section from Shaw's Bridge
is probably the most attractive, with
a fine stand of beech trees at
Minnowburn, rich meadowland
and a profusion of wild flowers in
early summer.

Lahinch, Co Clare

Map Ref: 124 R08

The name of this resort on
Liscannor Bay is almost a synonym

for golf with its 18-hole
championship course nicely
situated behind a long sandy beach.
Lahinch is four miles south-east of
the Cliffs of Moher. At O'Brien's
Bridge, where the R478 crosses the
northernmost tip of the bay between
Lahinch and Liscannor, are the
ruined nave and chancel of the
15th-century Kilmacreehy church,
and of Dough Castle.
    In **Liscannor** are the ruins of an
O'Connor (later O'Brien) castle,
and nearby in Castle Street is the
birthplace of John P Holland
(1841–1914), often called the
inventor of the submarine; these
craft, in fact, had existed before his
time, but he produced a design far
superior in rapid diving and
mobility to anything before it.
Holland was a Fenian, and his work
was financed in the USA by the
Fenian movement, for use against
Britain. However, after the US
Navy adopted the model in 1900,
Britain's Royal Navy built four
vessels, its first submarines, to his
design the following year.

AA recommends:
Hotel: Aberdeen Arms, 3-star,
tel. (065) 81100
Campsite: Lahinch Camping & Caravan
Park, 4-pennant, *tel.* (065) 81424

Larne, Co Antrim

Map Ref: 123 D40

The Scottish coast is often clearly
visible from Larne's Promenade
and from the Curran, a long
tapering gravel spit curving
southward from the town between
10 and 20ft above high water mark.
The scenic Antrim Coast Road
begins here. Olderfleet Castle is
13th century, unoccupied since
1614, and now a ruin; the Chaine
Memorial Tower, a 92ft modern
replica of a round tower,
commemorates James Chaine MP
who at his own request was buried
standing up in a niche in the cliffs.
Larne is the starting point for the
scenic Antrim Coast Road.

The wide sweep of Liscannor Bay fronts the popular holiday resort of Lahinch

A climber's paradise where mountains rise steeply around the lovely Killary Harbour at Leenane

Leenane, Co Galway

Map Ref: 122 L86

Leenane, a small angling and climbing resort in a lovely setting, stands where the Clifden to Westport road crosses Killary Harbour – a ten-mile arm of the sea between steep mountains, often referred to as Ireland's only fjord. In British times the Killary was often the haunt of warships, and Queen Victoria sailed up it. Mweelrea (2688ft) and Bengorm (2303ft) rise from the northern shore.

Gravel terraces, numerous minerals and glacial relicts will interest geologists, while the Joyce Country stretches to Loughs Mask and Corrib in the east and south-east. The impressive Aasleagh waterfall, near Leenane, is worth a pause.

Linen

Although linen of some sort has been made in Ireland since the Bronze Age, it was not until the arrival of Huguenot refugees at the end of the 17th century that the development of the linen industry began. They brought the distinctive damask cloth, a mix of warp-face and weft-face fabric, which was later elaborated with embroidery, crochet edging and hand-painting. Although the linen industry is chiefly associated with Armagh and the Lagan Valley, as a rural activity it was widespread throughout Ulster and Connaught. Flax was usually grown alongside the other crops. It was harvested by pulling it up by the roots, by workers in teams or 'boons', sheaved, then 'retted' or steeped in warm, stagnant water, creating a once familiar, un-pleasant, Ulster smell. The slimy beets were then grassed to dry, then broken, scutched, hackled, spun, woven and bleached. The women would 'flower', or sprig and em-broider the cloth in their own cottages.

Inevitably, mechanisation took over with the added process of 'beetling', or polishing, the cloth. Some of the mills were small, water-powered operations, handling one process and tying in with other mills in the neigh-bourhood, but large scale mills developed in the towns, and Belfast became the world's major linen-producing city.

Linen's very durability and high quality told against it in competition with man-made fibres, but although most flax is now imported, linen is still manufactured in Ireland, in large factories and through small-scale 'cottage' industries, using traditional and modern patterns. Its high quality still enjoys a world-wide reputation.

Manufacturing techniques may have changed over the centuries but the popularity of the end product remains constant

Letterkenny, Co Donegal

Map Ref: 123 C11

Where the N56 and N14 meet at the winding River Swilly, which empties into the Lough of the same name, Letterkenny, with one of Ireland's longest main streets, can be seen on the hillside for miles.

The modern St Eunan's

Cathedral is a rather free interpretation of neo-Gothic, with round-headed transept doorways and a profusion of Celtic carvings. The decorated ceilings are by Amici of Rome, and the church is mainly built of sandstone from Mount Charles, on Donegal Bay.
Killydonnell, to the north, has a ruined 16th-century Franciscan friary, whose bell is said to lie in the lough. Cowal cemetery, to the west, has many ancient tombstones, and an ancient stone fort, Conwal Dun. Letterkenny is a salmon angling centre.
Glenveagh National Park to the north-west is well worth a visit with its castle, lough, gardens, walks and other attractions.

AA recommends:
Hotel: Gallagher's, 2-star, *tel.* (074) 22066
Garages: P Doherty & Sons, Pluck, *tel.* (074) 57116
Hegarty's Auto Services, Ballymacool, *tel.* (074) 21282

Limerick's Sarsfield Bridge was styled on the Pont de Neuilly, Paris

Limerick, Co Limerick

Map Ref: 124 R55

The Republic's third city is built where the Shannon enters its estuary. Limerick's older and major part, on the river's left bank, is the sum of three former towns, Englishtown (the oldest), Irishtown and Newtown Pery. These names are not nowadays used, though fragments of the separate wallings of Englishtown and Irishtown remain. Englishtown, on an island bounded by the Shannon and its looping tributary, the Abbey, is still sometimes called 'the Island', and was settled by the Vikings in 831. When they were evicted by Brian Boru, it passed to the O'Briens, and later to the Anglo-Normans. This area contains St Mary's Cathedral and King John's Castle, while Irishtown, beside Garryowenen, is dominated by the lofty spire of St John's Cathedral. Newtown Pery is easily identified by its Georgian terraces, and is named after the developer, Edward Sexton Pery.

The library, art gallery and museum are to be found in the People's Park. Of particular interest in the museum is the well-known 'nail' or pedestal which once stood in the exchange. The city's merchants used to discharge their debts on this. A monument in the park honours the liberal Protestant

An elegant Georgian façade in a Limerick city street. Below: Although much altered since 1210, King John's Castle is still an impressive pile, with five drum towers, a 200ft-long river frontage and walls 10ft thick

landlord Thomas Spring-Rice, Lord Monteagle of Brandon, who devoted himself to justice for Catholics.

St Mary's Cathedral, begun in 1168 or 1180, is a mixture of styles, with a squat, battlemented west tower and a fine four-order Romanesque doorway. The house, where Cromwell's General Ireton died of plague, stood in the churchyard but has been demolished. Nearby a school is named after Gerald Griffin, whose novel *The Collegians* was the basis of the play *The Colleen Bawn* and the opera *The Lily of Killarney* – based on the murder of Garryown girl, Ellen Hanly, in 1820.

King John's Castle, from 1210, is still awesome with great drum-towers, but council houses have been built in its courtyard. The neo-Gothic St John's Cathedral, from 1854, has a 280ft spire, one of Ireland's tallest. Near it is an exquisite, stone Georgian square of the same name, and in the grounds of the similarly-named hospital a gatehouse of the Irishtown walls survives.

Limerick is famed for lace, also for the doggerel form, 'the limerick', devised in a pub in Limerick Street. The pub no longer exists. There is a racecourse, two 18-hole golf courses nearby and good salmon and trout fishing at **Castleconnell**.

AA recommends:
Hotels: Jury's, Ennis Road, 3-star, *tel.* (061) 55266
Limerick Inn, Ennis Road, 3-star, *tel.* (061) 51544
Limerick Ryan, Ennis Road, 3-star, *tel.* (061) 53922
New Green Hills, Caherdavin, 3-star, *tel.* (061) 53033
Two Mile Motor Inn, Ennis Road, 3-star, *tel.* (061) 53122
Royal George, O'Connell Street, 2-star, *tel.* (061) 44566
Restaurant: Merryman, Glentworth Street, 2-K & F, *tel.* (061) 43466
Garages: Elm Motors, Coonagh Cross, Ennis Road, *tel.* (061) 51577
Gleeson Bros, Ellen Road, *tel.* (061) 45567
Frank Hogan, Dublin Road, *tel.* (061) 46000
Pat Keogh, Castle Street, *tel.* (061) 43133

Lisdoonvarna, Co Clare

Map Ref: 124 R19

This inland resort on N67 is the country's premier spa, with several mineral springs; it once boasted that its sulphur water contained more than three times as much hydrogen sulphide gas as that at Harrogate. Gowlane spring is the most popular, with sulphur and lithium, and recommended for rheumatism; at the Twin Wells sulphur and iron-rich water issue from the rock within a few inches of each other,

and the Rathbaun spring supplies iron and 'magnesia' (manganese) water.

This is the area of the Burren (see page 48). The resort is noted for its conviviality in summer and 'match-making' festivals have taken place. Bathing is at the sandy cove of **Doolin**, a fishing village five miles away with a reputation for traditional music. **Milltown Malbay**, south of Liscannor Bay, has a nine-hole golf course and is adjacent to two good strands. The curious Spectacle Bridge on the River Aille, with an open circle over its arch, is near Lisdoonvarna.

AA recommends:
Hotels: Imperial, 2-star, *tel.* (065) 74015
Keane's, 2-star, *tel.* (065) 74011
Lynch's, 2-star, *tel.* (065) 74010
Spa View, 2-star, *tel.* (065) 74026
Guesthouse: Ballinalacken Castle, *tel.* (065) 74025

Lismore, Co Waterford

Map Ref: 125 X09

Sitting on the River Blackwater, this village once contained 20 churches. St Carthach founded a monastery here in the 7th century, and within 100 years it was famed throughout

Lisdoonvarna Spa has all modern comforts as well as age-old mineral springs

Europe as a university. It suffered the usual assaults and burnings from Vikings, and was finally ravaged by Raymond le Gros in 1173. St Carthach's Cathedral incorporates the fabric of one of the old churches, but this was rebuilt by the Earl of Cork in 1633.

Lismore Castle, Irish seat of the Dukes of Devonshire, stands in a commanding position on a sheer cliff overhanging the river, and is renowned for the magnolias in its gardens. It was built by King John in 1185, supposedly on the site of St Carthach's monastery, and was an episcopal residence before passing to Sir Walter Raleigh, who sold it to Richard Boyle, 'Great' Earl of Cork, in 1602. Robert Boyle, the chemist who gave us Boyle's Law, was born here. In 1753 it passed to the Devonshires, one of whom rebuilt it from a ruin in 1812.

AA recommends:
Hotel: Ballyrafter House, 2-star (country house), *tel.* (058) 54002

Magnolia blossom in full bloom outside Lismore Castle

Londonderry's fine 19th-century Guildhall is today the venue for plays, festivals and concerts

Londonderry,
Co Londonderry

Map Ref: 123 C41

Londonderry enjoys one of the most beautiful situations in Ireland, rising evenly on both sides of the River Foyle. Its name, popularly known as Derry, comes from the Irish 'doire' which means 'a place of oaks'. These grew on the mound which overlooked the marshy land known as the Bogside, with views to the Sperrins and the Donegal hills. It was here that St Columba chose to found his first abbey in 546 and his great love for the place is reflected in a translation of his verse:

The Guildhall's beautiful stained-glass panels depict the city's history

'If all Alba were any land,
Ben and glen and golden strand
Gladly would I give it but
To build in Derry's glades a hut.'

   This idyllic setting was vulnerable to raids by sea and there began a succession of attacks on the city which recurred for a thousand years, ending with a famous 105-day siege in 1689 when James II surrounded the city and placed a boom across the river. The siege was raised when the ship the

---

Castles

An engraving of Blarney Castle, Cork

Early Norman 'castles' were usually a motte-and-bailey fort, the timber building surmounting a circular earthen mound whose base was surrounded by a moat; the bailey was an adjoining cattle pen. Prehistoric burial mounds sometimes provided ready-made sites, as at the Millmount in Drogheda, having been used in the interim as Viking ceremonial meeting places.

   The Norman colonists soon gave up this tradition, replacing the flimsy fort with a stone castle when their rule of an area was sufficiently established. Their peak building years were between 1190 and 1215, and their finest castles were of the city type, as in Dublin, Limerick and Kilkenny. These consisted of four ranges of buildings surrounding a courtyard, without a central tower but with a massive circular one at each corner. The idea was that even if the walled city outside had fallen, this central area could be defended.

   A smaller castle, similar in basic appearance, but actually simply a fortified house with corner towers, was also built, such as at Enniscorthy, Co Wexford, and Malahide, Co Dublin. The more conventional idea of a castle, a great, high-towered building on rising ground, with a stout gated wall around its lands, was built in more open areas, such as at Trim, Co Meath.

   A boom in castle-building took place in the mid-15th century among influential native-Irish families, such as the MacCarthys (Blarney, Co Cork), Mac-Conmaras (Bunratty, Co Clare) and MacNamaras (Knappogue, Co Clare). Thick walls were still essential; guns designed to destroy masonry had been in use since 1326. Knappogue Castle and Bunratty Castle have been restored and are venues of mediaeval banquets. The smaller Enniscorthy Castle in Co Wexford houses a museum. Tullynally Castle, Castlepollard, Co Westmeath, is really a decorated mansion.

   By the end of the 17th century the notion of a castle as a stately home rather than a fortress was coming into vogue. Some purely residential mansions were, in the early 19th century, given crenellations and reborn as 'castles'.

Mountjoy broke the boom, and Derry remained inviolate, thus earning the title, 'the Maiden City'.

These impregnable walls begun in 1613 still remain Derry's most notable feature, and are the most complete city walls in Britain. Bastions and gatehouses are built into the walls, including the Coward's Bastion, 'Being most out of danger, cowards restored here – 1689' and Church Bastion, where the 18-pounder gun 'Roaring Meg' was placed.

In 1613, James II granted a charter by which the city became the responsibility of the City of London, which then gave the prefix to Derry. The streets within the walls were laid out in a formal grid with four streets leading to a square, the Diamond, and this pattern still forms the heart of the city.

St Columb's Cathedral was built in 1633 in a style described as 'planter's gothic'. Stained-glass recalls the popular hymn writer, Mrs Cecil Frances Alexander, who wrote *There is a green hill far away* and *Once in Royal David's City*. An inscription in the porch reads:
If stones could speake then
London's prayse should sounde
Who built this church and city from
the grounde.
The chapter-house of the Cathedral contains relics of the city's history.

St Eugene's Cathedral is the work of the major figure in Irish Gothic church design, J J McCarthy, and has a spire soaring to 256ft. The Guildhall in Shipquay Place recalls the influence of London and has been rebuilt five times. The courthouse is an early 19th-century building, mostly of Dungiven sandstone, and there are interesting town houses, including that of the Irish Society, good factories, warehouses and banks in and around the centre of the city.

On the road to Belfast is the prominent modern building of Altnagelvin Hospital, which has *Princess Macha*, a fine example of the work of sculptor, F E McWilliam. According to legend, Princess Macha was foundress of the first Irish hospital.

North-east of the city at the mouth of the Foyle river is Culmore Fort, which was built first in 1610 as a triangular artillery fort.

Lough Foyle is a very good area for birdwatching and there are good view points at rising tides (RSPB).

AA recommends:
Hotel: Everglades, Prehen Road, 4-star, *tel.* Londonderry 46722
Garages: Desmond Motors, 173 Strand Road, Pennyburne, *tel.* Londonderry 267613
Eakin Bros, Maydown Road, *tel.* Londonderry 860601
A McGeady & Sons, 43 Barry Street, *tel.* Londonderry 261255
Tullyally Car Breakers, Tullyally Road, Ardmore, *tel.* Londonderry 49395

Game fishing is a popular sport on Lough Corrib

Longford, Co Longford

Map Ref: 122 N17

Set in flattish country on the Camlin a Shannon tributary Longford was once called Longford O'Farrell, and its county called Teffia, Annaly. The O'Farrell family built a castle and Dominican friary here, probably in 1400. The castle stood at the bridge between Main and Bridge Streets and its last remnant was not removed until recent years. The Pakenhams of Tullynally Castle in Co Westmeath (see Fore) lived in it until 1816, abandoning it because of a family suicide.

St John's Church (Anglican), with its delightful octagonal spire, stands more or less on the site of the friary.

Longford was a terminal of a branch of the Royal Canal, founded in 1789 and called the 'Shoemaker's Canal'. Its founder, Long John Binns, had quit his directorship of the Grand Canal Company because he said he had been insulted for being a shoemaker, and founded a rival company; it was doomed from the start because of near duplication of routes. Longford's harbour has been filled in.

St Mel's Classical limestone cathedral dates from 1856, and is by J B Keane. **Ballymahon,** southward was Oliver Goldsmith's last Irish home before his departure in 1752. He was born in nearby Pallas in 1728.

AA recommends:
Garage: Longford Auto Service, Little Water Street, *tel.* (043) 41046

Lough Corrib and Lough Mask, Co Galway and Co Mayo

Map Ref: 122 M14 and M16

An underground river and a canal link these loughs, which are both noted for fishing and for their scenery; the Partry and Maumturk Mountains and the Joyce Country lie to the west. The system stretches south from Ballintober to Galway city, if we include the short Corrib River. Lough Corrib has many islands in its 68 square miles, including Inchiquin and Inchagoill; on the latter are the remains of the ancient Teampall na Naomh and the tiny Templepatrick. On Inishmaan in Lough Mask are the ruins of a church built by St Cormac in the 6th century and enlarged in the 1100s.

Joyce Country and the Maumturk Mountains stretch westward beyond Lough Mask

Lough Erne, Co Fermanagh

Map Ref: 123 H15 and H33

Fifty miles of navigable water sprinkled with 154 islands makes up Lower and Upper Lough Erne, an area of religious settlements, castles and nature reserves among lakes teeming with fish.

Although there are plenty of car parks, viewpoints and a few loughside roads, the best way to see Lough Erne is by boat. Cruiser hire, daily boat hire, a passenger pleasure-boat and ferry services are available.

Fermanagh has been described as a fisherman's paradise. The Department of Agriculture owns the lakes and there is no close season. Roach, bream, pike, gudgeon, eels and some rudd are said to be queuing up to be caught while salmon are found mostly in the rivers. Lough Melvin is noted among anglers for its three varieties of trout – the gillaroo, the sonaghan and the ferox.

Of the islands, several have special ecclesiastical interest. At Devenish are the remains of a monastery founded by St Molaise in 564 or 571 and including one of Ireland's finest round-towers, 81ft high and remarkable for an intricately-carved cornice of faces

with beards and moustaches intertwining. The tower dates from the 10th to 12th century. On White Island are eight uncanny stone-carved figures which were found at various times between 1840 and 1958, seemingly deliberately hidden or buried; some are definitely Christian in appearance while others, among them the grotesque female fertility figure, Sheila na gig, appear pagan. At Boa Island are two very pagan double-sided idols.

One of the best castles, a well-preserved 17th-century edifice, with barrel-towers, corbelling and musket loops, is set back a little from the Lough at **Monea**. Closer to the water is Castle Caldwell with castle

Eight mysterious stone-carvings were discovered on White Island amid the moody waters of Lough Erne

ruins and chapel, wildfowl hides (RSPB), nature reserve and sandy beach, while at Castle Archdale and Country Park there are caravan and camping sites, boating and fishing as well as nature trails. The lower lake has the biggest breeding colony of black scoters in the British Isles and is rich with coot, moorhen and many varieties of grebe. The corncrake can often be heard.

Lough Gur, Co Limerick

Map Ref: 124 R64

The Lough, a small crescent lake near Sixmilebridge (or Grange), is the centre of a very important prehistoric site.

There are two fine stone circles, an Early Bronze Age tomb, two stone forts of the Viking period, an early Christian earthen ring fort, two crannogs and Bourchier's Castle, a well-preserved 15th-century building.

The area is known for the variety of its bird life, and caves above the lake have yielded remains of species now extinct in Ireland, including reindeer, bear and giant Irish deer.

Lough Neagh

Map Ref: 123 J07

Lough Neagh, the largest inland lake in the British Isles, with an area of 153 square miles, borders five counties. There are marinas at Ballyronan, Maghery, Sixmilewater and Oxford Island. An old Belfast rhyme used to go:
'Lough Neagh hones, Lough Neagh hones
You put 'em in sticks and you take 'em out stones'
because of the petrified wood, which looks like pumice stone, found on the shore.

At the north-west corner is the Toome Eel fishery, where the tiny eels are caught which faithfully make the journey across the Atlantic from the Sargasso Sea each year. Baskets, made in the traditional way from sally rods, are still available near Aghagallon.

At **Arboe**, on a rocky height, is one of the finest northern High Crosses which marks the site of a monastery. Lough Neagh is an extremely important area for duck.

Loughrea, Co Galway

Map Ref: 124 M61

Loughrea was the site of a 1300 de Burgh Castle on the once wild northern shore of the little Lough Rea, which gives this market town its name. The same family endowed a Carmelite priory, some remains of which survive at the centre of the town. The town's south-eastern

The shores of Lough Gur have yielded some major archeological finds

gate-tower, which became a museum, is the only surviving fragment of the ancient walls; it stands beside the entrance to the cathedral, which was completed in 1903 and has stained-glass by leading artist Evie Hone.

Souterrains are a feature of the district and many crannogs (lake dwellings, in this case stockaded) exist on the lough. At Monument Hill, to the east, are a crowning dolmen and stone circle. The noted Turoe Stone is at nearby **Ballaun**, with fine La Tene sculpturing; the stone is regarded by experts as pre-Christian. The Ferwore ring fort and Mason Brook stone circle are close at hand. Excavation of the ring fort in 1938 showed evidence of habitation from about 100 BC to AD 100. The Turoe Stone formerly stood beside it.

Macroom, Co Cork

Map Ref: 124 W37

Macroom stands on the edge of a Gaeltacht, without actually being part of it, and Gaelic is often heard spoken here. The town and its huge square castle were once owned by Admiral Sir William Penn, whose son, William, founded the State of Pennyslvania on land granted to him in discharge of Charles II's

debt to his father, as a refuge for oppressed Quakers. The admiral may have been born in the castle, which dates from King John's reign and was burnt out four times in the 17th century.

The town is picturesquely situated in the valley of the River Sullane, a Lee tributary. The N22 (T29) on its way west to Killarney, beyond the Derry Assagart Mountains, passes through the Gaelic-speaking area which includes Ballyvourney, Coolea and Ballingeary. This is the homeland of composer Sean O'Riada and of Father Peadar O Laoghaire (Peter O' Leary 1839–1920), one of the most devoted advocates of a Gaelic revival. He was born at Liscarrigane. Near Ballingeary a clapper-bridge of stone slabs spans the Lee.

Carrigaphouca Castle, left of the Killarney road three miles from Macroom, is an old MacCarthy fortress on a high, 'whaleback' ridge of rock, with a ruined dolmen near it. A *pucà* or mischievous sprite was said to haunt the rock, hence its name.

AA recommends:
Hotels: Castle, 2-star, tel. (026) 41074
Victoria, 1-star, tel. (026) 41082
Garage: Kellehers, Main Street, tel. (026) 41029

Net mending is an important part of the Lough Neagh fisherman's work

This picturesque half-timbered clockhouse can be seen in Mallow town centre

Mallow, Co Cork

Map Ref: 124 W59

This prosperous town, in rich agricultural land on the north bank of the Blackwater where N20 crosses N72, is a former spa, once known as 'the Bath of Ireland'. The uninhibited behaviour of some of its visitors in those days inspired a popular song, *The Rakes of Mallow*. The town is nowadays best-known for angling and for its racecourse, also as a rail junction and sugar beet processing centre.

Mrs Henry Wood of *East Lynne* fame lived here, as did Anthony Trollope, and Sir Walter Scott visited the spa. Patriot and poet Thomas Davis, who founded the Young Ireland movement, William O'Brien MP and author Canon Sheehan were born in the town. The Elizabethan Clock House and the spa well are among the earliest survivals, and there are some good 18th-century houses.

Ruined Kilcoman Castle, home of Edmund Spenser for eight years, and where he wrote three books of *The Faerie Queen*, is reached by way of Old Twopothouse Crossroads and Doneraile. At nearby **Buttevant** on the Awbeg (the Mole in *The Faerie Queen*) are a ruined 13th-century Franciscan friary and modernised Buttevant Castle, a

one-time seat of the Barrys, whose warcry, 'Routes-en-avant' (press forward) gave the town its name. **Rathluirc** (Charleville), further north is a modern town; celebrated Gaelic poet Sean Clarach MacDomhnaill (1691–1754) is buried in the churchyard; at **Liscarroll**, to the south-west, is a massive 1280 castle ruin.

AA recommends:
Guesthouse & Restaurant: Longueville House, 2-K & F, *tel.* (022) 27156
Garage: Blackwater Motors, Ballydaheen, *tel.* (022) 21436

Manorhamilton, Co Leitrim

Map Ref: 122 G83

Sir Frederick Hamilton's ruined 1638 mansion still recalls the origins of this town, built at the meeting of four mountain valleys and surrounded by the region's striking limestone ranges. Steep hillsides, fertile valleys and narrow ravines contribute to beautiful scenery. The drive north-west to Kinlough (T54) is a delight, going up the Bonet valley, through a deep glen past Glenade Lough and passing, on the left, Truskmore (2113ft) and Cloghcorrach (2007ft), with ground rising to over 1700ft on the right. **Kinlough** is an attractive village on the north shore of Lough Melvin.

Marble Arch, Co Fermanagh

Map Ref: 123 H13

Under the beautiful, brooding mountain of Cuilcagh is the Marble Arch Cave, the largest and best-known of the system of limestone caves in Fermanagh. Streams which have flowed down the mountain disappear under ground when they reach the soluble limestone and combine at Marble Arch to resurface and run down the fine Marble Arch Glen. The 'Arch' itself is a high, underground bridge, with lakes, stalactites and stalagmites, and is now open as a show cave.

Nearby is Florence Court (NT) an exuberant piece of Georgian architecture with unorthodox, rusticated, external detail and fluent rococo plasterwork within. The home of the Earls of Enniskillen it is now set in fine parkland within a Forest Park. Not far away grows the Florence Court yew which is the mother of all Irish yews. It is one of a pair found on Cuilcagh mountain in about 1767 by George Willis, a tenant on the estate, and can be propagated only by cuttings.

The Forest Park provides some challenging and remote walks in the foothills of Cuilcagh Mountain.

Visitors can take a guided tour of the Marble Arch Cave

Mellifont Abbey – the first and greatest Cistercian house in Ireland

Mellifont Abbey, Co Louth

Map Ref: 123 O07

South-east of **Collon** village, with its picturesque former courthouse, these ruins are best reached by N51 from Drogheda. Their provenance is more interesting than their physical remains, though the foundation has not entirely disappeared. This was Ireland's first Cistercian abbey, built in 1142 by St Malachy O'Morgair, archbishop of Armagh and a former monk; he was so impressed by St Bernard's establishment at Clairvaux that he selected this site on the Mattock River because he found the surroundings similar.

The square gate-house still stands to a height of about 50ft, but the ruins of the abbey church are slight and not improved by concrete markers. Four sides of a once-octagonal lavabo remain, and this and the chapter-house, with a beautiful groined roof, are the best-preserved of the relicts. Queen Dervorgilla (see **Dromahair**) died here late in the 12th century. A gold ring believed to belong to her was excavated in Mellifont, sold by a workman for drink money and never recovered. New Mellifont (formerly Oriel Temple) in Collon, is a modern Cistercian establishment.

Midleton, Co Cork

Map Ref: 125 W81

Close to Cork Harbour on N25, Midleton is an area of limestone caves, underground streams and dripstone formations. The Owenacurra River valley to the north is a pretty, sylvan gorge. John Philpot Curran, 18th-century

orator and statesman, was educated at Midleton School. Sir Walter Raleigh was unsuccessfully ambushed at **Ballinacorra**, a mile south of the town.

Midleton's distillery, now the manufacturing headquarters of Irish Distillers Group, with almost all the Republic's distilling being done there, has become far more famous than the town's late 12th-century abbey. It was begun in 1826 by James, Daniel and Jeremiah Murphy. In 1854 two Murphys left the firm to become brewers in Cork.

Midleton had the world's biggest pot still, of 31,648 gallons capacity, which was used until 1975. One of its famous products, Paddy whisky (until recently, unusually in Ireland, spelt without an 'e'), took its name from Patrick J. O'Flaherty, a resourceful 1920s sales representative of the company.

AA recommends:
Farmhouse: Wilton House, Loughaderra, *tel.* (021) 667327
Restaurant: Searsons, 55 Main Street, I-K & F, *tel.* (021) 631559
Garage: Lee, Broderick Street, *tel.* (021) 631306

Mitchelstown, Co Cork

Map Ref: 124 R81

Famed for its cheese, this dairyland town is in a high valley south of the Galtee Mountains, on the Dublin to Cork road (N8, T6), while R665 leads to **Ballyporeen** and Ronald Reagan's ancestral home. The limestone Mitchelstown Caves, actually in Co Tipperary at **Coolagarranroe**, ten miles from Mitchelstown and three miles north of Ballypooreen, include the biggest chamber in the British Isles, 390ft long land 40ft high.

The Old (or Desmond) Caves are harder to reach. The 'Sugan' Earl of Desmond hid here in 1601 with a £1000 price on his head, and was betrayed by his relative Edmund Fitzgibbon, last White Knight of Kilomallock. The New Caves, discovered in 1833 by a quarryman, have such names as House of Commons, Lords, Organ, Drum, Pyramid, Closets, Lot's Wife, Victoria. The 240ft straight Kingston Gallery has coloured walls; pillars are formed by stalactities meeting stalagmites, and porrhomma myops, a rare spider, frequents the place. Part of the 170ft descent is vertical, requiring a ladder, and a guide's services are essential.

AA recommends:
Garage: Murphy's, Church Street, *tel.* (025) 24611

Moher Cliffs, Co Clare

Map Ref: 124 R09

Three miles west of **Liscannor** (R478), the cliffs extend for about five miles, and form one of the grandest coastal stretches in the British Isles. At O'Brien's Tower at the northern end they reach their maximum height of 668ft. Exceptional views of the Atlantic shore can be had from here, and from Hag's Head (400ft) at the southern end. The circular tower, erected in 1835 by Cornelius O'Brien, was an obvious look-out point until its spiral staircase was destroyed; below it a huge ridge called Goat Island runs seaward. The cliffs are dark sandstone, topped by black shale, with a stratified layer between containing unusual fossils. Offshore from the tower is a 200ft stack.

An exhibit from the extensive collection of the award-winning Monaghan county museum

Monaghan, Co Monaghan

Map Ref: 123 H63

Monaghan retains little of antiquity, but has a lot of fine, more recent architecture, much of it Victorian. Traces of a 1462 friary exist below ground in the Diamond, from which an ancient High Cross – looking more like a box spanner – on a bluestone plinth was moved to the town's edge to make way for the Rossmore Memorial, a highly ornate, canopied Victorian drinking fountain commemorating a Baron Rossmore who died in 1874. Equally unfortunate was the erection against the memorial of a steel anchor pole, with 41 guys.

The county museum in the 1829 Classical courthouse won an EEC museum award in 1980. The needle-spired, late English Gothic St Patrick's Church dates from 1836. St Macartan's Cathedral in French-revival Gothic, atop a series of terraces, is a splendid limestone building with a rich interior. It is by JJ McCarthy ('the Irish Pugin') and was completed in 1882. The small, Classical, granite market-house dates from 1792.

The St Louis convent girls' school grounds contain a crannog lake-dwelling. A myth exists that Dawson Street, running from the grounds to a spot near St Peter's Lake – the town pond – will one day split open and unite the lakes, causing an earthquake which will wreck the town.

Rossmore Castle forest park includes a golf course. The Fiddler of Oriel festival of Irish music and dance is held in the park each July.

AA recommends:
Hotel: Hillgrove, 3-star, *tel.* (047) 81288
Garage: Mullins, North Road, *tel.* (047) 81396

Mourne Mountains

The *Mountains of Mourne* really do sweep down to the sea in just the way Percy French's famous song describes, because the highest of the peaks, Slieve Donard, 2796ft, is only a mile-and-a-half from the coast. Ten of the peaks are above 2000ft and they lie in a compact ring, their peaks making a handsome profile. Most are smooth and regular but Slieve Binnian, Slieve Bernagh and Doan are topped with great granite crags. The Mournes are still 'young' mountains so their steep sides, deep valleys and occasional cliffs are not yet worn away, and they have great appeal for the walker. Only one road crosses the Mournes, by Spelga Dam, so there are plenty of remote areas.

The Mourne Wall, a ribbon of dry-stone wall about 6ft high, built 1910–22, goes up mountains and down mountains, encircling 10,000 acres and marking Belfast's water catchment area. Sheep graze the thin peaty soils which cover the mountain leaving heather and coarse grass which provide good nesting habitat for meadow pipit, skylark and red grouse while ravens, kestrel and sparrowhawk keep to the high lands. The foothills of the Mournes have small whitewashed cottages which look as if they are built into the landscape, and fields of an infinite variety of shades and shape bounded by dry-stone walls with granite or round-topped gateposts. This can be a place of contrasts as Ulster poet W R Rodgers wrote:

'Of the Mournes I remember
  most the mist,
The grey granite goose flesh,
  the minute
And blazing parachutes of
  fuchsia . . .'

There are several good access points and car parks and walks: from Donard Park (Newcastle), by the Glen River, woodland, the Saddle and Slieve Donard; from Bloody Bridge (south of Newcastle) up Bloody River and the Brandy Pad (an old smuggler's route; from Carrick Little near Annalong) to Blue Lough and Ben Crom valley; and from Trassey Road near Bryansford to Hare's Gap. The Mourne Countryside Centre (DOE) in Newcastle has good, walk leaflets and gives advice on codes of mountain safety and countryside practice.

The great bulk of Slieve Donard (2796ft) fills the skyline behind the popular seaside resort of Newcastle

Monasterboice, Co Louth

Map Ref: 127 O08

The ruins of the 5th-century monastery of St Buithe (Boice) here are noted for the excellence of the High Crosses. The site is a small, enclosed churchyard a mile left of the Drogheda to Dundalk road nine miles from Drogheda, near Timullen on a wooded by-way. There are two churches, a 9th-century round-tower, three of these sculptured crosses, a sundial and two early grave slabs.

The incomplete round tower, which must have been exceptionally tall, has had a modern flight of external steps and series of interior floors added. The church ruins are also incomplete; the older church is 9th century.

The Muireadach Cross (17ft 8in) and the West (or Tall) Cross (21ft 6in) have sculptures on every surface, including scenes of Christ Crucified and the Last Judgment; the North Cross's head is now supported on a modern stem, the original shaft, lying broken nearby.

Mostrim (Edgeworthstown), Co Longford

Map Ref: 123 N27

A tidy town on the Dublin to Sligo N4, Mostrim's best-known association is with the Edgeworths who settled here in 1583, and became noted for their interest in social affairs. Richard Lovell Edgeworth was an eccentric inventor who designed an early central-heating system for Tullynally Castle (see **Fore**). His daughter Maria (1767–1849) is best-known for her novel *Castle Rackrent*; Sir Walter Scott and Ivan Turgenev acknowledged her as an inspiration. Scott visited Edgesworthstown in 1824 and William Wordsworth did so in 1829. Richard and Maria are buried in St John's churchyard. Edgeworthstown House, their residence at the eastern end of the town, became a nursing home.

Oliver Goldsmith attended a classical seminary in Edgeworthstown. South-west of the town is wooded **Ardagh** village, and the convent school beside it is the house Goldsmith mistook for an inn in 1744, thus inspiring the comedy *She Stoops to Conquer*.

Mullingar, Co Westmeath

Map Ref: 123 N45

The Royal or 'Shoemaker's' Canal (see **Longford**) almost encircles this town on the N4 from Dublin to Sligo, and the railway line from here to Dublin is adjacent to the canal; in

St Buithe Monastery, Monasterboice, has magnificent High Crosses

1844 the Midland Great Western Railway bought the struggling canal company for £289,000, so that it could lay its tracks on the fringe land instead of having to negotiate with individual farmers. Mullingar is the centre of a cattle-rearing district. Its most striking architectural landmark is the 1939 Classical cathedral of Christ the King, designed by Ralph Byrne, with twin 140ft towers and some good sculpture.

Mullingar's 18-hole golf course is at **Belvedere** on Lough Ennell, and this and other lakes in the vicinity hold brown trout. **Delvin,** to the north-east was the scene in the 1920s of the public burning of *The Valley of the Squinting Windows*, an incisive novel by Brinsley MacNamara, who was born nearby in **Ballinvalley**; Delvin was believed to be the setting for the novel.

AA recommends:
Hotel: Bloomfield House, 3-star, *tel.* (044) 40894
Garages: Mullinger Autos, Dublin Bridge, *tel.* (044) 41241
Westmeath Motors, Dublin Road, *tel.* (044) 48806
Campsite: Lough Ennel Caravan Park, 3-pennant, *tel.* (044) 48101

Mulrany, Co Mayo

Map Ref: 122 L89

Also known by the older name of Mallaranney, this resort stands where the N59 from Newport turns north towards Ballycroy, ancestral home of late Princess Grace (Kelly) of Monaco. It is on an isthmus connection with the 'mainland' with the Curraun Peninsula, leading to Achill island. Mulrany stands between broad Clew Bay and little hook-shaped Bellacragher Bay. It has an exceptionally mild climate, and rhododendrons, tender fuchsia and Mediterranean Heather (*erica Mediterrania*) flourish. Prehistoric finds have been made in the 'kitchen middens', or ancient refuse dumps, in the sand dunes.

For bathing, fishing and boating in a lovely environment the place is ideal. Claggan Mountain (1256ft) is a little to the north beside Bellacragher Bay. Mulrany has views of island-peppered Clew Bay.

AA recommends:
Guesthouse: Avondale House, *tel.* (098) 36105

The twin-towered Cathedral of Christ the King, Mullinger

The field clear a hurdle safely at Punchestown racecourse near Naas

Naas, Co Kildare

Map Ref: 125 N81

Nowadays Naas is almost a suburb of Dublin, standing on the city's link with Cork and Limerick. (The short M7 motorway link by-passes Naas.) The large North Mote was the site of a palace when Naas was the seat of the ancient kings of Leinster. St Patrick is said to have camped on the site of St David's Church, and the rectory here was a Norman castle, part of the town fortifications attacked in 1316 by Robert and Edward Bruce. There is now no trace of several old monasteries. Jigginstown Castle, really an immense brick mansion, a mile from the town, was begun in 1632 by Thomas Wentworth, Earl of Strafford; Wentworth was beheaded in London, and the project left incomplete. Naas has its own racecourse and the fashionable Punchestown racecourse is nearby. **Droichead Nua** (Newbridge), a little south-west and adjacent to the Curragh (see **Kildare**) has rope and cutlery industries and is the headquarters of Bord na Mona, the national peat board. The 676ft Hill of Allen, north-west of it, is a reputed dwelling-place of Fionn MacCool, leader of the legendary 3rd-century Fianna.

AA recommends:
Farmhouses: Setanta, Carragh, *tel.* (045) 76481
Westown, Johnstown, *tel.* (045) 97006
Restaurant: Stables, *tel.* (045) 79925
Garage: T Hennessy & Sons, Sallins Road, *tel.* (045) 79251

Navan Fort, Co Armagh

Map Ref: 123 2824

Navan, or Emain Macha, near Armagh, was the great palace built by Queen Macha in 300 BC, which became the residence of the warrior kings of Ulster and of the legendary Red Branch Knights (the equivalent of King Arthur's Knights of the Round Table). Their great feats, especially those of the hero, Cuchullain, are told in the songs and stories of the Ulster cycle. However in AD 300 three brothers – the Cullas – destroyed Emain Macha and now only the massive earthworks remain to tell of its greatness.

AA recommends:
Farmhouse: Balreask House, *tel.* (046) 21155
Garage: Mac-Rei, Commons Road, *tel.* (046) 29040

Nenagh, Co Tipperary

Map Ref: 125 1817

The Dublin to Limerick N7 goes through Nenagh, which has the Silvermine Mountains to the south, Keeper Hill (2278ft) being the highest point, and the Arra Mountains and Lough Derg to the west. The east gable of a Franciscan friary, founded by the Kennedys in 1240 and said to be one of the greatest such establishments in Ireland, survives, with three tall lancet windows. Nenagh Castle, built about 1200 by Theobold Fitz-Walter, first Butler of Ormond, is noted for its circular, four-storey 100ft keep, with winding wall-stairs. Its crenellations were added in the 19th century when restoration work was undertaken by a bishop of Killaloe.

AA recommends:
Garages: Cleary's, *tel.* (067) 31310
Frosts, Dublin Road, *tel.* (067) 31120

Newcastle, Co Down

Map Ref: 123 J33

Newcastle is a seaside resort with a sandy beach which forms a three-mile crescent. At the southern end is the harbour with the Mournes sweeping to the sea behind. Further on round the coast is Maggy's Leap, a dark chasm 90ft deep and 6ft wide, said to derive its name from a local beauty who, pursued by an unwanted admirer, bounded across the gap, and reached the other side with all the eggs in her basket unbroken. A little further south is Bloody Bridge, scene of a massacre

---

Myths and Legends

In Ireland's mythological heroic age, around the birth of Christ, there are all the elements of the great sagas — courage, honour, loyalty, beauty, friendship and treachery, dishonour, jealousy and ambition. At the centre is the elite of Ulster's manhood, the warrior aristocracy of the Red Branch Knights, ruled by Conor MacNessa with fabled mighty warriors such as Fergus MacRoy. The greatest hero was Cuchullain, whose single-handed might defended the Red Branch Knights in the face of Queen Maeve and the men of Connaught intent of capturing the great bull of Cooley. The exploits of Cuchullain, the Hound of Ulster, are many and magnificent, and his death, standing strapped to a stone, overcome by sorcery, is of heroic quality.

With many Irish stories, there is a sense of doom hanging over the central figures. Such a one is Deirdre, the loveliest woman Ireland had ever seen, and the sons of Usnach, fated to die through treachery because of her fatal beauty. The story of the Children of Lir, who were changed into swans for hundreds of years, is hauntingly evocative, and Grania's tragic elopement with Dermot, from Finn, has echoes in the Arthur, Guinevere, Lancelot triangle.

Finn was the leader of another warrior race, the Fianna, and their heroic deeds are revered in myth and legend. He has come down to us, however, as a rather jolly giant, Finn MacCool, who in popular story-telling is often seen in fights with giants in Britain. During one of these, he is said to have picked up a clod of earth from where Lough Neagh is now and to have hurled it into the sea to make the Isle of Man.

during the 1641 rebellion. A path leads along the coast to Annalong, passing the ruins of St Mary's church.

To the north the beach runs right round to Dundrum, past the championship golf course of Royal Country Down.

In the centre of the town is a broad promenade on which stands the Percy French fountain, commemorating the man who made the Mournes famous in song. At the end of the promenade is the Annesley Mansions, now a recreation centre; the castle which gave the town its name stood here in different forms from 1433 to 1831. The town is well-equipped with parks, including Donard Park, which takes the walker from the heart of the town, up the Glen River, to the Mournes.

West of Newcastle is Northern Ireland's most popular Forest Park, Tollymore. Originally the home of the Magennis family, and of the Earls of Roden, it is sprinkled with pretty Gothick gates and follies, including a hermitage. The park offers a wide variety of walks.

AA recommends:
Hotels: Slieve Donard, 3-star, *tel.* Newcastle 23681
Enniskeen, 2-star (country house), *tel.* Newcastle 22392
Campsites: Newcastle Caravan Trailer Park, Tullybrannigan Road, 3-pennant, *tel.* Newcastle 22351
Tollymore Forest Park, 3-pennant, *tel.* Newcastle 22428

Geometrical symbols in the Newgrange tomb continue to baffle the experts

Newgrange, Co Meath

Map Ref: 123 O07

Newgrange's tumulus, or passage grave, in the Boyne Valley is over 4000 years old. (Strictly speaking there is only one tumulus at Newgrange, as the two others within sight of it are at **Dowth** and **Knowth**. The whole area is called Bru na Boinne, but it is often loosely referred to as Newgrange.)

Twelve standing stones remain, from a possible 35 to 38, of the most celebrated tumulus's Great Circle. The mound over the tomb is over 36ft high at the front, and white quartz stones were used as the outside layer. A roof-box, the only one to have been found so far was discovered in 1963 in the passage roof (see below). One ancient high king, Cormac MacAirt, is buried at Ross na Righ, across the Boyne from Newgrange, because he considered Newgrange, Dowth and Knowth a 'cemetery of idolators'.

Prehistoric Graves

The grand court graves of Ireland are the most spectacular legacy of Irish prehistoric man. For years seen as objects of mystery, they were explained as Giant's Graves, or Druid's Altars and there are still elements which archaeologists cannot explain. Outstanding are the majestic court graves of the Boyne Valley, including the famous Newgrange, which some claim is the oldest man-made 'building' in the world, some 4000 years old. A stone passage runs right into the heart of the mound, and on several stones intriguing examples of megalithic art can be seen. Spirals, concentric circles, rays, and serpentine twists are pecked or engraved in a design which has come to be regarded as specifically Irish in character, and has echoes in later Celtic decoration. A roof-box with a lintel embellished with lozenges is placed above the doorway. A narrow slit allows the rising sun to shine briefly on the floor of the chamber only on one day each year — the Winter Solstice (December 21). Early man's ingenuity in engineering this stone structure without the aid of machinery was matched by his scientific knowledge of nature.

About 1250 megalithic 'tombs

Legananny Dolmen is a notable tripod chamber tomb

survive in Ireland. The monuments commonly known as Dolmens are impressive. Perhaps they were not meant to be seen, exposed, as they are now, with two or three huge stones bearing a horizontal slab, but they are familiar landmarks scattered throughout the countryside, with some interesting and contrasting examples at Proleek, Co Louth; Poulnabrone, Co Clare; Legananny, Co Down; Browne's Hill, Co Carlow.

Omagh is a popular fishing centre situated alongside the River Strule

New Ross, Co Wexford

Map Ref: 125 S72

New Ross's streets wind up a hill overlooking the tideway of the River Barrow where it is crossed by the Waterford to Wexford N25. An inland port, it was once Waterford city's commercial rival, with sea-going barges among its more recent manufactures. Its waterway link with Dublin is via the Barrow navigation and Grand Canal. A river trip from here to Waterford, down the Barrow then up the Suir, is memorable.

Strongbow's daughter, Isabella de Clare, who died in 1220, was the town's founder in a secular sense, though St Abban had a 6th-century monastery here. Its Norman wall was over a mile long, but only fragments of the gates remain. One of these, Three-Bullet Gate, is so named because in 1649 three Cromwellian cannonballs lodged in it. The town was a focal point of the 1798 rebellion. The Church of St Mary stands on the site of the 1212 St Mary's Abbey (parts of which are preserved), and also the 6th-century monastery. Isabella de Clare's cenotaph is here.

John F Kennedy's ancestral home at Dunganstown is about four-and-a-half miles south. The home is now John F. Kennedy Park. Its 480 acres, opened in 1968, comprise an arboretum, a forest garden and a Kennedy memorial.

AA recommends:
Hotel: Five Counties, 3-star, *tel.* (051) 21703
Guesthouse: Inishross House, 96 Mary Street, *tel.* (051) 21335
Garages: Priory Lane, Priory Lane, *tel.* (051) 21844
D P Services, The Rookery, Stokestown, *tel.* (051) 22114

Newry, Co Down

Map Ref: 123 J02

A handsome town and port on the Dublin-Belfast road (A1), Newry is connected by canal with Carlingford Lough. The canal was opened in 1741. Pleasantly fringed by hills, the town has been called the Gap of the North because of its position as the main crossing between hills into Ulster from the south. It is an ideal centre for exploring the Mourne Mountains and Carlingford Lough area. The Roman Catholic cathedral by John Duff is a fine Perpendicular-style edifice. St Patrick's Church in Church St. retains part of a 1578 tower and is said to have been the first Protestant church built in Ireland.

Oldcastle, Co Meath

Map Ref: 123 N58

A small town between Loughs Sheelin and Ramor, Oldcastle is primarily a base for fishing the Sheelin and the River Inny. The Loughcrew Hills, three miles south-east, include Hag's Mountain (904ft), Patrickstown Hill (885ft) and Carnbane (824ft). Since this ridge is on the edge of the Central Plain of Ireland, the views from their summits are more extensive than their height suggests. About 30 cairns of passage graves are scattered over these slopes. Among them, a huge carved rock with a seat-like cavity is known as Ollamh Fodla's Chair, after a law-giver who died before 1000 BC and whose tomb is believed to be here. **Virginia**, over the Cavan border on N3, has a nine-hole golf course and sits on the north shore of Lough Ramor, which has several islets and good coarse fishing.

Omagh, Co Tyrone

Map Ref: 123 H47

Omagh, the county town of Tyrone, sits on a hill above the point where the rivers Camowen and Drumragh join to form the Strule. It is a good centre for visiting the Sperrins and a circle of interesting Forest Parks. To the north is Gortin Glen, where a five-mile forest drive affords the motorist splendid views at vista parks which look out over the Strule Valley and the Donegal Hills. There are wildlife enclosures with Sika deer, a children's play area and a nature trail. To the north-west is Barons Court Forest Park, near the home of the Duke of Abercorn, whose family gave names to two hills, Bessy Bell and Mary Gray. From Bessy Bell there are splendid views of Donegal, the Sperrins and Lough Erne. The Forest Park at Seskinore, south of Omagh, has a collection of ornamental birds and domestic fowl.

The Ulster American Folk Park, at **Camphill**, is an outdoor museum which vividly tells the story of Ulster's links with America. It shows the conditions which emigrants left behind in the Old World and the kind of life the pioneers would have found in the New. The Park has grown up around the ancestral home of the Mellon family, who founded the Mellon Bank of Pittsburgh. Traditional crafts, such as shoeing and candle- and soap-making are carried out by guides in costume in a reconstructed forge and cottage.

AA recommends:
Hotel: Royal Arms, 51 High Street, 2-star, *tel.* Omagh 3262
Garages: Johnston King Motors, Derry Road, *tel.* Omagh 41520
Sean Duncan, 52 Brookmount Road, *tel.* Omagh 44161

Oughterard, Co Galway

Map Ref: 122 M14

Oughterard, a rallying point for anglers, stands beside Lough Corrib (N59) on the Owenriff River at the northern end of the Iar (West) Connaught district, where the road turns west towards the starkness of the Connemara Mountains, the Maumturks and the rocky Twelve Bens (Pins). The district between here and Clifden especially Maam Cross, Recess and Ballynahinch, is noted for the little Connemara pony.

Ross Lake and Ross Castle lie five miles south-east of Oughterard. The castle was the home of Martin Ross, whose real name was Violet Martin. She collaborated with her cousin Edith Somerville to write *Some Experiences of an Irish RM* and other novels; 'Humanity Dick' Martin, a founder of the RSPCA. also lived here in the late 18th and

The mild Gulf Stream climate has produced a subtropical paradise in the charming resort of Parknasilla

early 19th centuries. He explained the inconsistency of being both an animal lover and noted duellist by declaring 'An ox cannot hold a gun', but was said to have made his reputation by contesting drunks.

At Lough Corrib's north-west extremity near Maam Bridge is Castlekirke, or Hen's Castle, fine remains of a 13th-century keep built by Rory O'Connor, the last High King. However, according to legend it was built overnight by a witch and her hen.

AA recommends:
Hotels: Connemara Gateway, 3-star, *tel.* (091) 82328
Corrib, Bridge Street, 2-star, *tel.* (091) 82329
Egans Lake, 2-star, *tel.* (091) 82205

Parknasilla, Co Kerry

Map Ref: 121 V66

Where the estuary of the Sneem and other small rivers meet the long inlet known as the Kenmare River, Parknasilla (N70) only lacks a sandy beach to make it the ideal resort. Gorgeous scenery, sylvan walks and boat trips are its main attractions. Excursions to the islands are popular, though Garinish Island should not be confused with the namesake near Glengarriff. The resort has good sea fishing and nine-hole golf, and bathers frequent the pier and nearby coves in the absence of a beach. Blackwater Bridge, a little to the east where the river runs through a romantic ravine in splendid woods, is noted for its beauty.

AA recommends:
Hotel: Great Southern, 4-star, *tel.* (064) 45122

Portaferry, Co Down

Map Ref: 123 J55

The long shore-front of Portaferry looks over the narrows of Strangford Lough where green meadows and parkland are flanked by wooded hills. Five tower-houses stand watch over the narrows, one of them in Portaferry itself, some built by the Savages, a Norman family, in the 16th century. The town is full of modest, good buildings and the Northern Ireland Housing Executive's development along the sea front is in keeping with the old fishermen's cottages. A ferry links Portaferry and Strangford.

The local hotels specialise in fish and on the other side of the Ards peninsula at Portavogie a large fishing fleet is based. It is a curious sight to watch two or three scavenging seals follow the fleet right into the harbour.

Kearney (NT) is a pretty village, with many holiday cottages, which has excellent walks. At Temple Cowey holy wells are still visited by pilgrims, while Derry Churches recalls an 8th-century monastery,

and Millin Bay, close to a fine beach at Ballyquintin, is a neolithic burial chamber.

Portarlington, Co Laois

Map Ref: 125 N51

A former Huguenot colony, this pleasant town still has a 'French' church and good, Georgian architecture, though after 1948 the massive cooling equipment of a peat-fuelled power sation became an unsightly landmark. The 4000-acre Clonsast Bog is four miles north. The 1250 Lea Castle ruin, once a Fitzgerald stronghold, is two miles east of the town. The ubiquitous Edward Bruce put a torch to it in 1315. Emo Park estate, with its Palladian mansion designed by James Gandon in 1790 for the Earl of Portarlington, is to the south; its dome covers a very lavish blue and gilt saloon ceiling. The house was a Jesuit college for a time, and later bought privately.

A colourful frontage in the tiny, picturesque village of Portaferry

Portlaoise, Co Laois

Map Ref: 125 S49

This town's former name, Maryborough, is retained in the Great Heath of Maryborough to the north-east on N7. An esker, or great ridge of sand and gravel, runs north from Portlaoise to Mountmellick and Tullamore, the N80 roughly following its course. Portlaoise was fortified in the reign of Philip and Mary, but only the outer wall of a tower remains. Four miles east on the Rock of Dunamase are the ruins of a 12th-century castle of Dermot MacMurrough, king of Leinster. Ballybrittas, beyond the Heath, is called the 'Pass of the Plumes' after a 16th-century battle in which Essex's defeated troops had the feathers cut from their helmets.

AA recommends:
Hotel: Killeshin, Dublin Road, 3-star, *tel.* (0502) 21663
Garages: Frosts, Dublin Road, *tel.* (0502) 22333
Laois Motors, Dublin Road, *tel.* (0502) 21392
Portlaoise Service Station, Dublin Road, *tel.* (0502) 22048
Campsite: Kirwans Caravan & Camping Park, Mountrath Road, 3-pennant, *tel.* (0502) 21688

Portrush, Co Antrim

Map Ref: 123 C83

Portrush, bounded by the sea on three sides with three beaches, is a popular seaside resort with all the usual amenities, including a championship golf course. In the first half of this century it was known for the purity and recuperative quality of its air and guide books extolled it as 'singularly efficacious in driving away distemper of mind and body, and specially recommended for sufferers from insomnia and nervous diseases'.

Off Lansdowne Crescent, below the Recreation Grounds, is Portandoo Countryside Centre (DOE). The stretch of shore close by is a geological nature reserve, noted for fossils of ammonites.

East of Portrush is Dunluce Castle, dramatically perched on the edge of a rocky headland. During the late Middle Ages it was held by the MacDonnells, but after a stormy night in 1639, when half the kitchen fell into the sea, taking servants with it, the Countess of Antrim declined to live there any longer and the castle fell into disuse and disrepair. Now it is being skilfully restored (DOE).

AA recommends:
Guesthouse: Mount Royal, 2 Mount Royal, *tel.* Portrush 823342
Farmhouses: Islay View, 36 Leeke Road, Ballymagarry, *tel.* Portrush 823220
Loguestown, *tel.* Portrush 822742
Restaurant: Ramore, The Harbour, *tel.* Portrush 823444
Campsite: Golf Links Caravan Park, Bushmills Road, 2-pennant, *tel.* Portrush 82288

Portstewart, Co Londonderry

Map Ref: C83

Portstewart is a pleasant resort rather overshadowed by its neighbour, **Portrush**. The town centre, with rock pools, dinghy pool and children's pool, is dominated by a cliff-top Gothic castle which, built by Mr Henry O'Hara in 1834, is now a Dominican Convent school. Portstewart Strand is a magnificent two-mile beach backed by dunes (NT) stretching from the town to the mouth of the Bann.

AA recommends:
Guesthouses: Links, 103 Strand Road, *tel.* Portstewart 2580
Oregon, 118 Station Road, *tel.* Portstewart 2826
Garage: Cahore Motors, Station Road, *tel.* Portstewart 2221

Poulaphouca, Co Wicklow

Map Ref: 125 N90

Noted for its cataracts at a 150ft drop in the River Liffey, Poulaphouca Waterfall lost some of its volume when a dam and power station were built and a large reservoir created as part of a hydro-electric scheme. But the fall, in its wild, natural setting, retains most of its beauty. A path leads to the south bank of the river where an excellent view can be had. Humphrystown Bridge spans an arm of the lake and leads to the woodland scenery of the eastern shore. The most spectacular part of the falls is directly under the Liffey road bridge, where the water cascades into the Pool of the Pooka (mischievous spirit).

Rathdrum, Co Wicklow

Map Ref: 125 T18

Rathdrum is high on the western side of the lovely valley of the Avonmore, with T7 passing through. North of the town is the wooded Vale of Clara, with particularly fine views from Clara Bridge. Nine miles south-west and west of the Vale of Avoca is **Aughrim**, situated at a junction of several mountain valleys, near where the River Ow and Derry Water meet to form the Aughrim River. The scenic valley of the Ow extends north-west of Aughrim for about ten miles to the foot of the 3089ft Lugnaquilla, crowning glory of the Wicklow Mountains.

Just over a mile south of Rathdrum is **Avondale House**, once the residence of patriot Charles Stewart Parnell, now part of a State forestry estate. Parts of the house may be visited. There are picnic facilities nearby. Parnell, who was born here in 1846, is more often remembered for his affair with Kitty O'Shea, which ruined him politically, than for his great work for social reform.

AA recommends:
Guesthouse: Avonbrae House, *tel.* (0404) 6198

Sea bathing and a two-mile long sandy beach are the main attractions in Portstewart

T & C: Abhainn Mor House, Corballis,
tel. (0404) 6330
St Bridgets, Corballis, *tel.* (0404) 6477

Rathlin, Co Antrim

Map Ref: 123 D15

'Like a drowned magpie' was
Charles Kingsley's description of
Rathlin, or Raghery, noting the
startling contrast between the black
basalt and the white limestone of
this L-shaped island which lies
about seven miles off **Ballycastle**.
The island has about 100
inhabitants; it can be reached by
boat from Ballycastle and has
facilities for visitors.

It is said that the islanders have
more in common with Scotland
than Ireland. Once the Scottish
custom of harvesting seabirds and
eggs was common. A famous Scot,
Robert the Bruce, taking refuge
here after his defeat at Perth in
1306, was said to have meditated
upon the efforts of a persistent
spider, whose web continually
broke, and was inspired to 'try, try
again'.

At Doon Point are geological
formations similar to those at the
Giant's Causeway. Rathlin has a
sweat house where the girls went to
enhance their complexions before
their annual excursion to the
Lammas Fair at Ballycastle.

The island has a huge bird
population (RSPB). The rocks near
the west lighthouse are the best
vantage point for watching
guillemots, razorbills, shearwaters,
fulmars, kittiwakes and puffins.

Rathluirc, Co Cork

Map Ref: 124 R52

On the N20 near the Limerick
border, this town, also called
Charleville, was the scene of an
unhappy meal in 1690. The Duke of
Berwick was guest of the Lord
President of Munster in his

Birthplace of Parnell in 1846, Avondale House is now a State forestry school

mansion here, and repaid the
hospitality by burning the house to
the ground. **Bruree**, five miles
north over the county border, was
the childhood home of Eamon de
Valera, 1916 revolutionary and later
Taoiseach (prime minister) and
President of the Republic. He was
born in New York. Here a
picturesque six-arch bridge crosses
the Maigue; there are scant remains
of a de Lacy fortress, and the place
was a residence of Munster kings
and, until 1746, a meeting place for
Ireland's bards.

AA recommends:
Garage: Park, *tel.* (063) 367

Rathmullan, Co Donegal

Map Ref: 123 C22

Red Hugh O'Donnell was lured
aboard a ship at Rathmullan in 1587
and taken to Dublin Castle,
escaping four years later. It was also
from here that the earls of Tyrone
and Tyrconnell fled to France in
1607.

The town stands on Lough
Swilly's western shore, and has the
remains of a 15th-century
Carmelite friary. Inland are
Craoghan (1010ft) and
Crockanaffrin (1137ft), with the
Knockalla ridge or Devil's
Backbone a little more distant

(1203ft). All offer striking views.
There is salmon fishing in Lough
Swilly, with brown trout in local
lakes.

AA recommends:
Hotels: Rathmullan House, 3-star
(country house), *tel.* (074) 58188
Fort Royal, 2-star (country house),
tel. (074) 58100
Pier, 1-star, *tel.* (074) 58178

Renvyle, Co Galway

Map Ref: 122 L66

Almost the entire northern shore of
the Renvyle peninsula and the coast
eastward to the Little Killary is lined
with sandy beaches, offering safe
bathing at all stages of the tide.
Reached from N59, this is also a
fishing and shooting area. Renvyle
Hill (Tully Mountain) 1172ft high,
overlooks the small Tully Lough.
Renvyle Castle was in turn the
property of the Joyces, O'Flaherties
and Blakes, and was unsuccessfully
besieged by Grace 'lady pirate'
O'Malley. Near it are a holy well
and a small dolmen with three
uprights. Offshore lie the small
Crump Island, with bigger
Inishbofin to the west.

AA recommends:
Hotel: Renvyle House, 3-star,
tel. (095) 21122

Rathmullan is an attractive resort on the west bank of Lough Swilly

Colourful houses surround the tiny village green at Sneem

Ring of Kerry, Co Kerry

Map Ref: 124

The Ring of Kerry is the colloquial name of the coast road along the shores of the lovely Iveragh Peninusla in Co Kerry, one of the most picturesque areas in Ireland for mountain and marine scenery. The beginning and end are not clearly defined, but a good route is to start from Kenmare.

Go 17 miles west to the pretty village of **Sneem**, passing through Parknasilla, a renowned beauty spot with fine mountain, sea and island vistas and good woodland walks. The road winds south-west from Sneem for nine miles to **West Cove**, with nearby **Staigue Fort**, arguably the finest ancient stone fort in Ireland, noted for the staircases within its immense walls. It then winds 13 miles north-west to **Waterville**, with angling, golf, grouse, snipe, duck, plover and a beautiful strand at **Ballinaskelligs Bay**. Ballinaskellings is a Gaelic-speaking village. The late Charlie

Chaplin fished regularly here.

Cahirciveen is 11 miles north of Waterville, with the ruin of Carhan House where patriot Daniel O'Connell was born in 1775, and an ancient stone fort. A little to the west is Valentia Island, seven miles long, two miles wide and hilly, a centre of deep-sea fishing. The first successful Atlantic telegraph cable was laid from here in 1866.

From Cahirciveen it is 17 miles north-east to Glenbeigh, a pleasant fishing and bathing village. From the right turn north of Kells into **Glenbeigh** which has magnificent views of Dingle Bay. The **Glenbeigh Horseshoe** of mountains includes 2541ft Coomacarrea. The route finishes, via Killorglin, at Killarney.

Robertstown, Co Kildare

Map Ref: 125 N72

The Grand Canal Company's Hotel of 1801 still stands, and in recent times has been used for

banquets is connection with horse-drawn barge trips on the waterway, which is no longer used commercially. The waterfront has been restored to its early 19th-century character. A local falconry, said to be the biggest in Europe, may be visited. This is the canal's highest point above sea level. North-east is **Celbridge**, with Castletown House, a magnificent 13-bay Palladian mansion by Allesandro Galilei, built in 1722 for William Conolly, Speaker of the Irish House of Commons. It is now the Irish Georgian Society's headquarters and may be visited.

Roe Valley, Co Londonderry

Map Ref: 123 C62

The heart of the Roe Valley is **Limavady**, a neat town where the original Georgian architecture has been treated with 'good manners' by later builders.

The name means 'the dog leap', said to be derived from the story of a mighty bound of a dog sent to fetch help with a message in its collar from a besieged castle. This was O'Cahan territory and O'Cahan's Rock is one of the landmarks in the lovely Roe Valley Country Park (DOE). The Park has a range of old watermills and Ulster's first hydro-electric domestic power station; it was started by a local inhabitant for his own house and later extended to the rest of the town.

It was in Limavady that Ulster's best loved tune 'The Londonderry Air', also known as 'Danny Boy', was heard and noted down by a Miss Jane Ross.

Many Irish placenames are of Gaelic derivation

a black pool, Limerick, a bare spot, Cork, a marshy place, Sligo, a shelly river, Carlow, a fourfold lake and Youghal, a yew wood. Some are romantically descriptive, like Labasheeda in Co Clare, which means 'a bed of silk', or Coolbaun, Co Tipperary, 'a white recess'. Clonmel, in the same county, means 'a honey meadow'.

Some names are ascribed to individuals or groups. Kilkenny means 'church of (St) Canice', Slievenamon, Co Tipperary, is 'mountain of the women' and Donegal denotes 'a fort of foreigners'.

The prefix 'bally', denoting a town, comes from a Gaelic word which literally means a home; it was originally used more in a domestic than administrative sense, and thus still refers mainly to smaller places, and some city suburbs.

Rath, meaning an earth-banked ring fort, is a common prefix. *Kil* (church); *dun* (fort); *knock* (hill); *slieve* (mountain); *drom* or *drum* (height or

hillock); *ard* (also meaning height); *carrick* (rock); *ath* (a ford) and *inis* or *inch* (island) are also often found. *Inis* sometimes appears as *ennis*, as in Ennis, Enniscorthy, Enniscrone.

Some purely English names have been changed back to older Gaelic designations, such as Kingstown becoming again Dun Laoghaire (pro-ounced Dunleary). In some such cases both names are used. So we have Edgeworthstown/Mostrim, Bagenals-town/Muinebheag, Charleville/Rath-luirc, Newbridge/Droichead Nua and Maryborough/Portlaoise.

Waterford and Wexford were the Norse Vatnfjordhr and Waesfjord (sea-washed town), but their respective Gaelic names are Port Lairge (Lairge's landing) and Loch Garman (Gorman's Lough). The casual rule that names ending in *ford* are of Norse origin is not infallible. Longford, for instance, comes from the Gaelic Longphort, meaning 'a fortress'.

Common suffixes are *beg* (small), *more* (great), *derg* (red), *duff* (black), *boy* (yellow) and *roe* (red).

Placenames

Most placenames in the Republic are Anglicised forms of Gaelic words. Some are physical descriptions, such as Dublin,

Tiny boats dot the harbour at Bertraghboy Bay overlooked by Roundstone village

Roscommon, Co Roscommon

Map Ref: 122 M86

In a landscape of meadow, bog, bush and lake, where the Galway to Longford and Sligo to Athlone roads cross, Roscommon is a colourful town. However, there is no trace of the 6th-century monastery of St Coeman, after whom it is named, unless we assume that some Romanesque pillars in the ruin of the 1253 Dominican friary, otherwise hard to explain, are part of the rebuilt Coeman foundation. The ruins of this Dominican establishment mainly date from a 1453 reconstruction, and there are many interesting sculptures.

Ireland's last hangwoman, coyly called 'Lady Betty', is commemorated by a plaque on the 18th-century jail where she worked, and which was disused after 1822. The market house by George Ensor has been restored, but Robert d'Ufford's 1269 castle was partly dismantled with explosives by Ironsides in 1652, and never recovered.

Roscommon has a nine-hole golf course and a racecourse.

AA recommends:
Hotel: Abbey, 3-star, *tel.* (0903) 6505
Farmhouse: Munsboro House, Munsboro, *tel.* (0903) 6375
Garage: P Casey & Sons, *tel.* (0903) 6101

Roscrea, Co Tipperary

Map Ref: 125 S18

The N7 from Dublin to Limerick threads through this picturesque and historic little town, passing first between a capless round-tower and something more unusual, a remnant of an 1100 Augustinian priory, used as gateway to the churchyard of St

Cronan's 1812 church (Church of Ireland). The 60ft tower has been capless since 1135, and lost another 20ft in 1798 when a cannon mounted on it backfired. Over the doorway of the priory façade is a well-worn figure of St Cronan, a 7th-century monk.

The churchyard entrance of St Cronan's Roman Catholic church is the square, castellated tower of the 1490 Franciscan friary, founded by Mulrooney O'Carroll, an Eli chief, and his wife Bibians (Vivien). Beside the 13th-century castle gate tower the splendid 1715 Queen Anne-style Damer House was saved by the Irish Georgian Society. The ornate Victorian fountain in Rosemary Square is worth a pause, as are some of the town's fine shop fronts. The Timoney Standing Stones are within reach of the town, and the Slieve Bloom Mountains and Devil's Bit Hill afford good climbing.

AA recommends:
Hotels: Racket Hall, 2-star, *tel.* (0505) 21748
Pathe, 1-star, *tel.* (0505) 21301
Farmhouse: Streamstown House, *tel.* (0505) 21519
Garage: Spooners, *tel.* (0505) 21063

Rosslare, Co Wexford

Map Ref: 125 T11

Rosslare, at Ireland's south-eastern corner, became an important harbour when the silting-up of the harbour at Wexford forced the move south; it has grown in prominence as a car and truck ferry terminal for Welsh and French ports. The town is also a resort with a splendid six-mile arc of sand and a famous 18-hole golf course fringed with sand dunes which shelter it, thus keeping it nearly always in good playing condition. Lady's

Island, connected by causeway to the mainland, is a place of pilgrimage where there are ruins of an Augustinian priory and a Norman castle with a leaning tower.

A little west is **Tacumshane**, with a well-preserved windmill, and at neighbouring **Ballysampson** Commodore John Barry, founder of the American navy, was born.

AA recommends:
Hotels: Kellys, 3-star (red), *tel.* (053) 32114
Casey's Cedars, 3-star, *tel.* (053) 32124
Golf, 2-star, *tel.* (053) 32179

Roundstone, Co Galway

Map Ref: 122 L74

South of Clifden, this quiet, small resort stands beside a sound which runs out to the mouth of Bertraghboy Bay, where fishing is the way of life. Nearby Dog's Bay (Port-na-Feadog) has an unusual porous strand. The 987ft Urrisbeg, just inland, overlooks a northward tract with about 300 small lakes. To the south, many islands can be seen, including Inishlacken and Deer Island; most of them have ecclesiastical remains. St MacDara's Island has a 6th-century oratory.

The rare heather *Erica Mediterrania* grows on Urrisbeg's slopes, and *Erica Mackaianna* is found on the shore of nearby Craiggamore Lake. The Clifden road swings west and north by Ballyconneely and Mannin Bays, with a wilderness of rock, bog and water to the right. The air is so bracing here that the route has been nicknamed the 'Brandy and Soda road'. Mannin Bay's Coral Strand has myriads of bleached coral fragments.

AA recommends:
Hotel: Seal's Rock, 1-star, *tel.* 15

Roundwood, Co Wicklow

Map Ref: 125 O10

Between Lough Dan and the Vartry reservoir, Roundwood is set in wild scenery on the Vartry River, and the village is a fishing centre for the reservoir, the Annamoe River and Loughs Dan and Tay. Lough Tay, overhung by a granite precipice, is the prettier of these lakes; Lough Dan is a mile-and-a-half long, also with precipitous shores, and sandy beaches. These granite and schist heights are outliers of the Wicklow Mountains.

The wooded **Annamoe** village towards Glendalough is where Laurence Sterne claimed to have fallen through a millrace as a boy and escaped unhurt. The mill ruin survives.

South of here is **Laragh**, where the road turns for Glendalough and where the Avonmore and Glenmacnass rivers meet. The Glenmacnass Valley is of striking beauty. The waterfall at the northern end of the glen is seen to full advantage when approached from Laragh.

AA recommends:
Campsite: Roundwood Caravan Park, 4-pennant, *tel.* (01) 818163

Russborough House, Co Wicklow

Map Ref: 125 N91

Between Blessington and the Poulaphouca waterfall, this Palladian mansion, begun in 1741 and completed by Francis Bindon after the death of Richard Cassels, has outstanding plasterwork, much of it by the famed Francini brothers. It is also renowned for its furnishings, with some of the Gobelin tapestry covering the chairs as fresh now as when made during Louis XVI's reign. The house's Beit collection of paintings, founded at the turn of the century by an uncle of the house's last owner, Sir Alfred Beit, is now in the national trust, and it includes works by

Russborough House, sumptuous plasterwork decorates a work in the Beit art collection. Left: The House itself, overlooks fine woodland gardens

Gainsborough, Goya, Rubens, Vermeer, Velazquez and Frans Hals.

St Mullins, Co Carlow

Map Ref: 125 S73

A charming village where a by-road skirts the winding River Barrow, and the ground has not yet begun to rise towards the Blackstairs Mountains in the east, St Mullins has at least four ancient churches, a holy well and an oratory 12ft long whose door has inclining jambs, suggesting great antiquity. Launches run between the village and New Ross; the Barrow's wooded banks, rising in places to nearly 300ft, are best seen from the water. The shapely Mount Brandon rises to 1694ft in the north-west, while the Blackstairs climb to over 2400ft. North-east of Ballymurphy the ground rises again to the 2610ft Mount Leinster.

Salthill, Co Galway

Map Ref: 124 M22

This suburb of Galway city has become one of the country's leading seaside resorts; stretching west along Galway Bay with good bathing. The promenade offers good views south to the hills of Clare and south-west to the Aran Islands. Good bathing is available at all tide stages. Galway Golf Club's 18-hole course adjoins the promenade and tennis, pitch-and-

Curragh fishermen, Kilkee, 1870s

Currachs

A curragh is a light sea-going vessel, fashioned from tarred canvas stretched over a wooden frame, although the earliest boatbuilders probably used animal skins. The oars of the curragh are each shaped from a length of sturdy timber and include a block fixed near the handgrip. An eye in the block fits over a wooden pin fixed in the top side frame of the boat and this provides manoeuvrability even in rough seas. The curragh is still in use today by the skilful boatmen of the Aran Islands and along the west coast.

putt, squash and badminton are also available, while there are indoor amusements for all ages, including a heated swimming pool. Salthill has a gallery of contemporary Irish art. Curragh racing championships have been held here and Galway Bay's International Sea Angling festival is held in September.

Shillelagh, Co Wicklow

Map Ref: 125 S96

The name of this village and its river means 'family, or issue of Ealach', but has become internationally known as a synonym for an Irish blackthorn stick. Shillelagh is almost surrounded by hills, with the Fitzwilliam estate of Coollatin Park to the east. A great oak forest here supplied the roofing of St Patrick's Cathedral in Dublin, and King Turloch of Leinster is said to have sent Shillelagh oaks to William II (Rufus the Red) in London in 1098 for the roofing of Westminster Hall. This claim is also made by Oxmantown Forest in Dublin but is equally doubtful since that hall's splendid oak roof was erected sometime after 1394 by Richard II. Shillelagh's lovely scenery, however, is an undisputed fact.

AA recommends:
Garage: Shillelagh Motors, tel. (055) 29127

Silent Valley, Co Down

Map Ref: 123 J32

Recently re-opened to the public, Silent Valley provides the only vehicle access into the inner Mournes. Covering an area of lake of 240 acres, the reservoir was opened in 1933. With Ben Crom

reservoir, Silent Valley supplies 30,000,000 gallons of water to the Belfast area per day. During the construction work 600 people were employed and lived in a village, now dismantled, called Watertown.

In contrast to the natural grandeur of the mountains is the park laid out near the dam, with gardens, shrubs, lawns and ponds.

Skerries, Co Dublin

Map Ref: 123 O26

This seaside resort off the N1 has a good sandy beach, a notably dry climate and an established fishing industry. The name is Norse and really applies to the rocky offshore islands rather than the town. The islands are St Patrick's Island, Colt Island and Shenick's Island - which is accessible by foot at low tide. St Patrick's Island has ruins of an ancient church, and the saint is said to have begun his Irish mission here, commuting to Red Island, now a part of the mainland, where 'his footprints' are carved in rock. Red Island was the site of the first permanent holiday camp in the Republic.

Inland is a tiny village with the curious name of **Man o' War**, and south at **Lusk** is a farm machinery museum. Lambay Island, off Portrane, rises to 418ft and is very picturesque, but can only be seen from a boat as access is restricted because of the bird sanctuary on it. **Swords**, a little south on the Dublin to Belfast road, has a 75ft round-tower and a rambling castle of about 1200, but there is no trace of St Colmcille's (Columba's) 6th-century foundation.

AA recommends:
Restaurant: The Red Bank, Church Street, 1-K & F, tel. (01) 491005

Skibbereen, Co Cork

Map Ref: 124 W13

This market town stands on the Ilen River where the stream widens to form a creek and unite with an inlet of Baltimore Bay. Its hinterland is rather desolate. The Grecian pro-cathedral dates from 1826 and west of the town, by the river, is the ruin of the 14th-century Cistercian Abbeystrowry, where hundreds of victims of the Famine, which began with the 1846–47 potato blight, lie buried.

The O'Driscoll family crops up frequently in the district. Over Baltimore Harbour, south-west on R595, their old cstle is perched on a rock; north of Sherkin Island the smaller Hare Island is also called Inishodriscol, and on the larger Clear Island, west of Sherkin, the ruined Dunamore Castle was an O'Driscoll stronghold. A pirate named Fineen O'Driscoll had his headquarters, which were based on a neighbouring islet, wrecked in 1538 by a galleyful of 400 enraged Waterford seamen, in reprisal for his affiliation with merchant shipping in the city.

From Cape Clear's headlands and cliffs there are striking views of 'Carbery's Hundred Isles'. This stretch of coast known as the Carbery Coast, and provided the setting for Somerville's and Ross' novels, including *The Real Charlotte* and *Some Experiences of an Irish RM* Edith Somerville's home was in **Castletownshend**, just south-east of Skibbereen (R596).

AA recommends:
Farmhouse: Abbeystrewery, tel. (028) 21713
Garage: Hurley Bros, tel. (028) 21555

The busy fishing fleet is a familiar sight at Skerries harbour

Sligo, Co Sligo

Map Ref: 122 G63

Sligo, though not officially a city, counts as a minor one by Irish standards. It is called the centre of the Yeats Country, but W B Yeats was neither born nor bred here. He came with his parents, both Sligonians, on holidays and his relatives the Middleton and Pollexfen families, owned a shipping firm, the Sligo Steam Navigation Company. Yeats wrote *Innisfree* and *The Fiddler of Dooney* about nearby Lough Gill.

The ruined Sligo Abbey is really a remnant of a 1252 Dominican friary, but nothing remains of a castle built by Maurice Fitzgerald seven years earlier. Sligo has some exquisite, traditional shop fronts, and opposite the amazing 1878 Venetian Gothic courthouse a firm of lawyers bears the incredible name of 'Argue and Phibbs' on its window. The Perpendicular Gothic St John the Baptist church, with its square early 17th-century tower, repays inspection.

Coney Island, beyond Rosses Point, a resort with a sandy beach and 18-hole championship golf course, (L16), inspired the naming of New York's Coney Island. The captain of the Sligo-registered *Arethusa* noticed that both islands swarmed with rabbits. 'Coney' in English, like 'coinin' in Gaelic, means rabbit. The rare bee-orchid is among the wild flowers of Sligo's Coney Island, which can be reached on foot at low tide. Near it is the 'Metal Man', a gigantic statue of a seaman cast in 1819 by John Clark and similar to one at **Tranmore** (q.v.). It marks Perch Rock for ships. Rosses Point and Coney Island figured in an archaeological wrangle when alleged paleolithic implements were found to be of recent make.

Carrowmore, two miles from Sligo, has the largest group of megalithic remains in the British Isles. **Ballymote**, to the south, (R293) has extensive remains of a castle once owned by Red Hugh O'Donnell. (see also **Drumcliff**).

AA recommends:
Hotels: Ballincar House, Rosses Point Road, 3-star, *tel.* (071) 5361
Sligo Park, Cornageeha, 3-star, *tel.* (071) 60291
Silver Swan, Hyde Bridge, 2-star, *tel.* (071) 3231
T & C: Aisling, Cairns Hill, *tel.* (071) 60704
Tree Tops, Cleveragh Road, *tel.* (071) 60160
Farmhouse: Hillside, Glencar Road, *tel.* (071) 2808
Garage: Henderson's Motors, Bundoran Road, *tel.* (071) 5286

Strabane, Co Tyrone

Map Ref: 123 H39

Strabane is a border town just across the River Mourne from Lifford in Co Donegal. The town has strong associations with America; John Dunlap, who emigrated from Strabane printed the American Declaration of Independence in 1776, and it is claimed that he learned his trade at Gray's Printing Shop which is still in existence (NT) above its pretty shop front, in Main Street. A fellow apprentice was James Wilson, grandfather of President Woodrow Wilson, whose home at Dergalt is well restored and furnished (Ulster Historical Trust). Wilsons still farm the land around the house.

A few miles south is Sion Mills, a model village of half-timbered buildings laid out on the hill above the fine mill in a chestnut-tree-clad valley. St Teresa's Roman Catholic Church is of excellent 1960s design, with a slate sculpture of the *The Last Supper* on the façade.

AA recommends:
Hotel: Fir Trees Lodge, Melmount Road, 3-star, *tel.* Strabane 883003
Garages: J Sayers Motors, 107 Melmount Road, Sion Mills, *tel.* Sion Mills 58232
R A Wallace & Sons, 85 Fyfin Road, Victoria Bridge, *tel.* Strabane 58334

Strangford, Co Down

Map Ref: 123 J54

As its name suggests, Strangford sits at the point where the water rushes through the narrow neck of the lough. It is a small, pretty village with a tower-house of the 16th century. Close by is the 18th-century Castle Ward (NT) built by Lord Bangor in a style half Classical (to please himself) and half Gothick (to please his wife, 'the whimsical Lady Anne'). It is set in fine parkland with an ornamental watermill, tower-house, saw-mill, corn-mill and Victorian laundry. Audley's Castle, another tower-house to the north, is built in an outstanding position.

Near Strangford is the de Ros family estate, the first Baroness was created in 1264; there is a coastal walk past a Victorian bathing place.

Strangford Lough

Map Ref: 123 J56 and J55

The best place to view Strangford Lough is from Scrabo Tower, a monument built by Frances Anne, third Marchioness of Londonderry, to her husband, Charles.

The lough, 20 miles long, and in places three miles wide, is studded with islands and stretches out below Scrabo Country Park (DOE). At the head of the lough is **Newtownards**, which has a fine square with a late Georgian Town Hall (1770) and an interesting Market Cross (1636). On the outskirts are the ruins of a Dominican Friary (1244) and 15th-century Movilla Abbey. Beside Newtownards the mud flats are often exposed, affording excellent feeding for wintering birds. Two-thirds of the world's population of Brent geese come to Strangford between September and January. Good viewpoints are at Ballyreagh (NT) and **Castle Espiê** where there is also a good, private wildfowl collection and art gallery. The islands and the many sheltered harbours make Strangford ideal for sailing and deep-sea fishing is popular.

The lough supports large colonies of seals which can easily be seen from Cloghy rocks when the tide is right, basking in the rocks. The National Trust operates the Strangford Lough Wildlife Scheme and organises boat trips which highlight the lough's interesting natural features, including its rich marine biology.

Monks chose the isolation of Mahee Island and left interesting ruins at Nendrum, including three cashels (monks' cells) and a church whose gable has a carved sundial. The Norsemen left little except the name Strangford (the violent fjord), and the Anglo-Normans left the tower-houses which are prominent at the water's edge.

Seals and birdlife find sanctuary in the island-studded Strangford Lough

Tara, Co Meath

Map Ref: 123 N95

The Hill of Tara was Ireland's royal acropolis in ancient times, and the religious, political and cultural capital. A modern statue of St Patrick and some mounds and earthworks remain for today's visitor. St Patrick came here at the beginning of his mission, but with the spread of Christianity the importance of Tara waned. However, it was a prestigious centre until the reign of the last pagan king in the 6th century, and was certainly the royal residence of Malachi II, who died in 1022.

A pillar stone on the hillcrest is reputedly the Lia Fail, coronation stone of the early kings. Much excavation of earthworks has been carried out. A human figure depicted on Adarnan's Stone in the churchyard is said to be Cernunnos, horned god of the Celts. The 'Mound of Hostages' turned out to be a 2000 BC passage grave containing the skeleton of a boy wearing a bronze, amber and jet necklace.

Tara has a stud farm entirely devoted to breeding donkeys.

Thomastown, Co Kilkenny

Map Ref: 125 S54

A pleasing, mellow town (on the T20 from Kilkenny) set in a lovely part of the Nore Valley, Thomastown is an important hunting centre. The Kilkenny Hunt kennels are at Mount Juliet estate, two miles away, which has a mansion of 1780. Thomastown is Anglo-Norman in origin, and has a ruined 13th-century church. The ruined Grianan Castle, also 13th-century, is just outside on the riverside. The Roman Catholic church contains the old high altar of Jerpoint Abbey. Philosopher Bishop George Berkeley, after whom Berkeley University of California is named, was born in nearby **Dysart Castle** in 1685.

Thurles, Co Tipperary

Map Ref: 125 S15

A cathedral town (N62, off N8 at Horse and Jockey) on the Suir, Thurles is a sugar-manufacturing and a marketing centre. It is well laid out with a fine central Liberty Square, which includes Hayes's Hotel, birthplace of the Gaelic Athletic Association in 1884. The cathedral's (1857–75) 125ft square campanile is a conspicuous landmark. Thurles has a racecourse and there is 18-hole golf at **Turtulla**, just over a mile south.

The Suir here has brown trout, as have its tributaries, the Drish and Clodagh. Black Castle and Bridge

The 512ft Hill of Tara was of religious and political importance for over 2000 years

Castle are two medieval remnants, and Brittas Castle, two miles north, is an incomplete replica of Warwick Castle in England.

AA recommends:
Hotel: Hayes, Liberty Square, 2-star, *tel.* (0504) 22122
Farmhouse: Ballynahow Castle, Ballycahill, *tel.* (0504) 21297
Garage: Haydens, Loughbeg, *tel.* (0504) 22403

Tipperary, Co Tipperary

Map Ref: 125 R83

Lying in the rich Golden Vale, this was a centre of Land League protests in the 19th century, but is best known for the song 'It's a long way to Tipperary' which was written in 1914 by Jack Judge, an

Englishman who had never been here.

John Sadleir founded a hugely successful bank here with his brother; his entanglement with the beautiful London dancer, Clara Morton, led him to a £1,500,000 fraud. He committed suicide on Hampstead Heath, London, by drinking poison from a silver ewer. Both Charles Dickens and Charles Lever made fictional use of the event.

AA recommends:
Hotel: Royal, 8 Bridge Street, 1-star, *tel.* (062) 51204
Guesthouse: Ach-na-sheen, *tel.* (062) 51298
Farmhouse: Barronstown House, Emly Road, *tel.* (062) 55130
Garages: Sean Crowe Motors, *tel.* (062) 51219
Galtee Service Station, *tel.* (062) 51689

Gaelic Games

Ireland's traditional games, which include hurling, football, camogie and hand-ball, are known as Gaelic Games.

Hurling, the national game, by far the oldest and said to date from pre-Christian days, is mentioned in the legends of the Red Branch Knights and the Fianna. It is played between two teams of 15, each side having a goalkeeper, six backs, two midfields and six forwards. Play is similar to field hockey but it is a much faster game with fewer restraints. The sticks, with curved striking blades, are usually three-and-a-half-feet long and made from ash wood. Goals are scored by sending the leather ball under the crossbar; points (three to a goal) are scored by sending the ball over the bar. The ball may be hand-caught, but not thrown, and must be picked up off the ground with the stick.

Gaelic football, which has features of both soccer and rugby, and in which all players may handle the ball, has the same team make-up and scoring system as hurling.

Both games, together with hand-ball, are administered by the Gaelic Athletic Association, founded in 1884, which organises hundreds of clubs throughout the country. They are strictly a male preserve, but a

Senior Hurling Final at Corke Park, Dublin

separate organisation administers a women's hurling game called camogie. This is played with 12 in a team and shorter sticks. Unlike hurling, camogie is popular in cities.

Traditionally, the strongest hurling counties are Kilkenny, Wexford, Cork, Tipperary, Waterford, Limerick and Galway: football is more evenly distributed at top level.

The all-Ireland finals of the Gaelic Games inter-county championships are played every September, almost always in Croke Park, Dublin.

Tralee, Co Kerry

Map Ref: 124 Q81

Renowned for its annual 'Rose of Tralee' beauty contest, named after a song by local man William Mulchinock, the port of Tralee has a beautiful setting, is tastefully laid out, and has a long history. It was the principal seat of the Earls of Desmond; their castle stood where the Mall joins Denny Street, which, with its lovely Georgian houses leading to the town park, is one of Ireland's most elegant thoroughfares.

Sir Richard Morrison's Ionic limestone courthouse, with monuments to Kerrymen who died in the Crimea and in the Indian Mutiny (1857–8) is now, sadly, roofless. Holy Cross Dominican Church was designed by A W Pugin, though it was begun nine years after he died. The striking modern Church of Our Lady and St Brendan is built in the shape of a wide-bodied canoe, in memory of this saint who sailed to America.

Tralee, as gateway to the Dingle Peninsula, is an established base for climbers. It has nine-hole golf, horse and greyhound racing, many bathing strands on Tralee Bay and shooting at Derrymore sloblands. **Spa**, four miles west, was once popular for its chalybeate spring.

AA recommends:
Hotels: Earl of Desmond, 3-star, *tel.* (066) 21299
Mount Brandon, 3-star, *tel.* (066) 21311
Restaurant: Cordon Bleu, The Square, 2-K & F, *tel.* (066) 21596
Garage: Ruane's, 13 Princes Street, *tel.* (066) 21838

Tramore, Co Waterford

Map Ref: 125 S50

Facing a long headland on broad Tramore Bay, this hillside resort is well-developed, with a fine pier and three-mile sandy beach. Other bathing venues are the Pier, Guillameen Cove and Newtown Cove. The mile-long 18-hole golf

Trim by name, trim by nature – a neat beflowered street in Trim, Co Meath

course is supplemented by miniature golf.

Tramore has a racecourse and a 50-acre amusement park, and is washed by the Gulf Stream. Surfing has latterly challenged bathing for the attentions of the young. Along the Doneralie Cliffs, often smothered in campion and sea pinks, is the 'Metal Man', a huge iron figure acting as a marker for ships, on Great Newtown Head (see **Sligo**). Legend says that girls who managed to hop around its base three times without touching ground with the other foot will be married in a year.

AA recommends:
Hotel: Sea View, 2-star, *tel.* (051) 81244
Campsite: Atlantic View Caravan Park, Riverstown, 3-pennant, *tel.* (051) 81330

Trim, Co Meath

Map Ref: 123 N85

On the approach to Trim cattle and horses abound as this is among the best grazing areas in Ireland. The town has substantial relics, the most conspicuous being the enormous, 75ft-tall 16-sided castle keep which now lies in a sad state of neglect. Built by Hugh Tyrell between 1190 and 1200, and occupied by King John from 1210 to 1215, it was once Ireland's biggest and strongest Norman fortress.

The 125ft Yellow Steeple is a

remnant of the 13th-century St Mary's Augustinian Priory, the rest of the building having been blown up in 1649 to prevent Cromwellian occupation. Tiny St Patrick's Cathedral, was opened in 1802, but its 60ft tower remains from an edifice built by Richard of York in 1449. His arms can be seen near the top of the tower.

The 1415 Talbot's Castle, off the medieval curve of High Street, became a school which the Duke of Wellington attended as a boy. He lived in Emmet Street, Trim, and was born in 24 Upper Merrion Street, Dublin. Across the Boyne, two miles south of Trim, is **Iaracor**, where Jonathan Swift was incumbent of the church; his Communion silver is preserved. **Navan**, north of Trim, also called An Uaimh, lies in a mining district and has a racecourse.

Tuam, Co Galway

Map Ref: 122 M45

On the N17 from Galway to Sligo, Tuam has a racecourse and a sugar factory, but is best-known as a centre of church affairs, ancient and modern; it has two cathedrals. The town owes its foundation to a monastery established here in the 6th century by St Jarlath; ruins of a Temple Jarlath date from around 1360. Immediately west of the town is the reputed site of a 1000 BC battle; sepulchral tumuli and stone circles found in the area may bear this out. The name Tuam itself means a burial tumulus.

The 14ft, 12th-century High Cross of Tuam, a decorated sandstone piece, was once broken in three, with each piece in different ownership. The rebuilt (1878) Church of Ireland cathedral has a magnificent red sandstone chancel arch in laboured Romanesque, erected certainly between 1128 and 1152. To the north, **Ballyhaunis**, Co Mayo, (N83, T11) has an Augustinian friary of 1641, restored in 1938.

AA recommends:
Garage: Hi-way Services, Dublin Road, *tel.* (093) 24215

The idyllic Lady Elizabeth Cove, in the peaceful resort of Tramore

Tullamore, Co Offaly

Map Ref: 125 N32

At the crossroads of the N52 and N80, Tullamore more readily brings the Grand Canal to mind. The canal reached the town in 1798, 13 years after another essay in transport history had ended in disaster. A hot-air balloon's brazier ignited the bag and 100 houses were destroyed in the fire; Patrick Street owes its width to the subsequent rebuilding.

The canal carried huge cargoes of yellow brick, made in Tullamore, to Dublin during its expansion in the 19th century. Rising labour costs, a change in brick fashion and increased use of cement ended this source of prosperity. Distillers D E Williams of Tullamore, whose initials are immortalised in 'Tullamore Dew', had their own barges. Some canal barges remain; Williams's now distils 'Irish Mist'.

A small church at Hop Hill and Charleville House, are by well-known architect Francis Johnston. There is an 8th-century church at nearby **Rahan**.

AA recommends:
Garage: Edgar J Hurst, Arden Road, *tel.* (0506) 21783

Ulster Folk and Transport Museum, Co Antrim

Map Ref: 123 3438

The Ulster Folk and Transport Museum at **Cultra** records the wealth of Ulster's folk life. Its

This spade mill can be seen in action at the Ulster Folk and Transport Museum

practice is to rescue important examples of vernacular buildings and, by carefully numbering each stone and recording each structure, to re-erect the buildings at Cultra. Most of the examples are rural, but there is a terrace of Belfast street houses. Other examples include schools, a church, water-powered mills, a market house and a range of dwellings from the most modest one-roomed house to a substantial 1717 rectory. All are furnished with meticulous authenticity. A modern gallery has changing displays of the wide range of material held by the museum, which is also an important research and teaching institution, recording oral traditional, folklore and craft.

The Transport Museum, on the same site, has displays which particularly relate to Ulster's contribution to shipbuilding and aircraft-making, as well as a full history of the development of vehicles. Outdoor exhibits include a three-masted schooner, *Result*, built across the Lough at **Carrickfergus**.

The Irish Cottage

The Irish cottage can look very much a part of the landscape, and this is mainly because traditionally the materials used were close to hand. Clay, rubble or local stone was used for walls; earth, sand or lime used for plaster or mortar, and thatch was made from whatever was available and suitable — wheat straw, rye, flax and marram grass — with an underthatch of sods of turf. The widespread use of limewash, built up over the years to form a skin, disguises the construction in most cases. Finely-coursed masonry is rare, because good local stone is rare in Ireland, but the skill involved in building a dry-stone house without mortar is apparent in cottages in Galway, and the operation of moving immense stones to the sites of such houses, when the builder was designer, labourer and client, can be imagined.

There are almost no examples now of the one-roomed cabin of the landless farm labourer once so prevalent in Ireland, but there are remnants of cottages in which animals and humans shared accommodation. This practice can still be remembered by the older

Interior of a traditional Irish cottage

inhabitants in the remote north-west.

Half-doors, which are typically associated with the Irish cottage, were not actually all that common and were probably on loan from the stable doors of the local Big House. Very common, however, was a 'jamb wall' with a spy window set into the door to keep draughts in check, to let light in and to enable the approach of visitors to be observed.

In the north and west a bed alcove beside the fire provided additional accommodation for the elder generation, but it was the open hearth which was the hub of the house — a place for cooking fresh and frequent meals, with a pot-hook or perhaps a brick-lined oven, and space for the family to sit round to work, tell stories and sing.

Waterford's 80ft-high Reginald's Tower became a civic museum in 1955

importance to the capital. Its harbour receives the waters of the rivers Barrow, Nore and Suir, attractive to the Norse for upriver forays. They called the place Vatnfjordhr. Near the AD1003 circular tower built by Reginald McIvor, a pub wall is claimed to date from 850, but most of the Norse walling was of timber, and has disappeared. Much of the later Anglo-Norman city wall remains, including towers, in the dark red sandstone. The Beach Tower, dating probably from 1212, has had a water tank placed on top.

A fragment of St Olaf's Viking church remains; nearby Keyser Street is claimed to have a Norse name, but it is really a polite corruption of 'kiss arse', from the posteriors of inebriated seamen 'kissing' the ground on their way back from inns. Spired Christ Church was rebuilt in 1773. The original church of 1050 was built to the same plan as Dublin's first Christ Church, as the kings of these cities were cousins. The roofless French Church was a 1240 Franciscan friary, and after 1693 became a Huguenot chapel.At Blackfriars a belfry tower of a 1226 Dominican priory remains.

Cherry's brewery, now part of Guinness, was originally Strangman's, founded to provide good lunch beer for the boys and girls of Newtown School, a 1798 Quaker co-educational college still in existence but now housed in a Georgian mansion. Waterford has some splendid Georgian architecture. The crystal factory may be visited.

Valentia Island, Co Kerry

Map Ref: 124 V37

Reached by bridge from a sideroad off N70, Valentia, named by Spaniards, is seven miles long and two miles wide, with a mainly rocky surface. Its most prominent features are Geokaun Mountain (880ft) and Bray Head at its south-western extremity, with 792ft cliffs. Both are splendid vantage points, with good cliff scenery. The island is popular as a resort, especially for deep sea fishing, and there is an excellent harbour. Boat excursions can be made to **Church Island**, which has an ancient oratory and some beehive huts, also popular are the gardens and fuchsia glade of **Glanleam**.

Waterford, Co Waterford

Map Ref: 125 S61

Waterford is an industrial city of unspectacular appearance; it was a Viking settlement second only in

---

Waterford Glass

The making of Waterford Crystal is a traditional craft which reached a peak before the end of the 16th century, but lapsed in 1851, and was not revived until 1947: thus two kinds of the crystal now exist, modern and the rarer antique pieces.

Skilled craftsmen at work in the Waterford Glass Factory

Only the chemical part of the production has changed, however, as the crystal is still made by hand. Though definite ranges are produced, no two pieces are exactly alike. The larger, more complex creations received a huge boost in American popularity when the late Bing Crosby, impressed by their beauty, ordered one as a golf tournament prize, setting a fashion which was copied by organisers of all kinds of sporting events.

Prices of Waterford Crystal do not vary greatly in Ireland. It is the availability of specific pieces, sometimes needed to complete a set, which sends enthusiasts from shop to shop. Antique Waterford is very scarce indeed. There is a widely-held belief that old Waterford must have a blue tint; this is untrue. Every piece of modern Waterford crystal has the word 'Waterford' in script somewhere below the surface, though this may take a few minutes to find.

The original Waterford factory, whose most famous owners were George and William Penrose, achieved world-wide repute from 1783 until 1851, when heavy duties forced it to close. For most of those years Cork had three similar factories, producing items ranging from ewers to scent bottles; the most famous firm was Atwell, Burnett and Rowe in Hanover Street.

The McGrath family of Irish Hospital Sweepstakes is responsible for the Waterford revival, which began in 1947 with a small training factory. The modern factory, which may be visited, is on the Cork Road, Waterford. The firm has no cheap line in 'seconds', as some such undertakings have, as all sub-standard items are destroyed. The big chandelier in Waterford City Council's chamber has a twin in the Hall of Independence, Philadelphia.

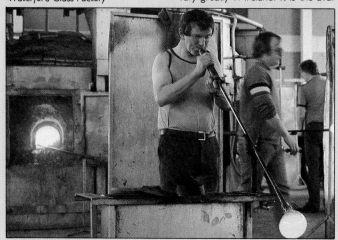

Waterford holds an international festival of light opera every September.

AA recommends:

Hotels: Ardree, 3-star, *tel.* (051) 32111
Granville, The Quay, 3-star, *tel.* (051) 55111
Tower, The Mall, 3-star, *tel.* (051) 75801
Dooleys, 30 The Quay, 2-star, *tel.* (051) 73531
Guesthouse: Diamond Hill, Slieverue, *tel.* (051) 32855
T & C: Bleinham House, *tel.* (051) 74115
Dunroven, 5 Cluain-a-Laoi, Cork Road, *tel.* (051) 74743
Farmhouses: Ashbourne House, Slieverue, *tel.* (051) 32037
River View House, Golfclub Road, Ferrybank, *tel.* (051) 32785
Knockboy House, Dummore Road, *tel.* (051) 73484
Garages: Sheridans Motor Garage, Cork Road, *tel.* (051) 72891
Tom Murphy, Morgan Street, *tel.* (051) 76614
C J Deevy, *tel.* (051) 55719
McConnell Bros, *tel.* (051) 74037

Waterville, Co Kerry

Map Ref: 124 V46

Between Ballinskelligs Bay and Lough Currane on the Ring of Kerry, this is a famed salmon fishing resort. It also has a fine sandy beach on the bay and a nine-hole golf course. East of the scenic lough, mountains rise to 2000ft. The lough's Church Island has a 12th-century ruin and a beehive cell, believed to have been used in the 6th century by St Finan Cam. **Ballinskelligs**, around the bay, is a Gaelic-speaking village situated beside a four-mile strand.

Cahirciveen, further north at the foot of Bentee mountain, overlooks Valentia Harbour. Near it is Leacanabuaile Fort, a massive, circular, stone rampart with steps at intervals along the inner side; excavations in 1939–40 uncovered chambers and house sites, with whetstones, quern stones and bone

combs suggesting an early Christian occupation.

The Skelligs Islands (or Rocks), about nine miles off Valentia Island, are called Lemon Rock, Little Skellig and Great Skellig. The last-named rises precipitously to 700ft. On top are two churches, two oratories and six beehive cells, all pre-10th-century. The ascent is made by crude stone steps. Pilgrims used to be required to kiss a projecting cross-inscribed rock above 'Christ's Saddle'.

AA recommends:

Hotel: Bay view, 1-star, *tel.* (0667) 4122
Restaurant: Huntsman, 2-K & F, *tel.* (0667) 4124
Guesthouse & Restaurant: Smugglers, 2-K & F, *tel.* (0667) 4330

Westport, Co Mayo

Map Ref: 122 L98

Westport, near the south-east corner of island-flecked Clew Bay, is reached by N59 or N60. Thackeray declared the view of Clew Bay to be the most exquisite in the world, and in fact the scenery around Westport can compare with that of any county in Ireland. The town was an important distributing centre from about 1780, ironically declining with the railway age, since railways from larger ports replaced the earlier sea-and-road trans-shipment arrangement. Westport has an international sea angling festival in June.

The central octagon is an exquisite piece of town planning. Its central pillar, limestone on an octagonal granite base, formerly topped by a statue of a local banker, has happily had an ill-placed public loo removed from its side. The Carrowbeg River is flanked by twin malls planted with limes; this, like most of the town centre, was planned by James Wyatt.

Westport House, whose estate adjoins the town, was designed by

Intricate carving at Westport House

Richard Cassels; despite a tendency to Teutonic heaviness, it is one of Ireland's noblest mansions, with a really exquisite interior. Its attractions include a zoo and shopping arcade, the revenue from which has probably saved the house from demolition. It was built in 1731 for John Browne MP, ancestor of Lord Sligo and descendant of Grace O'Malley, Queen of Connaught. An O'Malley castle had previously stood on the site. Wyatt designed the dining room later, and many say it is Ireland's most beautiful room.

Louisburgh is a fishing village with sandy beaches, and nearby Roonagh Quay is the departure point for Clare Island, with its high cliffs and ruin of Grace O'Malley's castle. However, the ferry service is notoriously erratic.

AA recommends:

Hotels: Hotel Westport, 3-star, *tel.* (098) 25122
Clew Bay, 2-star, *tel.* (098) 25438
Railway, The Mall, 2-star, *tel.* (098) 25090
Westport Ryan, Louisbourgh Road, 2-star, *tel.* (098) 25811
Farmhouse: Rath-a-Rosa, Rossbeg, *tel.* (098) 25348
Restaurants: Ardmore House, The Quay, *tel.* (098) 25994
Asgard, The Quay, *tel.* (098) 25319
Garage: Executive Coachworks, *tel.* (098) 25244

Ballinskelligs Bay and the green and pleasant countryside around Waterville

A memorial to James Barry, founder of the American Navy, stands in The Crescent, Wexford

Wexford, Co Wexford

Map Ref: 125 T02

Wexford was the Norse Waesfjord. It is built on three levels, the long narrow main street on the middle level, being a very charming thoroughfare with picturesque old shop fronts. Behind the Talbot Hotel stands St Doologue's Church (formerly a Viking church of 1035); with only three acres it became the smallest parish in the world. Selskar Abbey ruin, whose square west tower is the most well-preserved, was an Augustinian foundation, where the first Anglo-Irish treaty was signed in 1169. Wexford's West Gate, built in about 1300 in red sandstone by Sir Stephen Devereaux, is the sole survivor of five. It still has a stretch of wall attached to it and the little prison inside has survived.

St Peter's College has an exquisite 1838 chapel by A W Pugin. One of Wexford's hilly, narrow streets is called Keyser's Lane, a polite corruption of 'kiss arse' (see **Waterford**). Oscar Wilde's mother, 'Speranza', was born in the Bull Ring in what is now a fashion shop; her cousin Sir Robert McClure, discoverer of the North-West Passage, was born in a house now incorporated into White's Hotel.

Fishing and boating are available in the harbour, where the Slaney enters the sea; silting has long prevented ships bigger than trawlers using it. There is a maritime museum in a disused lightship. The October international opera festival is famed.

Puffins, razorbills, gannets, guillemots and other bird species inhabit the two Saltee Islands, about five miles out, in great numbers. The southern Wexford harbour slob-reserve of whitefront Greenland geese (wintering) was partly reclaimed for farming, to the needless alarm of naturalists; the birds took happily to the crops.

AA recommends:
Hotels: New Whites, 3-star, *tel.* (053) 22311

Talbot, Trinity Street, 3-star, *tel.* (053) 22566
Ferrycarrig, Ferrycarrig Bridge, *tel.* (053) 22999
Guesthouse: Whitford House, Clonard, *tel.* (053) 24673
Farmhouse: Rathaspeck Manor, *tel.* (053) 42661
Garages: Ferrybank Motors, Ferrybank, *tel.* (053) 22107
Rockland Service Station, *tel.* (053) 43372
Campsite: Ferrybank Caravan Park, Ferrybank, 3-pennant, *tel.* (053) 24378

Wicklow, Co Wicklow

Map Ref: 125 T39

This is a seaside town off N11 looking out on a wide bay fringed by a crescent of coast. The Vikings called it Wykinglo. Today the old 'Viking's Lough' is a resort, its narrow streets much modernised. The long spit of land called the **Murrough**, with a railway line along part of it, has a sand and shingle beach and a promenade. The Silver Strand is just south of the town, as is the nine-hole golf course. There is sea-fishing, trout fishing in streams nearby and a regatta is held annually.

There are slight remains of a 13th-century Franciscan friary, and the Black Castle ruin on a rocky promontory at the town's eastern end, begun in 1176 by Maurice Fitzgerald, is picturesque rather than threatening. The ruined Dunganstown Castle, six miles south, was visited by Sir Francis Bacon. An obelisk in the town commemorates Captain Robert Halpin, commander of the cable-laying 'Great Eastern', who was born here.

AA recommends:
T & C: Marine Villa, Church Hill, *tel.* (0404) 3252
Thomond House, St Patricks Road Upper, *tel.* (0404) 2940
Farmhouse: Lissadell House, Ashtown, *tel.* (0404) 2458
Restaurant & Guesthouse: Old Rectory, 2-K & F, *tel.* (0404) 2048
Garage: Vartry Service Station, New Street, *tel.* (0404) 3127

Woodenbridge, Co Wicklow

Map Ref: 125 T17

Between Avoca and Arklow, at the junction of three valleys, this is an idyllic spot. The Aughrim and Avoca rivers join here to form the 'Second Meeting of the Waters' (see **Avoca** for the first). Croghan Kinshela (1987ft), to the south-west, at the head of the Gold Mines River, was a mineral source for the goldsmiths of ancient Ireland, and in 1796 the finding of a nugget there led to a 'gold rush'. In a few months 2600 ounces were found; since then there have been small finds, but the pine-scented air of this little retreat is nowadays a more sought-after commodity.

Youghal, Co Cork

Map Ref: 125 X17

Straggling along N25 at the mouth of the Blackwater, Youghal's old, mile-long main street forms a herringbone pattern with its side streets. The 1771 Clock Gate, an archway crowned by a clock lantern, divides it. Street names incised on little marble tablets are a pretty touch. The new town is built on the fringe of the bay.

Golf, fishing, boating and a long, wild strand are among the attractions, but the antiquities overshadow these. The Collegiate Church of St Mary, built in the reign of King John, restored in the mid-15th century and again in 1851–58, is Ireland's largest medieval parish church. Its monument to Richard Boyle, Earl of Cork, which includes figures of his family, was erected in 1619 by the earl himself. There is a monument to Catherine, Countess of Desmond, who is reputed to have fallen to her death from a cherry tree at the age of 147. The church has an Early English west doorway and a separate belfry-tower, with walls 8ft thick.

Youghal has remains of a 1268 Dominican priory, and some of the town walls survive around St Mary's churchyard. North is Myrtle Grove, home of Sir Walter Raleigh, warden of the town in 1588 and 1589. It is a splendid, Elizabethan, gabled house; Raleigh is said to have planted Ireland's first potatoes and smoked Ireland's first tobacco in its garden, and his clay and brass pipe is preserved. Here he entertained Spenser, but a folk tale that Shakespeare, was also a visitor, is hard to confirm. The house is not open to the public.

AA recommends:
T & C: Carriglea, Summerfield, *tel.* (024) 92520
Farmhouse: Cherrymount, *tel.* (024) 97110
Restaurant: Aherne's Pub, 163 North Main Street, 1-K & F, *tel.* (024) 92424

Directory

INFORMATION

Getting There

By air: Major international airlines operate scheduled services from Canada, the USA, Britain and Europe, direct to these airports:
Belfast International *tel* (0232) 229271
Belfast Harbour *tel* (0232) 56463
Cork *tel* (021) 965388
Dublin *tel* (01) 370191
Shannon *tel* (061) 61666
By sea: Car ferry companies and routes:
Belfast Car Ferries: Liverpool – Belfast
Isle of Man Steam Packet Company: Douglas – Belfast
B+I Lines: Pembroke – Rosslare; Holyhead – Dublin; Liverpool – Dublin.
Sealink: Fishguard – Rosslare; Holyhead – Dun Laoghaire; Stranraer – Larne
Townsend Thoresen: Cairnryan – Larne
Irish Continental Line: Le Havre – Cork; Le Havre – Rosslare; Cherbourg – Rosslare
Britanny Ferries: Roscoff – Cork

Public Transport

Buses: Comprehensive networks cover the whole of Ireland, including cross-border routes and special excursions.
Northern Ireland: Ulsterbus *tel* Belfast (0232) 220011
Republic: CIE (Coras Iompair Eirann) *tel* Dublin (01) 787777
Trains: A two-hour Belfast – Dublin express service is run jointly by NIR (Northern Ireland Railways) *tel* Belfast (0232) 230310 or 230671 and CIE *tel* Dublin (01) 787777. Rambler and Overlander tickets give unlimited bus and/or train travel throughout Ireland for eight or 15 days. Contact Ulsterbus, NIR, CIE and travel agencies.

Car Rental

Cars are available for hire at the airports above. Lists of approved firms throughout the country are available from Bord Failte and the Northern Ireland Tourist Board. A full driving licence, issued in your country of residence, is required. Prior arrangements are necessary for persons under 23. Special documentation is needed to cross the border.

Principal AA Offices

Fanum House, 108–119 Gt Victoria St, Belfast *tel* (0232) 244538

23 Suffolk St, Dublin *tel* (01) 779481
9 Bridge St, Cork *tel* (021) 505155

National tourist organisations

Information and literature on every aspect of touring in the Republic of Ireland can be obtained from the Irish Tourist Board – Bord Failte Eireann, Baggot Street Bridge, Dublin 2 *tel* (01) 765877; tourist information 747733, or Bord Failte Eireann, PO Box 273, Dublin 8 for written enquiries. Information on Northern Ireland can be obtained from the Northern Ireland Tourist Board, River House, 48 High Street, Belfast BT1 2DS *tel* (0232) 246609.

Money

Northern Ireland: Sterling, *Republic:* Irish pound (IR£) – also called the *punt*. The two currencies are not interchangeable and may be quite different in value. Travellers' cheques and leading credit cards are widely acceptable throughout Ireland. You may import as much currency into Ireland as you wish, but export from the Republic is limited and no bank notes may be sent from there by post.

Banks

Open 1000–1230 and 1330–1500 (1530 Northern Ireland), Monday to Friday (except public holidays). Dublin banks stay open until 1700 on Thursdays.

Public Holidays

Holidays falling at weekends are taken the following Monday.
Throughout Ireland: 1 January, St Patrick's Day (17 March), Good Friday (unofficial in the Republic), Easter Monday, Christmas Day and 26 December (Boxing Day in Northern Ireland, St Stephen's Day in the Republic).
Northern Ireland only: Orangemen's Day (12 July), May Day (first Monday in May), Spring Bank Holiday (last Monday in May), Late Summer Holiday (last Monday in August).
Republic only: June Holiday (first Monday), August Holiday (first Monday), October Holiday (last Monday).

Post

Northern Ireland Post Offices open from 0900 to 1800 weekdays and 0900 to 1230 Saturdays. British stamps must be used. Post boxes are red.

Republic Post Offices are open from 0900 to 1730 Monday to Saturday (sub-post offices close at 1300 once a week). Republic of Ireland stamps must be used. Post boxes are green.

Telephones

Northern Ireland: Booths are red or the new-style glass and steel, and all are on STD. Dial 100 for the operator.
Republic: Booths are blue and cream. Most of the large towns are on STD, but some country areas have not been converted. Dial 199 for the operator, or 0 in a press-button box.
Please note: The telephone codes given are applicable only within each country. To telephone to the Republic from Northern Ireland and vice versa consult your dialling code book.

Time

Greenwich Mean Time: last Sunday in October to last Saturday in March. 1200 in Belfast and Dublin is 0700 in New York. British Summer Time: rest of the year (one hour ahead of GMT).

Electricity

Standard current is 220 volts AC (50 cycles). Most hotels have 220/110 sockets for shavers.

Licensing Hours

Northern Ireland 1130 to 2300 except Sundays when pubs are closed all day (restaurants and hotel bars are open).
Republic 1030 to 2330 in summer, 1030 to 2300 in winter at time of publication. Legislation to extend the licensing hours is proposed. In Dublin and Cork pubs close from 1430 to 1530. Sundays 1230 to 1400 and 1600 to 2200.

Emergencies

Throughout Ireland dial 999.

St Patrick's Day in Dublin – always an occasion for a parade

CALENDAR OF EVENTS

*These dates may vary. Check
locally with Tourist Board.*

February
Cavan International Song Contest
Cork City Opera Season
Ulster Motor Show, Belfast
Ulster Harp National, Downpatrick
    Racecourse

March
Belfast Music Festival
Horse Ploughing Match & Heavy
    Horse Show, Ballycastle
Irish Motor Show (RDS),
    Ballsbridge (biennial)
St Patrick's Day (Mar 17): national
    holiday with many parades
Hurst Cup Motorcycle Trial,
    Bangor
Irish International Boat Show
    (RDS), Dublin

April
Silk Cut Festival of Country Music,
    Belfast
Dublin Grand Opera Society
    Spring Season
Galway Arts Festival
Circuit of Ireland International
    Motor Rally, Belfast

May
Belfast City Marathon, Maysfield
    Leisure Centre
Sealink Classic Fishing Festival,
    Erne Waters
Spring Show (RDS), Ballsbridge
Cork International Choral & Folk
    Dance Festival, City Hall
North West 200 (motorcycle race),
    Portstewart
Pan Celtic Week, Killarney
The Lord Mayor's Show, Belfast
Belfast Civic Festival
Dublin Grand Opera Season,
    Dublin & Cork
Tipperary Remembers Weekend,
    Tipperary town
International 3-Day Event,
    Punchestown Racecourse
Dundalk Amateur Theatre Festival
Fleadh Nua (traditional Irish dance,
    music, song) Ennis
Royal Ulster Agricultural Show,
    Belfast
Listowel Writers' Week

June
Carling Country Music Festival,
    Cork
Festival of Tipperary
Music Festival in Great Irish
    Houses
Glengarriff Festival
Spancilhill Horse Fair, Ennis
An Tostal (dance, ballads, singing),
    Drumshanbo
Dun Laoghaire Summer Festival
Ballybunion Bachelor Festival
Dublin International Organ
    Festival
West Cork Festival, Clonakilty
Annual Northern Ireland Game &
    Country Fair, Clandeboye
    Estate, Bangor
World Championship 125cc Moto
    Cross Grand Prix, Killinchy

Wexford Strawberry Fair,
    Enniscorthy
Ulster Games, held throughout
    Northern Ireland

July
International Rose Trials (Jul–
    Sep), Belfast
Willie Clancie Summer School,
    Miltown Malbay
Drimoleague Festival
Festival of Humour, Shannon
Schull Festival
Cobh International Folk Dance
    Festival

*Folk dancing has its own international
festival at Cobh, Co Cork*

Kerry Summer Painting School,
    Cahirciveen
Bridge Congress, Ballina
Glens of Antrim Feis (music,
    dancing, sports), Glenariff
Queen of Connemara Festival,
    Oughterard
Bandon Week
Skibbereen Annual Show
Open Amateur Golf
    Championship, Royal Portrush
Orangemen's Day (Jul 12), parades
    throughout Northern Ireland
Ulster Harp Derby, Down Royal
    Racecourse
Ulster Steam Traction Rally,
    Antrim
Mary from Dungloe Festival,
    Dungloe
Sham Fight (re-enacts Battle of the
    Boyne), Scarva
International Ulster Motor Rally,
    Belfast
Galway Races (Jul–Aug)

August
Ballyshannon International Folk
    Festival
O'Carolan Harp & Music Festival,
    Keadue
Stradbally Steam Rally
Claddagh Festival, Galway
International Summer School,
    Sligo
Irish Antique Dealers' Fair, Dublin
Dublin Horse Show (RDS)
Granard Harp Festival

Relief of Derry Celebrations,
    Londonderry City
Puck Fair, Killorglin
Ancient Order of Hibernians'
    Celebrations, several towns in
    Northern Ireland
Connemara Pony Show, Clifden
Ulster Grand Prix World
    Championships (motorcycling),
    nr Belfast
Percy French Festival, Newcastle
Oul' Lammas Fair (one of Ireland's
    oldest and biggest fairs),
    Ballycastle
Wild Rose Festival, Manorhamilton
Schull Regatta
Carroll's Irish Open Golf
    Tournament, Royal Dublin Golf
    Club
Birr Vintage Week
Merriman Summer School,
    Lahinch
Limerick Show
Carlingford Oyster Festival
Rose of Tralee Festival
Letterkenny International Folk
    Festival
Fleadh Cheoil na hÉireann,
    location changes every year
Kilkenny Arts Week
Vintage Car Rally, Inistioge
Wexford Mussel Festival
Ideal Home & Do-It-Yourself
    Exhibition (Aug–Sep), Belfast

September
Salthill Festival
Harp Cork Folk Festival
Belfast Folk Festival
City of Belfast Flower Show
Cobh International Sea Angling
    Festival
Waterford International Festival of
    Light Opera
Dublin Theatre Festival
Cork City Opera
Lisdoonvarna Folk Festival
Listowel Harvest Festival and
    Races
All Ireland Hurling & Football
    Finals, Dublin
Galway Oyster Festival
Phoenix Park Motor Races
European Surfing Championships,
    Rossnowlagh
Castlebar International Song
    Contest (Sep/Oct)

October
Kinsale Gourmet Festival
Fruits de Mer Festival, Kenmare
Flower Festival, St Nicholas
Ballinasloe October Fair
Cork Film Festival
Wexford Opera Festival
Guinness Jazz Festival, Cork
Royal Ulster Academy of Arts
    Exhibition, Botanic Gdns,
    Belfast
Irish National Stamp Exhibition
    (RDS)

November
Ulster Fine Art and Antiques Fair,
    nr Belfast
International Ploughing
    Championships
Belfast Festival at Queen's Belfast
Dublin Indoor International
    Showjumping (RDS)

ANGLING

Coarse Fishing

This is possible all year in Ireland as there is no close season. In the Republic no licence is needed and permits are only required on a few private fisheries. Maximum of two rods permitted. In Northern Ireland a Coarse Fishing permit and a Rod licence are required. These are available (for 15 days or a season) from local tackle shops, hotels or the Fisheries Conservancy Board for Northern Ireland, 1 Mahon Road, Portadown, Co Armagh (0762) 334666. There are many miles of well-stocked waters in the Republic, and the Dept of Agriculture Fisheries in Northern Ireland have excellent facilities.

Game Fishing

A State licence is required for salmon and sea trout, but not for brown or rainbow trout. The seasons vary slightly from county to county: salmon 1 Jan to 30 Sep; sea trout 1 Jan to 12 Oct; brown trout 15 Feb to 30 Sep. Some salmon fishing is free, as are many brown trout waters, but almost all sea trout fisheries require a permit. Salmon are found in most rivers flowing north, west and east, but are most prolific in Galway; sea trout frequent the shorter coastal streams and their acid lakes; hundreds of brown trout waters are scattered throughout the country.

Tackle for all freshwater fishing is difficult to hire. Bait can often be purchased locally, or can be pre-ordered from Irish Angling Services, Ardlogher, Co Cavan *tel* (049) 26258. Boats may be hired on most still waters at a reasonable cost. More information from the Central Fisheries Board, The Weir Lodge, Earl's Island, Balnagowan Mobhi Boreen, Glasnevin, Dublin 9 *tel* (01) 379206 and the NITB.

To game fish in Northern Ireland you must obtain a rod licence from either the Fisheries Conservancy Board (address above) or from the Foyle Fisheries Commission, 8 Victoria Road, Londonderry, *tel* (0504) 42100. In addition you must obtain permission from the owner of the water. In the case of Department of Agriculture waters this permission takes the form of a permit, or a daily ticket from an angling club. Licences and permits are available from NITB, the visitor centre Enniskillen and from tackle shops around the province. More information from the Department of Agriculture, Fisheries Division, Stormont, Belfast *tel* (0232) 63939.

Sea Fishing

A tremendous variety is available: different types depend on the time of year – shore, from rocks, piers, beaches and promontories; inshore, within bays and inlets; deep sea, usually from small motor vessels. Natural bait not generally stocked, but salted bait obtainable locally. All

A fine brown trout caught on Lough Corrib, Co Galway

sea fishing is free and does not require permits or licences. Over 250 competitions and festivals take place from February to November. Most are open to all-comers. Details of tides, boats and centres in *Sea Angling*, published by *Bord Fáilte*. Information from the Irish Federation of Sea Anglers (Secretary), 67 Windsor Dr, Monkstown, Co Dublin and the Dept of Agriculture, Fisheries Division, Stormont, Belfast.

BIRD WATCHING AND NATURE RESERVES

Although there are fewer breeding species here than in the rest of Europe, some of them are of particular interest, including the corncrake, the chough, gannets, Manx shearwaters and storm petrels. Many more birds pass through Ireland than spend the winter or summer: peak migration times are Apr to May and Sep to Oct. The best places to see migrating birds are coastal headlands and offshore islands.

There are at present over 60 bird sanctuaries where the shooting of wild birds is prohibited. Many are privately owned and prior permission to visit must be sought. Details from Forest & Wildlife Service, Conservation Sections, Leeson St, Dublin 2. There are fewer nature reserves and not all are open to visitors. Information about these and other birdwatching sites is available from Irish Wildbird Conservancy, Southview, Church Rd, Greystones, Co Wicklow *tel* (01) 875759; RSPB, Belvoir Forest, Belvoir Park, Belfast 8 *tel* (0232) 692547; The National Trust, Rowallane House, Ballynahinch, Co Down *tel* Saintfield 510721.

CANOEING

This all-year-round sport is becoming increasingly popular in Ireland which has hundreds of navigable lakes and rivers free from restrictions. Slalom, down-river racing, rough water and surfing is available in winter; sprint, long-distance, marathon and surfing in summer. Canoe touring – on streams, rivers, canals, lakes and the

sea – is probably of most interest to visitors: organised trips include exploring, camping and adventure training. Details from the Association of Adventure Sports, Tiglin Adventure Centre, Ashford, Co Wicklow *tel* (0404) 4169. More information available from Irish Canoe Hire, c/o 82 Upper Georges St, Dun Laoghaire, Co. Dublin *tel* (01) 807517 (office), the Irish Canoe Union, 4/5 Eustace St, Dublin 2 *tel* (01) 719690 and the Canoe Association of N. Ireland, House of Sport, Upper Malone Rd, Belfast *tel* (0232) 661222.

CLIMBING

Most of the summits in Ireland can be reached without climbing gear, but Muckrish and Errigal in Co Donegal and the Mountains of Mourne provide challenging climbs. The Federation of Mountaineering Clubs of Ireland (Secretary), 20 Leopardstown Gdns, Blackrock, Co Dublin *tel* (01) 881266 and the NI Mountain Centre, (Warden) Tollymore, Newcastle *tel* (03967) 22158 can provide information.

CULTURAL HERITAGE

Houses and Gardens

The Historic Irish Tourist Houses and Gardens Association and the National Trust for Northern Ireland are the two main bodies concerned with the preservation of the stately homes and castles open to the public in Ireland. Their publications and details of opening times and charges are available from the Bord Failte and NITB. Many of these famous houses also have beautiful gardens open to the public (see feature on page 80).

Museums

There are 150 museums in Ireland (including Northern Ireland), ranging from the large National Museum in Dublin (Kildare Street) to the small specialist museums such as the Toomevara Folk Museum in Co Tipperary with its display of 19th-and 20th-century exhibits. Details of all of these are contained in an illustrated guide published by Ward River Press in

Playing golf on the shores of the Atlantic Ocean at Ballybunion

association with The Irish Museums Trust. It is available from booksellers or direct from The Irish Museums Trust, Gardner House, Ballsbridge, Dublin 4.

Art Galleries
The National Gallery of Ireland, Merrion Square West, Dublin 2 *tel* (01) 608533 is open weekdays 1000–1800 (2100 Thur) and Sun 1400–1700. It houses a fine collection of Old Masters, most notably of the Italian and Dutch schools, an American collection and Irish paintings and sculpture from the 18th century to the present day.

There are many other galleries throughout Ireland displaying all aspects of early and contemporary art and sculpture by international and local artists. Details from Bord Failte and NITB.

CYCLING
The quiet, generally fairly flat, country roads are ideal for cycling. Raleigh operate a Rent-a-Bike scheme through over 100 of their dealers and details are available from their head office: Irish Raleigh Ltd, The Collen Industrial Estate, Broomhill Rd, Tallaght, Co Dublin *tel* (01) 521888 telex 24523. Rent-a-Bike have rental offices at the main bus/rail/air terminal in Dublin, at 58 Lower Gardiner St, Dublin 1 *tel* (01) 725931 telex 33527 (contact this address for information) and at Rosslare Harbour from Jun to Sep. Bicycles hired in Northern Ireland cannot be taken into the Republic, or vice versa. More information, including suggested routes, from the Irish Tourist Board and the NITB offices.

The Youth Hostel Association of Northern Ireland (YHANI), 56 Bradbury Pl, Belfast *tel* (0232) 224733 and *An Óige*, the Irish Youth Hostel Association, 39 Mountjoy Sq, Dublin 1 *tel* (01) 745734, offer various cycling holiday packages.

FIELD SPORTS
Beagling
This can be enjoyed by anyone who likes walking. No special expertise or clothing is required and hunts welcome non-members. The season extends from Oct to Mar and meets are usually held on a Sunday or mid-week. Contact the Irish Masters of Beagles Association (Hon Secretary), Tipper Rd, Naas, Co Kildare *tel* (045) 76251.

Fox Hunting
This is obviously not so easy to participate in, but visitors are welcome at meets. Horses can be hired for a day's hunting from some stables. A special holiday package, including two days' hunting with the East Down Foxhounds is available: contact Miss Diana Kirkpatrick (Hon Secretary), Church Hill, Newcastle, Co Down *tel* (03967) 23217. The Irish Masters of Foxhounds Association (Hon Secretary), Rockmount, Kilmacthomas, Co Waterford *tel* (051) 91183 (home).

Shooting
Facilities for visiting sportsmen are limited and strictly regulated. In Northern Ireland it is mainly confined to the State forests. Visitors must possess a current Irish firearm certificate for each shotgun carried, and an Irish hunting licence (free) is required to hunt game species during open seasons. Applications for both can be made, by post only, to the Forest and Wildlife Service, Leeson St, Dublin 2, at least one month in advance. A number of organisations provide shooting trips and holidays for tourists; details in the Irish Tourist Board's booklet, *Shooting in Ireland,* or from The Irish Fieldsports Agency, 174 Castlereagh Rd, Belfast *tel* (0232) 59248. Further information about field sports in Northern Ireland from the Chief Wildlife Officer, Forest Service Dept of Agriculture, Dundonald House, Belfast 4 *tel* (0232) 650111 or the NITB, and in the Republic from the National Association of Regional Game Councils (Secretary), Gorta Cleva, Bushey Park, Co. Galway *tel* (091) 24266 (home).

GOLF
Over 250 courses throughout the country welcome visitors and most have plenty of accommodation nearby. Clubs are not generally available for hire and caddies must be booked in advance. There are several open competitions. The International Championships are held at Royal Portrush and Royal County Down. Information and leaflets on all courses from the Irish Tourist Board and the NITB Travel Trade Dept.

Details of golfing holidays are obtainable from any Irish tourist office, travel agents, or direct from JP Murray, Golf Promotion Executive, Irish Tourist Board, Dublin 2 *tel* (01) 765871 and The Irish Golfing Agency, 174 Castlereagh Rd, Belfast *tel* (0232) 59248.

There are pitch and putt courses in practically every town in Ireland. A list of clubs is available from The Pitch and Putt Union of Ireland, rear of 32 Shandon Gdns, Philsboro, Dublin 7 *tel* (01) 301245.

HANG-GLIDING
Ireland provides nearly perfect conditions for this increasingly popular sport. It can take place all year round at the hundreds of sites available. Thermal activity, however, is best from Mar to Oct. Visiting flyers must contact the Irish Hang-Gliding Centre, Wits End, Drumbawn, Newtown, Co Wicklow *tel* (01) 819445, for information about air traffic lanes etc. Flying in the Republic is controlled by the Irish Hang-Gliding Association (Secretary), 41 Newlands, Wexford *tel* (053) 41276 (home); in Northern Ireland by the Ulster Hang-Gliding Club, which is affiliated to the British Hang-Gliding Association. Contact Alan Watson, 21 Brentwood Way, Newtownards, Co Down *tel* (0247) 816985.

HOLY PLACES
With its long unbroken tradition of Christianity, Catholicism in particular, Ireland is one of the more important places of pilgrimage in Europe today. The country's religious tradition is not a thing of the past, buried in the annals of history, the spirit is very much alive today.

The three major places of pilgrimage are: *Knock Shrine, Co Mayo* where an apparition of the Blessed Virgin was witnessed on the evening of August 21, 1879. Pilgrimage enquiries to Rev Parish Priest, Knock Shrine, Co Mayo *tel* (094) 88100, or Knock Shrine Bureau, 29 South Anne Street, Dublin 2 *tel* (01) 775965. *Lough Derg, Co Donegal* Ireland's greatest and most important place of pilgrimage. Station Island, or St Patrick's Purgatory as it is known, has been a place of pilgrimage for at least 1500 years. A monastery flourished here in very early times. Pilgrimage enquiries to Rev Prior, Lough Derg, Pettigo, Co Donegal. *Croagh Patrick, Co Mayo* In AD441 St Patrick spent 40 days of fasting and prayer on this holy mountain, a graceful isolated cone rising above the shores of Clew Bay. Pilgrims have come to pray on its summit for more than 1500 years. A national pilgrimage takes place each year on the last Sunday in July. A special train service runs to Westport (6 miles from Croagh Patrick) on Pilgrimage Sunday.

HORSE-DRAWN CARAVAN HOLIDAYS

This unique form of travelling must be one of the nicest ways to see Ireland. Current operators are: Mr J O'Reilly, Blarney Romany Caravans, Blarney, Co Cork *tel* (021) 85700 telex 26047; Mr J Desmond, Ocean Breeze Horse Caravans, Bayview House, Granreigh, Kilbrittain, Co Cork *tel* (023) 49731; Mr D Slattery, Slattery's Horse-Drawn Caravans, Slattery's Travel Agency, Tralee, Co Kerry *tel* (066) 21722 telex 26823; Mr D Clissmann, Dieter Clissman Horse-Drawn Caravan Holidays, Carrigmore Farm, Co Wicklow *tel* (0404) 8188 telex 33599.

HORSE RIDING

Many establishments throughout the country offer facilities ranging from hacking and trekking to top-class tuition. In the Republic, *Bord na gCapall* – the Irish Horse Board – has established a scheme whereby many stables are registered in categories according to what they offer and standards are strictly maintained. Each displays a plaque with the *Bord's* symbol on it. Details can be found in the Irish Tourist Board's booklet *Where To Ride in Ireland. Bord na gCapall*, The Irish Farm Centre, Naas Rd, Dublin 14 *tel* (01) 501166 telex 30452/33338. For more information about riding in Northern Ireland contact the NITB Travel Trade Dept or the Sports Council at The House of Sport, Malone Rd, Belfast *tel* (0232) 661222.

INLAND CRUISING

This is particularly enjoyable in Ireland as the waterways are extensive, uncommercialised and free from pollution. The three navigable rivers – the Shannon, the Erne and the Barrow, the Grand Canal and Lower and Upper Lough Erne are the chief cruising areas. The Grand Canal and the Barrow Line are under the control of CIE and a permit is required.

Several companies provide self-drive, luxury cabin cruisers for hire and all craft have been inspected by the Irish Tourist Board, which can supply full details. Extras such as fishing tackle or bicycles are usually available. Guide books and basic navigation charts are provided. For details of annual boat rallies to which visitors are welcome, contact Mrs R Heard, Inland Waterways Association of Ireland, Stone Cottage, Claremont Rd, Killiney, Co Dublin *tel* (01) 852258.

SAILING

Sailing is a very popular pastime here and facilities and opportunities are plentiful. The Irish Yachting Association, 4 Haddington Terr, Dún Laoghaire, Co Dublin *tel* (01) 800239, governs the sport (including boardsailing) and can supply information to visiting yachtsmen. The racing programme is extensive and open to craft of many types and classes: visitors are welcome to compete. Yachts or sailing dinghies may be brought into Ireland on holiday without liability for tax or duty. The Irish Association for Sail Training, IFMI, Confederation House, Kildare St, Dublin 2 *tel* (01) 779801 telex 24711, is the national organisation representing professional sailing schools, voluntary sailing organisations and the State Sail Training Committee: contact the secretariat for information about tuition and hire of craft.

TRACING YOUR ANCESTRY

Tracing your ancestry is a fascinating occupation but can also be very time-consuming, so it is important to assemble as much information as possible at home before making explorations in Ireland itself.

The initial stages consist of talking to relatives, examining family papers, bibles, letters, diaries and military service records, as well as consulting emigrant shipping lists, local church and state records, newspapers and your nearest genealogical society. In the USA the National Archive contains many useful records, from which you may be able to trace your family's history back to the port and date of arrival. Important facts to ascertain are: the full name of your emigrant ancestor; date of birth, marriage and death; occupation; background; date of emigration from Ireland and the county of origin. Useful here is the tradition of emigrants naming their American homes after the parish or town they lived in.

Once in Ireland there are many sources of valuable information. It is often a good idea to start enquiries by post in advance. Send a stamped addressed envelope or international reply coupon.

The General Register Office *8–11 Lombard St East, Dublin 2, tel (01) 711000*, holds the general civil registration of births, marriages and deaths from 1864. Some non-Catholic marriages are recorded from 1845. A small fee is payable. You can make the search yourself or have it done for you.

General Register Office *Oxford House, 49–55 Chichester St, Belfast BT1 4HL, tel (0232) 235211*, holds the above records for Northern Ireland (marriage registrations since 1922).

Lough Erne, scenically studded with islands, offers 50 miles of uncongested waterway

The National Library *Kildare St, Dublin 2, tel (01) 765521* has a major collection of genealogical material, including historical journals, directories, topographical works and local histories, plus an extensive collection of parish records – births and marriages. Free.

The Public Record Office *Four Courts, Dublin 7, tel (01) 725275* has many valuable documents, including wills, abstracts of wills and tithes dating from 1800. The returns for the 1901 census may be seen here. Research can be carried out on your behalf for a fee. **The Public Record Office of Northern Ireland** *66 Balmoral Ave, Belfast BT9 6YN, tel (0232) 661621*, has a public research room open 0930–1645 Mon–Fri and holds the Tithe Applotment Books. The Ulster Historical Foundation in the same building has a searching service.

The Genealogical Office *2 Kildare St, Dublin 2*, holds records of official pedigrees, coats of arms and will abstracts. Research can be carried out on your behalf for a fee.

The Registry of Deeds *Henrietta St, Dublin 1*, has documents from 1708 regarding property transactions, e.g. leases, mortgages and settlements. A small fee is payable.

The Irish Genealogical Association *164 Kingsway, Dunmurry, Belfast BT17 9AD, tel (0232) 629595*, undertakes research on a mail-order basis and employs a professional genealogist to assist people doing their own research. Tours are available.

A good place to start is with the relevant parish records (if it is known); apply to the priest or minister. Also look at the headstones in the graveyard.

Other useful sources of reference are county records, local libraries and historical or archaeological societies. There are also several books available on the subject.

Research agencies, of which there are a number in Ireland, can be employed to undertake searches varying from basic reports to extensive investigations. Some addresses are: *Hibernian Research Co Ltd*, 22 Windsor Rd, Dublin 6; *M O'Connor*, 31 Rushbrook Way, Templeogue, Dublin 12; *Historical Research Associates*, 7 Lancasterian St, Carrickfergus BT38 7AB, *tel* (09603) 67544; *Heritage Research*, 8 Powerscourt Town Centre, Dublin 2; *Ulster Historical Foundation*, 66 Balmoral Ave, Belfast *tel* (0232) 661621; *Ulster Pedigrees*, 5 Heathermount Court, Comber, Co Down *tel* (972) 873155.

WALKING

Walking in Northern Ireland is rather more organised than in the Republic. The Ulster Way covers about 500 miles around the province. Much of it is waymarked but some sections require reference to a map. Information about the path is obtainable from the Sports Council of Northern Ireland, The House of Sport, Malone Rd, Belfast

tel (0232) 661222. The many State forest parks, several with nature trails, exhibitions, picnic sites etc, provide very enjoyable walking. Walking and rambling tours are organised by the YHANI (see page 118 **Cycling**).

The Republic offers less formalised walking with very few restrictions. Generally speaking it does not have a network of footpaths but long-distance footpaths include the Wicklow Way, which runs from Moyne to Clonegal and stage one of the South Leinster Way, which runs from Clonegal to Graiguenamagh. Many more routes are in the process of being established: contact the Irish Tourist Board for current information. More information about walking is available from The Wayfarer's Association, 26 Waterloo Rd, Dublin 4 *tel* (01) 683863 (home) and *An Óige* (see page 118 **Cycling** for address).

WATER SPORTS
Boardsailing

There are many centres where tuition and board hire are available and numerous events take place throughout the year. Contact the Irish Yachting Association (see page 119 **Sailing**), the Irish Boardsailing Association, 5 East Beach, Cobh, Co Cork *tel* (021) 811237 and the Irish Windsurfing Class Association, c/o Gary Matthews, 1 Havelock Sq, Donnybrook, Dublin 4 *tel* (01) 684703, for details.

Sub-aqua Diving

Every conceivable form of diving and underwater swimming can be enjoyed here and conditions are virtually ideal. Information is available from the Irish Underwater Council (Hon Secretary), 60 Lower Baggot St, Dublin 2 *tel* (01) 785844 (office) and Peter Wright, Norsemaid Enterprises, 154 Portaferry Rd, Newtownards, Co Down *tel* (0247) 813457.

Surfing

The waves off Ireland's coast are comparable to any on the world's top surfing beaches. Visitors are advised to bring their own equipment although boards may be hired at some resorts. Information is obtainable from the Irish Surfing Association (Secretary), Tigh-na-Mara, Rossnowlagh, Co Donegal *tel* (072) 51261 (home); (073) 21053 (work).

Water-skiing

The Irish Water-Ski Association (President), 7 Upper Beaumont Dr, Ballintemple, Cork *tel* (021) 292411, which controls water-skiing in the Republic, and the Northern Ireland Water-Ski Association, form the Irish Water-Ski Federation. These authorities promote this fast-growing sport through affiliated clubs – many of which offer facilities to non-members – located throughout the country.

Opposite: Georgian houses in the Mall, Waterford – a reminder of the town's late 19th-century prosperity

Ireland Legend

ATLAS
1:1,020,400
Approx. 16mls to 1 INCH

TOURS AND WAYMARKED WALKS
1:250,000
4mls to 1 INCH
(unless shown on plan)

IRISH GRID REFERENCE SYSTEM

The map references used in this book are based on the Irish Grid. They comprise of one letter and two figures, and are preceded by the atlas page number.
Thus the reference for Belfast appears
123 J 37

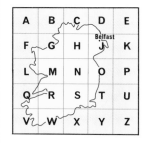

123 is the atlas page number. Each square is identified by a letter eg. J The 100 kilometre squares are then subdivided into 10 kilometre squares and are numbered left to right 0 to 9 and bottom to top 0 to 9. This reference is used to locate gazetteer entries. The 10 kilometre squares can be further divided into tenths to give a place of reference to the nearest kilometre.

The references to walks can be further subdivided into tenths of a kilometre square to allow for a more precise reference to locations on the larger scale maps.

REPUBLIC OF IRELAND

Motorway	M1
National primary road	N1
National secondary road	N61
Regional road	R352
Other roads	

NORTHERN IRELAND

Motorway	M2
Primary road	A2
A road	A45
B road	
Spot height in feet	▲ 2284
Customs	N.Ireland / Rep of Ireland
Distances in miles	8
Place of interest	■ Giant's Causeway
International boundary	

REPUBLIC OF IRELAND

Motorway	M1
National primary road	N4
National secondary road	N54
Regional road	R248
Other roads	

NORTHERN IRELAND

Motorway	M2
Class A road	A4
Class B road	B39
Other roads	
Spot height in metres	·112
Approved frontier crossing point	★
International boundary	•—■—•
Parking	P
Picnic site	🛉

IRELAND

Atlas

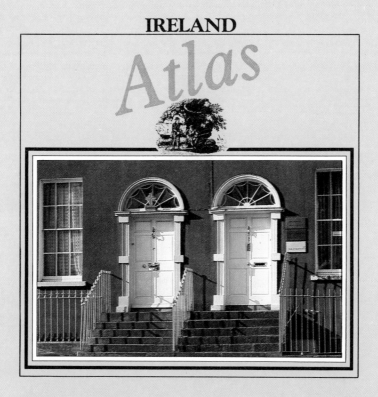

The following pages contain a legend and atlas of Ireland, twenty-four circular motor tours, nine planned walks and a selection of waymarked walks in the Irish countryside.

WALKS 1 to 4 1:35,000 0:55mls to 1 INCH		WALKS 5 & 6 1:25,000 0.40mls to 1 INCH		WALKS 7 & 8 1:35,000 0.55mls 1 INCH	
				WALK 9 1:47,000 0.74mls to 1 INCH	
Motorway	M2	Class A road	A35		
Class A road	A8	Class B road	B8I	National primary road	N11
Class B road	B197	Class C road	C446	National secondary road	N81
Minor road		Minor road		Trunk road	T61
		Track		Link road	L161
Parking	P	Path		3rd class road	
Picnic area	✕			Other roads	
Caravan site	🚐	Parking	P	Footpaths	
Public telephone	✆	Toilets	WC	Heights in feet	·112·
Spot height in metres	·112	Bird sanctuary		Woods and state forests	
Woods		Picnic site			
Park or ornamental grounds		Wildfowl observation point			

Start point of Waymarked walk	W1	Route of walk	→	Route of tour	→
Start point of walk	1	Alternative route	▸▸	Alternative route	▸▸
Line of walk		Start point of tour	1	Line of tour	

Blacksod Bay

Achill Head
Keel
SLIEVE MORE
2204
Achill Island

Mulrany
Newport
Clew Bay
Clare
Caher
Westport
CROAGH PATRICK
2510
Louisburgh
R335

Inishturk
Inishbofin
Inishshark
Renvyle
Cruagh
Letterfrack
KYLEMORE ABBEY
2395
Clifden
Mannin Bay
Ballyconneely
Slyne Head
Roundstone
Croagnakeela
Glinsk (Glinsce)
Kilkieran (Cill Ciaráin)
Gorumna Island

2369
Lough Conn
NEPHIN 2646
R315
Foxford
Swinford
Turlough
Castlebar
Ballyhean
Balla
Ballintober
Claremorris
Ballinrobe
Partry
Neale
Clonbur (An Fhairche)
Cong
Cornamona
Lough Corrib
Headford
Oughterard
Annaghdown

Crossmolina
Lough Corr
N17
Tobercurry
Curry
Charlestown
Carracastle
Ballaghaderreen
Swinford
Kilkelly
Kiltimagh
Knock
Ballyhaunis
Dunmore
Glenamaddy
Creggs
Castlerea
Ballinlough
Ballindine
Tuam
Mount Bellew
Monivea
Caltra
Ahascragh
Shrule
Kilmaine
Ballinrobe

Rock
Inishmore
Aran Islands
Inisheer
North Sound
South Sound

Galway Bay

Galway
Salthill
Oranmore
Clarinbridge
Kilcolgan
Craughwell
Loughrea
Athenry
Kinvarra
SLIEVE AUGHTY
1207
MTS
Woodford
Lough Cutra
Lough Graney

The Burren
Ballyvaughan
Gort
W7
Lisdoonvarna
Kilfenora
Cliffs of Moher
Kilconnell
Hags Head
Lahinch
Corofin
Ennistymon
Crusheen
Feakle
Scarriff
Tuamgraney
Mountshannon
Inishcealtra
Tulla
Mal Bay
Milltown Malbay
Ennis
Mutton
Doo Lough
KNAPPOGUE CASTLE
Broadford
Killaloe
Ballina
Silvermines
Clarecastle
Doonbeg
Newmarket-on-Fergus
Sixmilebridge
Cloonlara
Newport
Donegal Point
Kilkee
Cooraclare
Killadysert
Shannon Airport
BUNRATTY CASTLE
Ardnacrusha
Kilrush
LIMERICK
N7
Loop Head
Mouth of the Shannon
Killimer
Tarbert
Foynes
Glin
Loghill
Askeaton
Patrickswell
Caherconlish
Pallasgreen
Ballylongford
Shanagolden
Adare
Croagh
Croom
Herbertstown
Ballybunion
Rathkeale
Ardagh
Ballingarry
Bruff
Hospital
Tipperary
Ballyduff
Listowel
Newcastle West
Kilmeedy
Bruree
Kilmallock
Causeway
Duagh
Ardfert
Abbeyfeale
Kilcolman
Rath Luirc (Charleville)
Kilfinnane
Ballyheige
Ballyheige Bay
Abbeydorney
Kilinlea
Broadford
Dromcolliher
Rough Point
Kerry Head
1170
Tralee
Castleisland
Freemount
Liscarroll
Buttevant
Mitchelstown
BRANDON MTN
3127
BEENOSKEE 2713
2796
Camp
Scartaglen
Newmarket
Kildorrery
Brandon Bay
BAURTREGAUM
Castlemaine
Farranfore
Ballydesmond
Kanturk
Doneraile
Glanworth
Sybil Point
Dingle (An Daingean)
Gallerus Oratory
Anascaul
Milltown
Boherbue
Castletownroche
Inishtooskert
Inch
Cloonbannin
Mallow
Fermoy
Great Blasket Island
Conor Pass
Killorglin
Killarney
Rathmore
Nad
Mourne Abbey
Rathcormack
Slea Head
Glenbeigh
Beaufort
Millstreet
BOGGERAGH MTS
Glenville
Inishvikillane
Lough Leane
Muckross
MUCKROSS HOUSE
2118
Carriganimmy
CARRANTUOHILL 3414
MANGERTON MTN 2756
Cloonkeen
Ballymakeery
Blarney
Doulus Head
2539
MULLAGHANATTIN
Cloonkeen
Macroom
Dripsey
Coachford
Glanmire
Valentia
Molls Gap
Kilgarvan
Ballingeary (Béal Átha an Ghaorthaidh)
Inchigeelagh
CORK
Cahirciveen
Kenmare
Ovens
Crookstown
Fota Island
Passage
Waterville
Sneem
Tahilla
KNOCKBOY 2321
GOUGANE BARRA
Kilmichael
Cross Barry
Carrigaline
Parknasilla
Kilbrittain
Ballinspittle
The Skelligs
Bolus Head
Castle Cove
Caherdaniel
Lauragh
Glengarriff
Dunmanway
Ballineen
Bandon
Inishannon
Kinsale
Scariff
Ardgroom
Enniskeane
Dunderrow
Belgooly
Cod's Head
2251
Adrigole
BANTRY HOUSE
Drimoleague
Timoleague
Old Head of Kinsale
Allihies
Castletownbere
Bantry
Clonakilty
Courtmacsherry
Dursey
Bear
Durrus
Leap
Ross Carbery
Ballydehob
Glandore
Galley Head
Sheep's Head
Schull
Skibbereen
Toormore
Castletownshend
Mizen Head
Goleen
Baltimore
Toe Head
Crookhaven
Clear
Roaringwater Bay

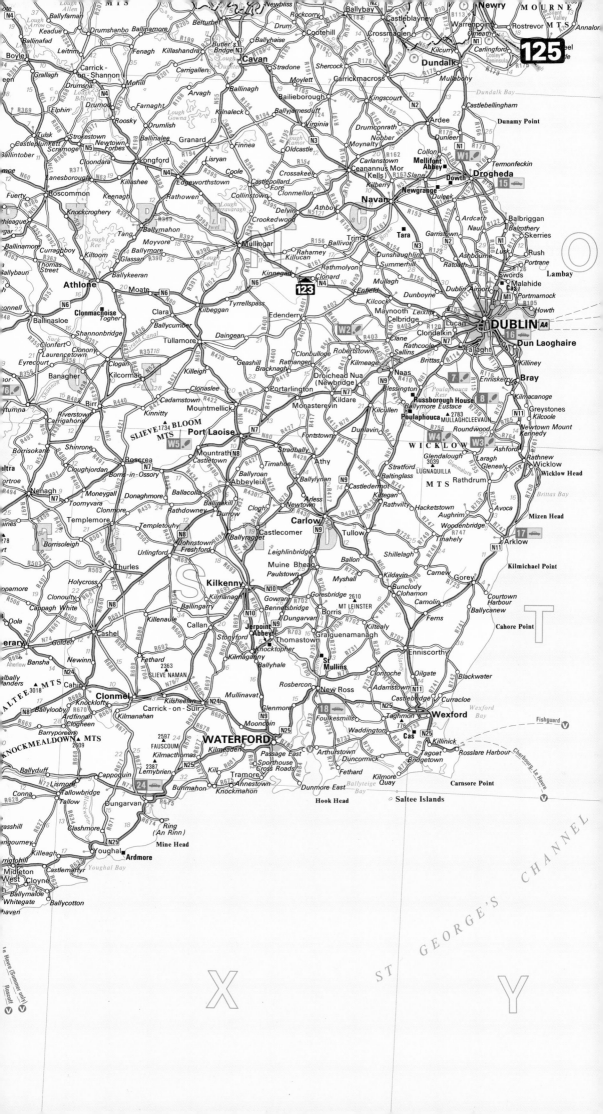

To the Blue Stack Mountains

'All hands on deck' – a fishing boat is spruced up in Killybegs harbour

The drive starts at Donegal. From The Diamond in **Donegal** follow SP 'Killybegs, Mountcharles' N56. Drive alongside Donegal Bay, passing Mountcharles after 3¾m, and ascend inland for several miles. Rejoin the coast at Inver Bay. After 7m (from Mountcharles) pass through Dunkineely, which lies at the base of a narrow peninsula separating Inver and McSwyne's Bays. This peninsula can be explored by an unclassified road. In 1½m pass through Bruckless, and 1¾m farther bear left and shortly keep left onto the R263 before driving alongside Killybegs harbour and entering the town. In ¼m bear right and ascend, then in 1¼m descend to the edge of sandy Fintragh Bay. After 2¾m bear right SP 'Kilcar', and climb a low pass between Croaghbeg (260mtrs) and Crowarad Hill (491mtrs). Descend along Glenaddragh Valley into **Kilcar**. Meet X-roads and keep forward SP 'Coast Road' on to an unclassified road. In ½m ascend steeply, with distant views of the Co. Mayo mountains to the left. Summit views extend across Teelin Bay to the famous Slieve League (598mtrs). Rejoin the R263 and in 1m reach Carrick, a village which provides access to Teelin and Slieve League. Pass through Carrick, following signs for Glencolumbkille, shortly enter the Owenwee Valley, then climb to 180 metres before descending sharply towards **Glencolumbkille**. At the edge of the village keep forward on an unclassified road SP 'Ardara'. A left turn here allows a detour to the Folk Village. In ¼m bear left over a river. Meet a T-junction and turn right SP 'Ardara', then in 1m cross a river and bear right. Climb to a 210mtr pass between Croaghnaleaba (271mtrs) and Croaghloughdivna (310mtrs) then

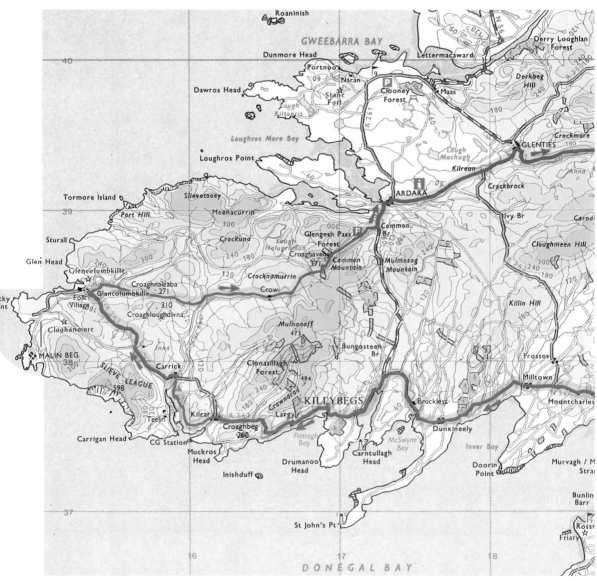

descend to the Glen River valley. Bear left SP 'Ardara' then drive forward to cross the river and enter the Crow River valley.

Follow an easy ascent past Crow village, with mountains ahead and to the right, and climb 271 metres below Croaghavehy (371mtrs) at the head of Glen Gesh. Descend, with maximum gradients of 1 in 4 and hairpin bends. meet a T-junction and turn left on to the N56 SP **Ardara**. In 1¼m enter the town of **Ardara** and bear left SP 'Glenties', then ascend and bear right. Continue for 6m to reach Glenties. Pass the school and church on the right, and immediately turn right on to an unclassified road, keeping the town to the left. Follow the Owenea Valley and after 3¼m cross a river bridge and keep right. In ¾m the road affords views of Aghla Mountain (592mtrs) on the left, plus Carnaween (519mtrs) and Silver Hill (600mtrs), Lough Ea lies to the right after several more miles. In 2¼m (from the loch) reach a 241 metre summit, then make an easy descent into the Reelan Valley. Ahead is Gaugin Mountain (566mtrs) and views to the right include the Blue Stack Mountains. Continue for 4m and bear right across a river, then in 1m join the valley of the River Finn. Follow the river for 3¼m and drive forward on to the R252 then proceed to **Ballybofey**. Turn right here on to the N15 SP 'Donegal', and skirt Lough Mourne after 4m. The mountains beyond this include Croaghnageer (544mtrs) on the right plus Croaghconnellagh (523mtrs) and Barnesmore (451mtrs) ahead. Drive between the latter two mountains via Barnesmore Gap. Once clear of the range pass Lough Eske (right), and later re-enter Donegal.

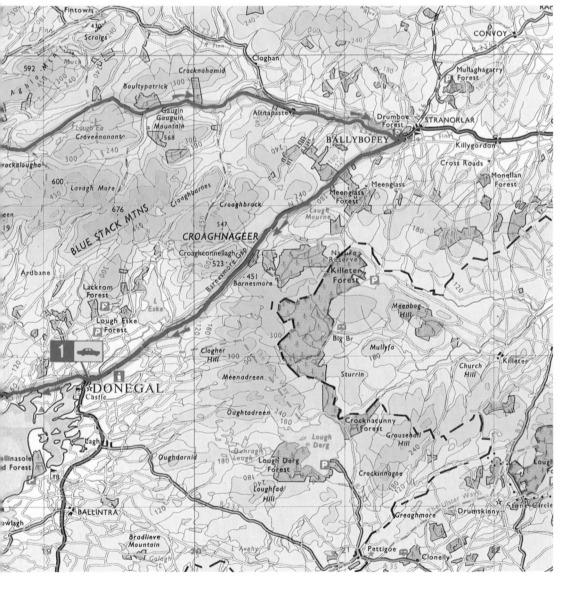

Over The Derryveagh Range

The drive starts at Dunfanaghy. Leave
Dunfanaghy via the N56 with SP 'Portnablagh and
Carrigart', then in 1½m reach Portnablagh. In ¼m
reach a garage and turn left uphill on an unclassified
road SP 'Marble Hill Strand'. After 2m join Marble
Hill Strand (left) and shortly pass a well-wooded
hillside (right) as the route turns away from the beach.
In 1m turn left to rejoin the N56, and in ½m pass
through **Ballymore**. After a further ¾m pass the Ards
Forest Park entrance (left). In 2m, close to a new
church at the edge of Creeslough, branch right on to an
unclassified road and ascend. Later pass beneath
(667mtrs) Muckish (right), and in 4¾m at a
T-junction turn left; the right turn here leads to the
241 metre high Muckish Gap. In ¾m cross the
Calabber River and immediately turn left on to the
R251. Skirt Kingarrow (322mtrs) on the right, cross
the Owencarrow River at the end of Lough Veagh, and
in ¼m pass the Glenveagh National Park entrance.
Continue for 1½m to a T-junction, and turn right. In
½m bear right SP 'Gartan', then in 1¾m reach the
bottom of a small valley and turn sharp right uphill.
Continue above the west shore of Lough Akibbon,
later obtaining views of Gartan Lough, then descend
past another Glenveagh Park entrance (right). Bear
left, pass between the two loughs, then in ¼m drive
forward on to the R251. Cross a river, bear right, and
in ½m turn right on to an unclassified road to follow
the shores of Gartan Lough. Brown Mountain stands
at 224 metres on the left and Leahanmore (442mtrs)
rises to the right. After 1¼m pass the entrance to
Church Hill Wood. Half a mile farther keep forward
SP Doochary. Drive forward past the end of Gartan
Lough and enter the Bullaba Valley. Later climb to a
241 metre high pass, with Leahanmore and Farscollop

(420mtrs) to the right and the Glendowan range left.
Ahead the peaks of Dooish (652mtrs) and Slieve
Snaght (680mtrs) rise from the Derryveagh
Mountains, and views right extend towards Lough
Veagh. Follow the road left and descend into the Barra
Valley between Moylenanav and Slieve Snaght, then
continue past Lough Barra with high ground to the
right. In 5¼m reach the nearside of **Doochary**. Turn
sharp right on to the R252 SP An Clochan Leith then
ascend steep Corkscrew Hill. Isolated
Croaghleconnell rises to 266 metres on the left.
Proceed, with small lakes on both sides of the road, and
after 5¼m turn right on to the N56 'Dungloe' road. In
2½m reach a garage on the nearside of Dungloe and
turn right SP 'Gweedore'. Follow a broad road, and
after 4¾m pass **Loughanure** village and lough. In
2¼m turn right then continue and shortly pass
through Crolly. In ¾m keep forward with the N56 and
gradually ascend. After 1¼m cross the end of Lough
Nacung Lower, then in ¼m reach Gweedore. At the
T-junction turn right SP Gort-an-Choirce
(Gortahork) follow the shores of Lough Nacung
Lower, and pass the peat-fired Gweedore Power
Station. Half a mile farther keep forward on the N56
and ascend; the R251 right turn here leads to Dunlewy
and the famous Poisoned Glen. Magnificent views
right extent over Lough Nacung Upper and take in the
highest mountain in Co Donegal – the conical 749
metre high Errigal. Continue to a low summit, with
Tievealehid and Carntreena (396mtrs) on the left,
then gradually descend and turn right continuing on
the N56. In ½m pass through **Gortahork,** then in 2m
proceed through Falcarragh and re-enter Dunfanaghy
in further 7¼m.

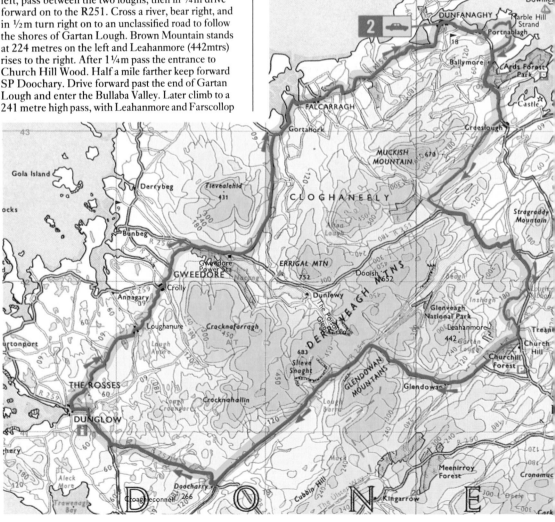

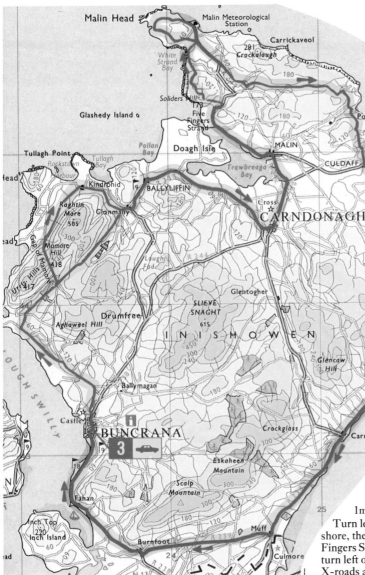

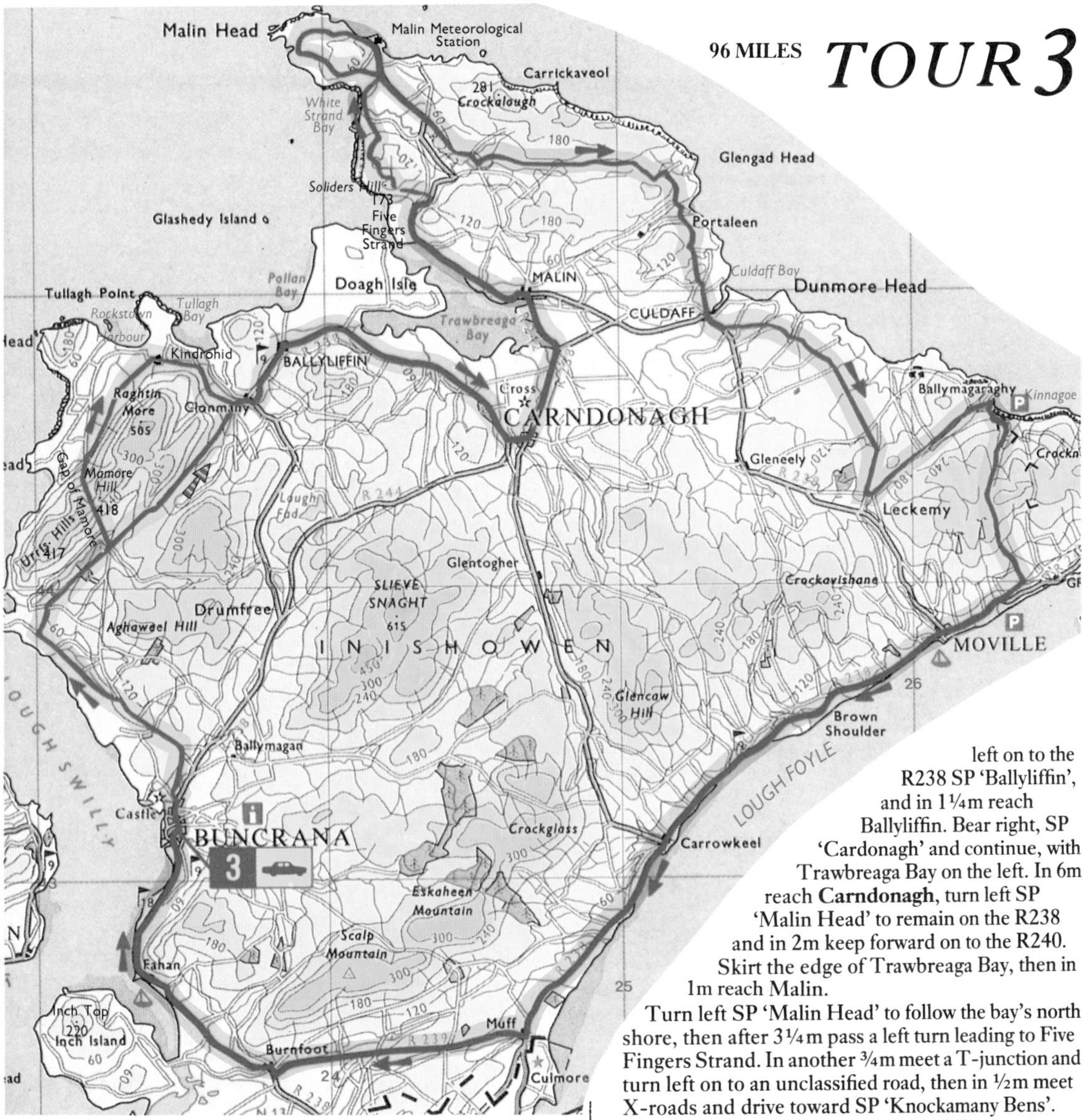

Over The Mamore Gap

The drive starts at Buncrana. Leave **Buncrana** with SP 'Carndonagh R238 and at the end of the town turn right. In ½m turn left on to an unclassified road SP 'Gap of Mamore', and in ¼m bear right. After another 1m meet X-roads and bear left SP 'Dunree'. Ascend and in 1½m bear left SP 'Dunree, Mamore Gap'. The 365 metre high Knockalla Mountains can be seen on the far side of Lough Swilly (left), and the Urris Hills rise to 417 metres ahead. After 2¼m turn right SP Clonmany then in ½m at a T-junction turn right. Drive along the Owenerk River valley and in 1¾m at X-roads turn left for the Gap of Mamore. To avoid the Gap's gradients, keep forward along the direct road to Clonmany.

Climb to the Gap's 259 metre summit, with Mamore Hill (418mtrs) on the right and Dunaff Head (207mtrs) ahead, then descend steeply through hairpin bends. Views extend left over the mouth of Lough Swilly to Fanad Head, right across Rockstown Harbour and Tullagh Point, and ahead to Dunaff Head. In 1m reach the foot of the descent and bear right SP 'Clonmany'. Continue, with Rockstown Harbour on the left, then in 2½m bear right SP Clonmany. In ½m reach **Kindrohid**. Bear right here, with views of Tullagh Bay (left) before entering the Clonmany River valley. After 1½m (from Kindrohid) meet X-roads and turn left. Cross a river into Clonmany, turn right in the village, and in ¼m turn

left on to the R238 SP 'Ballyliffin', and in 1¼m reach Ballyliffin. Bear right, SP 'Cardonagh' and continue, with Trawbreaga Bay on the left. In 6m reach **Carndonagh**, turn left SP 'Malin Head' to remain on the R238 and in 2m keep forward on to the R240. Skirt the edge of Trawbreaga Bay, then in 1m reach Malin.

Turn left SP 'Malin Head' to follow the bay's north shore, then after 3¼m pass a left turn leading to Five Fingers Strand. In another ¾m meet a T-junction and turn left on to an unclassified road, then in ½m meet X-roads and drive toward SP 'Knockamany Bens'. Climb past Soldier's Hill (173mtrs), following signs for 'Malin Head', to a carpark and viewpoint.

Descend towards White Strand Bay, and on reaching the foot of the incline bear left SP 'Malin Head'. Shortly pass the edge of the bay, then in ½m meet a T-junction. Turn left, reach a hotel, then immediately turn sharp left. After another ½m bear left and shortly right. In 2m reach Malin Head – the most northerly point in Ireland – and after another ½m pass a left turn leading to Banbas' Crown tower. Shortly pass the Malin Meteorological Station (left). Farther along, this road becomes the R242. In 1¾m (from the Meteorological Station) meet X-roads and drive forward SP 'Glengad'.

In another 1½m turn left SP 'Glengad', then proceed through farmland. After 4½m bear right, then in 1¼m meet a T-junction and turn left SP 'Culdaff'. Climb then descend with Culdaff Bay on the left. Reach **Culdaff** village and turn left on to the R238 SP 'Moville', pass a hotel, then bear right. In ½m (from Culdaff) turn left on to an unclassified road and gradually ascend. After 4m at a X-roads keep forward and in ½m bear right, then in a further 1m turn left and immediately left again. Reach a low summit, descend to Kinnagoe Bay, then turn sharp right SP 'Moville' and climb to a 305 metre summit. Follow a long descent, meet a T-junction and turn right to follow the shores of the lough, and in ½m turn right on to the R241. In 1¼m enter **Moville**, go forward on to the R238 and continue alongside the lough for 13½m to reach **Muff**. Drive to the end of this village and turn right on to the R239 SP Burnfoot. Continue through farming country, and after 5½m reach Burnfoot. At a T-junction turn right on to the R238 'Buncrana' road, and in ¼m bear left. In 2½m rejoin the shores of Lough Swilly and proceed to Fahan. Continue alongside Swilly and in 3½m re-enter Buncrana.

The Lower Erne Shoreline

The drive starts at Enniskillen. Enniskillen is an island town strategically sited in the River Erne between Upper and Lower Lough Erne. Its position has made it of great military importance for hundreds of years; as such it has been the centre of numerous battles and the site of several castles. From **Enniskillen** follow SP 'Omagh' to leave the town on the A32. In 3¼m branch left on to the B82 SP 'Kesh' and pass the road to Devenish Island. This is situated in beautiful Lough Erne and boasts one of the most complete monastic settlements in Ireland. St Molaise first founded a monastery here in the 6th century, and the small, rectangular oratory which carries his name is typical of many such structures built by the early-Irish church. Other interesting remains to be seen on the island, which can be reached by passenger ferry, include the Great Church and an 85ft round tower of 12th-century date. After another 1½m pass Ballycassidy Post Office and cross the Ballymallard River via a hump-backed bridge. Beyond this the road affords a fine view over the island-studded waters of Lower Lough Erne. Continue through the small angling resort of Killadeas and follow the wooded shores of attractive Rossclare Bay, then after a further 1m pass the road to Rossigh Bay Picnic Area on the left.

Continue through the village of **Lisnarrick** and in 1m turn left on to an unclassified road SP 'Kesh Scenic Route', passing the entrance to Castle Archdale Forest Recreational Area, Loughshore Paths and Picnic Areas on

Clear sky over Ballyshannon Harbour at the mouth of the River Erne

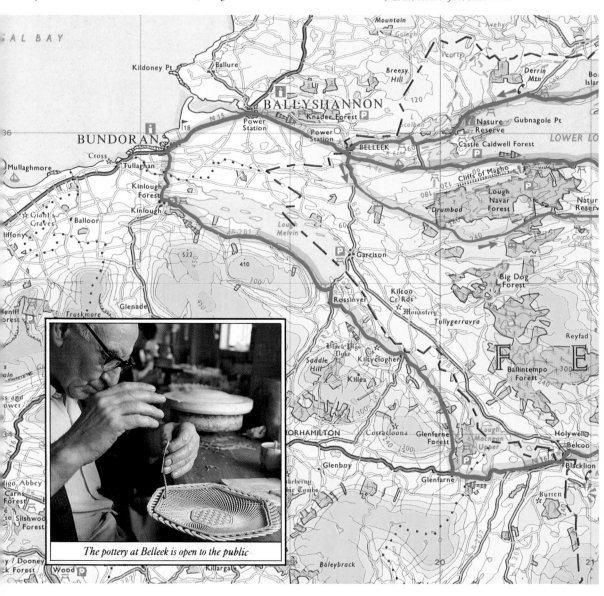

The pottery at Belleek is open to the public

the way. This castle now serves as a Ministry of Agriculture Grassland Experimental Centre. Ascend through part of the Castle Archdale Forest and reach a stretch of road which offers further excellent views of Lough Erne. Drive through more open undulating countryside, still with views of the lough. In 1¾m bear right and in 1¾m at T-junction turn left SP 'Kesh' and proceed to the sailing and angling centre of **Kesh** village, then turn left on to the A35, cross the Kesh River and pass Muckros Quay Recreation Area. In a further ¾m turn left A47 SP 'Boa Island, Belleek' to pass through pleasant scenery alongside the N shore of Lower Lough Erne. In 2¼m cross a bridge on to narrow Boa Island, the largest of the many islands in the lough, and in another 5m cross over to the mainland.

In ½m at a T-junction turn left SP 'Belleek', and in 3½m pass the entrance to Castle Caldwell Forest Recreation Area and Wildlife Park (left). Beside the park gate is the 18th-century Fiddle Stone, which carries a curious inscription. The castle which gave its name to this park was one of the numerous 'Plantation' structures which dot the shores of Lough Erne. Continue to **Belleek**, which is noted for its pottery, then leave this small town on the A46 SP 'Enniskillen' to cross the River Erne. After ¼m follow SP 'Garrison, Forest Drive' on to the B52.

Ascend, and in 1½m turn left on to an unclassified road SP 'Derrygonnelly Forest Drive'. Continue through barren, hilly countryside with distant views of Lough Navar Forest and Corral Glen Forest ahead, plus Big Dog Forest to the right. After 5¼m proceed along a pleasantly tree-lined road, and in 3m pass the Lough Navar Forestry Office and then the entrance to the circular Lough Navar Forest Drive. The latter offers an interesting diversion from the main drive and visits two viewpoints, the first at Aghameelan with Picnic Area and Walks, and second at Magho Cliffs.

The magnificent panorama includes Lough Erne, the distant Donegal Hills, and far off Donegal Bay on the W coast. The signposted return follows a descent past Lough Achork with Picnic Area and Walks and rejoins the main road, where a left turn is made to complete the circuit SP 'Enniskillen' and once again pass the forestry office. A road opposite the entrance to the Forest Drive leads into wooded Glen Corral.

Continue along the unclassified road which forms part of the main route, and in ¾m pass picturesque little Carrick Lough. Follow SP 'Lough Erne', then in 2¼m meet crossroads and keep forward. After another 1½m turn right on to the A46 SP 'Enniskillen'. In 1m pass the road to Camagh Bay on the left, then after another 1½m pass the road to Carrickreagh Viewpoint on the right. Skirt the shore of Lower Lough Erne and pass the entrance to Ely Lodge Forest Loughshore Trail and Picnic Area on the left, then drive through part of the Ely Lodge Forest. Later pass a road leading right to Monea Castle ruins, and continue along the A46 for the return to Enniskillen. Portora Royal School can be seen on the hill before the route enters the town.

OPTIONAL CROSS-BORDER DRIVE   71 MILES

Along the Shores of Lough Melvin and Lower Lough Erne

From Enniskillen follow signs Sligo A4. In 2¾ miles the A32 on the left leads to Florence Court (5 miles) and Marble Arch Caves (9 miles). Continue with the A4 to Belcoo then cross border N16 to reach Glenfarne. Turn right R281 and continue via Kiltyclogher to Rossinver. At crossroads turn right then in ¾ mile turn left shortly alongside Lough Melvin. In 6¼ miles branch right to reach Kinlough. Turn right R280 to Bundoran. Turn right again to reach Ballyshannon. On nearside of River Erne turn right R230 and later cross border to the edge of Belleek. Keep forward A46 and later pass alongside the southern shore of Lower Lough Erne for the return to Enniskillen.

The Tyrone Forests

The drive starts at Omagh. The county town of Tyrone, Omagh is home of the Royal Inniskilling Fusiliers which boasts a fine regimental museum. Follow signs B48 'Gortin' to leave **Omagh** SP 'Gortin Glen Forest Park'. After 2¾m bear right and continue with Slieveard (419mtrs) and Tirmuty Hill (336mtrs) on the right. In 3¼m pass Gortin Heritage Site on the left then enter the Gortin Forest. In ¼m cross the Pollan Burn, and in a further ¼m pass the entrance to Gortin Glen Forest Park (right). A signposted, 4½m forest drive can be taken through the park's fine scenery, which boasts numerous carparks, planned forest walks and a deer enclosure. There are also camping and recreational facilities within the confines of the park. The park exit joins the B48 on the 'Omagh' side of Pollan Bridge.

To continue with the main drive, ascend through the forest on the B48 to a 256 metre summit between Curraghchosaly Mountain (415mtrs) and a high spur of Mullaghcarn (539mtrs). In 1¾m descend past an unclassified road (right) SP Gortin Lakes 'Scenic Drive' (right). In 1¼m reach the edge of **Gortin** and turn left B46 SP 'Newtownstewart'. Proceed along the valley of the Owenkillew River, and after 3¼m bear right. In ½m cross the river, then at T-junction turn left SP 'Newtownstewart'. In 2¼m reach another T-junction and turn left. Cross Abercorn Bridge into the small market town and angling resort of **Newtownstewart,** which is situated beneath Bessy Bell (420mtrs). Turn right A5 SP 'Strabane' and in ½m bear right. In ¾m turn left (296mtrs) B164 SP 'Ardstraw', and 2½m farther bear right into Ardstraw. At X-roads forward to cross the River Derg SP 'Castlederg'. Continue along the valley with glimpses of the Derg on the left. After 3¼m at T-junction turn left B72 SP 'Castlederg'. In a further 2¼m bear left SP Ederny to enter Castlederg a renowned salmon and trout fishing centre. Turn left B72 SP 'Ederny'. Shortly cross the river, then climb out of the valley and after 2¾m pass through Killen. High ground to the left includes Bin Mountain (332mtrs), Bolaght Mountain (338mtrs), and Lough Hill (324mtrs). Continue the gradual ascent, and after 4m reach a 215 metre summit. Gradually descend, and in a further 2¾m turn left unclassified road SP 'Drumquin, Lough Bradan'.

Continue through hilly country with forested areas which give way to peat bogs. In 2¼m enter Lough Bradan Forest. In ½m pass Lough Braden Forest car park and Lake on the right, then begin a descent into the valley of the Black Water and skirt part of the forest for about 1m.

After 3¾m (from Lough Bradan) at T-junction turn right B84 SP 'Dromore'. Ascend, and after 1¾m reach a low summit between Pollnalaght (296mtrs) and Dooish (338mtrs). In 2½m at X-roads keep forward, in 1¼m bear left, then in a further 1¾m reach X-roads and turn right into **Dromore.** The area around Dromore features a number of ancient earthen forts. Turn right A32 'Enniskillen, Fintona' road and in ½m forward to join B46 SP 'Fintona'. After 1m cross a river bridge, bear left SP 'Fintona', and in a further 5m turn left to enter **Fintona.** At T-junction turn left along the main street SP B122 'Omagh' then right. In ½m bear right across a river and at X-roads forward B46 SP 'Seskinore, Beragh', then in ¾m bear left SP 'Beragh'. In 1½m proceed through Seskinore with its game farm and small reserve of mixed woodland. After ¾m at X-roads turn right. In another 1½m at staggered X-roads turn right A5, then left B46 SP 'Beragh'. In 2½m reach Beragh. At X-roads turn right into the village. Continue along the B46 with SP 'Sixmilecross' and cross the Cloughfin River. After 2m enter Sixmilecross, then leave by following SP 'Carrickmore' on the B46. Pass high ground on the right.

After 4m bear left across Pound Bridge. In a further ¼m cross Nine Mile Bridge. At T-junction turn left B4 SP 'Carrickmore'. Proceed through wooded country 1¼m to reach Carrickmore and turn right B46 (No signs). Ascend into wild hill and bog country, with Copney Hill (281mtrs) on the left, and after 4m at X-roads turn left A505 SP 'Omagh'. Pass Greggan Forest on the right, then continue with magnificent hill and forest views. Proceed, with views of Mullaghcarn (539mtrs) ahead, and in 3¼m (from the X-roads) drive between a series of small lakes. In 3m views to the right take in Mountfield village beneath Mulderg (314mtrs). In a further ¾m pass an unclassified road on the left leading 4m to Lough Macrory.

Continue past Mullaghcarn, gradually descending towards Omagh. In 5m cross the Camowen River on the outskirts of Omagh. After another 1m re-enter the town centre.

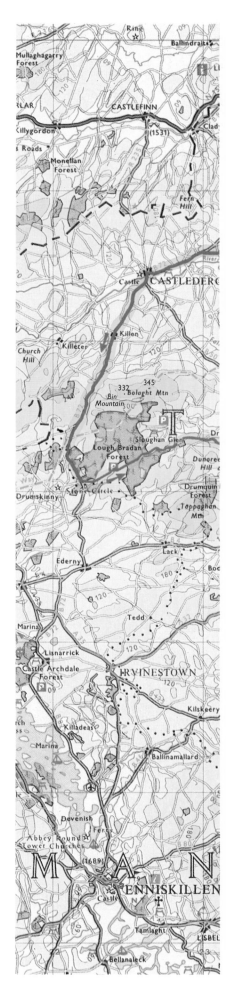

A dramatic sunset over Omagh and the River Strule

TOUR 6 74 MILES

To the Giant's Causeway

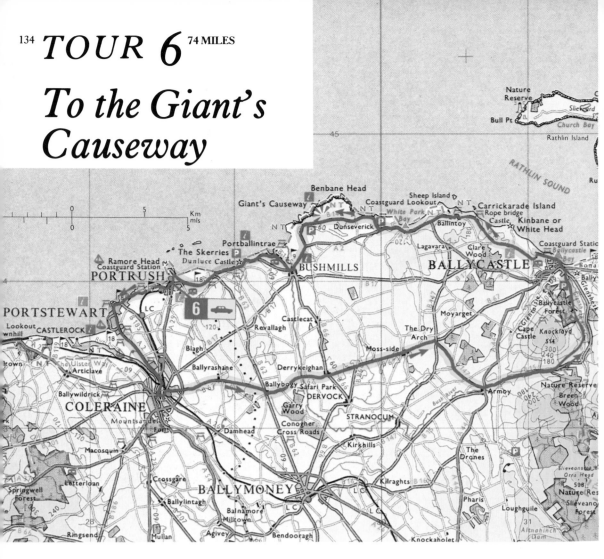

The drive starts at Portrush. Follow SP 'Portstewart' to leave **Portrush** on the A2. Continue, with seascape views which include Ramore Head and Co Donegal's Inishowen Head, and reach the Derry resort of **Portstewart** – noted for its extensive sands. Follow SP 'Coleraine' to remain on the A2 and turn inland with the road along the Bann estuary. Pass the new University of Ulster on the left and Marina on the right to enter the commercial and market centre of Coleraine, on the River Bann. Leave the town by following SP 'Ballycastle B67', and go over the level crossing and immediately turn right into Ballycastle Rd passing The Showgrounds. In ¾m at roundabout take 2nd exit. Continue through pleasantly pastoral country. After 3m cross the county boundary to enter Co Antrim, then ½m farther in Ballybogy at T-junction turn right then left, still following SP 'Ballycastle B67'. In 1¾m cross the Bush River then pass the Causeway Safari Pleasure Park on the right. This 62-acre reserve holds free-ranging lions and other species of wild animals. In Derrykeighan at staggered X-roads turn right then immediately left. Proceed along a straight but undulating road and pass through pleasant countryside to reach Moss Side. Drive through this village and in 1¼m turn right SP 'Armoy B147'. Ascend to a T-junction and turn right, then immediately left on to the B147. Continue through hilly country, with views left of Knocklayd Mountain (513mtrs) before Armoy.

To leave Armoy follow SP 'Glenshesk B15', then in ¾m at X-roads forward. After another 2¾m turn left on to an unclassified road (no signs). Climb through picturesque hill country with Knocklayd Mountain to the left and the Glenshesk River below. To the right is Ballypatrick Forest.

In 2¾m enter Ballycastle Forest. Continue along the 'Ballycastle' road and descend while fine seaward views to the N encompass **Rathlin Island**. Here exiled Robert Bruce was taught a lesson in perseverance by a spider. In 2m at T-junction turn right then immediately left SP Town Centre to join B15 and A2 and enter the resort of **Ballycastle**. Leave by the harbour road and follow SP 'Portrush B15'. In 1½m turn right SP 'Ballintoy, Bushmills' in order to continue through hilly country with intermittent sea views to the right. After another 1m pass road to Kenbane Castle then in 2m pass a picnic area on the right. After another ¼m pass the entrance to Carrick-a-Rede rope bridge, a precarious bridge which links Carrick-a-Rede island to the mainland across a coastal chasm measuring 18 metres wide and 24 metres deep.

Continue through the village of **Ballintoy**; beyond this the route offers good views of White Park Bay and Benbane Head. In a further 1m join the A2 SP 'Bushmills, Giant's Causeway', then in 1¼m pass the road to White Park Bay. In another 1m turn right B146 SP 'Currysheskin, Giant's Causeway' to continue through Dunseverick. Beyond the latter pass the ruins of Dunseverick Castle to the right. Veer inland with the road for 2½m, then pass the road to the world-famous **Giant's Causeway**. This feature is one of the most remarkable natural phenomena known in Britain, and comprises a virtual cascade of geometric basaltic columns which march down the cliff to the sea in their thousands. Continue with the 'Bushmills' road, and in 1m turn right to rejoin the A2. Proceed to **Bushmills**, a community noted for its distillery and fishing, and at roundabout take 2nd exit. SP 'Portrush'. Cross the Bush River, then turn right again to B145 SP **Portballintrae**. In 1m turn left to enter Portballintrae.

Leave this pleasant little resort by following SP 'Portrush', and in ¾m turn right to rejoin the A2 once again. After ¾m pass the ruined, cliff-top **Dunluce Castle** on the right. This strange structure is precipitously perched on a detached basaltic rock far above the sea. Complete the drive by returning to Portrush with its magnificent long sandy beaches.

A Spectacular Sea Drive

The drive starts at Larne. This route follows part of the **Antrim Coast Road** – rightly considered to be one of the finest marine drives in the whole of Europe – through some of the spectacular scenery around the famous nine **Glens of Antrim**. Most of these glens are accessible from the road and comprise a series of deep, wooded rifts which cut across a range of coastal hills. The most distinctive is Glenariff, which extends 5m inland from Waterfoot and includes attractive waterfalls.

From **Larne** follow SP 'Glenarm' to leave by the A2 along the Antrim Coast Road. In 2m pass through Black Cave Tunnel to drive along the bays of Drains and Carnfunnock, then round the 92 metre high Ballygalley Head and in 3m reach Ballygalley. The fine fortified manor house in this village is now used as a hotel. Continue along the coast for 6½m to enjoy lovely hill and sea views before reaching Glenarm, a village on the Glenarm River at the head of one of the Nine Glens of Antrim. The village's chief attraction is the beautiful park and glen which adjoin its imposing castle, built by the Earl of Antrim in 1636 but subsequently altered. Leave the village by following SP 'Carnlough' and cross the Glenarm River, then continue along the coast to Carnlough. The latter is beautifully situated at the foot of Glencloy – famous for its waterfalls – and features one of the mesolithic raised beaches for which this coast is famous. On leaving Carnlough pass beneath a stone arch, with the harbour to the right, following SP 'Cushendall, Waterfoot'. In 4m pass Garron Point Post Office, where Garron Point itself towers above the road and offers views which extend to the Scottish coast.

Veer west with road to follow shoreline of Red Bay. After 4½m reach Waterfoot. Drive to the end of the village, cross the Glenariff River, and at T-junction turn left on to the A43 SP 'Glenariff Forest Park, Ballymena'. Begin the ascent of Glenariff, often considered the most beautiful of the nine Glens. A particularly attractive feature of this place is the contrast between the green of cultivated land and the black of basalt cliffs. Keep the Glenariff River on the left and wind along the cultivated, tree-shrouded slopes of Lurigethan Mountain (349mtrs) which rises to the right. This road affords fine views across the glen to the left, and to imposing cliffs with several waterfalls on the right. After 4½m pass the entrance to Glenariff Forest Park on the left. Parkmore Forest is later seen to the right, and north of this is Trostan Mountain, at 551 metres the highest of the Antrim Hills. Proceed through rugged hill country with views of Cargan Water to the right, then descend through pastoral scenery to reach the village of Cargan. In 2½m cross the Clogh River, and after another 2m (at X-roads) turn left B94 SP 'Broughshane'. Continue through undulating countryside for 4m, then cross the Braid River. In ¼m turn left A42 to enter Broughshane.

Turn right B94 SP 'Ballyclare'. Drive through pleasant, hilly country along a stretch of road which affords views of Slemish Mountain (435mtrs) to the left, then after 6m at X-roads turn left A36 SP 'Larne'. Follow the valley of the Glenwhirry River and in 1¾m bear right. In 2m cross the Glenwhirry River. Ascend through hilly countryside with fine views of the river, now on the left. In 1m pass Killylane Reservoir and in another ½m reach Ballyboley Forest. Beyond the forest climb for a short distance and attain the 309 metre Shane's Hill Summit, then descend over bleak moorland. Later pass the Kilwaughter House Hotel, and in 1m farther turn left A8 for the return to Larne.

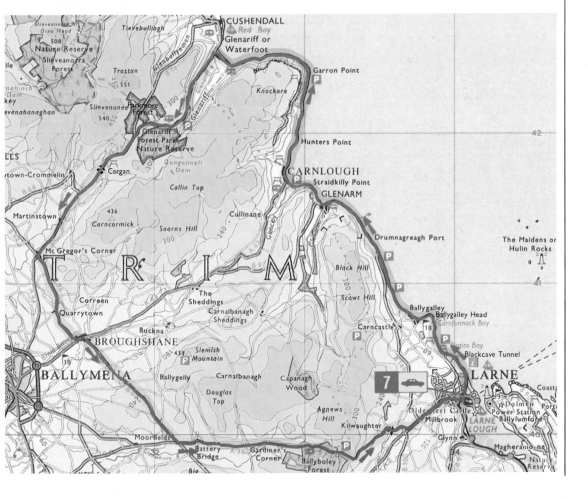

TOUR 8 63 MILES

Through the Mourne Mountains

Old cornmill and waterwheel, Annalong

The drive starts at Newcastle. Leave **Newcastle** with SP 'Bryansford B180'. First the forest slopes of Slieve Donard (849mtrs) and later Tollymore Forest Park beneath Shan Slieve (669mtrs) are visible to the left. After 1¾m (from Newcastle) pass the park entrance, then in ½m meet a T-junction and turn left. In a further ½m follow SP 'Hilltown' through Bryansford and pass Tollymore Forest Park below the **Mourne Mountains**. After ¾m pass a road to 'Dromena Cashel and Souterrain' (AM) on the right. In ½m pass the entrance to the Northern Ireland Mountain Centre (left), with Moneyscalp (246mtrs) on the right. Gradually ascend with further summits on the left and views of Lough Island Reavy below Tullynasoo Mountain (279mtrs) on the right. After several miles reach a 204mtr summit and descend along the Kinnahalla Valley, then after 1½m pass the road to Goward Dolmen (AM) on the right. Views to the left extend across the upper Bann Valley to Hen (360mtrs) and Cock (505mtrs). In ½m turn right on to the B27 SP 'Hilltown', and in 1m turn left on to the B8. Shortly cross the River Bann to enter Hilltown, then continue on the B8 SP 'Newry' and proceed with high ground on the left. After 1½m bear right and continue the ascent for ¾m, then descend into Mayobridge. At X-roads turn left on to the B7 SP 'Warrenpoint', then climb through hilly country beneath Craignamona (286mtrs) and Slieveacarnane (295mtrs). Descend and in 3½m pass through Burren. After another 1m at X-roads turn left SP 'Warrenpoint'. After 1½m turn left A2 Warrenpoint. The Carlingford Mountains rise to over 460mtrs on the south side of Carlingford Lough and include the isolated summit of Slieve Foye (587mtrs). Follow SP 'Rostrevor' through Warrenpoint. Proceed along the lough shores with mountain views to the right and Rostrevor Forest on the slopes of Slievemartin (487mtrs) ahead. After 1m cross the Moygannon River, and in a further 1m cross the Ghann River into Rostrevor.

Here the main drive route keeps forward with SP 'Hilltown B25', and in ½m branches right on to an unclassified road SP 'Spelga Dam' before crossing the Kilbroney River in ½m. However, Rostrevor town centre offers an attractive alternative route through the Rostrevor Forest Park. To follow this turn right on to the A2 SP Kilkeel and in ½m turn left on to an unclassified road SP 'Rostrevor Forest Drive'. Enter the forest and follow the signposted, one-way route. Climb steeply, with views of Carlingford Lough, and cross several mountain streams on the way through the forest. After 1¼m reach a picnic area and descend with fine views over Rostrevor, Carlingford Lough, and the Republic of Ireland. Warrenpoint can be seen in the distance. After 2m leave the forest and turn right on to an unclassified road SP 'Hilltown' to rejoin the main drive. Climb the Kilbroney Valley, with part of Rostrevor Forest ahead and to the right; Leckan More (351mtrs) rises to the left. After 1¾m cross a bridge and enter the forest. In 1½m pass a picnic area on the right and reach a 205mtr summit. Gradually descend along the valley of Shanky's River, with views of Rocky Mountain (402mtrs) ahead, and after 1½m pass picnic area to a fork and bear right SP 'Spelga Dam'. Pass Rocky Mountain on the right and in 1¼m cross the Rocky River to a further picnic area. In ¾m cross the River Bann, meet X-roads, and turn right on to the B27 SP 'Spelga Dam, Kilkeel'. Follow the Bann River past Hen Mountain and the wooded lower slopes of Kinnahalla, then ascend steeply (10%) into barren country between Spelga (454mtrs) and Cock Mountain. This section of road is part of the Spelga Pass hillclimb route. Shortly reach the edge of the Spelga Dam reservoir, with some of the higher points in the Mourne range ahead. In ¾m at T-junction turn right SP 'Kilkeel' to continue at over 380mtrs above sea level.

In ¾m cross the infant River Bann, then pass between Slieve Muck and Pigeon Rock Mountain (531mtrs) towards 'Kilkeel'. After 1¾m skirt a small forest, with picnic area on the right, and in another 1½m branch right on to an unclassified road SP 'Attical'. Descend through agricultural country, and in ¾m reach the small village of Attical. After another ½m cross the White Water River, with Finlieve (573mtrs) ahead and the wooded slopes of Knockchree (306mtrs) on the left. Follow the White Water past Knockchree and the woods of the Mourne Park Estate, then continue the descent with some views of Carlingford Lough to the right. At T-junction, turn right A2 SP 'Warrenpoint', and in 1½m turn sharp left on to the unclassified 'Cranfield' road. Skirt Mill Bay with views of the Carlingford Mountains. In a further 2½m cross the White Water bridge, then at X-roads turn left SP 'Kilkeel'. In ¾m bear left then turn right SP 'Kilkeel'. In ½m at T-junction turn left to proceed to Kilkeel. Enter this town and follow SP 'Newcastle' to join the A2. The road to the right leads to the Kilkeel Harbour. Reach the end of the town, cross the Kilkeel River, and in ¼m pass an unclassified road on

the left leading to the *Silent Valley* reservoirs – situated deep in the Mourne range. The lower reservoir lies to the left of Slieve Binnian (743mtrs). In 1¾m pass through Ballymartin, descend almost to the shore, then after 2m (from Ballymartin) enter the straggling fishing village of **Annalong**. In 1m pass the harbour (right) also Marina Park and Cornmill (right).

Cross the Annalong River and continue along the A2 with views of Slieve Binnian to the left and Chimney Rock Mountain (653mtrs) ahead. Follow the coastline, with views across Dundrum Bay to St John's Point, and after 4m (from Annalong) cross Bloody Bridge. Slieve Donard, the highest of the Mourne Mountains, rises to 849 metres on the left. Rejoin the cliff edge, and in ¾m pass a ravine known as Maggie's leap. Beyond this is the edge of extensive Donard Lodge Forest, and to the right are further views over Dundrum Bay. After 1m (from Maggie's Leap) pass Newcastle Harbour, and in ¾m re-enter the town.

Newcastle harbour is now used purely for pleasure fishing and yachting

Peninsula Villages

The drive starts at Belfast. Leave **Belfast** by following SP 'Bangor A2'. In 2¾m pass Belfast Harbour airport on the left. In 1m at roundabout take the first exit, then continue along a stretch of road which affords views over the coastal Belfast Lough to the left. In 2m skirt Holywood and stay on the 'Bangor' road. After another 1½m pass Cultra Manor on the right. The manor and its grounds form the **Ulster Folk Museum**, which was originally created to illustrate traditional Ulster life. Re-erected buildings in the 136-acre park include a thatched barn, a farm, and a spade foundry.

Paintings by William Conor can be seen inside the house, and other interesting exhibits include a fine collection of transport vehicles. From the same exit the Transport Museum can be reached and visitors can view the exhibits while riding on a miniature railway. In 2m turn left B20 SP 'Crawfordsburn', then follow a pleasantly tree-lined road to the attractive village of this name. In ¼m pass Crawfordsburn Country Park on the left and drive to the outskirts of **Bangor**. This town is Northern Ireland's largest seaside resort and boasts all the usual amenities, including good sandy beaches and the annual regatta of the Royal Ulster Yacht Club. Bangor is also of historical interest as it was an important ecclesiastical centre at the time of St Columba.

Drive into the town by Bryansburn Rd, and at roundabout keep forward. At T-junction turn right along the sea front. Views from here extend over Bangor Bay. In 1m pass Ballyholme Yacht Club on the left, then at the end turn left on to Ballyholme Esplanade to run alongside Ballyholme Bay. In ¼m turn right into Sheridan Drive, then left, no signs. In ½m at roundabout take the first exit SP B511 'Groomsport' to reach the small resort of Groomsport. Turn left A2 SP 'Donaghadee'. Fine seascape views which now open up to the left include the off-shore Copeland Island. Enter the resort of **Donaghadee**. Leave by turning right then left SP 'Portaferry' to stay with A2. Follow the eastern coastline of the fertile Ards Peninsula to Millisle. To the west of this small resort is the restored Ballycopeland Windmill of 1784, which stands on the B172. Remain on the A2 and continue, with fine sea views, for 5¼m to pass through Ballywalter – a little resort noted for its extensive sands. Proceed to Ballyhalbert; on entering this village the drive affords views of the off-shore Burial Island, which marks the extreme eastern limit of Irish soil. Leave Ballyhalbert keeping forward SP Portavogie Coastal Road. Continue into the small fishing village of Portavogie. On entering the village turn right then left and drive to the harbour.

After ½m turn left to rejoin the A2 SP Portaferry. Follow a stretch of road which offers views of Kirkistown Castle to the right, and reach the little resort of Cloughy – situated on Cloughy Bay. Drive through the village and in ¼m turn left SP 'Kearney'. Continue along this undulating road for 1¾m, then turn left SP 'Kearney, Quintin Bay'. After another 1½m meet a T-junction and turn right SP 'Portaferry'. A diversion (¾m) can be made from this point by turning left to visit the restored fishing village of Kearney (NT). Drive alongside Knockinelder Bay for ½m and turn left to continue along the coast. Pass the much-restored Norman stronghold of Quintin Castle on the left, and in ¾m pass Millin Bay Cairn (National Monument) on the right. ¾m further at T-junction turn left SP 'Bar Hall'. After another 1¼m pass the Ballyquintin Point Road on the left and continue along the 'Bar Hall' road.

On reaching the shores of Bar Hall Bay proceed northwards along the narrow straights of **Strangford Lough**, an important bird sanctuary. In some places the lough is as deep as the section of English Channel between Dover and Calais. Continue, with fine views across the water, and drive into the small port of **Portaferry**. Leave this town via the unclassified Lough Shore Road (no signs) passing **Strangford** car ferry on the left, and skirt the edge of Strangford Lough. In 5½m turn left A20, and after a further ½m reach Ardkeen Post Office. Proceed along the western arm of the Ards Peninsula. Views from here take in part of Strangford Lough which has broadened to form an inland sea studded with numerous small islands. In 5½m pass through the village of Kircubbin and continue to **Greyabbey**, which features one of the most complete Cistercian abbeys in Ireland. Turn left SP 'Newtownards', then after 1½m pass the entrance to the 18th-c Temple of the Winds and ½m farther beautiful Mount Stewart Gardens (both NT). The Mount Stewart estate grounds are rich in prehistoric remains, including three raths and a perfect dolmen. Continue along the 'Newtownards' road with views which extend across the lough to the Londonderry Monument on distant Scrabo Hill. Enter Newtownards and follow SP 'Belfast' to leave by the A20 passing the Ards Shopping Centre. Pass through undulating countryside, and after 4¾m reach Dundonald. Beyond Dundonald drive through increasingly urban areas to a point where views to the right take in Stormont Castle – the parliament buildings of Northern Ireland. Proceed to Belfast city centre.

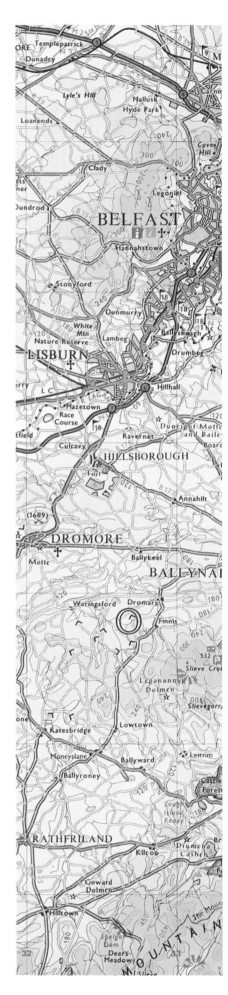

Stricklands Glen – a tranquil retreat near Bangor

An ideal picnic spot overlooking Strangford Lough where basking seals may be spotted in summer

TOUR *10*

To the Shores of Lough Conn

The drive starts at Castlebar. Historic **Castlebar** is the county town of Mayo and has many interesting associations with Ireland's past. It was here, at the Imperial Hotel, that Michael Davitt founded the Land League during the time when the notorious Lord Lucan was forcing eviction on his tenants. Lucan was a member of the hated Bingham family. Leave the town centre by Shamble St R311 and cross a river bridge. Turn right SP 'Foxford, Ballina' into Chapel St and pass a church on the right, then at X-roads turn left into an unclassified road. Keep straight on to enter hilly, rather infertile country, then in 2m look left for distant views of Croagh Patrick (762mtrs) and the Connemara mountains. Croagh Patrick is one of the most famous mountains in Ireland, and is traditionally the place where St Patrick withdrew to fast for the Lent period. After a further ½m pass through extensive forestry plantations, and shortly ascend to the top of a low rise. This affords views of Lough Sallagher to the left. Some 4m from Castlebar is a right turn which leads up to the TV transmitter on the 427-metre summit of Croaghmoyle, the highest peak of its range and an excellent viewpoint.

The next section of the route becomes undulating and offers forward views of Lough Beltra, which lies in front of the Nephin Beg Mountains. The main heights visible from here include Bengorm (580mtrs) above Lough Feeagh, Buckoogh (587mtrs) and Birreencorragh (697mtrs). Pass Glenisland Wood on the left and descend to reach the R312. Go forward onto it, and in 1m cross a river bridge to reach the shores of Lough Beltra. To the right are the wooded slopes of Birreen (326mtrs), while Knockaffertagh (514mtrs) and the conical peak of Nephin (804mtrs) rise ahead. Birreencorragh is visible to the left. Pass the end of the lake and continue for ¾m, with the Crumpaun River valley separating the two mountains ahead, and meet staggered X-roads at the edge of **Beltra** hamlet. Turn right on to an unclassified road SP 'Lahardaun', and drive along Glen Nephin with bogland stretching back to the forested slopes of Nephin Mountain to the left. Rocky slopes rise to the right. Make a small ascent for forward views over Lough Conn, and in 1½m at a T-junction turn left SP 'Crossmolina'. In 1m drive straight ahead, and again in 1m keep forward. Pass extensive forestry plantations to the right, and beyond these enjoy good views over Lough Conn. Shortly go forward on to the R315 SP 'Crossmolina', and pass through the village of **Lahardaun**. In 1¾m bear right to cross undulating grazing land, then in 1¼m meet a junction and bear right. In ¼m pass an unclassified road to the right allowing access to ruined Errew Abbey on a long, narrow peninsula in the lough.

Continue the drive through pleasant countryside and scrubland, then after 2¼m reach **Crossmolina** on the River Deel. Considered one of the most progressive towns in N Mayo, this Lough Conn and River Deel community owes its prosperity to Bord na Mona and the Electricity Supply Board. These bodies have been intelligently exploiting the local boglands without detrimental effect to the countryside. On reaching the centre of the village turn right at the statue on to the N59 SP 'Ballina'. Drive over more grazing land at the north end of Lough Conn, and in 2m enter a belt of dense woodland. After a further 2m at X-roads turn right on to a narrow unclassified road, with Nephin Mountain visible to the right. In 2m meet a T-junction and turn left, then in 1¾m bear right to pass fairly close to the shores of Lough Conn. In 2m bear right and pass a ruined castle on the left, then continue across predominantly flat grazing land. In 3¼m reach **Knockmore** village and turn left on to the R310 then right on to an unclassified road. Climb this narrow section of the drive through scrubland, crossing the edge of Stoneparkbrogan Hill before descending to pass over a level crossing. Meet a T-junction and turn right on to the N58. Proceed through boggy countryside, with the Moy River to the left in front of the distant Ox Mountains, and dense forest to the right. Drive to the edge of **Foxford** and before reaching the river bridge turn sharp right on to the R318 SP 'Pontoon', then bear left. In ¾m go over a level crossing, then immediately turn right on to an unclassified road SP 'Scenic Route'. Follow this narrow road and gradually ascend through extensive woodland, with good views over Foxford to the right. After 1½m turn sharp left and continue to climb. After a further ¾m reach the road summit below the top of Stoneparkbrogan Hill. Panoramic views from here take in Lough Conn and the Nephin Beg Mountains ahead, with Lough Cullin to the left. In just over

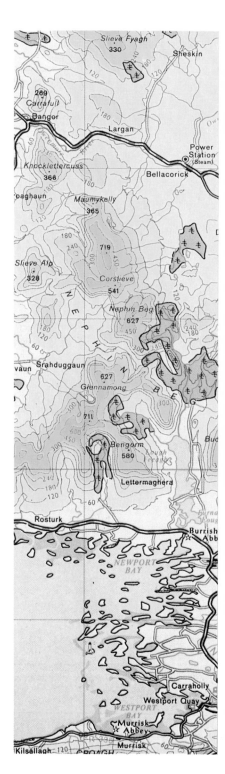

½m turn left SP 'Scenic View Carpark' and ascend. Meet a T-junction and turn right, then in ¼m reach the Scenic View carpark. Descend steeply to the lake shore and at the T-junction turn left on to the R310. In 1m keep forward SP Pontoon then 1m farther cross the stream which separates Lough Conn from Lough Cullin, via Pontoon Bridge.

Follow the shores of Lough Cullin to the forest-backed village of **Pontoon**, and at the T-junction turn left SP 'Castlebar'. In 1m follow the route away from the lake through scenery which gradually changes to moorland and hills to the right, and poor grazing land to the left. After 5m (from Pontoon) climb a rise in the road for views ahead over Castlebar to the distant Partry Mountains. Croagh Patrick rises to the right. Pass bogland to the right, with Clydagh Wood and Picnic Site on the left, and cross the Clydagh River. Gradually descend past Tucker's Lough. After a further 3m pass through extensive forestry and go forward onto the N5 to re-enter Castlebar.

Lough Conn offers free fishing and boats and boatmen can be hired

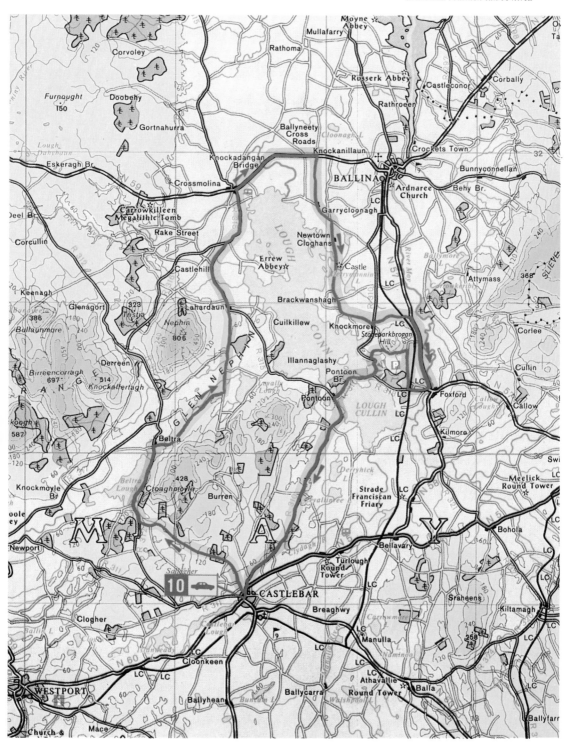

Into Joyce's Country

The drive starts at Clifden. Take the unclassified Sky Rd to leave **Clifden**, and follow the coast of a peninsula which is bounded to the south by Clifden, Bay. Climb above the bay to cliff tops, which afford superb island views and Atlantic seascapes. In 4m keep right in order to return along the north side of the peninsula, and later follow the shore of Streamstown Bay. This part of the drive affords distant views of the *Twelve Bens*, or *Pins*; the highest of these mountains rises to 727 metres. After 3¾m turn left on to the N59 SP 'Westport' and continue through barren countryside. In 1¾m bear right to cross open moorland, with further views of the Twelve Bens to the right. After another 1¾m the views to the left take in Ballynakill Harbour, backed by Tully Mountain (355mtrs). Continue and later drive alongside Barnaderg Bay to reach **Letterfrack** in the shadow of Diamond Hill (442mtrs). Leave Letterfrack and continue, with Doughraugh (526mtrs) ahead, before following the valley of the Dawros River and entering the Pass of Kylemore. The late 19th-c Kylemore Abbey, a castellated granite structure which was one of Ireland's last castle houses, is later passed on the left. This was built in 1860 for a rich Liverpool merchant and is constructed of stone from Dalkey quarry, Dublin.

Proceed to the attractive shoreline of Kylemore Lough. The stretch after the lough affords views of the Maumturk Mountains to the right. After 3m it is possible to catch a glimpse of Lough Fee to the left. Descend to the shores of picturesque Killary harbour, from which views of the Mweelrea Mountains can be obtained. The 816 metre high Mweelrea dominates the range to which it gave its name and is the highest peak in Connacht. Continue to **Leenane**, which is pleasantly situated near the head of Killary Harbour, and branch right on to the R336 SP 'Maam Cross and Galway'. Cross higher ground for short distance then gradually descend through moorland scenery to enter the area known as *Joyce's Country*. This unofficially-named region derives its title from a Welsh family who moved here in the 13th-c. Many of the local people count these early settlers among their ancestors. Follow the valley of Joyce's River with the Maumturk Mountains prominent to the right. Later on keep forward with the R336 to Maam Bridge, then turn right on to the 'Maam Cross' road. Cross Joyce's River and continue over higher ground with Leckavrea (610mtrs) to the right.

Proceed through rather barren countryside to **Maam Cross**, and at X-roads go forward SP 'Carna'. In 5½m keep forward on to the R340 and skirt the numerous inlets of the Atlantic Ocean which form a main feature of the South Connemara coast. In 4¾m cross a river bridge, then keep left and later follow the west shores of Kilkieran Bay to reach the village of **Kilkieran**. Continue with the R340 to the outskirts of Carna, meet a T-junction, and turn right SP 'Cashe' to turn inland. More views of the Twelve Bens are offered ahead. After 3½m rejoin the coast and skirt Bertraghboy Bay.

In a further 4m turn left on to the R342 SP 'Cashel and Roundstone', then after 1m pass Cashel Bay. In 4m turn left R341 SP 'Roundstone', then in 1m turn left again. The next section of the route offers extensive coastal views before taking the drive to the little fishing village of **Roundstone**. Continue along the Clifden road and later skirt Dog's and Ballyconneely Bays to reach Ballyconneely.

Proceed northwards and shortly pass Mannin Bay. In 3¼m pass a track to the right which leads to the spot where famous aviators Alcock and Brown landed after the first trans-Atlantic flight in 1919. A memorial and viewpoint commemorating the event lie ½m to the left. In order to complete the drive, cross Ballinaboy Bridge and turn left, then later pass Salt Lake before returning to Clifden.

Clifden is a handsome early 19th-century market town and fishing harbour

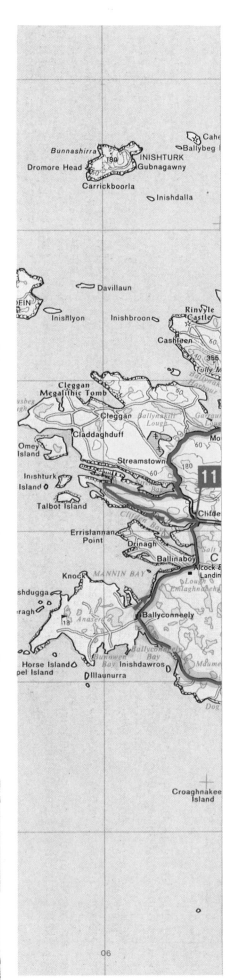

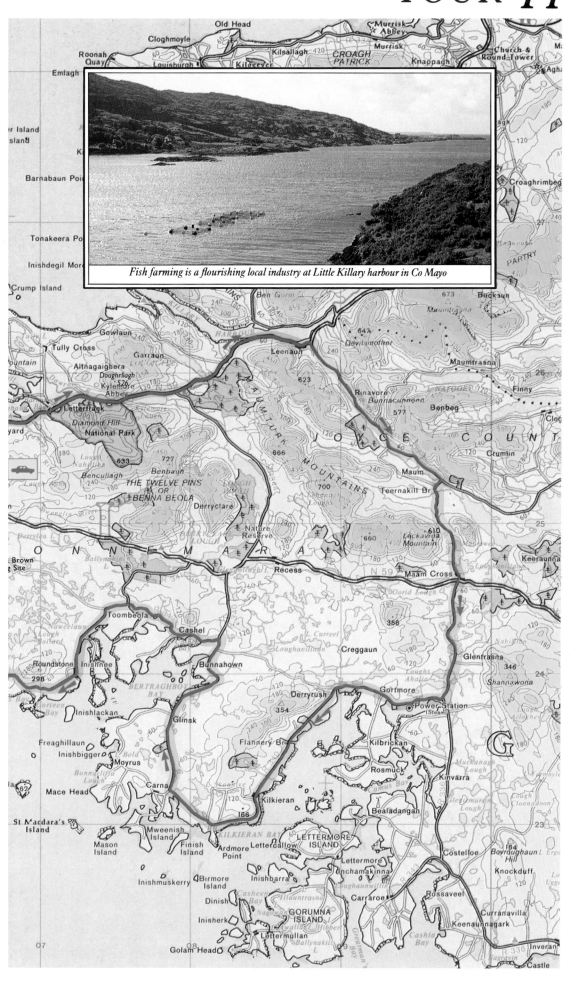

Fish farming is a flourishing local industry at Little Killary harbour in Co Mayo

TOUR *12*

The Shores of Lough Corrib

The drive starts at Galway. Follow SP's 'Salt Hill' to leave **Galway** by the R336 and drive to the seaside resort of Salt Hill. Continue on the 'Spiddle' road, and in 1½m keep left SP 'Carraroe Barna'. Follow the north coast of Galway Bay and pass through Barna before reaching the small angling resort of **Spiddle**. Views afforded by this part of the drive extend across the waters of the bay to the distant mountains of Co. Clare.

Seascapes beyond Spiddle encompass the Aran Islands, while landward views take in a patchwork of little stone-walled fields – a prominent feature of this part of Ireland. After 8m branch right SP 'Costelloe', and turn inland to pass through barren rocky countryside. In 2½m turn right on to an unclassified road SP 'Oughterard'. After a short distance the scenery becomes mountainous and the drive route affords views of numerous small lakes as it winds through the hills of the Iar Connaught district. After 8m enter a pine plantation, and later make a gradual descent towards Oughterard for fine views of distant Lough Corrib. On reaching **Oughterard** turn left on to the N59 then immediately right SP 'Clifden'. Cross the Owenriff River and drive alongside it for a short distance.

Enter the Connemara district, then after 10m reach **Maam Cross** and turn right on to the R336 SP 'Maam Bridge'. Drive over barren, open countryside before crossing higher ground with Leckavrea Mountain (613mtrs) prominent to the left. Continue to Maam Bridge with the Maumturk Mountains to the left and the hills of Joyce's Country ahead. Cross the Bealanabrack River at Maam Bridge and turn right SP 'Cong' onto the R345. After a short distance there are views of Lough Corrib's west arm -- including the island-ruins of Castle Kirke, which is also known as Hen's Castle. After 1½m turn inland for a short distance and cross more high ground before continuing to Cornamona. Drive beyond this village and run parallel to the shore of attractive Lough Corrib for 2½m before once again turning inland. Make a winding ascent and turn right on to an unclassified road SP 'Cong', then continue through agricultural country criss-crossed with stone walls and studded with little farms. In another 2½m pass through Cong Woods, then keep forward to reach **Cong**.

One of the major features offered by this interesting village is its largely-rebuilt Augustinian friary, a royal foundation dating from the 13th-c. Drive to the old Market Cross in Cong and keep left SP 'Galway'. Leave the village, and after ½m pass the impressive gates of 19th-c Ashford Castle, which now serves as a hotel but was originally built for Arthur E Guinness. Keep forward with the R346 'Headford' road, and in 2½m turn right onto the R334 at the village of Cross.

Continue along this road through undulating livestock-grazing country and after 1½m keep left. After another 4¾m pass the ruins of Ross Abbey on the right and proceed into the small country town of **Headford**. Join the N84 SP 'Galway', and continue the drive through flat, rather uninteresting countryside for almost 11m before crossing the River Clare. This river flows into Lough Corrib, which lies only 1m to the right but is not clearly visible from the road. In 2¾m pass the remains of Ballindooly Castle, then complete the drive by continuing along the N84 to Galway.

'Salmon for dinner, anyone?' – game fishing on Lough Corrib

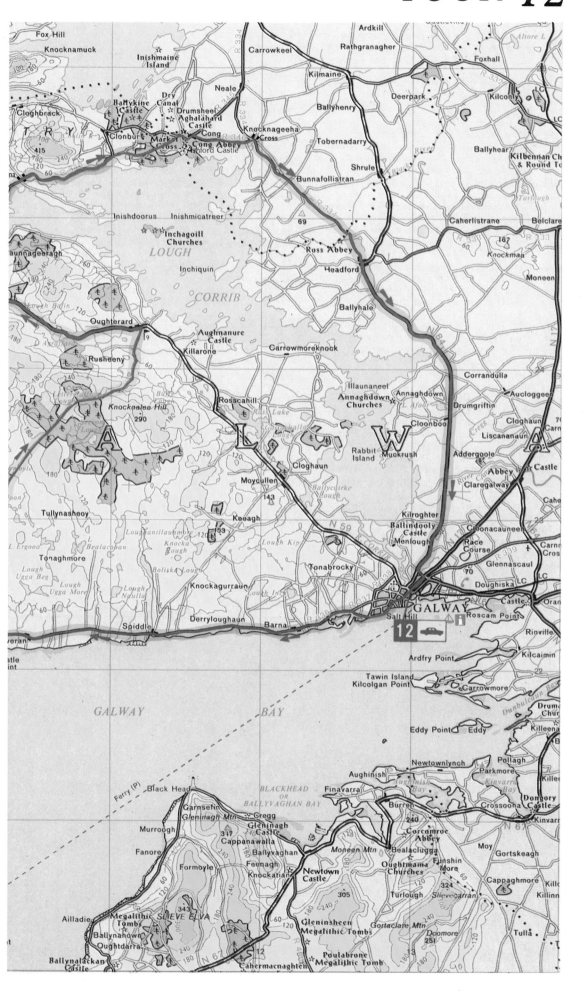

Burren
Moonscapes

The drive starts at Ballyvaughan. Depart from the monument in **Ballyvaughan** with SP 'Black Head' on the R477 and drive along the shores of Ballyvaughan Bay. Pass beneath Cappanawalla (309mtrs) and Gleninagh Mountain (315mtrs), then after 6m round Black Head for views of the Aran Islands. In 1½m pass through the tiny village of Fanmore, and in a further 2m pass Craggagh Post Office on the right, with Slieve Elva (342mtrs) to the left.

Continue, passing Knockauns (294mtrs) on the left, then after 4m (from Craggagh) turn inland and ascend with 15th-c Ballynalackan Castle visible ahead. Galway Bay and the Aran Islands can be seen behind during the climb. After 1¾m reach the castle gates and turn right on to the R479 SP 'Cliffs of Moher'. Pass through farmland with distant forward views of the famous 180-metre high Cliffs of Moher. Descend to **Roadford**, cross the River Aille, and in ¼m turn left SP 'Cliffs of Moher'. The road ahead leads to Doolin Strand (1m). In 1¼m at X-roads turn right on to the R478. Ascend with fine views to the right and Knocknalarabana (204mtrs) on the left, then after 4½m pass a right turn leading to the Cliffs of Moher carpark. Steps from here lead up to cliff-top O'Brien's Tower, which affords magnificent views of the 3m cliff range. After another 1¼m along the R478 pass St Bridget's Well and a monument on the right. In ¾m meet a T-junction and turn left SP 'Liscannor, Lahinch', then in 1½m enter Liscannor on the shores of Liscannor Bay. Continue with the R478 along the shore and in 1m pass a fine (but dangerous) beach. Follow SP 'Lahinch', cross the Inagh River by O'Brien's Bridge with castle ruins on the left, then skirt Lahinch Championship Golf Course among the sand dunes on the right. At a T-junction, turn right on to the N67 then immediately left into the main street of **Lahinch**. Drive to the church, then turn right, then immediately left SP 'Kilkee, Milltown Malbay'.

Ascend and in 1m turn right SP 'Kilkee' to continue along the coast road. Proceed through farmland with hilly country to the left, and, after 4m views ahead of Mutton Island. After a further 2½m turn right into **Milltown Malbay**, continue to the end of the town, and turn left on to the R474 SP 'Inagh, Ennis'. In 1½m turn left on to the R460 SP 'Inagh' and follow a winding road. After another 4m pass between several loughs as the drive approaches Inagh. Enter the village and turn left on to the N85 SP 'Ennistymon' to follow the valley of the Inagh or Cullenagh River. Reach **Ennistymon**, go forward through the town and climb on the N67 SP 'Lisdoonvarna', and in 1m branch right on to the R481 SP 'Kilfenora' to enter low, hilly country. In 4½m enter Kilfenora, drive to the end of the village, and turn left on to the R476 SP 'Lisdoonvarna'. Climb steadily with views ahead and right of the Burren – a vast moonscape of bare limestone. After about 2m pass bogland. Continue, and in another 1m turn right on to the N67 across the Aille River. Enter the spa town of **Lisdoonvarna**, follow SP 'Galway, Ballyvaughan', and in ¼m bear left. In another ½m meet a T-junction and turn right SP 'Galway' to follow a narrow road between stone walls with rocky fields on both sides. Slieve Elva – the highest point in the area – rises to the left as the route climbs steadily into the heart of the Burren. After 6m (from Lisdoonvarna) reach Corkscrew Hill, which affords magnificent views. Descend steeply through hairpin bends, and in 3½m re-enter Ballyvaughan.

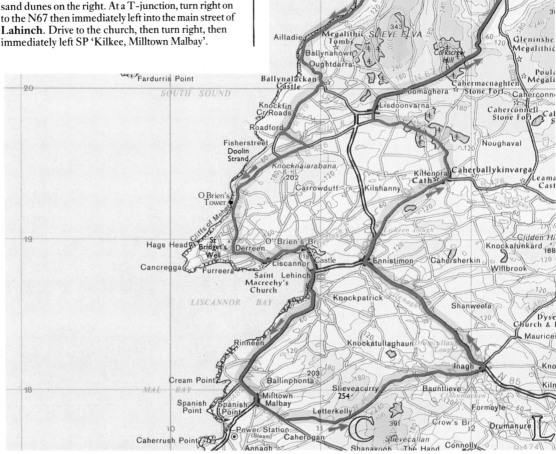

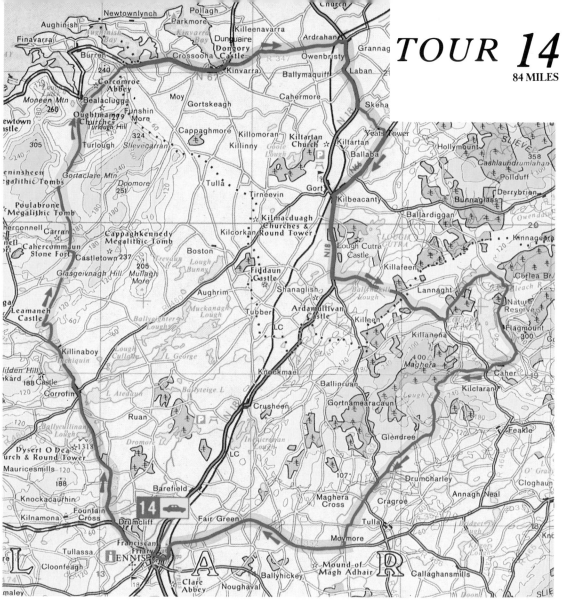

Through Clare and Galway

The drive starts at Ennis. Follow SP 'Ennistymon' N85 from **Ennis**, and in 2½m branch right on to the R476 SP 'Lisdoonvarna, Corofin'. In ¾m turn right. Reach Corofin and keep forward to the Grotto, then bear right SP 'Ballyvaughan, Kilfenora'. Shortly pass Inchiquin Lough and 15th-c castle ruins (left). After 2½m (from Corofin) turn right on to an unclassified road.

In ½m ascend through several hairpin bends, and 3¼m farther bear left. In ½m at a T-junction turn right then ½m farther pass through the hamlet of **Carran**, and in a further 2m begin a long descent. Pass through a deep, rocky gorge into a wide valley, then later drive between Moneen Mountain (260mtrs) and Turlough Hill (279mtrs). Lough Luick lies a short distance from the road on the left. Shortly beyond this pass the road to Bealaclugga (on left) which leads to the entrance to Corcomroe Abbey (NM). After another 1m pass close to the abbey buildings and climb to a low pass. The summit affords forward views over the islands in Galway Bay. In ½m turn right on to the N67 'Galway' road and continue with fine views of the Burren hills on the right. After 4m reach **Kinvarra**. Follow SP 'Galway' to round the head of Kinvarra Bay, with 16th-c Dunguaire Castle ahead to the left. Reach the castle gate and turn right on to the R347 SP 'Andrahan'. Continue, and in 1¾m bear right. In a further 3¾m enter Ardrahan and turn right on to the

N18 SP 'Ennis' then in 1¼m reach **Laban** and turn left. In 1¾m at X-roads bear left on to an unclassified road SP 'Thoor Ballylee-Yeats Tower'. In ½m bear right, then after 1m pass the Thoor Ballylee-Yeats Tower (right). In ½m meet a T-junction and turn right on to the N66 SP 'Gort'.

Proceed for 3½m to the edge of Gort, turn left SP 'Ennis' to rejoin the N18 and in 2¼m pass the entrance to Lough Cutra Castle (left). After another 1¼m turn left on to an unclassified road SP 'Scarriff', and shortly follow SP 'Lough Cutra Drive' to pass close to Ballynakill Lough (right). In just over 1¾m bear right SP 'Feakle, Scarriff'. In 2½m bear left, and in ¼m left again. In 3¼m at a T-junction turn right. Descend and shortly cross the Bleach River, then bear right and in ½m pass the entrance to Lough Graney Wood on the right. After another ¾m reach the shores of the lough and continue between high hedges. Shortly pass Flagmount Post Office on the left, turn away from the lough, and in 1m bear right. In a further ½m meet a T-junction and turn right SP 'Feakle', then in ¾m rejoin the shores of Lough Graney and enter **Caher** village. Continue for ¾m and turn right SP 'TV Station'. Ascend steeply for 1¾m to the entrance of Maghera TV Station, then continue the climb to a 240-metre summit.

Descend, then in 1m meet X-roads and go forward and in 1m bear right. In 2½m at a T-junction turn right, then in 1m bear left onto the R462 SP 'Tulla'. After another 1m meet X-roads and go forward on to an unclassified road SP 'Quin'. In 1¼m reach a T-junction and turn right, then in ¼m bear left and continue for 1m to X-roads. Turn right on to the R352 SP 'Ennis' and return to Ennis.

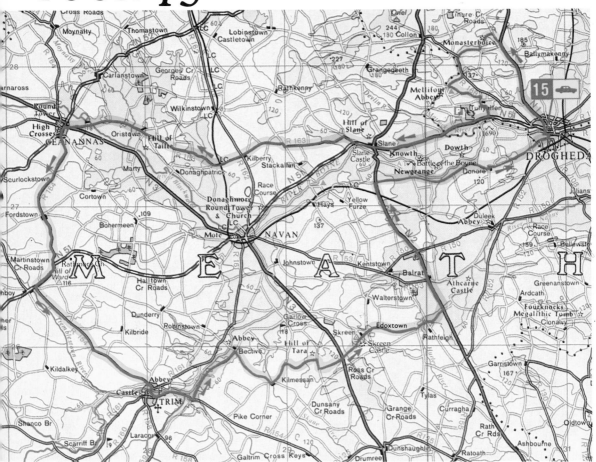

The Historic Boyne Valley

The drive starts at Drogheda. Leave central **Drogheda** via West St and turn right into George's St N1 SP 'Dundalk, Belfast'. In 4½m turn left on to an unclassified road SP 'Monasterboice Abbey, Round Tower', and in ½m turn left again. In ½m pass ruined Monasterboice Abbey on the right. Continue with SP 'Mellifont Abbey' and in 1½m turn right. After another 1m go forward on to the R168 SP 'Dublin, Drogheda'. In 1m turn right on to an unclassified road SP 'Mellifont Abbey', and in another 1m meet X-roads. Go forward for ¼m to ruined Mellifont Abbey, beside the Mattock River. Return to the X-roads and turn right. In 1¾m at a T-junction turn right and shortly at X-roads go forward SP Newgrange into King William's Glen, then in ¾m turn right on to the N51 SP 'Slane'. In ¾m pass an unclassified road on the left leading to the prehistoric tumuli at Dowth, Newgrange, and Knowth.

Follow the main road along the Mattock Valley and after 1½m cross the River Mattock. After ¼m pass another left turn leading to Knowth and Newgrange, then in a further 1¼m pass a third, similarly signposted road. After another 1¾m enter **Slane** and at X-roads keep forward with the N51 SP 'Navan'. In 1m with the Slane Castle estate on the left, turn right on to the R163 SP 'Kells'. In ½m turn left, and in 2½m meet a T-junction. Turn right SP Kells then in ¼m turn left. In 1m bear left, and in a further 1m reach Kilberry. At staggered X-roads turn right then immediately left and in 1m drive forward over a level crossing. In 2¼m at X-roads keep forward then in 1½m bear right then shortly left through Oristown. In a further 2½m cross the River Blackwater and in 1m bear right into the town of **Kells**. Pass the Headfort Hotel, branch left, then turn left on to the N52 SP

Mullingar. In ¼m branch left and in a further ¼m turn left R164 SP Athboy. In 6½m turn right on to the N51; the left turn here leads to Rathmore Church (NM). In 1¼m, on entering Athboy, pass an unclassified left turn which leads to the Hill of Ward. Immediately beyond this road turn left on to the R154 SP 'Trim' and follow the line of the Athboy River. In 2½m bear right and continue to the charming market town of **Trim**.

Continue forward, and on meeting a T-junction turn right into the High St. Cross the River Boyne into the town square, and follow SP 'Dublin R154. Pass castle ruins (left) and in ¼m bear left to follow the River Boyne. After 1¾m turn left, cross a bridge, then turn left again on to an unclassified road SP 'Bective'. Continue along the Boyne Valley, then after 3m enter Bective and at X-roads turn right SP 'Kilmessan'; the left turn here leads to a ruined fortress abbey. In 2¼m reach **Kilmessan** and turn left SP 'Tara, Navan' to cross a river bridge. Keep straight ahead, and in 1m turn right SP 'Tara'. Climb towards the ancient royal hill of Tara, once the seat of the High Kings in pre-Christian Ireland, then in 1½m meet a T-junction and turn right. In ½m turn left, and in 1m cross the N3 SP 'Skreen Cross Church'. In a further 1¼m pass the ruins of Skreen Castle on the right. Shortly pass Skreen Church and Cross (NM) on the left, meet X-roads and go forward, then in ½m at the next X-roads go forward again and later descend. After 2¼m reach Edoxtown X-roads and turn left SP 'Dunleer' then in ¾m meet more X-roads and drive forward, in ¼m bear left SP 'Duleek, Dogheda'.

In 1m at X-roads turn left on to the N2 SP 'Slane'. Keep forward for 6¼m along the N2 to McGruder's X-roads and turn right on to Drogheda. In 1¾m pass an unclassified left turn SP 'Battle of the Boyne' – site of a crossing made by part of the Williamite force. Shortly bear left to reach the Boyne, then in 3¾m enter **Donore** and turn left SP 'Drogheda'. After another ¼m pass another unclassified left turn SP 'Battle of the Boyne' – the site of the main battlefield. In 2¾m re-enter Drogheda.

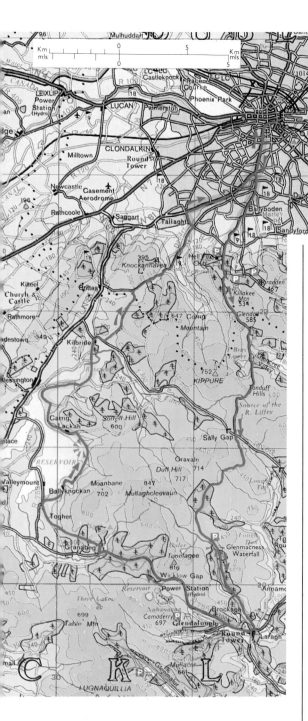

Wicklow Summits

The drive starts at Dublin. Follow the N81 Rathmines Rd to leave **Dublin** and proceed to the suburb of Rathmines. Bear right, and in 100yds bear left into Rathgar Rd. In ¾m bear right through Rathgar on to Terenure Rd East, and in a further ½m enter Terenure. Meet traffic signals and turn left, then in ¾m reach Rathfarnham. Bear left into Main St, and at the church turn right on to the R116 SP 'Glencree'. In 1¼m turn right onto the R115 SP 'Sally Gap', then shortly left into Stocking Lane and ascend. Views to the left take in Tibradden (467mtrs) and Kilmashogue (405mtrs). Pass close to Mount Pelier, or Hellfire Club Hill, and the entry to the Hellfire Club Wood on the right. Continue the ascent, and in 1m reach Killakee carpark and viewpoint. Bear right up an ascent, then in

¾m pass a left turn leading to Cruagh Forest and carpark.

Continue along the side of Killakee Mountain (534mtrs) and emerge high above the Dodder Valley. Within 1½m reach a 485 metre summit between Glendoo (585mtrs) and Kippure (751mtrs). Descend to a minor road junction known as Glencree Cross. Magnificent views from this 393 metre point extend along the Glencree Valley to the conical, 499 metre Great Sugarloaf in the distance. The Welsh mountains can be seen in clear weather. Continue along the R115 to a 519 metre summit between Kippure and the two Tonduff hills – 620 and 640 metres respectively. A right turn here leads to a TV transmitter on Kippure. In 1m cross the Liffey Head Bridge, with the source of the River Liffey on the left. In a short distance the drive affords panoramic views of the Liffey Valley as far as Blessington. A 681 metre hill rises ahead above Sally Gap and in front of Gravale (714mtrs). In a short distance gradually descend to X-roads at **Sally Gap** (714mtrs) and drive forward on to the unclassified 'Glendalough' road. Views from this old military road extend left across the Clochoge Valley to War Hill (683mtrs) and Djouce (724mtrs). In about 1m descend, then later pass through plantations below Duff Hill (717mtrs) and an un-named 794 metre summit. Climb to 424 metres at the head of the Glenmacnass River. In ½m descend to a carpark at the head of Glenmacnass Waterfall. Continue along this unclassified road for 4¾m and reach **Laragh**.

Turn right on to the R755 cross a bridge, then branch right again on to the R756 SP 'Glendalough'. In ¼m bear right up an ascent. The left turn here leads to the Vale of Glendalough. Ascend the Vale of Glendasan, with rocky slopes on the right and views of the Glendalough lakes to the left. Climb past Camaderry (697mtrs) with Tonelagee (815mtrs) rising on the right, and after 4m pass a left turn leading up to the Turlough Hill pumped-storage electricity station. Immediately beyond this reach the 454 metre summit of Wicklow Gap. Descend into the King's River valley, and after 3¾m turn right on to an unclassified road SP 'Valleymount Lake Drive'. Climb through a plantation at first, then after 1¾m reach a summit and descend with views over the Poulaphouca reservoir – or Blessington Lakes. After 2m turn right SP 'Lake Drive', and continue above the reservoir with Moanbane (702mtrs) on the right. In 7½m meet a T-junction and turn left. In ¾m reach a bridge and keep forward SP 'Manor Kilbride'.

Follow the shore for another 1¼m, then later cross the River Liffey. In 1¼m reach **Manor Kilbride** and turn right on to the R759 SP 'Sally Gap'. After another ½m at the second junction turn left up an incline on to an unclassified road. Climb to over 305 metres then descend to meet the R114. Turn right onto it SP 'Dublin, Rathfarnham' and climb to about 300 metres. Descend into the Dodder Valley, cross a river bridge, then in 1½m at X-roads turn left onto the R113 Old Bawn Rd for Tallaght. Recross the River Dodder and in 1m enter **Tallaght**, then turn right onto the N81 to pass along the main street. Return to central Dublin via Templeogue, Terenure, Rathgar, and Rathmines.

TOUR *17* 64 MILES

Sea Views and the Wicklows

The drive starts at Arklow. Leave **Arklow's** main street with SP 'Dublin' N11 and cross the Avoca River. In ½m branch right on to the R750 SP 'Brittas Bay', and continue with the sea visible to the right. Ballymoyle Hill rises to 278 metres on the left, and low Mizen Head can be seen ahead. After 6m reach the shores of Britass Bay, and 5m farther turn right SP 'Coast Road' to pass Wicklow head and lighthouse on the right after 3m. At this point the road affords views to the coast and mountains of North Wicklow. Shortly descend into **Wicklow**. Go forward through the town and on reaching the hotel bear right SP 'Dublin, Rathnew'. In 2m enter Rathnew and bear right on to the N11 SP 'Dublin'. After another 1½m approach Ashford and pass the Mount Usher Gardens on the right. Shortly cross the Vartry River into Ashford. Turn left on to the R763 SP 'Devil's Glen, Roundwood'. In ¾m descend and bear left, then recross the Vartry River and ¾m farther pass the entrance to Glanmore Castle on the right. In ¼m bear right SP 'Annamoe' up an ascent. Shortly pass the entrance to Tiglin Adventure Centre on the right, Carrick Mountain rises to 380 metres on the left. Pass the entrance to the Devil's Glen Woods, gorge and waterfall on the right. Continue the steep ascent through dense woodland to a summit of 213 metres and continue for several miles with the Vartry River and Devil's Glen on the right. Ahead are views of the hills around Annamoe. Descend, with fine views down the Avonmore Valley to Laragh ahead and turn left on to the R755 into **Annamoe**. Cross the Avonmore River and follow a broad main road which affords tree-framed views of the Wicklow Mountains. After 2m pass the entrance to Trooperstown Wood, which offers forest walks, a carpark, and a picnic site, on the left. Proceed to Laragh, with a magnificent view into the Vale of Glendalough ahead, and bear left across the Glenmacnass River – then left again with the R755 SP 'Rathdrum, Wexford'. In ½m pass the Glendalough Craft Centre and Museum on the right. Bear right SP 'Glenmalure, Rathdrum' and cross a river bridge, then in ½m branch right uphill on to an unclassified road SP 'Aghavannagh'. Climb along an old military road with views along the Vale of Clara (Owenmore Valley) ahead. Great Sugarloaf (501mtrs) is distantly left and Trooperstown Hill (430mtrs) lies across the valley. Reach a 337 metre summit with Kirikee (472mtrs) on the left and Cullentragh (466mtrs) to the right then descend towards the Avonbeg River. Reach the valley bottom, and at X-roads go forward SP 'Aghavannagh, Rathdrum'. Cross Drumgoff Bridge; to the right is Lugnaquilla (923mtrs), the highest mountain in the Wicklows. Climb through forestry to a 448 metre summit, with Coraghanmoira (662mtrs) on the left and Slieve Maan on the right. Descend to **Aghavannagh** X-roads, turn left SP 'Aughrim', and in ½m bear left. To the left is Carrickashane (503mtrs). Ascend through dense woodland on the slopes of Croaghanmoira to a 366 metre summit. In 2m descend and meet X-roads. Go forward SP 'Ballinaclash' and continue the descent into the Avonbeg Valley. After 3m keep forward, and in ¼m reach Ballinaclash. Turn left on to the R757 and cross a river bridge, then turn left again SP 'Rathdrum'. In 1m turn right on to an unclassified road, and in ¼m cross a main road SP 'Avondale House'. After a further ¼m bear right; the road on the left leads to Avondale House. Follow a ridge between the Avonmore and Avonbeg Rivers, then make a steep descent through woodland with the mansion of Castle Howard visible across the river on the left. At a T-junction turn left on to the R752 and shortly cross the Avonbeg River at the Meeting of the Waters.

Enter the Vale of Avoca and pass a former copper-mining area on the right after 1½m. In another ¾m reach the edge of Avoca village and turn right SP 'Woodenbridge'. Continue, and in 2m reach **Woodenbridge**. At the hotel, turn right on to the R747 SP 'Aughrim', and follow the Aughrim River. In 2¼m bear left, and after another 1m turn left then right across the Aughrim River. In ¼m bear right again and in 1¼m pass the edge of Aughrim town. Continue forward with the R747 to follow the Derry Water with Croghan Mountain (604mtrs) on the left. In 6½m (from Aughrim) meet X-roads and turn left on to an unclassified road SP 'Gorey'. Ascend, and in 3½m bear left SP 'Gorey'. Enter the low Wicklow Gap, with Annagh Hill (454mtrs) on the right, then descend and meet X-roads. Turn left, ascend to over 245 metres then descend. Climb again to 245 metres with coastal views, then descend and continue for 1½m to Ballyfad Post Ofice. Meet a T-junction here and turn left SP 'Coolgreany'.

Continue the descent and in 1½m enter **Coolgreany**. At a T-junction turn left SP 'Arklow', and in 1m turn right. In ¼m bear left along a quiet road, with views of Ballymoyle and other hills beyond Arklow. After 3¼m meet a roundabout and bear left to re-enter Arklow.

Remains of an 11th-century monastic city can be seen around the shoreline at Glendalough

Valley Woodlands

The drive starts at New Ross. Take the N25 west from **New Ross**, cross a river bridge, and turn right on to an unclassified road SP 'Rosbercon'. Enter Rosbercon and shortly turn left, drive over a level crossing, then begin an ascent from the Barrow Valley. In 2m bear left, and in ½m bear right SP 'Inistioge'. In ¾m descend through wooded country into the Nore Valley, with Brandon Hill (516mtrs) ahead. Shortly bear left, keep forward, and in ¾m being a long ascent with SP 'Inistioge'. In 2m the route affords panoramic views over the Nore Valley ahead and to the right. From this point descend for about 1m, passing a ruined castle on the right, and shortly climb round the heavily wooded lower slopes of Mount Alto (277mtrs). Once clear of woodland the route affords good views before a further descent. In ¾m bear right and in ½m descend steeply into **Instioge**. Turn left on to the R700 'Thomastown, Kilkenny' road, follow the River Nore for 1¾m to Brownsbarn Bridge and at the nearside of the bridge turn left on to an unclassified road. Enter dense woodland and in 1¼m meet a road junction. Bear right and descend through more woodland, then shortly bear left to cross the Arrigle River. In 1m keep forward with good views ahead along the valley towards Thomastown. In 2m reach the edge of Thomastown and turn left on to the N9. Ascend, with views of Slievenamon (719mtrs) ahead, and in 1¼m pass the remains of 12th-century Jerpoint Abbey on the left. This is considered one of the most interesting first-generation Cistercian houses in Ireland, and carries typically-Irish battlements. The church which serves this monastic complex incorporates many interesting features, including a number of fine early carvings. In a further ½m turn right SP 'Stonyford' and cross the Little Arrigle River. In 1½m enter heavy woodland, with Mount Juliet Wood on the right, then in ¼m meet a forked junction and bear right SP 'Stonyford'. In 1½m enjoy further views over the attractive countryside towards Kilkenny. In ¼m turn right on to the N9 SP 'Kilkenny' to enter the village of **Stonyford**. In ¾m cross the King's River and immediately turn right on to an unclassified road SP 'Bennettsbridge'. Continue along an undulating, partly tree-bordered road which affords distant hill views to the right. Later continue alongside the River Nore, with dense woodlands to the left of the road. After 4½m reach Bennettsbridge, and at X-roads go forward on to the R700 SP 'Kilkenny'. Continue along the Nore Valley, and in 4¼m reach Quarry Hill. Fine views extend over the city of **Kilkenny** from here. In ¾m enter the city – passing the castle on the right – then proceed to traffic signals and turn right into Rose Inn St. Follow SP 'Carlow, Dublin' to cross the River Nore via John's Bridge. Keep forward, and in ½m go forward under a railway bridge on to the N78 Castlecomer Rd Bear left, and in ¾m turn right on to an unclassified road SP 'Balleyfoyle'. Follow a narrow, hilly road through dense woodland. After 2m a scenic section of the drive affords good views, which include the Slieveardagh Hills in the distance on the left. After another ½m turn left and shortly right SP 'Castlecomer'. In 1½m pass a road on the left leading to the Cave of Dunmore (NM), a natural limestone cave which is considered one of the finest to be found anywhere in the country.

In ¾m go forward on to the N78 SP 'Castlecomer' and follow the valley of the Dinin River. In 2½m cross Dysart Bridge, and in a further 1¼m enter **Castlecomer** – a pleasant town which serves as a centre of the Leinster anthracite coalfield. Meet X-roads and turn right SP 'Athy, Carlow', then in a short distance recross the Dinin River and enter dense woodland. In 1¼m turn right on to an unclassified road SP 'Coon, Gowran'. Ascend gradually, with good views extending over the landscape behind and to the left. In 1½m at X-roads keep forward SP Coon, Paulstown to enter more woodland. Descend gradually into the valley of another Dinin River, and at the nearside of the bridge turn left SP 'Coon, Carlow'. Follow the valley and climb steadily for 1¾m to reach the village of Coon (or Coan). Turn right SP 'Bilboa, Carlow' and cross a river bridge, then keep forward with good views over the surrounding countryside. In 1½m meet X-roads, turn right SP 'Oldleighlin', and climb out of the river valley. Drive to a height of 281 metres for fine forward views of the Blackstairs Mountains and the prominent Mount Leinster (792mtrs). Follow a long, straight descent for 1¾m to Oldleighlin village, where remains of a 12-century Protestant cathedral can be seen to the right of the road. Continue through the village, and after 2m reach **Leighlinbridge**. Cross the N9 into the village and drive forward along the main street SP 'Dublin, Carlow', cross the River Barrow with the ruins of Black Castle on the right, then keep forward on the R705 SP 'Borris'. Proceed through rich pasture land along the Barrow Valley with fine views of Mount Leinster ahead. In 2½m reach Muinebheag (Bagenalstown) and bear right SP 'Kilkenny' then shortly turn left into the main street. In ¼m turn right SP 'Borris', then meet X-roads and go forward. In 2½m cross a river bridge and immediately branch right unclassified SP 'Goresbridge'. In a

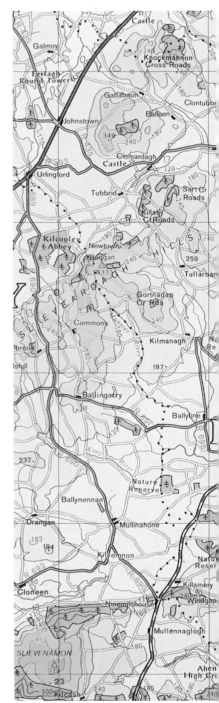

Impressive Kilkenny Castle

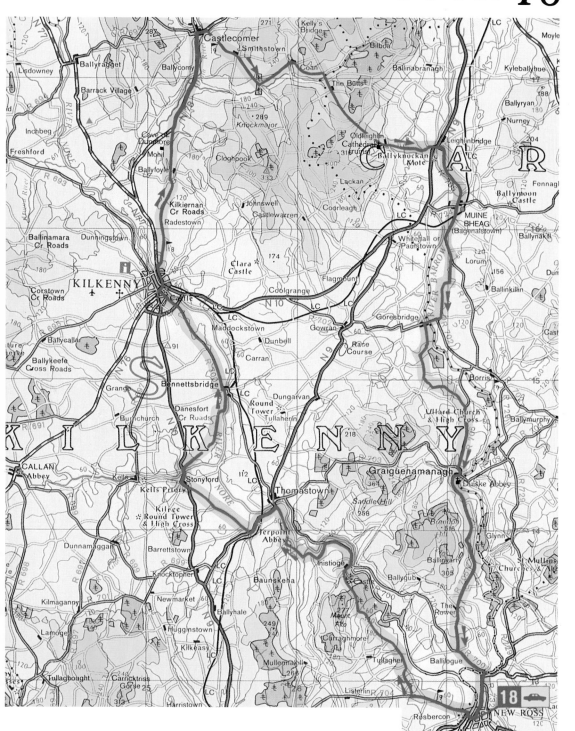

further 2½m at T-junction turn right to join the R702 and recross the River
Barrow into Goresbridge. At X-roads in the village centre turn left on to an
unclassified road SP 'New Ross'. Continue along an undulating road in 2m
pass Mount Loftus Wood on the left, with Brandon Hill rising ahead. In
2¾m turn right onto the R705 SP 'Graiguenamanagh'. The Blackstairs
range can be seen to the left. In 2m begin a descent into **Graiguenamanagh**
with the wooded slopes of Brandon Hill directly ahead. Meet a T-junction,
turn left into the town SP 'New Ross, Enniscorthy', and continue to the town
centre. A signpost to the left here indicates 'Duiske Abbey, Castle, and
Church ruins'. Turn right SP 'New Ross', and in ¼m keep forward on the
R705 SP 'New Ross, Waterford'. Continue alongside the River Barrow with
dense woodland on the right. Mountain views are afforded to the left, and
views ahead extend along the valley towards New Ross.

Later, pass directly beneath Brandon Hill, which rises to the right. After
7m (from Graiguenamanagh) reach the curiously-named village of The
Rower. Descend from here along a road which offers more views, and in
1½m turn left on to the R700. In a further 1½m turn right and cross
Mountgarrett Bridge, which spans the River Barrow, then immediately turn
right on to the N79. Pass through woodland, rejoin the river, and descend
into New Ross.

Eleventh-century Jerpoint Abbey

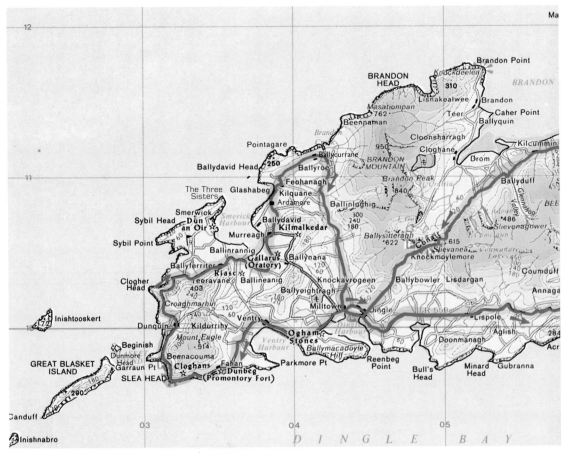

The Dingle Peninsula

The drive starts at Tralee. Leave The Mall in **Tralee** by turning left into Bridge St, then follow SP 'Dingle' R559 along Princes Quay for ¼m before turning right. Drive between a ship canal on the right and the River Lee, and in 1¼m turn left over the river to enter Blennerville.

Proceed along the R559 with the Slieve Mish Mountains on the left. In 7¾m reach the edge of Camp village and turn right on to an unclassified road SP 'Stradbally, Connor Pass'. Pass through **Stradbally** village. In 2m bear left SP 'Dingle, Connor Pass', and in 1½m cross the end of the deep Glennahoo Valley. In 2m climb steeply away from the Owenmore River valley to the upper slopes of Slievanea (615mtrs). Continue forward and shortly obtain views ahead of numerous small loughs, then meet a sharp bend where a small waterfall provides a high outlet for tiny Lough Doon.

After a further 1m reach the dramatic, almost knife-edged summit of the 454 metre Connor Pass. Follow a long descent for panoramic views which extend across Dingle Bay. On entering Dingle turn left and immediately right, then in ¼m turn right on to an unclassified road SP 'Ventry, Ballyferriter'. Drive out of the town and proceed alongside Dingle Harbour, then after ¾m reach Miltown and turn left SP 'Murreagh, Ballydavid' across the Milltown River. In ¼m keep straight ahead SP 'Slea Head', and in ½m keep forward again SP 'Slea Head' – with Dingle Harbour visible on the left. In 1½m continue along a stretch of route which affords views of Mount Eagle, rising to 514 metres beyond Ventry Harbour. After another 1¾m enter Ventry, in ½m turn left SP 'Slea Head, Dunquin', and in 1¼m turn right. In ¼m turn left again, then after 1¼m rejoin the coast. Continue for a short distnce and pass through **Fahan** – the site of some 400 of the stone bee-hive huts known as clochans, plus numerous other ancient remains. Opposite the village is the interesting Dunbeg promontory fort. After another 1m pass SP indicating 'Fahan prehistoric bee-hive huts' on the right. In a further 1½m drive round Slea Head, high above the shore and below the towering bulk of Mount Eagle.

Proceed for another 1m and pass through Coumeenoole. Pass behind Dunmore Head, before rejoining the coast. Continue to Dunquin – claimed to be the most westerly place of habitation in Europe – and at X-roads turn left. In 1½m pass Clogher Head on the left, with views ahead extending across a small bay to take in Sybil Point and a curious rock formation known as the Three Sisters. Meet a T-junction and turn right SP 'Ballyferriter', then in 2m keep forward through **Ballyferriter** village. In 1m meet another T-junction and turn left SP 'Murreagh, Ballydavid', then in ¼m turn right

Kilshannig cross slab forms part of the remains of a 6th-century monastery (NT)

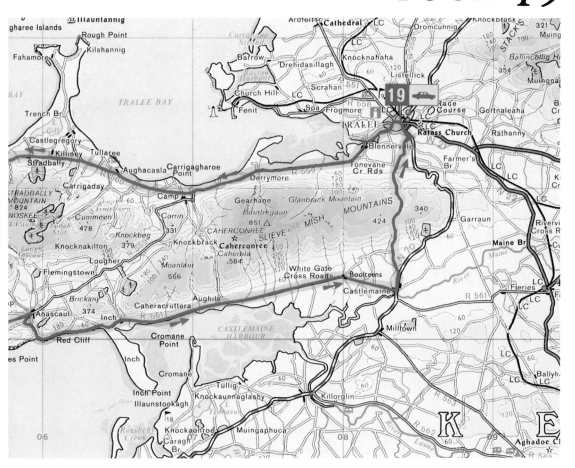

SP 'Dingle, Feohanagh'. Cross a bridge and keep forward. In 1¼m turn left SP 'Murreagh, Feohanagh, Gallarus Oratory', and proceed through barren, rocky countryside. In ½m at a T-junction turn left; the road to the right leads to the ancient Gallarus Oratory – the only perfect example of its type in Ireland. After a further 1m enter Murreagh, turn right, and keep forward with SP 'Feohanagh'. Pass a radio transmitter on the left beyond the village, and after 1½m drive past Ardamore. In a further ¾m keep forward for views to the left of the Dooneen Cliffs. In ½m enter Feohanagh and turn sharp left SP 'Ballycurrane'. Pass Ballydavid Head on the left, and proceed to Ballycurrane. Continue for ½m and at X-roads turn right SP 'Dingle'. The road to the left here leads to Brandon Creek. Climb to a low pass with views of the Brandon Mountains to the left, and continue to the summit for views which extend along the valley of the Milltown River to Dingle Harbour. In 4m reach Milltown and turn left, then in ¾m drive into Dingle via the main street. Proceed to the end of this street, cross a bridge, and immediately turn right SP 'Tralee'. In ¼m turn left on to the R559 SP 'Tralee, Anascaul'.

Ascend gradually for several miles, then descend to cross a wide valley which surrounds a coastal inlet. Afer 5½m pass Lispole and follow a long winding climb to a low summit then descend to the edge of Anascaul. At the nearside of the village turn right on to the R561 SP 'Inch' and follow the Owenascaul River between high hills. Meet the coast and drive along the Red Cliffs with Dingle Bay on the right and views of the mountains which rise from the Iveragh Peninsula. The Inch Peninsula with its fine sandy beach extending 3m out into the estuary can be seen ahead.

Pass through the village of Inch which lies at the base of the peninsula, then bear right SP Castlemaine. In a short distance drive close to the shores of Castlemaine Harbour. Pass on the left the main group of the Slieve Mish Mountains on the approach to Whitegate Crossroads.

Keep forward and in 1¼m reach Boolteens and bear right with the main road. Continue for another 2m and enter Castlemaine. Turn left on to the N70 SP 'Tralee' then immediately left again. In ¾m turn left on to an unclassified road SP 'Viewing Park'. In 2½m reach a carpark and 302 metre viewpoint on the left. Features that can be identified from here include the Maine Valley, Castlemaine Harbour, the Laune Valley as far as Killarney, and the Magillycuddy's Reeks mountains. Continue and after a short distance reach a second carpark which affords fine views to the north. Tralee Bay can be seen to the left with Tralee town and the Stack's Mountains ahead. Descend to X-roads and keep forward then in 1½m at a T-junction turn left on to the N70 for Tralee. In ¾m turn left into Castle street and drive into the centre of the town.

Top: Brandon Bay is overlooked by Mount Brandon. Bottom: Slea Head with the Blasket Islands beyond

TOUR 20 80 MILES

Through the High Passes

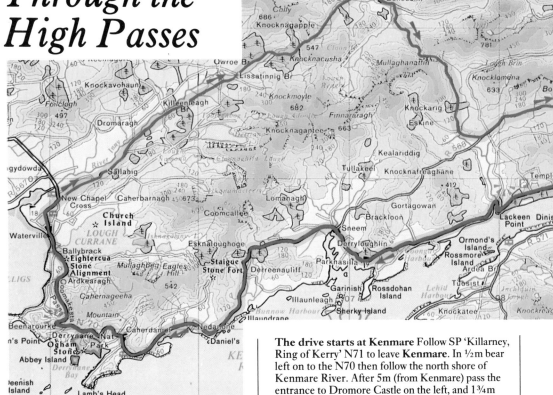

The drive starts at Kenmare Follow SP 'Killarney, Ring of Kerry' N71 to leave **Kenmare**. In ½m bear left on to the N70 then follow the north shore of Kenmare River. After 5m (from Kenmare) pass the entrance to Dromore Castle on the left, and 1¾m farther pass Dromore Wood Picnic Site on the left. In another 1m cross Blackwater Bridge and continue alongside the bay. After 6¼m pass another picnic site

---

TOUR 21 86 MILES

Peaks of Three Ranges

The drive starts at Killarney. Leave **Killarney** by the N22 'Cork' road, and in 2½m bear left onto the N72 SP 'Mallow, Rathmore'. Proceed with the Mangerton Mountains on the right, and in 5m pass through Barraduff. Drive to Rathmore, in ½m branch right on to the R582 SP 'Millstreet', and in 6¾m, reach **Millstreet**. At the memorial, turn right SP 'Cork, Macroom'. In 4m turn sharp right on to an unclassified road SP 'Ballyvourney'. Climb steadily through forestry plantations to a 405 metre road summit, then descend through dense forest.

In 2m turn left SP 'Ballyvourney', and in 1¼m at a T-junction turn left on to the N22. Pass through Ballyvourney, and in 1½m reach **Ballymakeery**. Turn right on to an unclassified road SP 'Ballingeary, Renaniree', and shortly enter the Douglas River valley. In 2¾m turn left SP 'Renaniree', pass through rocky countryside, then in 1m meet a T-junction and turn right. In ¼m reach Renaniree and turn right. Ascend gradually for 2¾m to a 302 metre summit and turn right SP 'Kilgarvan, Kenmare'. Follow the mountain side to a 347 metre summit and make a long, winding descent. Climb to a 319 metre pass and continue down into the Roughty Valley. Cross Inches Bridge and drive alongside the river for 1½m to Morley's Bridge. Turn

right across the bridge, then left on to the R569. Proceed to Kilgarvan and follow SP 'Kenmare' through the village. Continue down the Roughty Valley to reach **Kenmare**. Follow SP 'Killarney' on the N71 to drive along the Finnihy River Valley and ascend between low hills. Climb to the summit of a 259 metre pass known as Moll's Gap and bear right. Descend into the Owenreagh Valley; after 1½m pass the famous Gap of Dunloe – separating 832 metre Purple and 760 metre Shehy Mountains from the main part of the Macgillycuddy range – to the left. Beyond Looscaunagh Lough (on the right) pass Lady's View viewpoint, which lies to the left. Proceed through extensive woodland for several miles to the shores of Upper Lake, then pass the conical 333 metre Eagle's Nest Mountain before skirting the base of Torc Mountain (535mtrs) with Muckross Lake on the left.

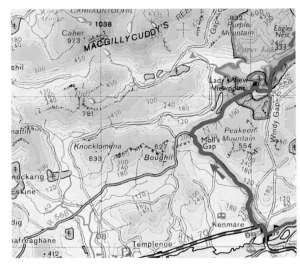

at Parknasilla Wood. Continue from here to **Sneem** along a tree-lined road, with glimpses of Kenmare River to the left. Approach Sneem with views of the mountains which ring the town. Cross the Sneem River by a narrow bridge and turn inland. Ascend along an afforested valley to the summit of a low pass,

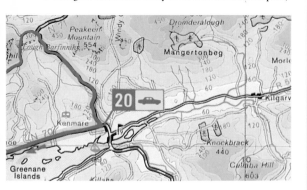

with Coomcallee on the right. Descend through wild, rocky scenery to rejoin Kenmare River. Views afforded by this stretch extend across the bay to the Slieve Miskish Mountains. Continue to Castle Cove; an unclassified road here leads to Staigue Fort (NM). Follow the coast to reach **Caherdaniel**. Restored, 17th-century Derrynane House (NM) can be visited from here. Ascend on the main road, and pass beneath Cahernageeha (497mtrs) and Farraniaragh (469mtrs). Magnificent seaward views include Scariff and Deenish Islands. Continue to the summit of Coomakista Pass. Descend gradually to the small resort of **Waterville**, with magnificent views of Ballinskelligs Bay and high Bolus Head, and Lough Currane on the right. Proceed to the north end of the town and bear left, then right. In 1¾m reach New Chapel Cross and go forward on to an unclassified

road SP 'Ballaghisheen, Glencar'. Follow the broad valley of the River Inny along a narrow but level road. Approach the head of the valley, and shortly reach a vantage point for views of Coomacarrea (771mtrs), Meenteog (713mtrs), and Colly (685mtrs). The foothills of Knocknagantee (683mtrs) and Kockmoyle (681mtrs) rise to the right. Ascend past extensive woodland to the 305-metre summit of Ballaghisheen Pass. Descend steeply through desolate bogland, along a narrow road with several difficult bends to the valley floor. Continue for 4m beyond the pass, cross the Caragh River at **Bealalaw Bridge**, and bear right. Follow the Caragh Valley with the foothills of Macgillycuddy's Reeks on the left. After 1¾m turn right SP 'Ballaghbeama, Parknasilla', and recross the Caragh River. Ascend between towering rock faces, with Mullaghanattin (771mtrs) on the right, to reach the 305 metre summit of Ballaghbeama Gap. The 464 metre summit on the left is part of Knockaunanattin. Pass the road summit and descend along the valley of the River Kealduff, with Knocklomena (636mtrs) ahead and Lough Brin to the left. On reaching the valley floor, continue through forestry plantations and cross the river. After 1m turn left SP 'Killarney, Moll's Gap', and follow a wide valley with Knocklomeana on the left, Boughil (634mtrs) and Peakeen Mountain (553mtrs) ahead, and the low hills of Knockanaskill and Letter South on the right. Climb to over 215 metres and join the top end of the Finnihy Valley, with Boughil towering on the left. Shortly pass little Lough Barfinnihy on the left, then skirt an unnamed 380 metre hill for views of the Owenreagh Valley to the north. Meet the main road and turn right on to the N71. Pass through Moll's Gap, situated between the unnamed hill and 490 metre Derrygarriff at a height of over 275 metres. Complete the drive by returning to Kenmare via a long, winding descent, which affords excellent views of Kenmare Bay and the surrounding mountains.

Shortly pass the entrance to magnificent Torc Waterfall on the right. Continue through dense woodland, and after 1m pass the entrance to Muckross House and Gardens on the left. In another ¾m pass ruined Muckross Abbey (NM) on the left, and shortly

catch sight of Lough Leane.
  In 1¾m cross the Flesk, and after ½m pass a left turn leading to ruined Ross Castle. Continue with the N71 to re-enter Killarney town centre.

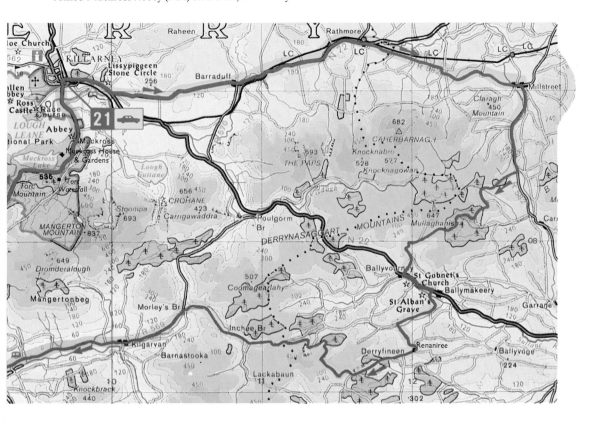

TOUR 22 84 MILES
Round Bear Haven

The drive starts at Glengarriff. From **Glengarriff** follow SP 'Castletownbere, Healy Pass' on the R572, skirting Poul Gorm pool and Glengarriff Harbour on the left. Continue above the Bantry Bay coast with the Sugarloaf (572mtrs), highest of the Caha Mountain foothills, to the right. Descend and skirt Adrigole Harbour. Continue to Adrigole, cross the river, and turn left SP 'Coast Road'.

After 2½m ascend with forward views of the 244-metre high Bere Island, then follow the shores of Bear Haven with the Slieve Miskish Mountains on the right. Enter **Castletownbere**, keep forward through the town on the R572 coast road, and in 1½m pass Dunboy Castle and Picnic Site on the left. After 1m bear left and ascend to a 152-metre summit. Descend for 1¼m and turn right on to an unclassified road SP 'Allihies'. Climb to a low pass and in 2¼m turn right on to the R575 then after ½m turn sharp right. In ½m enter **Allihies**, turn left on to an unclassified road SP 'Eyeries', and in ¾m turn right. Climb to another low pass and descend steeply. Follow SP 'Eyeries', and after 6m reach Kealincha River bridge and bear left.

Meet X-roads and turn left on to the R571. In ¼m bear right SP 'Killarney, Kenmare' and continue to the R571 to Ardgroom. Bear left, then turn right SP 'Kenmare'. To the right rise Coomacloghane (597mtrs) and Tooth Mountain. Shortly enjoy views of Kilmakilloge Harbour; in 3m reach Lauragh Bridge and pass an unclassified right-turn leading to the 305mtr-high Healy Pass. Ascend the Glantrasna River valley to a 182mtr-high pass, with mountain views to the right, and follow a long descent to **Ardea Bridge**. Continue along the river for another 8m to Kenmare Suspension Bridge, then turn right on to the N71 SP 'Glengarriff'. Drive along Sheen Valley, and after 7m cross the Baurearagh River. Climb through several short tunnels to reach a long tunnel which marks the summit of a 300-metre ridge. Descend, with the Caha Mountains to the right, into the densely-wooded valley bottom and pass the entrance to Barley Wood Picnic Site on the right before re-entering Glengariff.

TOUR 23 95 MILES
Seascapes and the Lee Valley

The drive starts at Cork. From St Patrick's Bridge, **Cork** follow SP 'Limerick' N20 along Watercourse Rd. After ¾m reach Blackpool Church, turn left, then immediately right SP 'Killarney' into Commons Rd R617. In 1¼m bear right and drive to **Blarney**. At the end of Blarney pass a hotel and bear left SP 'Killarney, Macroom'. In 1¾m bear right then left. In ¾m turn right on to the R579 and in ¾m left on to the R622 SP 'Inishcarra'. Descend for 1¼m and turn right on to the R618 SP 'Killarney, Macroom'.

Shortly follow the River Lee to Dripsey and turn left over a bridge SP 'Coachford'. In 2¼m at **Coachford** X-roads turn left on to the R619 Descend, cross the River Lee, and bear right SP 'Crookstown, Bandon' and ascend. In 1m bear left and after 1m at X-roads turn right. Descend to a T-junction, turn right on to the N22 and in ½m turn left on to the R585 SP 'Bealnablath'. Cross the river, and in 1m meet a T-junction. Turn right, then in ¼m left on to the R590 SP 'Bandon'. In 4m branch left (unclassified). After 3m reach the Old Mill Bar and bear left. Cross the Brinny River, and at X-roads turn right SP 'Bandon'. In ½m cross a main road SP 'Upton', then in ½m branch right. In 1½m bear right, then in ½m descend to Inishannon. Turn right on to the N71 and in ½m cross the Bandon River and bear right. In 3¾m bear left SP 'Clonakilty' then keep forward in to **Bandon**. Near the top end of the main street turn left SP 'Clonakilty'. In 1½m bear left and shortly left again on to the R602 SP 'Timoleague'. After 7m reach the edge of Timoleague and turn left on to the R600 to run alongside the Argideen estuary. After 3½m at X-roads

turn right, and 2m farther cross a river bridge then turn left. In ½m turn right SP Kinsale. Three miles farther at a T-junction turn left into Ballinspittle. Continue along the R600 SP Kinsale and in 1¼m turn right. Three miles farther cross Kinsale Bridge and turn right. Drive to the Trident Hotel in **Kinsale**, turn right on to the Quays and follow SP 'Cork' through the town. Meet a fork, bear left uphill, then in 2m cross a bridge. In a further ½m cross another bridge and turn left SP 'Cork'. Reach Belgooly X-roads and turn right on to the R611 SP 'Carrigaline'. In 4m reach Ballyfeard and bear right SP 'Cork'. Continue for 5m to Carrigaline and turn left. Keep forward for 1½m then at a roundabout turn right. In 1m turn left and immediately right R600 SP 'Monkstown' and proceed through Monkstown and **Passage West**. Five miles beyond Passage West turn right on to the R609 to re-enter Cork.

Charles Fort was a formidable harbour fortification in the 17th century

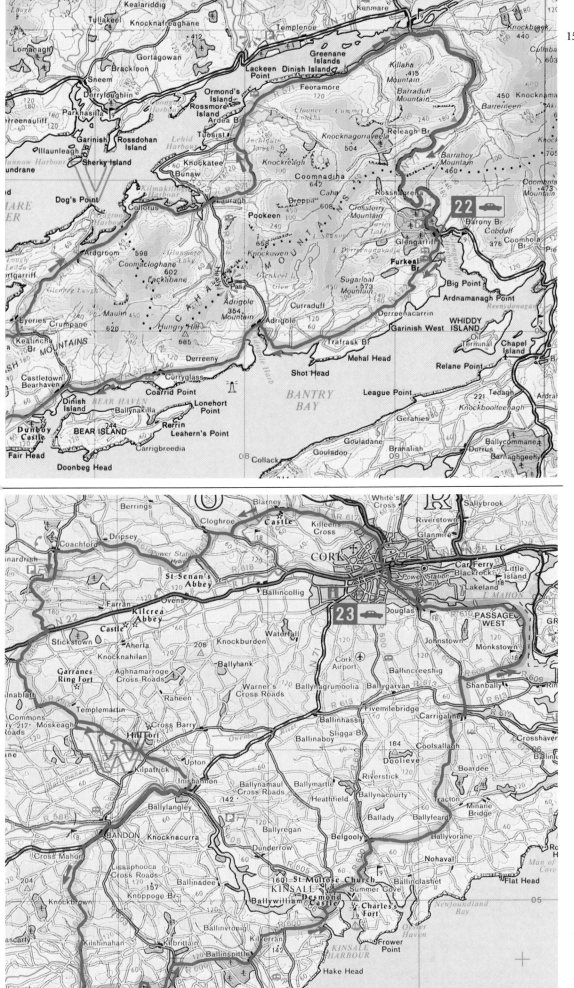

TOUR 24 96 MILES

The Blackwater Valley

The drive starts at Dungarvan. From the Square in **Dungarvan**, follow signs Cork N25, then in ½m join the shores of Dungarvan harbour. In 1¾m cross the River Brickey and climb on to high ground where there are good views over the harbour. Continue along the N25 through a gap in the Drum Hills. After 12m cross the Blackwater, then turn right on to an unclassified road SP 'Cappoquin, Lismore, Blackwater Valley Drive'. Follow the Blackwater, and after 1½m pass a ruined castle (right). Continue with SP 'Cappoquin, Scenic Route', and in ½m bear right. After a further ¾m bear right and ascend steeply. In 1m descend, then in another mile cross a bridge and keep left to follow a small valley. After another 2m climb past Carnglass Wood (right). Continue for 1m to a T-junction and turn right SP 'Cappoquin, Scenic Route'.

Descend for ½m to pass Strancally Wood on the left, and rejoin the Blackwater Valley. After a further ¾m meet a T-junction and turn right. In ¾m turn right SP 'Cappoquin, Scenic Route, Lismore' and shortly cross the River Bride. In 1m enter a gap and continue above the Blackwater. Killahaly Wood (left) faces Dromana Forest across the river. After leaving the river there are views ahead of the Knockmealdown Mountains. In 2¾m meet a T-junction and turn left into the tiny market town of **Lismore**. During the 12th century, Lismore was the site of a sizeable monastic settlement. Drive to the monument in the town centre and turn right SP 'Clogheen', then pass Lismore Castle, once owned by Sir Walter Raleigh, on the left and cross the Blackwater.

Take the second turning left on to the R668 SP 'The Vee, Cahir, Scenic Route' and enter the Owennashad Valley. Climb steadily to a 337 metre summit known as The Vee, where a carpark affords views of the Galtee and Comeragh ranges. Enter Bohernagore Wood then descend through numerous sharp bends. Three miles further, at the outskirts of Clogheen, turn sharp right on to an unclassified road SP 'Newcastle' and continue along the Tar Valley. In 5½m meet X-roads and go forward with the River Tar now on the left. In 2m meet a T-junction and turn right, then continue into **Newcastle**, an attractive seaside resort backed by the Royal County Down Championship golf course. Bear right, SP 'Clonmel'. In 2¼m meet X-roads and turn left SP 'Clonmel'. In ¾m at X-ways turn left onto R671. After 3m pass through a valley between Mountneill and Cannon Woods, then 2m farther meet a T-junction and turn right. In ½m go forward (no sign). In a further ½m keep left then right. Shortly run alongside the river and in ½m at the roundabout turn right on to an unclassified road SP The 'Nier Scenic Route'. Shortly climb along the Comeragh Mountain foothills. After 3½m pass Lyreanearca Wood (right). In a further ¾m

turn right SP 'Comeragh Drive', and in 1m – after a pair of hairpin bends – reach a carpark offering mountain views across the Suir Valley from over 330 metres. Later descend towards the Nier Valley. After 2½m pass Nier Wood (left), shortly cross the River Nier, and turn right SP 'Ballymacarbry'. Continue for 3m to the outskirts of **Ballymacarbry**. At X-roads turn sharp left, (still signed Comeragh Drive) and climb to 240 metres. After 5¾m turn left, then shortly right. In ¼m turn left and in 1¼m meet a T-junction and turn left SP 'Kilbrien, Comeragh Drive'. Descend to **Scart Bridge**, bear right, and ½m farther reach Kilbrien Church; keep forward SP 'Dungarvan' (leaving Comeragh Drive). In 1¾m keep forward again. In ½m turn right and cross a bridge. In 1¼m turn right again and cross another bridge, then in ¾m meet X-roads and bear right – still with SP 'Dungarvan'. Descend, and after 1¾m cross the Colligan River and turn left SP 'Dungarvan'. In ¾m pass through Colligan Wood, and in ½m turn left on the R672. In 1m turn left onto the N72 then branch right to re-join the R672 for the return to Dungarvan.

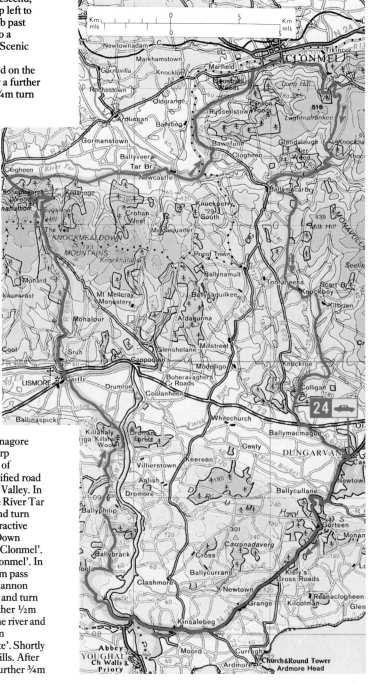

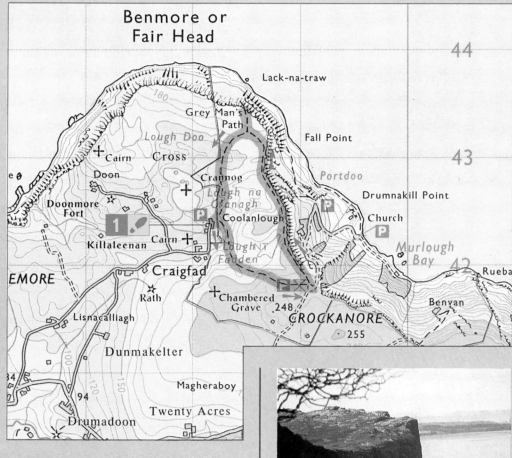

Benmore or Fair Head

The Incomparable Fair Head

Allow 2½ –3 hours

A walk along one of the most magnificent stretches of coast in Ireland.

Park at the National Trust's small car park at Coolanlough five miles east of Ballycastle, Co. Antrim. Coolanlough is a very old clachan or small cluster of houses formerly occupied mainly by members and relatives of one family.

From the car park pass through the metal gate and follow the route waymarked by yellow squares (not circles) painted on rocks. For much of the way there is no trodden path. After climbing over the stile about 100mtrs or so from the gate look out for a yellow square on the hill beyond a patch of long grass, sometimes marshy after rain. The route continues over a moor which is fairly easy going. About a quarter of a mile to the south of Lough Fadden you cross a high stile and make for a yellow square on a rock opposite. The square also has an arrow pointing to the right. Take this course for a few yards only and then go straight up the steepish bank to another square. Turn left here and, following roughly the contour of the ground, look out for the next square. From here to the car park at Murlough Bay there should be no difficulty. From the

Fair Head, Co Antrim from the path

car park at a height of about 230mtrs, you look down into a bay of unsurpassed beauty.

It is an area too of great interest to the geologist and to lovers of folklore. There are many tales and legends associated with the district – 'the sorrowful stories of Ireland' – like the fate of the Children of Lir who were turned into white swans for 300 years until restored to human form on hearing a Christian bell.

From the car park another Trust trail is marked by yellow circles. This leads us along the top of the cliffs to Fair Head, a magnificent headland 190mtrs high. Rathlin Island lies below and to the right the top of Goatfell on Arran Island may be seen above the low hills of Kintyre. In clear weather Merrick in Galloway and the Scottish islands of Islay and Jura may be seen. A little extension takes us to the Grey Man's Path, a steep track down a cleft in the rocks. It is possible to climb down to the shore below but great care is needed. *From the Grey Man, going south over the moor, a trail of yellow circles goes back to the car park.* On the return, look down to Lough na Cranagh with its man-made island, or crannog, built and inhabited 1000 years ago as a protection against wild animals or even wilder humans!

Trailing a giant

Allow 1½ – 2 hours

A riverside walk and the Giant's Ring.

Park at National Trust's Minnowburn Beeches car park on Edinderry Road, just off the B23 Belfast to Ballylesson Road (J324685). The car park is located at a delightful spot where the Minnowburn stream flows into the River Lagan. It is surrounded by wooded hills. Along one side of the river is National Trust property, while the other is Barnett Demesne, owned by Belfast City Council.

Go down the few steps to the path which runs by the side of the Lagan. Turn left. On the left is a grove of 77 larch trees planted to commemorate a visit there by Mr St Barbe Baker, founder of 'Men of Trees', then 77 years of age. Beyond a stile, which marks the boundary of the National Trust property, the path is flanked in autumn with masses of the pink and white flowers of balsam (*Fireman's Helmet*). If these are touched at the right time they explode, scattering seed in all directions. Close to the path on the left is an Anglo-Norman motte of about AD 1200.

At the outskirts of Ballylesson village take the road to the left and at the T-junction after a quarter of a mile, turn right on to Ballynahatty Road. Before the house take the field path to the right for Giant's Ring (a little over half a mile). This is a huge circular rampart of about 2000 BC enclosing a large dolmen about a third of a mile in circumference. *Go through the gate on the far side and take the road from the Ring. On reaching Ballynahatty Road turn left, and then right down Giants Ring Road to Ballylesson Road. Turn left here and walk back by way of Crooked Bridge to Ballylesson Road and the car park.*

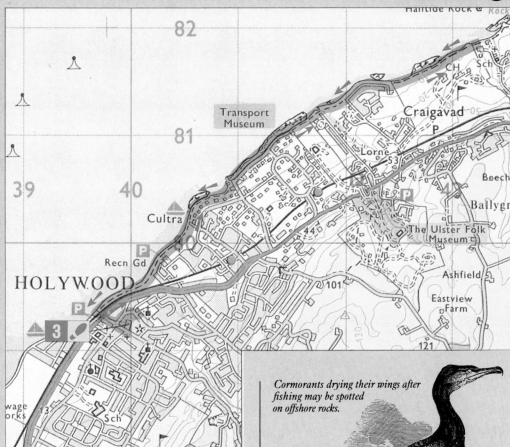

Sea Breezes

Cormorants drying their wings after fishing may be spotted on offshore rocks.

Allow 2½ – 3 hours

This very attractive walk goes along the southern shore of Belfast Lough by the North Down Coastal Path.

Park in the public car park (free) in Church Street, Holywood 100mtrs from the main Belfast–Bangor road (A2).

Walk down Church Street to the maypole at the crossroads. Nearly 70ft high with a weathervane at the top, this is the last surviving maypole in Ireland. There is a story that the first maypole here was the mast of a Dutch ship which ran aground in 1700 and was erected by the sailors.

Turn right, up High Street, for 200mtrs past a charming bronze statue of a boy playing a melodeon, to the Old Priory and its late 17th-century tower and clock. The main part of the building, now ruined, dates from the early 13th century. Holywood, or Santa Boscus as it was called by the Normans, goes back to very early times, an ecclesiastic establishment having been founded about AD 650 by St Laisren. It was connected with the older and larger abbey at Bangor six miles further along the coast.

Go back to the maypole and turn right towards the shore. Go under the railway bridge and turn right. A wide concrete path takes you along the lough shore. Wherever the path diverges, take the fork nearest the water.

Twenty minutes' walk brings you to the marina of the Royal North of Ireland Yacht Club at Cultra. Hundreds of yachts, from dinghies to ocean-going boats, may be seen in summer – out racing or on their moorings. The shore here is of geological interest; if the tide is out you can see remnants of the creamy permian dolomite quarried for a number of later 12th- and 13th-century buildings. The large chimney dominating the view across the lough is Kilroot power station.

At the Royal Belfast Golf Club course, the going gets slightly difficult for about 100mtrs. The path winds around little rocky headlands with fine views across the lough to the Antrim hills. At Craigavad, a 7ft-high concrete wall, covered with faded blue-and-pink murals, gives way to an equally-high stone wall. A short distance offshore seals and cormorants may be seen on Half-tide Rocks. The little sandy beach here is ideal for bathing. *Just past the end of the high wall a tiny path by a half-hidden stream marks the end of the walk. It leads up Rockport Road to Seahill rail station (frequent trains to Holywood) and the A2 (bus route).* However, if you walk back the way you came, there are interestingly different views, with the Belfast hills dwarfing the huge shipyard cranes prominent in the distance.

WALK 4
The Giant's Causeway

Allow 1–1½ hours (shorter route)
3–4 hours (longer route)

A spectacular walk which includes the famous Giant's Causeway.

Park at the public car park at Causeway Head (C945440). From the car park go up the roadway past the National Trust's information centre shop and cafe. Take the path running northwards along the top

A 19th-century engraving of the Giant's Causeway

of the cliff. Along the cliffs is a series of narrow headlands commanding magnificent views of the coastline. Weirs Snout overlooks Great Stookan and Little Stookan down on the shore. Airds Snout rises 91mtrs, above the Grand Causeway. Go out to the point of the snout to get the best view. *About 30mtrs beyond the snout, the Shepherd's Path, with steps at the steepest parts, leads down to the shore at Port Noffer. On reaching the lower path turn left.* You are then walking at the foot of a series of amazing rock formations. The Giant's Chair, or Boot, as it is sometimes called, is passed before reaching the Grand Causeway, which we saw from the top of the cliff. This is composed of some thousands of basaltic columns in the form of a honeycomb. According to legend it was built by the Irish giant, Finn MacCool, to reach his Scottish enemy. Just past the Grand Causeway are the Middle and Little Causeways with the popular wishing chair. *Follow the path to Little Stookan and Windy Gap.* In summer the National Trust runs a minibus to and from Causeway Head. *If you prefer to walk, or have to, it is uphill back to the car park.*

A worthwhile extension of the walk is along the cliff top path as far as Hamilton's Seat instead of going down the Shepherds Path. You will then see a remarkable series of cliffs and headlands, including Port-na-Spaniagh, where the treasure ship of the Spanish Armada was wrecked on 26 October 1588 with a loss of over 1200 lives. Much of the gold and silver and jewellery, including 400 gold coins, was recovered in 1967 and 1968 and is now in the Ulster Museum at Belfast.

Visitors are recommended to obtain a copy of the National Trust's brochure of the area.

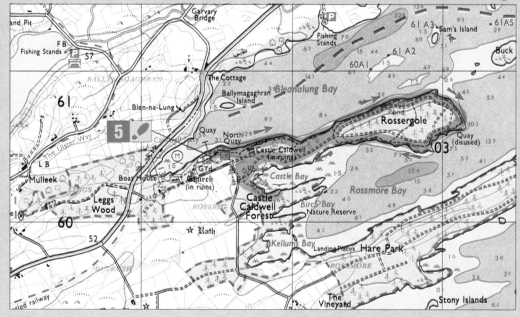

Lakeside Meandering

Great crested grebes, once very rare, are now found on many inland waters.

Allow 1½ – 1¾ hours

Fermanagh is a most beautiful county, with forests, lakes and mountains. It leads along the shore of a long wooded peninsula in Lower Lough Erne which forms part of Castlecaldwell Forest, the first state forest in Northern Ireland. A nature trail and ruined castle add interest. The walk can be extended to include an RSPB hide. The lake has about 366 islands – the extra one is not for Leap Year but to have two for Easter Sunday.

Take the A47 road west from Kesh across Boa Island. Follow the signs for Castlecaldwell Forest and go through the gates, past the quaint Fiddler's Stone (commemorating a local fiddler who drowned in the lake after drinking), and make for the car park (HO14603).

Walk to the lakeside path to the left of the visitor centre (open May–Sept). If the centre is open, you can pick up a nature trail leaflet. Against the wall of the centre is a Lough Erne 'cot', a 30ft-long flat-bottomed boat used to bring cattle to and from the islands. Ahead of you are the ivy-covered ruins of Castle Caldwell itself. *Follow the sign for the loughshore trail, bearing left.* The numbered posts refer to stations on the nature trail. Many of the young trees in the natural woodland are silver birch, the white bark a lovely sight against the blue water of the lake. *You pass on your left some big black rocks and, following the signs for Rossergole Point, you come upon an old lime kiln. Take a rest on the bench up the path or, if it's raining, keep on to the thatched shelter (40 minutes from the start) with a fine view down Lower Lough Erne. In a few minutes you reach the Point, the top of this little peninsula.* From the sheltered seat set into an old wall, look across at the big tree-covered peninsula.

The return route is along the southern shore of the peninsula, the path taking you in and out of the woodland. There is a variety of wild flowers by the wayside – lords and ladies, cranesbills and red campion. In autumn the russet leaves of Spanish chestnut cover the path like Indian canoes. There are lovely views across the lake patrolled by families of swans. Another thatched shelter breaks the journey in trees just off the path. As you walk along, a large bird hide is visible away off to the left, but you are already at the limit of the loughshore walk. *Turn sharp right through the trees and follow the car park signs, along a broad avenue and then through silver birch woods back to the castle and your car.*

Birdwatchers will find it rewarding to continue to the wildfowl hide by turning left just beyond the castle (well signposted). Among the birds which you might see on the lake are great-crested grebe, little grebe, red-breasted merganser, tufted duck, teal and common scoter – Lower Lough Erne is the main breeding ground in the British Isles for this species. *(Allow 40 minutes extra for this detour.)*

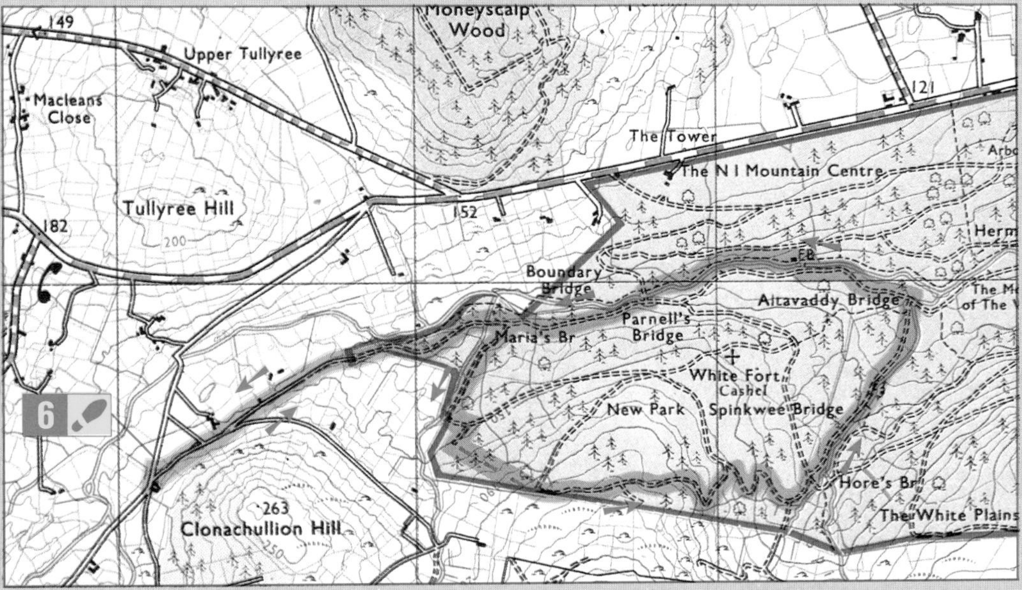

Map reference labels: 331 332 333 / 149 / Moneyscalp Wood / Upper Tullyree / Macleans Close / Tullyree Hill / 182 / 200 / 52 / 121 / The Tower / The N I Mountain Centre / Arbo / Herm / Boundary Bridge / Altavaddy Bridge / The M of The V / Maria's Br / Parnell's Bridge / White Fort / Cashel / New Park / Spinkwee Bridge / Hore's Br / The White Plains / 263 / Clonachullion Hill / 6

Forest Foray

Allow 2½ – 3 hours

A fairly strenuous steep walk, mainly by tracks through Tollymore Forest, which clothes the northern slopes of the Mourne Mountains. The path goes down the gorge of the Spinkwee River. There are some most lovely views of the mountains. A delightful walk for those not troubled with claustrophobia in forests!

Take the B180 Bryansford road from the south end of Newcastle town centre to Bryansford village, turn left (still B180). Ignore Tollymore Forest Park signs. After 2½ miles bear left down Trassey Road, cross the hump-back bridge and continue to the public car park on the left, near Kane's Farm (J311314). The farmhouse, hidden behind trees, isn't visible from down in the car park.

Park your car and turn left back on to the road and uphill a few yards. Take the narrow lane past the front of the farmhouse. After ¼ mile two old lanes branch off to the left. Take the right-hand one, past a large holly tree. After another ¼ mile there is a derelict single-storey cottage on the left. Leave the well-used part of the lane at this point and continue straight on along the track bordered with gorse for 10 yards, then cross the wooden stile. The lane is now largely overgrown with short grass. *Continue past the next gate to the high stile into Tollymore Forest.* From Kane's Farm and for the next two miles the route is part of the 500-mile Ulster Way and is waymarked by wooden posts with arrows and a walking man. Ignore all other arrows.

Reach the Salmon Leap view overlooking the valley of the Shimna River, with the hills of Tullyrea and Moneyscalp beyond. On the right is the King's (or Giant's) Grave, a large burial monument probably dating from the early or middle Bronze Age. Maria's Bridge lies ¼ mile further on with a 30ft waterfall above it. *Up the hill from the bridge, bear resolutely right, taking the route up past a tumbling mountain stream. About 10 minutes later,*

The pine marten lives only in mountainous or wooded country. It hunts squirrels and other small mammals

following the waymarks, leave the forest road and take the track up through the trees to the boundary of the forest. Here, at a height of over 200mtrs, is a magnificent view of the mountains rising steeply above – Luke's Mountain, Slievenaglogh ('mountain of goats') and Slieve Commedagh ('mountain of watching') (765mtrs, 2515ft). *Follow the waymarked forest road running parallel with the boundary fence.*

Just before Hore's Bridge take the road almost straight ahead, signposted 'Cascade'. This is where you part company with the Ulster Way's walking man sign. The route passes along the lip of the gorge of the Spinkwee River, which rushes down in a series of cascades and waterfalls. *At Altnavaddy Bridge turn left and after ¼ mile cross the footbridge (signposted 'rustic bridge') over the Shimna. Turn left and follow the riverside path to Parnell's Bridge. Cross the bridge and turn right. In a few minutes you are back to Maria's Bridge and the return to the car park.* Some 18 species of fauna can be seen in the forest – from pygmy shrew to pine marten. There are interesting plants like alpine enchanter's nightshade and common wintergreen.

West to Seahan

Allow 2½ – 3 hours

The south-west corner of Co Dublin is a land of agreeable contrasts – lofty moorland in sight of city streets, high pastures mixed with spreading forest, all with a 'through the looking glass' feeling, as you traverse hills usually seen in dark outline from Dublin itself.

There is a choice of parking places – at the Stone Cross (O07522) above Ballinascorney Gap, or at the forest gate under Black Hill (O077214). This latter route is considerably shorter than the walk from Stone Cross and involves retracing your steps for part of the route. Wellington boots are recommended in changeable weather. Please park carefully and remember that these are working forests on weekdays.

The walk goes south from the uninscribed Stone Cross, which recalls a fatal accident involving a haycart here about 1850. There follows a steady climb for nearly two miles (3km) to the crest of the road. The rounded summit of Slievenabawnoge will be seen on the left to eastward, separated by a sharp 'notch' from the long ridge of Ballymorefinn Hill. This notch is a glacial drainage channel, cut by torrents of melt water from the glaciers here when the Ice Age relaxed its grip. At the crest of the pass, look back north and north-west over the Brakes of Ballinascorney.

From the forest entrance on the left go east on a forest road for 7–10 minutes, passing picnic tables, which, like the entrance itself, are specially adapted for wheelchair use, then slant up right by a clear path, continuing in the same direction beyond the forest fence to the summit of Seahan. Seahan, at 2131ft (649mtrs) is the highest top completely within Co Dublin and is marked by a survey pillar (1953 vintage) set upon a prehistoric burial mound. This was a place of special importance, perhaps because of the tremendously wide view north-west and west over the central plains. There are at least three ancient burial sites on or near the summit, while on the summits looming up darkly in the south, beyond the hollow in which Kilbride Camp lies, there are other well-preserved burial cairns.

Descending northerly to the forest fence again, turn right and go down the stony firebreak, almost a road. On the left is a small rock-stack, which is signposted as an 18th-century Mass Rock, though this seems a most unlikely spot for a congregation to assemble (in sight of half the county), when public worship by Catholics was forbidden.

Those parked at Black Hill forest gate will turn left just past Ballymorefinn Hill at the Mass Rock signpost, down to a forest path, where another left turn retraces the outward route by the 'wheelchair gate'.

If making for the Stone Cross, keep on down the firebreak on Ballymorefinn ridge, heading north, with glimpses on the right of the reservoir in the depths of Glenasmole. When the forest fence bears right, cross it and continue northerly on a ride to leave the forest on the edge of the glacial notch that cuts off Slievenabawnoge. This is a grassy gully with a track at the bottom, and the remains of 'Famine Fields' above, traditionally the work of victims of the 1847 famine, who never survived to harvest their crops. Cross the stile on emerging from the forest and follow the line of the forest and later a wall down to the tarmac road where a right turn leads back to the Stone Cross.

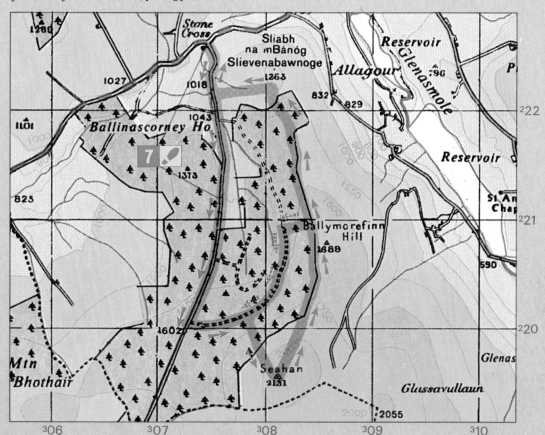

WALK 8
The Heart of Wicklow

Allow 3 hours

Though physically not quite in the centre of the Wicklow Mountains (it lies a few miles east of centre), this walk encompasses much that is best loved in the county. With its distant views grand and wild, yet close at hand reminiscent of the English Lake District, nowhere else in Wicklow has the beauty that this walk affords.

The walk starts at Pier Gates (O172064) on the west side of L161. There are two ways of getting there from Dublin. The route over the Military Road (L94) to Sally Gap, turning left there, traverses wild moorland scenery. That from the Glendalough road (T61) to the turn-off (L161) right towards Sally Gap is a better road but not quite equal in mountain scenery.

Park at Pier Gates, 4 miles from Sally Gap and 2 miles from the turn-off from T61. Here there are two sets of prominent pillars and plenty of room to park by the side of the road. Before starting to walk it is possible to envisage the route. Across the valley lie the giant cliffs of Luggala, over 1000ft high. To the left of Luggala lies the subsidiary valley of the Cloghoge Brook, and left again the rugged peak of Knocknacloghoge (1754ft). The route skirts Luggala and runs down the valley of the Cloghoge River to Lough Dan with Knocknacloghoge on the right.

The walk starts on tarmac, so take the road between the larger pair of pillars, following it down to the

valley floor. Lough Tay, just out of sight from here, lies at the foot of Luggala, and the house on it is owned by the Guinness family. Of this area Bertrand Russell once wrote, 'The beauty of the scenery made a profound impression on me. I remember especially a small lake in County Wicklow, called Lugala' (*sic*).

With these philosophical thoughts in mind, continue, at the bottom of your descent the road bends right, and you will approach a crossroads with a farmhouse to your left. Follow the track straight ahead where the tarmac ends, then cross the wooden bridge spanning the Cloghoge River. Keep on and cross a second wooden bridge across the Cloghoge Brook. About 200 yards beyond this bridge the track divides and you are faced with two gates. Pass through the gate to the right so that now the long stone wall is immediately to the left of you, and continue down through pastoral and wooded terrain on a track (occasionally muddy) to the two-storey house on Lough Dan.

Cross the river here by a set of stepping stones, the one difficult obstacle on the route. They are set some way apart and in rainy weather may be just below the level of the water. If they prove too daunting, retrace your steps back to the car park.

After the stepping stones walk away from the river and very soon turn left into a wood. Pick up the track in the wood; a low stone wall is on your right. Climb the hill following this path, past a derelict farmhouse on the right and shortly you will join the main track which leads back towards the car along a pleasant route enlivened by glimpses of Lough Tay. It may be possible to discern ridges of former 'lazy beds' (cultivated strips where the women augmented the poor soil with seaweed) ascending high up the slopes of Luggala and Knocknacloghoge, a testimony to the fact that this now thinly inhabited valley was once home to many. Poor people certainly, but in such an environment certainly not suffering from visual poverty!

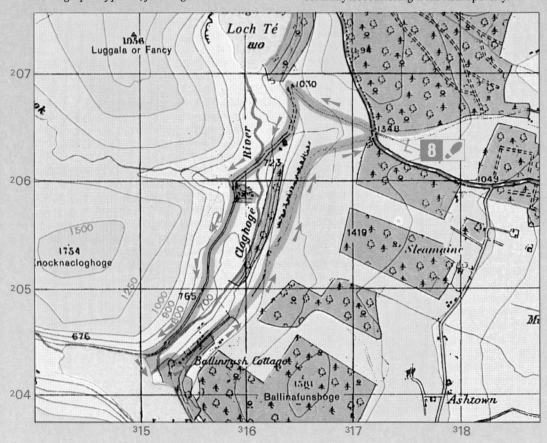

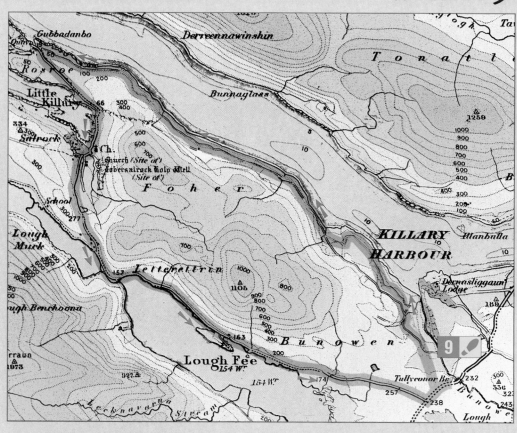

Hills and the Sea

Allow 4 hours

The time taken can be reduced by 1–1¼ hours if a car pick-up is arranged at the road junction at Lough Muck. There is parking in a large layby between Lough Muck and Lough Fee. This is a 'walk on the flat' that still manages to embrace the varied scenery of hills and the sea which is so typical of Connemara.

Park in the disused quarry just west of Tullyconor Bridge on the Leenane-Letterfrack road. Follow the road for about 100 yards, then turn right along the narrow road which curves down towards Killary Harbour. Killary is a long fjord, deep enough it is said locally, to house the British Fleet in pre-First War days, though cold truth suggests that nothing larger than a destroyer used it. From the far shore rises the imposing mass of Mweelrea 'the grey bald mountain', at 2688ft the highest mountain in Connacht. Even in fine weather, Mweelrea often wears a white cap of cloud.

After about 30 minutes' walk the road becomes a track and contours round the hill about 100ft above the sea. A further 1¼ hour's walk, with Killary beside you and Mweelrea always on your right brings you to the little harbour of Rosroe (Gubbadanbo on the map, but that name is locally unknown). The harbour is typical of the West of Ireland. Stone-built in the 19th century for fishing and local

goods transport, it is now hardly used except by a few local fishermen, and the very occasional Galway Hooker. These distinctive sailing craft were once the 'delivery vans' of the area; the few remaining are private yachts.

From Rosroe take the road which climbs out of the village and over the rocky spine of the Rosroe Peninsula to Little Killary. Follow the road round the head of the bay and into the wood beyond. Little Killary is a delightful miniature of its big brother. In the wood east of the road are the ruins of a medieval church, a holy well of St Roc (hence the name 'Salruck') and, almost completely overgrown, an old 'pipe graveyard'. Each mourner smoked a clay pipe over the grave, and left the pipe behind.

Climb the steep narrow road onto the open hillside, and continue to the crest of the ridge. This is wild country, a mixture of bog and bare rock. If you don't mind a bit of rough ground and are well-shod, it's worth leaving the road and climbing the little hill west of it for a view of the fine beaches and splatter of islands towards Renvyle.

The road descends past another little wood and joins the Tully Cross-Leenane road on the shore of Lough Muck (1 hour from Rosroe). Turn left and follow the road through the narrow gap to the shore of Lough Fee. The rafts on the lough are used for shellfish farming. Notice the peninsula and island covered in undergrowth – this is what the rest of the land might look like if there were no sheep to graze it.

The road continues along Lough Fee and then across bogland for a mile to a road junction; turn left, and a few minutes brings you to your starting point. This rather dull stretch is enlivened by fine views of the bare, sparkling quartzite domes of the Twelve Bens (or Twelve Pins), eight of which rise to over 2000ft, and the Maum Turk Mountains to the south.

Waymarked Walks in the Republic

The countryside in the Republic of Ireland is wild in places and often difficult of access. The type of terrain and the distance to be covered (to follow a circular route around a hill, for example), as well as the uncertain weather and the shortage of large-scale mapping, mean that many areas would be suitable for exploration on foot only by fit, well-equipped and experienced walkers.

For this reason we have included a selection of waymarked walks, developed by the Forest and Wildlife Service, which are geared to more casual walkers and families. Leaflets tracing the route and describing what can be seen at stops along the way can often be obtained on site. Please take care not to damage trees and plants, and do not light fires or leave litter. For further information on nature trails, contact the Forest and Wildlife Service, 22 Upper Merrion Street, Dublin 2, *tel* (01) 789211.

Townley Hall Wood, Co Louth

Location: 3½m (5.5km) west of Drogheda on the Navan road N51.
Distance: About 1 mile (½ hour).
Facilities: Car park, picnic site, forest walks, nature trail (leaflet available on site).

Situated in the Boyne Valley, the trail takes you to the site of the Battle of the Boyne, where in 1690 James II was defeated by William of Orange, later William III. Steep in parts and with some steps along the route, it is not suitable for pushchairs or wheelchairs.

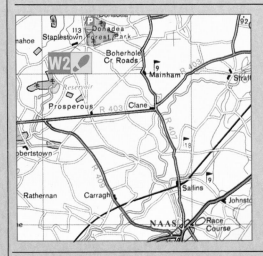

Donadea, Co Kildare

Location: 11¼m (18km) NNW of Naas via R407, then by unclassified road for 2¾m (4.4 km).
Distance: Under 1½ miles.
Facilities: Car park, picnic site, castle ruins, forest and lakeshore walks.

Donadea Castle, for centuries the home of the Aylmer family, is the start of this walk, which takes you through woodland of lime, beech, oak, ash and conifers, populated by red and grey squirrels, butterflies and moths. You pass a church and a lake with mallard, coots, moorhens and the occasional mute swan.

Devil's Glen, Co Wicklow

Location: 3½m (4km) NW of Rathnew on R763.
Distance: Under ½ mile.
Facilities: Car park, picnic site, forest walks, waterfall, nature trail (leaflet available on site).

The nature trail is a gentle circular walk with a fine view of the valley where you can see Glanmore Castle, the ancestral home of the playwright John Millington Synge. Other forest walks (unguided) take you further into Devil's Glen up to where the Vartry River falls over 30 metres into the steep-sided wooded chasm.

Glendalough Woods, Co Wicklow

Location: 2m (3.22km) west of Laragh on R757.
Distance: From 1 mile to 5½ miles.
Facilities: Car park, picnic site, forest walks, nature trail (leaflet available on site), 'wilderness' trek, boat trips, national monuments.

Glendalough, meaning 'valley of the two lakes', offers wild, spectacular scenery, a cathedral, several churches, a round tower, monastic remains and a variety of walks to suit most tastes and capabilities. The circular nature trail of about one mile provides steps for the steepest gradients and passes a waterfall.

Monicknew Woods, Co Laois

Location: Slieve Bloom Mountains, 13m (22km) WNW of Port Laoise via N7 to Mountrath then by R440 for 4½m (7.2km).
Distance: About 1¼ miles (2km).
Facilities: Car park, picnic site, forest walks, viewing points, nature trail (leaflet available on site).

The sandstone arch of Monicknew Bridge, dated 1840, begins this walk through hardwood trees, such as oak, ash, birch and elm. Later you pass through plantings of Sitka spruce and grand fir, part of a State programme of afforestation. You may see a badger's sett on your route and, if you are lucky, even a fallow deer.

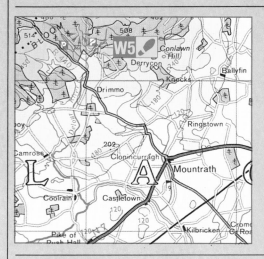

Portumna Forest Park, Co Galway

Location: Adjacent to Portumna. On north shore of Lough Derg.
Distance: Just over 1 mile.
Facilities: Car park (small fee), picnic sites, toilet/ information building, forest walks, deer herds, stands for viewing wildlife, wildfowl ponds, nature trail (leaflet available on site), marina.

The Forest Park's 1400 acres border on Lough Derg and are a sanctuary for 16 species of mammals, including many red and fallow deer, and 85 different kinds of birds. Binoculars would be an asset on the nature trail. After your walk you might like to visit Portumna Castle and the 15th-century priory.

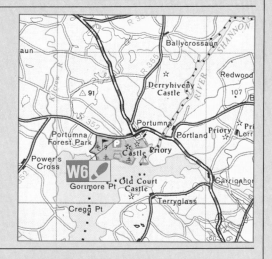

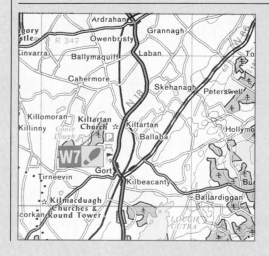

Coole Demesne, Co Galway

Location: 2m (3.2km) north of Gort via N18.
Distance: Just under 2 miles (some short cuts).
Facilities: Car park, picnic site, forest walks, nature trail (leaflet available on site), former estate of Lady Gregory, 'Autograph Tree'.

Coole House was a centre of the Irish Literary Revival around the turn of the century when Lady Gregory, herself a writer, entertained Yeats, Shaw, Synge and O'Casey among others. The walk takes you past the old orchard, now a home for deer, a disused lime kiln and quarry, near Coole Lake and its swans, and finally to the great copper beech on which many of Lady Gregory's literary guests carved their initials.

Acknowledgements

The publishers would like to thank the many individuals who
helped in the preparation of this book. Special thanks are
due to Bord Failte and the Northern Ireland Tourist Board.

The Automobile Association wishes to thank the following
photographers, organisations and libraries for their assistance
in the compilation of this book.

Nathan Benn 59 Brendan Voyage; *BBC Hulton Picture Library* 17 Sean O'Casey; *Board of Trinity College Dublin* Book of
Kells; *Bord Failte* Cover Nr Ardgroom, 1 Ardmore Round Tower, 3 Parknasilla, 6/7 Rock of Cashel, 16/17 Abbey Theatre, 18
James Joyce, 19 Joyce's Home, 27 Kenmare Bay, 31 Blarney Castle, 32 Adare, Achill Island, 34 Kilronan, Ardee, 35 Weaving, 37
Athlone, Road bowling, 38 Nr Avoca, Avoca, 39 Ballybunion, 41 Bantry Bay, 47 Birr Castle, Bray, 48 The Burren, Interpretative
Centre, Burren Flora, 49 Carlingford, 50 Carlow Lock, 52 Carrick-on-Suir, Carrick-on-Shannon, 53 Rock of Cashel, 55 The
Abbey, 56 Kells High Cross, 57 Clifden, 58 Clonmacnoise, Clonmel, 60 Cork City, River Lee, 61 Croagh Patrick, 64 St
Laurence's Gate, The Viaduct, 65 Dromahair, 66 St Patrick's Cathedral, Four Courts, Plaque, Phoenix Park, 70 Drumcliff
Church, Court House, 71 Dun Laoghaire, Dunmore East, 72 Enniscorthy, 72 Abbey Tavern, 73 Powerscourt Gardens, 74
Fermoy, 75 Gallarus Oratory, Lough Gur, Parrot, 76 Spanish Arch, 77 Glendalough, Galway City, 78 Glenmalure, 79 Glin
Castle, Gougane Barra, 81 Lighthouse, Malin Head, 82 Kilkee, National Stud Museum, 83 Kilkenny, 83 RDS Horse Show, 86
Kylemore Abbey, Lahinch, 87 Leenane, Irish linen, 88 Sarsfield's Bridge, Georgian houses, King John's Castle, 89 Lisdoonvarna
Spa, Lismore Castle, 91 Game fishing, Lough Mask, 93 Stone circle, 94 Mallow, 95 Mellifont, 96 Monaghan County Museum,
97 Monasterboice, Mullinger Cathedral, 98 Punchestown races, 99 Newgrange, 101 Parknasilla, 103 Avondale House,
Rathmullan, 104 Sneem, Gougane Barra, 105 Roundstone, 106 Russborough House, 107 Skerries, 109 Tara, Hurling, 110
Trim, Lady Elizabeth Cove, 112 Reginald's Tower, Glass factory, 113 Westport House, Nr Waterville, 114 James Barry
memorial, 115 St Patrick's Day parade, 116 Folk dance festival, 117 Game fishing, 118 Golf, 121 The Mall, 127 Motoring in
Donegal, 130 Ballyshannon Harbour, 141 Lough Conn, 142 Clifden, 144 Lough Corrib, 151 Glendalough, 152 Kilkenny Castle,
153 Jerpoint Abbey, 155 Slea Head, 158 Charles Fort; *Bushmills Distillery* 23 Labels; *W Capper* 161 Fair Head; *C
Douglas-Deane* 13 The Burren, 14 Gannet, Spotted slug, 15 Mountain hare; *Industrial Development Board* 11 Short
Brothers aircraft works; *The Mansell Collection* 65 The Baptism at Tara; *Mary Evans Picture Library* Back Cover Vale of
Avoca, 87 Irish linen; *Midleton Distillery* 24 and 25 Distillery; *G Morrison* 10 Turf House, 12/13 Lough Sheedagh, 14
Golden Vale, 26/7 Fish and shellfish, 28 Lamb and vegetables, 29 Cold buffet, 30 Smoked salmon, 42 Belfast, 46 Chiro pillar, 60
Cork, 62 Clifden, 63 Brandon Bay, 72 Fiddler, 84 Upper Lake Killarney, 85 Killybegs, 106 Curragh, 111 Cottage kitchen, 126
Fishing boat, 143 Fish farming, 154 Kilshannie cross slab, 155 Brandon Bay; *National Library of Ireland* 10 Dublin street scene,
66 Custom House, 84 Torc Waterfall, 90 Blarney Castle, 162 Giant's Causeway; *National Museum of Ireland* 8 Tara brooch;
Northern Ireland Tourist Board 5 Lough Erne, 15 Kingfisher, 20 Louis MacNeice, Birthplace of Patrick Brontë, 20/1 Yeats's
grave, 22 Distillery, 33 Horseshoe shop, Annalong harbour, 35 Lace, 36 Planetarium, 39 Ballintoy, 40 Lammas Fair, Ballycastle
strand, 41 Bangor, 42 Crown Bar, Botanic Gardens, City Hall, Queen's Arcade, Library, 51 Carrickfergus Castle, President
Grant, 53 Devenish Island, 54 Castlerock, 55 Castlewellan, 57 Cheese making, 62 Cushenden, 63 Windmill, 74 Fair Head, 76
Giant's Causeway, 78 Glencloy, 80 Mount Stewart, 90 Guildhall, 92 Lough Erne, White Island, 93 Fishermen, 94 Marble Arch
caves, 96 Newcastle, 99 Legananny Dolmen, 100 Omagh, 101 Portaferry, 102 Portstewart, 108 Strangford, 111 Folk Museum,
119 Sailing, 130 Belleek, 133 Sunset, 136 Annalong, 137 Newcastle harbour, 139 Stricklands Glen, Strangford Lough.

Other Ordnance Survey Maps of Ireland

Republic of Ireland

One-inch district maps, coloured for Dublin, Wicklow,
Cork and Killarney. Half-inch touring and general-
purpose maps, coloured and contoured—24 sheets
available. General map of Ireland: 9 miles to 1 inch.
Scenic areas and mileage chart. Folded and coloured. In
card covers. Tourist map of Ireland—12 miles to 1
inch—folded and covered. Wicklow Way map at
1:50,000. Street maps of Dublin (1:20,000) Cork
(1:15,000) Limerick and Waterford (1:900), all folded
and inclusive of street index. Available from Ordnance
Survey of Ireland, Phoenix Park, Dublin.

Northern Ireland

A fully-coloured street map with gazetteer of Belfast.
Coloured street maps of many of the major towns of
Northern Ireland at 1:10,000 scale. Outdoor pursuits
maps of Mourne Country, Lower Lough Erne and
Upper Lough Erne at 1:25,000, designed for those
whose leisure activities are to be found in the mountains
or on the water. Complete coverage of Northern Ireland
at 1:50,000, ideal for motorist and rambler alike.
Available from Ordnance Survey of Northern Ireland,
Colby House, Stranmillis Court, Belfast, BT9 5BJ.

Ireland

Four sheets covering Ireland at 1:250,000—'The
Holiday Map' each sheet packed with tourist
information. 'The Ordnance Survey Road Atlas of
Ireland' hand-bound and fully coloured maps at
1:250,000 with street plans of the major towns and
cities. Available from both outlets above.